FILMING THE COLONIAL PAST

Filming the Colonial Past
The New Zealand Wars on Screen
Annabel Cooper

OTAGO UNIVERSITY PRESS

Published by Otago University Press
Level 1, 398 Cumberland Street
Dunedin, New Zealand
university.press@otago.ac.nz
www.otago.ac.nz/press

First published 2018
Copyright © Annabel Cooper
The moral rights of the author have been asserted.

ISBN 978-1-98-853108-3

A catalogue record for this book is available from the National Library of New Zealand. This book is copyright. Except for the purpose of fair review, no part may be stored or transmitted in any form or by any means, electronic or mechanical, including recording or storage in any information retrieval system, without permission in writing from the publishers.

No reproduction may be made, whether by photocopying or by any other means, unless a licence has been obtained from the publisher.

Published with the assistance of Creative New Zealand.

Editor: Gillian Tewsley
Design/layout: Fiona Moffat
Indexer: Diane Lowther
Printed in China through Asia Pacific Offset.

Cover: *Utu: Redux*: Corporal Wīremu Te Wheke (Wī Kuki Kaa) and Lieutenant Scott (Kelly Johnson) ride to Te Puna.

Frontispiece: *River Queen*: Wiremu (Cliff Curtis) finds the body of his dead son (Brandon Lakshman). The episode was drawn from an incident before the battle of Te Ngutu o te Manu in 1868, when the son of the scout Kātene Tū Whakaruru was killed.

CONTENTS

INTRODUCTION

1 HAYWARD IN THE BAY OF PLENTY:
  The silent *Rewi's Last Stand* and *The Te Kooti Trail*   36

2 HAYWARD IN THE WAIPĀ:
  Rewi's Last Stand in the sound era   68

3 WARS IN THE LIVING ROOM:
  The Killing of Kane and *The Governor*   94

4 THE PŪHĀ WESTERN: *Utu*   128

5 DOCUMENTARY ADVENTURES: *The New Zealand Wars*   159

6 TELEVISION HISTORIES IN UNCERTAIN TIMES:
  Greenstone, Von Tempsky's Ghost and *Frontier of Dreams*   182

7 AFTERMATH AND MEMORY:
  In Spring One Plants Alone and *Rain of the Children*   201

8 ENCOUNTER, ROMANCE AND CONFLICT: *River Queen*   225

9 MĀORI CREATIVE CONTROL AND NEW SCREENS   247

CONCLUSION   273

NOTES   282

BIBLIOGRAPHY   301

ACKNOWLEDGEMENTS   309

INDEX   312

INTRODUCTION

One soldier turns in surprise to search the face of another. Clad in blue-black uniforms, rifles slung across their shoulders, they ride between tussock and clear sky, two figures picked out in a colonial army on the move. The Māori corporal looks straight ahead. Aware that he has startled the Pākehā lieutenant, he seems covertly amused at the reaction he is provoking. He sits easily on his horse, in command of the conversation as the lieutenant questions him, suddenly uncertain. Not for the first time, the corporal is reminding the lieutenant of the tensions underlying their friendship, and the ambiguities inherent in his own place as a Māori soldier in a colonial army.

OPPOSITE: Cast and crew on the set of The Te Kooti Trail, pictured near Whakatāne in 1927. Director Rudall Hayward stands with the megaphone at right, cameraman Ted Coubray centre. Hilda Hayward and the Pākehā leads sit at front, with Tina Hunt and Pātiti Warbrick (Te Arawa), the romantic leads from Rotorua. On horseback, centre right in the dark uniform, is the Tūhoe rangatira Te Pairi Tūterangi, who had followed Te Kooti as a young man and played him in the film. Completing the picture are the Ngāti Awa extras who played Te Kooti's followers. Peoples of the Bay of Plenty connected to all sides of the region's wars took part in the film.

Preserved and made available by Ngā Taonga Sound and Vision. Courtesy of the Hayward Collection. Ref S 3756.

This moment from Geoff Murphy's *Utu* (1983) is one of many in which screen stories have portrayed the cultural encounters, tensions and open conflict of the New Zealand Wars. Beginning with Rudall Hayward's silent *Rewi's Last Stand* (1925), filmmakers have made stories about these wars in feature film, television drama, documentary, phone app, website, music video and even sand and lightbox. Each film was shaped in a time and place, a present with its own preoccupations, agendas and terms of cultural exchange. Each production in turn reshaped its audiences, informing and engaging them and sending them away to rethink the past.

Filming the Colonial Past asks how a succession of screen stories about the New Zealand Wars came to be made, how filmmakers focused on different historical figures or events over time, how their portrayals of the wars altered, and how filmmakers and local communities, especially mana whenua, dealt with each other through the making of these shifting portrayals of the past. Over the 90 years in which they were made, beliefs about the colonial past altered unevenly but radically, and people's understandings about their own legacies from that past came to seem much less straightforward. Who were the goodies and the baddies? (And who was in between?)

Who won and who lost? Was this how 'New Zealand' was born? And whose side are we on, now? These screen productions, rolling out across the decades one after the other, illuminate the changing answers to these questions, the changing perspectives on the colonial past, and the changing understandings of Māori–Pākehā relationships.

To make a film about colonial war was to create a context in which many legacies came to the surface. Meetings between kaumātua and film crews, kōrero on marae, screenwriters' labours over drafts and revisions, debates on the film set about what should be done, how, and by whom – the spaces where arguments, negotiations and performances take place – these were contexts in which historical knowledge was put forward, contested and often reformulated as the meanings of the wars were remade. This body of screen texts represents a past portrayed to show shifting representations of heroism, injustice and suffering, but also a series of present 'cultural moments' of filmmaking. These cultural moments encompass the broader politics of the day, as well as the production processes themselves and how they reveal the cultural politics of their time – in the inclusion, exclusion or authority of Māori and Pākehā in decisions about casting, dialogue or the staging of historic events, in the relationships of filmmakers with mana whenua, and in the hierarchies of crew members.

Film's dependence on collaboration is a central element in this story. It is not a neglible fact that a single person can write a book but it takes many people to make a film. If the film is about the New Zealand Wars, a good proportion of those people must be Māori and the filmmaker depends on their willingness to participate. Although Māori have only very recently occupied the director's chair, this book shows that Māori influence has been exercised from the very first films – including through advising, performance, and having the filmmakers on their whenua. In general Pākehā filmmakers understood the extent of their reliance on Māori – and they had no doubt about the calibre of performance that Māori brought. Unlike the portrayal of Native Americans in some early Hollywood westerns, there was never any question that Māori actors would play Māori characters. Māori not infrequently felt angry or hurt at the making of screen stories that they saw as wrong or irrelevant or not yet appropriate for a public forum, but in other cases Māori knowledge was sought, willingly given and valued, and tangata whenua were increasingly involved in production decisions or hired in senior roles. The story of these interactions is far from simple – it varies from one production to another, and despite the rising seniority of Māori in the industry there is no straightforward progression from racism to enlightenment: instead, there are surprising continuities between some of the earliest and the most recent productions.

Making screen stories about Aotearoa's colonial wars – indeed, about the national past in general – has always been a risky endeavour. Raising funds for the always expensive historical fiction features is a formidable task, and documentary on these subjects is costly too. In a small nation's screen industries, money is scarce. Costs rise faster than budgets. And makers of historical films are faced with the persistent fact that many New Zealanders are indifferent to their past – unlike in America, where their history is a compulsory subject at school and is repeatedly retold through a screen industry with a global reach, so that it is folded intimately into their sense of nation. Added to this is the difficult emotional territory of colonial history: the most dramatic events of our past are often the least comfortable, reminders of the divisions and injustices that underlay colonial settlement and whose legacies continue.[1] As the recent struggle to establish a national day of commemoration of the New Zealand Wars has revealed, these are not easy events to incorporate into a national story.

Given these impediments, filmmakers have returned with surprising regularity to the subject of colonial warfare. Rudall Hayward, the most important of the country's early filmmakers, made not one but three New Zealand Wars features: the silent films *Rewi's Last Stand* (1925) and *The Te Kooti Trail* (1927) and, in 1940, a second *Rewi's Last Stand* with sound. The arrival of sound, which was far more costly to make than silent film, meant that very few further New Zealand films were made until the 1970s. But when the country's first colour television programme *The Killing of Kane* (1971) was made, it was about war in Taranaki. *The Governor* (1977), the great television series of its decade, dramatised the Northern War, the Waikato War and the battle of Gate Pā. Murphy's *Utu* (1983), which is loosely constructed around the campaign against the guerilla leader Te Kooti Arikirangi, has become one of the country's most highly regarded films, and *The New Zealand Wars* (1998) is one of our highest-rated documentary series. Other television came in its wake – both drama and documentary, concentrating in part or entirely on the wars. In the cinema, Vincent Ward's fiction feature *River Queen* appeared in 2005 and his drama-documentary *Rain of the Children* in 2008.

In the past decade a cluster of films centred partly or wholly on the wars has signalled the arrival of Māori creative control in documentary: these include Tearepa Kahi's *The Flight of Te Hookioi* (2009), Paora Joseph's *Tātarakihi: The children of Parihaka* (2012), the *Waka Huia* series documentaries on the 150th commemorations of the New Zealand Wars (2014), and *The Prophets* and *The Kiingitanga* documentary series (2013; 2016). On newer media platforms, alongside the efforts of iwi, historians and rangatahi to increase national awareness and understanding of the wars, online content is emerging in, for example, the Ruapekapeka website, phone apps on the Waikato, Taranaki and Wellington wars, online streaming of music video, and the RNZ online documentary *NZ Wars: Stories of Ruapekapeka*.

The New Zealand Wars: A historical overview

Conflict among settlers, imperial troops and colonial forces of various stripes and Māori – some of whom allied with the Crown and some who were resisting attacks on their land, sovereignty or rights – flared in different regions between 1843 and 1916.[2] The first incident, the only one to take place in the South Island, was the brief Wairau Affray of 1843. In the Northern War of 1845–46 Hōne Heke Pokai and Te Ruki Kawiti contested imperial sovereignty, sacked the town of Kororāreka and rapidly developed new strategies of defence that culminated in the devastating victory against the British at Ōhaeawai; they then built and later evacuated 'the bat's nest' – Ruapekapeka pā. The Northern War ended in a strategic truce and the British withdrew their forces to Auckland. In the same period fighting broke out over land in Wellington and Whanganui; and the colonial government grabbed the chance to extend its influence. These conflicts ended with the capture and imprisonment of the great Ngāti Toa leader Te Rauparaha and his ally Te Rangihaeata's withdrawal to the Manawatū.

The most protracted period of fighting involving the most troops took place in a series of interconnected campaigns right across the middle of the North Island through the 1860s and early 1870s. Through the 1850s settlers urged government to make more land available for purchase, and government sought to extend the spheres of its control beyond territory occupied by settlers, to land still occupied and essentially controlled by iwi. Over that decade iwi worked to create the Kīngitanga or Māori King movement as a means of establishing a form of joint Māori sovereignty through which laws for Māori might be agreed to, and government pressure to sell their lands to settlers resisted. The colonial government objected to what it interpreted as growing intimations of Māori self-government, especially when Pōtatau Te Wherowhero was crowned the first Māori king in 1858.

In 1860 the First Taranaki War erupted when the government purchased land in Waitara from a chief whose authority to sell it was disputed. Although it ended a year later, this war was the trigger for a series of increasingly bitter conflicts that lasted over a decade and spread across the North Island. The wars in Taranaki drew in hapū from the Waikato, some of whom were supporters of the king, and this provided government with an excuse for advancing on the fertile lands of the Waikato and seeking to bring the Kīngitanga under colonial control. Troops under General Duncan Cameron invaded the Waikato in 1863 by crossing the Mangatāwhiri Stream, the border of Māori-held territory. To do this they built the Great South Road and brought gunboats up the navigable section of the Waikato River. The Kīngitanga, mainly Tainui iwi, constructed a series of large defensive earthworks. A sequence of major battles was fought between 1863 and mid-1864, but the troops continued their advance into Māori-controlled territory, eventually circling behind the line at Pāterangi to attack the undefended village of Rangiaowhia. By the middle of 1864 there were 12,000 imperial troops in the colony.[3] The Battle of Ōrākau in the Waipā Valley south of modern-day Hamilton was the last battle in the Waikato. Cameron then turned to the Bay of Plenty and brought his troops into Tauranga. Māori crushed the imperial attack at Pukehinahina (Gate Pā) but lost to the British at nearby Te Ranga in mid-1864. Meanwhile the Kīngitanga established an aukati or border at the Pūniu River, immediately south of Ōrākau; the aukati stood until 1881.

War flared again on both sides of the island. The Second Taranaki War (1863–66) brought two developments: the Pai Mārire (Good and Peaceful) movement initiated by the Taranaki prophet Te Ua Haumēne; and, among other punitive government methods, the scorched-earth policy in which troops laid waste to settlements perceived as 'disloyal', depriving Māori communities of crops and shelter. Intertribal conflict in the Bay of Plenty spilled into war with government when Pai Mārire converts hanged the missionary Reverend Carl Völkner at Ōpōtiki in March 1865, for spying. This phase ended with government victory at Waerenga-a-Hika near Gisborne in November 1865, and the imprisonment of many of its defenders at Wharekauri (Chatham Islands) in 1866. In the Bay of Plenty, East Coast and Te Urewera, where there were already histories of inter-tribal conflict but also extensive patterns of intermarriage among iwi, historical allegiances and the involvement of various iwi in the Waikato War created complex legacies. Affiliation with the missionaries and traditional churches on the one hand, or with Pai Mārire on the other, tended to align with pro- or anti-government allegiance. Extensive raupatu or land confiscations by the government in Taranaki, the Waikato and,

---

The Governor (1977) dramatises the imperial bombardment of Pukehinahina (Gate Pā) in April 1864. The attempt to destroy the defences failed; in the following scenes, Ngāi te Rangi and their allies inflict a famous defeat on their enemy.

TVNZ Television Archive, Stills Collection, Ngā Taonga Sound and Vision. Courtesy of the Arthur Wrigley Collection.

later, the Bay of Plenty dispossessed and displaced thousands of people and caused great hardship. The spread of Pai Mārire, with its incorporation of Old Testament narratives of suffering and redemption, invested iwi with powerful forms of faith and drew them into alliances against the Crown.

By the end of the 1860s the 'self-reliant' policy that mandated that the colony should provide its own troops was in effect, and the last few imperial troops departed in 1870. The colonial troops consisted of settlers and native-born Pākehā in militia, ranger or armed constabulary units and Crown-allied Māori in units such as the Arawa Flying Column, which was led by Pākehā captains. Over time more Māori formed alliances with the government, and government placed greater reliance on tribal federations such as Te Arawa, Ngāti Porou, Ngāti Kahungunu and Whanganui. These federations were divided: some hapū supported government and others remained resistant.

Through the second half of the 1860s, the wars fought on both the west and the east coast became increasingly intertribal and even intratribal as much as between Māori and Europeans. As Britain withdrew the last of its military support to the colony, two conflicts – one on the east coast and one on the west – threatened colonial government. The first of these two wars flared when East Coast people who had been banished to Wharekauri after Waerenga a Hika made their escape in 1868 under the leadership of the prophet Te Kooti Arikirangi of Rongowhakaata. They captured a ship and returned to Poverty Bay, where they travelled inland. Colonial troops pursued and confronted them, and this sparked a series of raid-and-retreat attacks on settlements in Poverty Bay and the Bay of Plenty. The colonial troops and, later, bush-fighting contingents led by captains Gilbert Mair and George Preece and the kūpapa (Crown-allied) leaders Rāpata Wahawaha (Ngāti Porou) and Te Kēpa Te Rangihiwinui (Whanganui) pursued Te Kooti through the difficult country of Te Urewera and the Central Plateau – a vast territory to hide in – until 1872, when he took refuge with the Kīngitanga. As in Taranaki and the King Country, the higher, inland forested country provided refuge for resistant Māori who had not conceded defeat, and it remained an object of government anxiety. The earlier decision to protect Te Kooti came at great cost to Ngāi Tūhoe: the government decided to punish them by invading their lands in Te Urewera and systematically destroying their crops and settlements in another scorched-earth campaign.

On the West Coast, beginning north of New Plymouth, Ngā Ruahine chief Riwha Tītokowaru sought to resist settler encroachment on confiscated land. When peaceful strategies proved unsuccessful he put the fear of God into settlers, launching surprise attacks and sending letters that alarmed colonists. Tītokowaru's military strategies involved building expendable pā, inducing the military to attack, and using surprise elements to outwit his more numerous opponents. He won two victories at Te Ngutu o te Manu and Moturoa. With an increasing band of followers he advanced rapidly south to the outskirts of Whanganui, but apparently on the eve of a third great victory at Tauranga Ika in 1869 he suddenly and mysteriously retreated. The most common explanation for this is that he was found with the wife of an allied chief, and lost the support of followers.

The uneasy decade of the 1870s, punctuated by scares and alarms, was somewhat settled at Pirongia in 1881 when King Tāwhiao met with the Government Native Officer William Mair (brother of Gilbert Mair) and put down his weapons in a gesture of his commitment to peace. Two years later Te Kooti was included in a general pardon.

This was not the end of Māori independence, nor of government incursion. Two settlements showed signs of independent Māori leadership that generated colonial anxiety, leading to conflict. Te Whiti o Rongomai and Tohu Kākahi established a non-violent settlement at Parihaka in Taranaki. When government sent officials and troops to survey and build roads through their lands, their followers repeatedly pulled up survey pegs and ploughed up the roads. The government imprisoned and exiled waves of the ploughmen and, finally, invaded Parihaka in November 1881. Welcomed by women and children singing and offering food, the troops disobeyed orders, looting the village and raping women. Te Whiti, Tohu and others were arrested and imprisoned.

The final conflict of the wars occurred in 1916 when the government, uneasy at the growth of the prophet Rua Kēnana's settlement at Maungapōhatu in Te Urewera, sent colonial police to invade the settlement: they captured and imprisoned Rua and several of his followers and killed two people, including one of Rua's sons, in a panicked outburst of shooting.[4]

The wars did not end with the cessation of open hostilities. Their effects on families and communities continued over generations, especially in the ongoing impacts of dispossession and the consequent erosion of livelihoods and mana in their aftermath. These wars were, moreover, only one dimension of an ongoing process of settler colonisation that, as Patrick Wolfe observed, is 'a structure, not an event'.[5] The Treaty of Waitangi had been signed in 1840 but the subsequent waves of settler immigration resulted in the demographic 'swamping' of Māori by settlers keen to acquire land and to replicate familiar institutions in the new world. Extensive confiscations occurred at the time of the wars, but the individualisation of titles to land and the establishment of Land Courts alienated far more Māori land through to the twentieth century.

The long aftermath of these events continues in marked economic and social disparities between Māori and Pākehā. Iwi have made applications for redress over the generations since, and the legislative process for making claims through the Waitangi Tribunal is ongoing. These and other aspects of settler colonialism have meant that Māori, besides the historically-based disadvantages they have suffered, have had more limited access to ways of telling their histories in a public forum.

War histories and war stories

How filmmakers chose to tell stories about the New Zealand Wars varied from one to the next and over time. How they learned about what happened was circumscribed by what was handed down in oral and in written form, and by the way the stories were reshaped for new generations and new purposes in both Māori and Pākehā traditions of recording the past.

Iwi and hapū have always handed on knowledge of the past through oral and other forms – in formal ways such as through whaikōrero, waiata and haka, but also by each generation telling stories to following ones – kuia and kaumātua to their mokopuna. Other artforms also maintained traditions, such as the houses built to commemorate events – for example Te Whai a te Motu in Ruatāhuna, built to acknowledge the pursuit of Te Kooti across the central North Island. Māori petitions, letters, diaries and newspaper interviews left written records. Responsibility for maintaining the stories that were passed on might be assigned to kaitiaki, such as Raureti Te Huia of Ngāti Maniapoto. The stories were told and retold, in marae or domestic contexts and for purposes such as legal claims. James Cowan, the only historian who interviewed both Māori and

Pākehā veterans of the wars extensively, knew some of these kaitiaki well, which meant that some of their accounts crossed over into national history through publication in Cowan's writing. They made their way into film, sometimes from eyewitness or oral history accounts and sometimes mediated through the written histories. This is not to say that the stories passed on were uncontested or that they did not alter over time – as did Pākehā historical traditions. Among and within iwi and hapū, accounts varied, especially since wars are complex events that involve many people with different agendas. As political and legal circumstances placed changing demands on the past, stories were reshaped to respond to changing imperatives. There were some events people might be reluctant to recount, for a variety of reasons. As perspectives on the wars have shifted and as alliance with the Crown has come to be seen in a less positive light, tensions have reemerged about who was on what side. Historical work associated with the Waitangi Tribunal has sometimes meant a return to tensions that have long rumbled below the surface, and competing accounts have emerged in many Tribunal proceedings.[6]

Written history is another vehicle for maintaining cultural memory, and it dominates the sources of many of the films discussed here. The 'first draft of history' – the newspaper reports of the time – reflected the opinions of settlers, but those were diverse: James Edward FitzGerald's editorial on Ōrākau in the *Press* a few days after the battle slated the invasion of the Waikato, although this was unusual.[7] The Māori-language newspapers, too, offered different perspectives. Accounts written by ex-soldiers from the perspective of the government side, such as those by Alexander, Whitmore and Featon, were published within living memory of the wars: they betray few doubts about the colonial project, and deal largely with military matters. Early general histories devoted considerable attention to the wars, and again the perspectives varied. George Rusden's *History of New Zealand* and *Aureretanga: Groans of the Maoris* were highly critical of government actions, from the Waitara land purchase and the Taranaki War to Parihaka in 1881 – so much so that Rusden was sued for libel.[8] William Pember Reeves' *The Long White Cloud: Ao Tea Roa*, the standard history of the country for decades, is a relatively nuanced account; other historical accounts, such as Lindsay Buick's *New Zealand's First War, or The rebellion of Hone Heke*, followed the government line.[9] But in 1918, towards the end of World War One, cabinet responded to an appeal by the veteran Colonel Porter to fund an official history of the New Zealand Wars and to employ the journalist and amateur historian James Cowan to write it.[10]

The decision to commission an official history of past wars in the midst of an ongoing one reflected a sense of national duty to the fallen, after four years of the war overseas. It also reflected the respect that Māori contingents had earned while fighting alongside Pākehā in Gallipoli and France, and a recognition that there was much still to be resolved in the aftermath of the nineteenth century. While some iwi had volunteered in large numbers during World War One, others – including Waikato and Ngāi Tūhoe – pointedly refused to fight for a government that had treated them so poorly. It was nevertheless a striking decision to appoint an official historian, and the choice of Cowan was an adventurous and illuminating one. Cowan spoke fluent Māori, he grew up on a farm situated partly on the most famous of the battlefields, Ōrākau, and he had already established a reputation as a journalist who was well informed about Māori culture and history – including stories of the wars. Cowan had known some of the surviving Māori defenders of the Waikato War since childhood, and had already written

James Cowan interviewed veterans from all sides for his historical work on the New Zealand Wars – his official history, and numerous newspaper and magazine articles. Cowan's writing was an important source for generations of filmmakers.

Ivan Ruscoe Collection,
Ref PAColl-5877-5, Alexander Turnbull Library, Wellington

The Maoris of New Zealand (1910) and *The Adventures of Kimble Bent* (1911); the latter was based on interviews with the renegade soldier Kimble Bent as well as Māori veterans.[11] It must have been evident from his earlier work that he would write a history that took account of Māori perspectives. In employing Cowan, therefore, the Department of Internal Affairs showed itself willing to commission a history that acknowledged both resistant and pro-government Māori, in an invitation to greater national unity.

Cowan's two-volume *The New Zealand Wars: A history of the Maori campaigns and the pioneering period* (1922–23) profoundly shaped all subsequent histories of the wars for two reasons.[12] The first was that Cowan's history was often sympathetic to resistant Māori and elaborated their perspective on the conflicts – especially in the first volume; Cowan was more sceptical about the prophetic movements that arose in the later stages of the wars and notably about Te Kooti. The second reason was that Cowan's preference for oral sources created a detailed record of the testimony of veterans on all sides, while they were still living; often Cowan returned to the sites of battles with veterans and conducted his interviews there.[13] Over time, these interviews fed into Cowan's long string of popular books and articles on the wars, so that their contents were dispersed well beyond those who read the official history itself. Cowan's writing, moreover, was frequently anecdotal and sensitive to place and scene, lending itself readily to film. He saw the New Zealand past as a rich source of national stories, and encouraged this view with his lively nonfiction narratives.[14] Cowan's own active interest in film led to his being employed as historical advisor on several films, including Hayward's films about the wars. Largely because of his cultural and linguistic competence, and his predilection for detail and anecdote, his influence on film continues into the present, well after some of his interpretations have been overtaken by later scholarship. Cowan's position on the wars shifted throughout his career, and he became more critical of government and settlers. Some of his work sharply delineates the destructive impacts of colonisation, whereas on other occasions he idealises crosscultural relationships.

Before the arrival of feature film the wars had already inspired novelists and other storytellers, including the British author G.A. Henty's *Maori and Settler* (1890) and Australian Rolf Boldrewood's *War to the Knife* (1899). George Hamilton-Browne saw the advantages of posing as a veteran when he 'borrowed' soldiers' stories for his *With the Lost Legion in New Zealand* (1911) and *Camp Fire Yarns of the Lost Legion* (1913), and although he was later exposed as an imposter his books still sold well. Among the better known New Zealand novels were William Satchell's Waikato story *The Greenstone Door* (1914), published on the eve of World War One, and Mona Tracy's children's novel about Te Kooti, *Rifle and Tomahawk* (1927). In the 1960s, against a background of the increasing ferocity of colonial wars in Indochina, other novels appeared: Frank Bruno's potboiler about Tītokowaru, *Black Noon at Ngutu*, and an impressive trilogy by Errol Braithwaite that traced the rising intensity of interracial conflict from the First Taranaki War (*The Flying Fish*, 1964) through the Waikato War (*The Needle's Eye*, 1965) to Tītokowaru (*The Evil Day*, 1967).[15]

Despite these historical, journalistic and fictional treatments, collective memory of the wars in the broader national sphere, as opposed to in te ao Māori, diminished as the twentieth century progressed. As the last veterans died and living memory was replaced by collective memory, North Island iwi from the regions affected by the wars passed down through the generations detailed accounts of these events, which had had far more detrimental effects on them than on most Pākehā. As collective memories they were held largely within Māori contexts. On the broader national stage the world wars came to seem more attractive subjects of national memory, offering stories of the past that centred on unity rather than on internal conflict and injustice. The 'Māori Wars' were recalled through a few heavily mythologised snapshots – the 'interracial respect' supposedly arising from Ōrakau, or the repeated felling of the flagpole at Kororāreka.

The generation of historians that followed Cowan encompassed three main, sometimes overlapping strands: radical or polemical, professional, and military histories. Dick Scott's pamphlet *The Parihaka Story* (1954) was a sharp attack on colonial New Zealand, a polemical history of the invasion of Parihaka and a reminder to forgetful Pākehā about a shameful event. A much extended edition was published in 1975 as *Ask That Mountain*. By then the rise of professional history in the universities, which was finally turning sustained attention to the New Zealand past, had produced a series of studies of the New Zealand Wars. Keith Sinclair's *Origins of the Maori Wars* (1957) and *History of New Zealand* (1959) questioned the reputations of still-revered figures like Governor George Grey, and argued that the wars should occupy a more central place in nineteenth-century history. Ian Wards argued that the idea that land was alienated from iwi through 'moral suasion' was demonstrably false. Alan Ward damned the colonial policy of racial amalgamation as 'a show of justice' and made the case that the wars were fought over sovereignty rather than land.[16]

The work of these mid-century historians, written within a global climate of emerging decolonisation and indigenous liberation movements, challenged comfortable national myths of race relations in Aotearoa and helped to lay the ground for historiographic and broader political changes in the second half of the twentieth century. Except for Scott and Sinclair, their broadest readership was probably university students; but these histories were also read by the writers and creators of film and television, a rising generation of Māori scholars and activists, and the next generation of historians, some of whom were becoming more attentive to the politics of reaching a wider readership. These included more accessible histories such as Tony Simpson's *Te Riri Pakeha: The white man's anger* (1979), and military histories such as Tim Ryan and Bill Parham's *The Colonial New Zealand Wars* (1986).[17] The two most influential writers of this next generation are of central interest to this book, as they each worked between written and visual history and informed a generation of filmmakers.

Judith Binney's books were not histories of the wars but they dealt extensively with colonial conflict and its aftermath: *Mihaia* (co-authored with Gillian Chaplin and Craig Wallace, 1979); *Ngā Mōrehu* (with Gillian Chaplin, 1986); *Redemption Songs*, a biography of Te Kooti (1995); and her history of Te Urewera, *Encircled Lands* (2009).[18] Like Cowan, Binney made oral history her central mode of inquiry and she developed strong and enduring relationships with iwi, notably Tūhoe. She made extensive use of photographic images – *Mihaia* began with the discovery of a photographic archive, and both it and *Ngā Morehu* involved collaborations with photographer Gillian Chaplin. Binney later worked directly with film when she contributed to Ward's *Rain of the Children* and the documentary series *Frontier of Dreams*.

James Belich's *New Zealand Wars and the Victorian Interpretation of Racial Conflict* (1986) was instrumental in shifting conceptions of the colonial past, at least among those who read New Zealand history. Analysing European ideology in the Victorian era – which he argued assumed that Māori, as 'natives', were incapable of strategic thinking – he demonstrated its inadequacy as he produced evidence of the success of resistant Māori strategy. Drawing on his master's thesis on Tītokowaru, he wrote *I Shall Not Die* (1989), before turning to television documentary in *The New Zealand Wars* series (1998). Belich's argument that Māori developed innovative military and political strategies in response to British firepower and colonial encroachment brought certain figures into a new prominence, especially Te Ruki Kawiti and Riwha Tītokowaru. He sparked some hostile reaction, but the recasting of Māori resistance as a practice of agency rather than victimhood found support, not only among Māori.[19]

Both Binney and Belich were widely read in the Māori world as well as by sympathetic Pākehā. Ranginui Walker's *Ka Whawhai Tonu Matou: Struggle Without End* (1990), a general history of Aotearoa from a Māori perspective, pursues a similar, albeit brief interpretation of the wars.[20] *Wars Without End: The Land Wars in Nineteenth-century New Zealand* by Danny Keenan (Ngāti Te Whiti Ahi Kā, Te Ātiawa), concerned mostly with events in Taranaki, appeared in 2006. Keenan's shift in emphasis is apparent in his title: in this and other work he has argued for the necessity of seeing the wars as an ongoing reality rather than as events in the distant past, reflecting not only their continuing effects but a way of understanding the relationship between past and present. He has since written a biography of Te Whiti.[21]

Belich's work inspired a fictional trilogy by Maurice Shadbolt: *Season of the Jew* (1986, about Te Kooti), *Monday's Warriors* (1990, about Kimble Bent) and *House of Strife* (1993, on Hōne Heke). Over a longer period, Witi Ihimaera's fiction has taken up incidents from the wars: *The Matriarch* (1986), *The Trowenna Sea* (2009), *The Parihaka Woman* (2011) and, with Hemi Kelly, *Sleeps Standing Moetū* (2017), among others. Hamish Clayton's *Wulf* (2011) fictionalises the story of Te Rauparaha.[22]

In 1985 when the Waitangi Tribunal was mandated to consider historical claims against the Crown dating back to 1840, it opened up institutional inquiry into the history of invasion, confiscation and other injustices perpetrated by the state. Initially undertaken on a relatively small scale, the claims process expanded to create a substantial sub-field involving many historians. This work has largely been produced as reports in support of the respective claims. More recently, though, as claims have been settled, some of it has led to publication, including Binney's *Encircled Lands,* Vincent O'Malley's *The Great War for New Zealand: Waikato 1800–2000* (2016) and Michael Belgrave's *Dancing with the King* (2017) about the years following the Waikato War.[23] The emergence of a necessarily legally inflected approach to history has sparked much debate. Bill Oliver and Giselle Byrnes, both of whom had undertaken Tribunal work, argued that there were inherent problems of balance and breadth in this kind of single-purpose history; an exchange of unfriendly fire ensued and the debate continues.[24]

The naming of the wars has been contentious. The various names adopted reflect the stance taken, consciously or unconsciously, by the speaker or writer. Several terms had been tried by the time James Cowan explicitly rejected the then-current 'Maori Wars' and opted instead for 'New Zealand Wars'. Later writers veered towards 'Land Wars', which emphasised settler desire for land and government willingness to wage war for it as a primary cause of the conflicts. Many – especially many Māori – still prefer this name, as Danny Keenan observes.[25] Other terms that have come and gone are the 'Colonial New Zealand Wars', 'Anglo–Māori Wars' and 'Te Riri Pākehā' (the Pākehā's anger). In the 1980s James Belich argued for a return to 'New Zealand Wars' on the grounds that while land was a primary cause, so was sovereignty, which encompassed the issue of land – as Alan Ward had argued strongly. Belich also contended that these wars were formative nation-creating events – another good reason for 'New Zealand Wars'. His use of this name in the titles of his book and television series helped return it to its current standing as the one preferred by most historians. But popular usage is enduring: as I wrote this book I was often asked, 'Do you mean the Māori Wars'? The use of individual leaders' names to identify specific wars, such as 'Tītokowaru's War' or 'Te Kooti's War', entails the same problem as 'Māori Wars' in that it assumes that the source of the conflict resided on one side only – but these terms are still used, mainly to avoid confusion.

Film and history

Since the release of the silent *Rewi's Last Stand* in 1925 most New Zealanders – especially Pākehā but many Māori too – have been more likely to know about the New Zealand Wars through a screen story than by reading or hearing about them. Rudall Hayward made his films at a time when filmmakers were beginning to understand the screen's enormous potential for creating national origin stories. He had seen D.W. Griffith's disturbing paean to the American South, *Birth of a Nation* (1915); and his own New Zealand Wars silent films appeared in the same years as Sergei Eisenstein's revolutionary Soviet epics *Battleship Potemkin* (1925) and *October: Ten days that shook the world* (1927).[26] Filmmakers' persistent return to the New Zealand Wars derives from just this impetus: these were events that, reinterpreted in successive screen narratives, seemed to contain the deeper truths of national origin.[27] The filmmakers' pursuit of origins through events that disrupt, divide and trouble stood in marked contrast to governments' impulse to anchor national identity in the world wars, events that offer the far more acceptable face of national unity.

Can film offer us 'true' origin stories? Critics of film as a vehicle for history have pointed to historical inaccuracies, especially in dramatic genres; to film's habitual preoccupation with individual stories or a small group of figures in a historical landscape instead of covering a broad sweep of action; and to film's compression of many incidents into a few, arguing that it routinely simplifies the past at the expense of historical complexity. More recently, though, scholars have suggested that film should be understood as 'doing history differently' and should not be measured by the same standards as written history. Robert Rosenstone argued that filmed history is distinctive in drawing viewers into the experience and the emotions of the past: 'History on film is largely about emotion, an attempt to make us feel as if we are learning about the past by vicariously living through its moments.'[28] Dramatic film aims to recreate the look and sound of the past; it engages our senses so that we feel immersed in its world. And documentary, too, invites us to 'enter into' the past in a way that written history doesn't usually do. This capacity to call on the emotions gives film what cultural historian Peter Mandler has called a 'broad throw': a film, even only a moderately successful one, reaches a much greater audience than written history does – even historical fiction (which shares some of the characteristics of film history). By calling on our emotions and senses, film also has a memorability that written history can seldom match. James Belich, who was determined to take history to a broader audience, was startled to find that the screen could reach audiences many times the size of even the raciest historical book.

If film is the source of most people's knowledge of the past, it is important to ask how film *does* history. What claim is a given production making about its relationship to a real past? How does it render history visible and audible? How does it invite us to respond? And who is it speaking to?

The films discussed here offer different answers to these questions. Rudall Hayward made the boisterous claim that his films were an exact representation of history: he produced a flyer that shouted 'FILMED AS IT ACTUALLY HAPPENED!' 'NOT FICTION – FILMED FACTS!' But his films were, in fact, an eclectic mix of re-enactment, imagined scenes and conversations, and overtly fictional additions – and that was part of his implicit contract with his audiences. Fictional characters rubbed shoulders with real historical individuals in his films. Later films made a variety of implied claims to historical truth – from the feature films, whose claim was founded in the idea that fiction, by paring away irrelevance and chance, can cut to deeper truths about the past and the present, to the condensation of historical events in the documentary dramas, and the insistence on historical evidence, argument and artefact in the talking-heads documentaries. Across all these forms, filmmakers drew on written and oral histories and usually consulted the historians of their day personally.

Fiction and documentary are not mutually exclusive; each borrows from the other. Historical fiction anchors its credibility in references to recognisable historical events; and documentary draws on narrative devices borrowed from fiction, structuring past events in ways that are often thought of as specific to fiction. Hayden White observes that 'the discourse of the historian and that of the imaginative writer overlap, resemble, or correspond with each other ... [T]he techniques or strategies that they use in the composition of their discourses can be shown to be substantially the same, however different they may appear.'[29] White is discussing

Costume and set lend this character from *Utu* (1983) the look of the 1860s. But Kura (Tania Bristowe) has a directness recognisable to 1980s audiences. Although her speech has a nineteenth-century inflection, it is often casually modern. 'I can see your bum,' she laughs in one scene.

Frame enlargement from *Utu: Redux* (2013), Utu Productions

written history texts, but the same can be said of the screen. Across fiction and documentary, and overlapping between them, a range of techniques are used for screening the past. Stories both 'true' and 'fictional' are structured and interpreted for effect; the stories follow individuals with whom we are invited to align our sympathies; they are given beginning and end points as writers round off a plot in timeframes that would not have been recognisable to those living through these events. Cameras select objects for our attention and structure the way we look at them, shaping our empathy or antipathy. Narration and editing manage our attention and control a story that is pulled out of the chaotic jumble of the past.

Nevertheless, viewers make distinctions between types of historical film. A film's claim to represent real events is usually implicit in the genre it deploys, and this is understood by its audiences. No one expects a fiction feature film to stick exactly to documented historical facts. We expect a western, or a romance, or a melodrama to develop according to plot conventions that we are familiar with, against events that seem plausible for the time and place in which it is set. We expect characters to wear costume and occupy settings that look right for the period. But we are also accustomed to fiction features bridging then and now: hair, makeup and costuming may look vaguely appropriate to the 1860s but at the same time align with current fashions, and speech is likely to sit somewhere between speech patterns of the past and the way we speak in the present. This can vary even within a film, as filmmakers seek to engage audiences in a world that looks and feels plausibly 'then', while still making it familiar enough to draw in those who inhabit the 'now'.

There is, for example, no documented historical case of a white woman travelling alone in the war-riven parts of the North Island as freely as Sarah O'Brien does in *River Queen*. This female mobility is grounded not in history but in aspiration. It invites twenty-first-century viewers to engage in an imagined past; and Sarah's freedoms and desires speak to present-day

There are echoes of historical figures in these soldiers in *River Queen* (2005) – but nothing too precise. As leader of the kūpapa troops, Hōne (Mark Ruka) has the implacable determination of Te Keepa Te Rangihiwinui. Both the dashing style of Gustavus von Tempsky and the ruthlessness of Thomas McDonnell are apparent in Major Baine (Anton Lesser).

River Queen (2005), Silverscreen Films

audiences. This implausibility is countered in *River Queen* by the careful historical detailing: from the dark, heavy uniforms of the constabulary to the soft stirrings in a wharenui as sleepers wake, the sets and costumes convey a powerful sense of the look and feel of a particular past. The language of the characters in *River Queen* – as in other films – ranges from plausibly formal nineteenth-century phrasing to the plainly contemporary. Through these means we are drawn into the film's world as a world we experience. But to what extent are we asked to believe it as history?

Neither Vincent Ward nor Geoff Murphy, in their fiction features, claimed to be 'doing history'. Yet both were very interested indeed in creating stories about the past which seemed to them to illustrate important truths. Ward ventured into the past in pursuit of the idea that Aotearoa was created by people who moved between Māori and Pākehā worlds: he is interested in these cultural go-between figures as definitive nationbuilders. Bruce Babington uses the term 'fabulous history' to describe *River Queen*. Murphy's intention is not the same but it is just as deliberate. He states that 'the object of [making *Utu*] wasn't to represent history in any sort of real way', and goes on to discuss the considerations involved in deciding how to create a historical world in the film – while surveying the treatments of the past in other national cinemas:

> … that preyed on us quite a bit, how to do that, how not to make it too much like a western, and enough, but we were allowed to go some of the way into their territory, and some of the way into [Japanese director] Kurosawa's territory … but not much of the way into the way British or Europeans did history cause they, they're too theatrical. So we were trying to create a creative space in which … history could be commented on.[30]

Not history in 'any real way', but a 'creative space in which history could be commented on': this is a succinct summary of the way film may render the past in order to open up its questions and its meanings for a present moment – rather than claiming to have told a finite truth.

At the other end of the spectrum, in high-end documentary, credibility depends on more demanding academic criteria. In the *New Zealand Wars* documentary series, Belich as narrator contests earlier explanations for historical events and argues for a reinterpretation. The scholarly authority of the series was supported by its visual style and high production values. It did not use re-enactment – which is often perceived as a more accessible, but less trustworthy, means of portraying the past; rather, it relied on the spoken word to carry the argument, supported by archival images and detailed computer-generated models. Belich as narrator was a historian speaking to camera about his specialist area, narrating past events from the historical sites and anchoring the claim to the real in the ground itself. Other speakers from across the range of iwi involved endorsed the series' arguments through the authority of whakapapa.

Between these extremes of feature film and documentary, other films demonstrate a range of implied relationships to truth about the past. Several productions come into the category of documentary drama. In *Rewi's Last Stand*, footage of turning pages – supposedly from Cowan's histories – lends the solid authority of the written word to the uncertain truthfulness of film. Each of Hayward's films invents characters to provide the romantic interest that Hayward thought was essential to engage viewer sympathy – and to appeal to a female audience. And each of his films includes a colonial male 'everyman' figure with whom his Pākehā audience was expected to identify. *The Governor* kept to historical sources as a basis for dramatic enactment, with the occasional use of voiceover. But, like other docudramas, *The Governor* invents dialogue and compresses events – such as the many hui that led up to the decision to create a Māori king – into one or two. It displaces incidents from one setting to another for the purposes of narrative continuity. The documentary *Von Tempsky's Ghost* used dramatised sequences – some created especially for the film – but it also borrowed from past films' portrayals of Gustavus von Tempsky to chart the shifting reputation of its flamboyant subject. *Rain of the Children* dramatises events, too, cutting them into the film's other narrative methods of direct-to-camera narration, interviews, and archival footage from an earlier film. Its dramatisations are evocative and poetic, and are consistent with the film's elegiac tone – even its interviews are filmed in accordance with art cinema rather than documentary conventions.

Perspectives on colonial war and its aftermath – the past towards which these filmmakers gravitated – mutated and shifted as each production reflected prevailing agendas and changing ideologies, especially those of settler colonialism and the critiques surrounding it. These shifts unfold across each film and over time. In a broad sense they reflect the history of colonialism as an ongoing structure that is still lived and internalised by filmmakers and audiences. We can chart a trajectory from what might be termed the 'late colonial' period in Aotearoa through a period of decolonisation – a limited process in a settler colonial society where colonists do not depart again but remain, as Pākehā do in Aotearoa.[31] The reputation of empire alters across these films: it begins with a benevolent face and transforms into an overwhelming threat.

Associated with this overarching theme of the New Zealand Wars stories in these films is a cluster of interlinked cinematic themes, motifs and figures, borrowed from familiar genres such as the western, the melodrama, historical drama, documentary and dramatised documentary, adapted and inflected by their reformulation in Aotearoa. Pākehā fascination with crosscultural or in-between figures persists in the forms of the immigrant becoming native, or of Europeans born in Aotearoa: both are stories of the creation of the Pākehā. The character of the Pākehā is transformed over the 90 years of the films, usually but not always in the form of the colonial soldier. Romance and friendship tend to counter, mitigate or even reconcile conflict.

In general the portrayal of the warrior – which undergoes a series of transitions – marks a distinction between how Māori are rendered in New Zealand film and some of the more extreme portrayals of Native American masculinity in Hollywood film. Portrayals of the warrior as 'savage' are scarce – except occasionally as 'noble savage' – and there is little sense of Māori as a 'vanishing race'. The narratives of Māori women – and European women for that matter – sometimes challenge expectations, pushing against genre conventions that constrain rather than enable female characters. These women are most often defined by their bravery, and their roles are somewhat more central to the narratives than war stories often allow. Nor is there much evidence of any parallel to the 'celluloid Indians' of the earlier Hollywood westerns – homogenised mash-ups of tribal costumes and traditions, adorned with feathered war bonnets and facepaint.[32] Other sub-genres that emerged in the United States were more influential: a handful of the pro-Indian westerns, including some of the few made by Native Americans, came to New Zealand cinemas in the 1910s and 20s and, by the 1970s, the revisionist western (exemplified by *Little Big Man*, 1970) was well known to New Zealand filmmakers. Still, when the US critic Robert Sklar watched Hayward's films in the 1960s he was struck by the sympathetic, rounded treatment of Māori in comparison with Hollywood fare.

The historical context of a film off-screen also connects history and film. These two kinds of history – the history narrated and portrayed *in* the film and the history *of* the making of the film – are intimately connected in the films studied in this book. We look into the cultural, political, industrial and economic circumstances in which each film was produced and within which it has selected and reinterpreted historical events. Giacomo Lichtner calls this process the 'double historicity' of film: the 'simultaneous relationship between the present of its production and the past of its narrative'.[33] *Utu*, a film in which events that took place in the 1860s and 70s are shaped into a story in the contemporary context of the 1981 Springbok Tour, is a prime example of this relationship. *The Te Kooti Trail* was made in the aftermath of World War One; the second *Rewi's Last Stand* addresses a nation on the brink of a centenary and entering another world war. *The Killing of Kane*, made in 1971 after a decade of international upheaval and colonial wars of liberation, comes as much out of a new critical self-scrutiny among some Pākehā as it does out of an interest in the past; and *The Governor*, later in the 1970s, attacked the smugness of mid-century white New Zealand's view of race relations. That Belich was both attacked and praised for the *New Zealand Wars* documentary series in the 1990s says a lot about the series' capacity to engage with the moment of its production. In the *Kiingitanga* series the mana of King Tāwhiao, fighting for his people in the nineteenth century, stands behind the embattled King Tūheitea in the present day.

This idea that the past is always a product of the present aligns these filmmaking practices with the workings of memory. It is well established that collective memory moulds itself – at times notoriously – in response to each new present and re-forms as current needs and contemporary worldviews demand. Maurice Halbwachs, whose work initiated the modern study of how social groups remember, argued that collective memory is shaped in two distinctive ways: it always addresses the present, and is always formed within social frameworks.[34] The 90 years of film productions in this book can be understood as a series of acts of memory, each of which selects and re-presents historical events for a specific present, out of a specific social framework.

Responding to the erosion of collective memory of the New Zealand Wars through the middle of the twentieth century, the filmmakers from the 1970s onwards are all conscious, in one way or another, that they are dealing with events that have *not* formed part of the 'national story', or that Pākehā New Zealand especially has preferred to set apart from the national story or to forget altogether. One after another, as filmmakers ask audiences to re-examine the wars, their films arrive as bearers of unfamiliar and discomforting truths. Most strangely, as a group of works cropping up here and there over the generations they suggest how sporadic the cultural memory of the New Zealand Wars has been: 'we seem to be remembering about them at every opportunity, and then forgetting about them everyplace in between'.[35] The ongoing relationship between films and histories and memory can nevertheless be traced in the way historical reinterpretations come to be incorporated – often gradually and unevenly – into cultural memory, as changing interpretations of historical figures or events are taken on and acquire the status of a truth, or not.

A film's afterlife is another connection between film, history and memory. Its place in ongoing memory has to do with quality, of course, but other factors are in play too. Distribution and changing technologies affect a film's circulation and its accessibility to viewers. Hayward's film screenings were public occasions that took place sometimes decades apart; but his films are now accessible only through a visit to Ngā Taonga Sound and Vision, the New Zealand film and sound archive (although there are a few poor-quality video copies in limited circulation). Television dramas of the 1970s, made before recording from broadcasts was possible, disappeared rapidly from public access. Rescreenings were limited by copyright restrictions on availability, but some lived on in the cultural memory of viewers. The arrival of online streaming has brought some of them out of the archives and into the public arena again, especially with the establishment and growth of the NZ On Screen archive.[36] Later films sometimes gained an afterlife through video or DVD release, but what was made available depended on decisions made by production companies. There is still a great variation in availability, even of the most recent productions; and documentary especially is often subject to the short life of on-demand access.

Cultural authority, creative control and collaboration

Until the late 1990s, with only one exception, the directors of all the films about the New Zealand Wars were Pākehā men. This demographic has historically enjoyed seniority in the industry and a claim on funding that was far less accessible to female directors and Māori directors. And although there are Māori directors of the later productions, only in the most recent have there been women with creative control – in *Stories of Ruapekapeka*, initiated by Mihingārangi Forbes, and in Ria Hall's *Rules of Engagement* music video. The changes evident in Māori-led productions, discussed in chapter 9, support the view that a more representative set of directors would likely produce a different body of work. The bias of the narrow demographic is apparent in the persistence of particular themes and perspectives, including the interest in cultural go-betweens, real or fictional, as nation-forging individuals, and the underrepresentation of events that took place entirely in te ao Māori. These are symptoms of a settler–colonial legacy. It does not make the films any less worthy of discussion, however, and for several reasons the representational bias should not be overstated.

The first reason is the inherently collaborative nature of film, and its reliance on the willing participation of many people in a variety of capacities – a director is not the only person who makes a film.[37] While some Māori actors may just have been doing a job, others opted in to keep an eye on things. Some pushed back against stories they did not like and were successful in making changes, or intervened in other ways. They may have taken the role because they thought it was good; or they were explicitly invited to contribute to its crafting. Often, by virtue of their upbringing, the actors were not only performers but recognised experts on such things as language, dress, thought and tikanga. Across these screen histories a great variety of conversations took place between filmmakers, Māori casts and crews and iwi as they dealt with each other. Te Pairi Tūterangi, Raureti Te Huia, Ramai Te Miha, Don Selwyn, Napi Waaka, Merata Mita and Joe Malcolm contributed more than their nominal roles might suggest, although recognition of their expertise did not always come in the form of credits or payment. Since the late 1990s, Māori have come in at higher levels of creative authority. Tainui Stephens is the first prominent example, and has been followed in Māori-initiated productions by others such as Tearepa Kahi, Paora Joseph, Mahanga Pihama, Mihingārangi Forbes and Ria Hall.

The priorities of cultural advisors whose main aim was to protect the integrity of stories concerning Māori were sometimes at odds with those of writers or directors who were intent on creating compelling narratives and marketable films. Their roles in a production and their responsibilities – to hapū and iwi or to an understanding of the past; to the integrity of aesthetics or narrative or to investors – meant they had varying stakes in a film. There might be a range of opinions about the right to tell stories – especially, whether or not stories about tīpuna were common property that anyone could tell. European ideas about creative freedom do not always mesh with the wishes of iwi or hapū to protect how stories are told, ensure tīpuna are represented respectfully, or keep some knowledge private or sacred. Pākehā by no means always had their way. There is perhaps no more remarkable example of this than the political presssure Ringatū elders brought to bear on Rudall Hayward when he made *The Te Kooti Trail* in 1927: they used their parliamentary representatives to prevent its release until sections that they found offensive were removed or altered.

The authority of Pākehā men was further mitigated by the fact that most films were shot on or near historical locations. This meant that filming involved the very land that had been fought over. Filmmaking is time-consuming, so relationships between filmmakers and mana whenua unfolded over time, from early visits to consult and to seek out locations and visit marae, to shoots and on to local premieres. In the process, filmmakers talked with iwi about the past, about involving iwi members in the production and cast, about protocols during the shoot, and about onscreen representation of place, people and story. This could go well or badly and there were often blunders – but filmmakers had a lot riding on it going well.

Local Māori whose tīpuna were involved in the conflicts sometimes found that their knowledge was accorded a new value – as descendants of Wiremu Tāmihana did in the making of *The Governor*; or they discovered a past they were unaware of. Several productions involved Māori who gained a deeper knowledge of their own past, like the local extras on *Utu*. Locations could be sites of cultural encounter and of the production of knowledge as people exchanged historical information handed down orally or gathered from archives. By the same token, these encounters could create suspicion and disaffection among mana whenua about outsiders who seemed to arrive out of the blue to capitalise on local stories. Some local Pākehā were highly supportive of the filmmaking – including, for example, members of the Te Awamutu Historical Society who assisted with *Rewi's Last Stand* in the 1930s. Others were more wary: at one site in the late 1990s, anxious Pākehā landowners would not allow *The New Zealand Wars* to be filmed on a historical location.

The Pākehā filmmakers, moreover, were in varying ways relatively atypical, or they would not have been interested in filmmaking let alone in the troubling colonial past. They were all committed in one way or another to showing a neglected side of the national history, and they gave a more sympathetic hearing to Māori perspectives than was common at the time. They came shaped by their own histories and prejudices, naturally, and as filmmakers they also all wanted to make good films, to entertain, and to get good audiences, so they usually had diverse and sometimes conflicting agendas.

The filmmakers often found that their involvement in these films altered them and their careers. 'It radically changed me,' said Michael Noonan about his research on colonial history for *The Governor*. Rudall Hayward, after he had made three films about colonial conflict, went on to collaborate with the female lead of the last of them, Ramai Te Miha (who later became his wife) to make other films that engaged with te ao Māori. For Vincent Ward the process began early and took a more circuitous path. As a young man he found himself changed by living and filming in a Māori community, where he filmed *In Spring One Plants Alone*. The persistence of this experience in his life and imagination led him to make a series of films, both in New Zealand and elsewhere, that reflected on the effects of close encounter with another culture. Many years on, he returned to the subject of *In Spring* when he made *River Queen* and *Rain of the Children*.

These filmmaking engagements between Pākehā men and Māori worlds, while they took a variety of forms, could echo the experiences of the cultural go-betweens at the centre of their historical narratives: filmmaking itself became an instrument of cultural change. It is not necessary to idealise this process to recognise it as a catalyst. As Peter Limbrick has argued in his study of *Hei Tiki* and *The Seekers*, both made with Māori communities in the Bay of Plenty, 'film is pulled into settler and indigenous histories and narratives of belonging … [Māori and Pākehā] were agents in a messy process of colonial encounter in which many parties interacted and were thus transformed.'[38]

Māori directors, too, have found these films about the wars to be journeys of discovery. Tearepa Kahi inserts himself into the journey of the *Te Hookioi* press as a traveller in search of the past. For Mahanga Pihama the personal stories that came down through generations were revelations. The era of Māori writers and directors is just beginning. Lee Tamahori has recently discussed the idea of a Te Kooti story set in the present day: perhaps this will be the first fiction feature on the wars from a Māori director.[39]

Films about colonial warfare involved Māori cast and crew more than most films of their time, providing opportunities for Māori actors to play substantial parts and for crew to gain experience and seniority. Often this led on to other film work. *The Governor*, for example, offered serious roles to many Māori actors. George Hēnare, Wī Kuki Kaa and Don Selwyn, who were already accomplished actors, acquired experience and recognition through playing lead roles. Tamahori worked as a boom operator on *The Governor* and Geoff Murphy's *Goodbye Pork Pie*, but on *Utu* he was promoted to first assistant director. The advantages accrued less often to women, although Ramai Hayward and Merata Mita both went on to direct feature films. Tainui Stephens, who directed *The New Zealand Wars* and went on to work with Ward, speaks warmly of the way that through these films, his role changed from Māori 'fixer-upper' to a genuine collaboration.

The gains in Māori creative control, celebrated in Libby Hakaraia and Tainui Stephens' recent documentary *Hautoa Ma! The rise of Māori cinema* (2016), have resulted from several converging factors. The first is the increasing presence of Māori in the film and television industries; this gained some impetus through some of the productions discussed here. Digital media and diversifying platforms have increased flexibility and reduced costs. The documentaries *The Flight of Te Hookioi* and *Tātarakihi: The children of Parihaka* are a sign of a growing market for feature-length documentary that can begin with release in theatres – usually at festivals both in Aotearoa and internationally, especially indigenous film festivals – and move on from there, perhaps to the sale of television rights. The establishment of Māori Television in 2004 meant that there was now a broadcaster interested in Māori subjects as its main concern rather than as niche programming. Mainstream television's Māori programming – *Koha*, *Waka Huia* – had already provided Māori audiences, but Māori Television brought a substantial and committed Māori audience and potential for a wider range of commissions, although – as is the case for older media in general at present – it is under threat from other platforms.

TOP: On the set of *The Governor*, Don Selwyn talks about making historical television from Māori perspectives, and what Māori cast and crew are learning through involvement in the production.
BOTTOM: Director Geoff Murphy and first assistant director Lee Tamahori eat lunch in the cold and discuss the rest of the day's shoot on *Utu*.

The Making of the Governor (1977); *Making Utu*, Gaylene Preston Productions (1983).

Descent and connection

The connections between Māori performers or iwi speakers and their tīpuna were often the subject of serious consideration, especially in documentary or dramatised documentary, and these connections were taken seriously by Māori audiences. Frequently the matter of the appropriateness of an actor was raised. For the series *The Governor* there were many hui where casting was discussed. In *Rain of the Children* most of the performers in the film's dramatic sequences came from Waimana, like the film's subjects. When professional actors came in from outside, in this and other productions, there were mixed feelings and often negotiations to be undertaken. As early as 1925 and as late as 2007 there have been objections to performers from other iwi taking on roles that some felt they had no claim or connection to. These were never absolute dictates, though – distant whakapapa links or other justifications could be found to support an actor who was considered right for a part. Don Selwyn from Ngāti Kurī and Te Aupōuri in the Far North had the Māori Queen's blessing to play Ngāti Hauā leader Wiremu Tāmihana from the Waikato, for example. Selwyn pointed to the weight of responsibility involved in taking on the mantle of a major historical figure: 'that's who you're playing, *that's who you are*'. It was seldom done lightly. Even in fiction films, where casting was less stringently associated with descent, success attached to the fittingness between performer and a recognisably 'historical' character. Sylvia Kaa speaks of how comfortable her husband Wī Kuki Kaa was in his role as a soldier in the constabulary in *Utu*, for example, because he descended from a hapū that had been divided during the campaign against Te Kooti: it was a role that 'had to do with him'.

Performances captured on screen could acquire a resonance and value of their own. Merata Mita's influential essay 'The Soul and the Image' outlines the history of the relationship between Māori and photographic images and shows the value placed on a photograph or film as a sign of the continuing life of someone who has since died. For this reason, film screenings are often emotional or tearful events.[40] When films are a permanent record of tīpuna or of whenua, or even a reminder of community involvement in their local production, they are frequently accorded an intrinsic value quite apart from the story they tell or their aesthetic merits. But this may come and go, and the affections may be very local. Whakatāne welcomed *The Te Kooti Trail* home in 1964 with warm affection, and *Utu Redux*, rising anew on its 30th anniversary, was greeted by a noisy audience – Māori and Pākehā – in 2013.

'Our stories' and the economics of a small nation's screen industries

'These are our stories, our people. Our children need to learn about them,' says narrator Mike King as he launches into a documentary about the soldier Gustavus von Tempsky. The filmmakers in this book all express a similar sentiment as they embark on stories of colonial conflict, although they may mean different things by 'our stories'. From Rudall Hayward, who knew there were incidents in the New Zealand past just as gripping as those of the American West, to Mihingārangi Forbes (Ngāti Paoa, Ngāti Maniapoto) stitching together the past and the present of Northland, screen productions are driven by a sense that there are stories that should or must be told. In spite of these aspirations 'our stories' have always struggled with large controlling forces, both external – in the form of the great influx of films in English from larger industries, especially Hollywood, and internal – the shifting industrial and economic structures of the screen industries. Limbrick argues that we must understand such apparently 'national' stories as effectively transnational – as much the creations of California and London, as of Whakatāne or Wellington – since their industries are so powerfully circumscribed by global markets.[41]

Furthermore, where 'our stories' are imagined as 'New Zealand stories', the stories told here, one way or another, contest or trouble an easy sense of nationhood. Geoff Murphy recalled that in the 1970s 'we were very nationalistic, and very sort of conscious that we were creating the foundation of New Zealand's national cinema', but the nationalism he was talking about was far from being an uncritical endorsement of the state.[42] Instead, he and his collaborators' engagement with the nation is closer to what Paul Willemen refers to when he distinguishes between a narrow form of nationalistic cinema and a cinema that scrutinises the 'multilayeredness of specific socio-cultural formations'.[43] Duncan Petrie takes up Willemen's distinction in his discussion of the New Zealand film industry as a cinema of a small nation.[44] Petrie points out that film's re-emergence from the 1970s coincided with the period of decolonisation in New Zealand and a consequent reforging of national identity – in the framework of the unravelling of historical ties to Britain after 1973; the Māori renaissance from the 1970s on and its articulation of the issues of land, culture and language; the deregulation initiated by the fourth Labour government in the 1980s; and the associated impacts of globalisation. In this rapidly changing era, Petrie argues, the films that emerged routinely argued back to the state. Indeed, *Utu* bore signs of both forms of nationalism: it had no foreign stars and, while it adapted genres and styles from American and Japanese cinema, it was an assertive statement of what could be done in New Zealand; it was directed first to New Zealanders. Yet its engagement with the nation took the form of a sustained critique of the colonial foundations of the contemporary New Zealand state, and it persistently points to continuities between the past and a turbulent present.

Even Hayward's *The Te Kooti Trail*, which largely applauds the nation-forming bonds between newly formed colonial men and 'friendly' Māori, and endorses the imperial project, cannot help but express some nostalgia at the defeat of Te Kooti's resistance to Empire.[45] Hayward's second *Rewi* (1940), while it reiterates the dominant belief in 'mutual interracial respect' forged at Ōrākau, simultaneously tells a brutal story of colonial impact. Hayward's desire to put 'our own stories' on screen was an effort to mitigate the tide of Hollywood westerns, but it was not narrowly nationalistic: his films told a complex national story that incorporated considerable sympathy with Māori resistance. The history of colonial conflict has proven attractive to filmmakers because it confronted generations of viewers with a past that was just as exciting as anyone else's – as commentators on the documentary series *The New Zealand Wars* repeatedly point out – but it also engaged them precisely because it troubled the surface of nationhood. Most of these filmmakers set out to challenge a national self-satisfaction over race relations that they thought had endured for far too long.

Petrie's discussion of New Zealand cinema elaborates on an ongoing problem associated with creating nation-troubling films in a small nation's economy. The filmmakers who were creating these contestatory narratives were working in an expensive medium and selling to a small market, which meant that this argumentative national cinema required state intervention. This arrived in the form of the New Zealand Film

Commission in 1978. As Petrie explains, the Film Commission was the outcome of 'a long process of political lobbying … [I]n the New Zealand case, the most constant refrain in the public discourse was the contribution that film could make to a sense of national identity.' Yet far from consolidating a narrow nationhood, he argues, these state-supported films persistently undermined rather than endorsed a unified national identity.[46] This was especially true of films about the New Zealand Wars, which were always more or less liable to bite the hand of the state that funded them. The same issues applied in television.

This precarious situation highlights the way in which films – and especially historical films with their higher production costs – have consistently negotiated a complicated web of industrial, institutional, government and market factors. Funds must be found somewhere, and they come with commitments. Hayward had created local companies and sold shares to fund his films, which left him with some obligation to produce films that were acceptable to his shareholders – settlers, businessmen, local iwi. The cost of sound equipment and production, though, combined with competition from Hollywood, made local features effectively uneconomic through the middle of the twentieth century: the industry starved from the 1940s until the mid-1970s, nursed along by the creation of the National Film Unit in 1941 and the dogged persistence of John O'Shea's Pacific Films. Just a handful of films appeared over these years.[47] Television, which arrived in 1960, took some years to create drama but when it did, it acquired status as a cultural flagship. For a while, drama was generously funded by today's standards, and its creators had considerable freedom. *The Killing of Kane* and *The Governor* both emerged out of this system – and each levelled barbs at a nation overly contented with its colonial past.[48]

By the mid-1970s today's independent film industry was beginning to emerge – operating on uncertain budgets and on the back of a bohemian culture structured around clusters of families and friends, most of whom were prepared to work for little or nothing;[49] they borrowed equipment and 'borrowed' film stock. Television and film remained two worlds, flourishing for different reasons; but in practice, personnel from each side worked in both industries through the 1970s and early 80s, in an era of creative, financial and ideological possibilities. *Utu* emerged out of the first few years of the Film Commission's operation, when directors in film still had a fairly free hand – and, more importantly, it coincided with the 'tax shelter years' – a brief period in which a tax break designed for another purpose accidentally made possible unprecedented budgets for feature films.[50] None of these independent productions depended on overseas sales, although Murphy hoped for them. Free from dependence on international finance, their creators could address New Zealanders, speaking in local terms, assuming local knowledge and questioning cultural memory and the self-fashioning of national identities. Nor were they unduly tempted to exploit the exotic to hype sales.

The New Zealand Wars documentary series took viewers to parts of their country that many knew nothing about, and told them stories they had never heard. Episode 5 related the events of the East Coast Wars including the conflicts within iwi where some hapū fought with the Crown and some against. This tekoteko gives dramatic emphasis to these internal rifts. It represents the Ngāti Porou ancestor Tūterangiwhiu, and stands on top of the whare whakairo Porourangi at Waiōmatatini on East Cape. Porourangi was built after the wars by the famed Ngāti Porou leader Rāpata Wahawaha.

The New Zealand Wars (1998). Landmark Productions, courtesy of Colin McRae. With the permission of Marie Collier for the kaitiaki of Porourangi.

In 1989 the second major funding organisation for the screen industry in New Zealand was established. It emerged out of a different economic world from the Film Commission, which was set up in 1978 under a regime that assumed the need for state support if there was to be a film industry. The Broadcasting Commission, quickly renamed New Zealand On Air, by contrast, was established in 1989 as part of a massive government push to deregulation. In the case of television this meant dismantling the state broadcaster's inhouse system of television production and replacing it with a system of competitive bidding for funding by independent production houses.[51] As Petrie shows, the Film Commission was later reforged in the deregulated era, with greater expectation of return on investment. In parallel with the trend in television, the implications of attracting international funding and appealing to international markets were altering the economies of screen production. As Petrie says:

> *Whatever the beliefs and motivations of those in charge of funding bodies like the New Zealand Film Commission, they are now compelled to pay more than lip service to the economics of culture. However, delivering the goods, in terms of improving the share of the domestic market for New Zealand films, let alone building an international audience through increased sales and marketing, has proven a very tough nut to crack.*[52]

The end of the 1980s profoundly reshaped the screen industries, both film and television, and the changes have endured even though the cultures of the two industries remain quite distinct. International co-production became inevitable for larger television budgets and mid-sized film budgets – with the attendant implications that an international market is necessary, international backers are usually involved in creative decisions, and cast and crew are more likely to be drawn from a global workforce. There were some benefits in the increased size of the industry and the connections to a global industry – which undoubtedly extended expertise, some forms of opportunity and the international profile of the New Zealand industry.

The closing of the tax loophole in the early 1980s meant that funding for New Zealand film became very hard to raise locally. A great deal of talent left the country, and some directors began a transnational shuttle between the international productions that would pay the bills and the New Zealand ones they wanted to make – if they could fund them. Local production tended to narrow down to genres that could be produced within locally feasible budgets. This had an important implication for the funding of historical film, which was always notoriously expensive. In addition, the film workers, friends and families who had once worked for little or nothing now needed an income and wanted to be paid. Costs rose for this and other reasons. International financing was now effectively a prerequisite for historical drama. In the global market, international backers looked for assurance that films would address international audiences at well as local ones. They needed stars with international recognition – who certainly did not work for nothing. Large-scale historical drama, for film or television, now had to negotiate between the desire to create national stories that were 'our stories' and spoke to local audiences – which the productions of the 1970s and early 80s had been able to prioritise – and the demands of a global marketplace. Despite the establishment of a Film Fund in 2000 for mid-range productions, local funding lagged further behind ballooning costs.[53] Mid-sized fiction features steadily became less feasible than smaller-scale productions that could employ cheaper and more flexible technologies. Historical features always came in at the upper end of the budget range, and funding – a constant factor that controlled filmmaking more than other creative activities – became a more and more complex dimension of historical filmmaking.

Two productions that did tackle the challenge of creating expensive historical dramas within these global relationships were the television series *Greenstone* (1999) and the feature film *River Queen* (2005). It is no coincidence that these were the most ambitious and most costly historical productions in each medium in the period they were made in, and that each struggled with the problems of address to audiences and of creative control that international co-production brought.

Smaller productions grapple with other aspects of a deregulated industry. Support for historical documentary has waxed and waned – often reflecting changes in NZ On Air personnel and policy, and broadcaster interest and emphasis. Every documentary-maker I spoke with had a funding story to tell. Te Māngai Pāho which funds Māori language and culture content alongside NZ On Air, and Māori Television which began in 2004, expanded the avenues for broadcasting, but in the deregulated environment all broadcasters remain cautious in their commitments.[54] Historical documentary continues to compete on an uneven playing field against contemporary subjects both because of its higher costs and because of the perennial perception that it is 'worthy' material that will not rate well. Although NZ On Air is mandated to fund programming of cultural significance, the accompanying requirement of ratings performance means that broadcasters are reluctant to take a risk on historical programming when lighter, safer bets are on offer. It is not much of a stretch to say that, as a result, New Zealanders know a great deal more about the history of other countries than they do about their own.

In countries such as New Zealand that constitute part of the English-speaking global market for the much more lavishly funded US and British screen industries, a small nation's industry competes with films and television programming made on much grander budgets than the local ones. International television content in English comes cheap to New Zealand broadcasters, who do not have to commission it but can purchase screening rights after the content has recouped most of its investment in larger markets. This is not a two-way street for New Zealand production companies. Most filmmakers interviewed here hoped for international sales, but competing on the global market is hard for 'niche' small-nation industries. In order to pitch to international appeal, plot, writing and casting decisions may have to be compromised in ways that undermine the integrity of the local – such as ensuring that the local is made explicable to the international, and complying with generic codes and conventions that have their origins in other cultures. At some point, these are 'our stories' no longer: filmmakers must regularly decide where that point is and whether it is a price worth paying.

One measure of filmmakers' ability to sustain their orientation to the local context is the extent to which te reo Māori is spoken in New Zealand Wars stories. As early as 1927, Māori was appearing in intertitles on the silent screen, and it was used frequently in films about the wars. This was often a means of maintaining a historical record of well-known statements such as those made at Ōrākau – but it also indicated that filmmakers saw themselves speaking to Māori as well as to Pākehā audiences, and acknowledging the language itself. Often there is a conscious inclusion of te reo in these films – in the final words that become a tribute to Monika in *The Te Kooti Trail* or in the finely chosen wording of scenes in *Rewi's*

Last Stand; in Wiremu's final speech in *Utu*; in the extensive use of te reo in Episode 4 of *The Governor* – but also in the increasingly frequent inclusion of interview material in te reo in documentaries, especially those made for Māori Television. Over time, the subject of the wars has provided many opportunities for normalising the onscreen use of te reo – but its use is more frequent in locally funded productions.

*

It has been said that the New Zealand Wars are the object of systematic cultural amnesia in much of Pākehā New Zealand: certainly governments have been reluctant to incorporate the wars into formal national remembrance, and only after a sustained campaign given impetus by calls for a national day of commemoration in 2014, the petition initiated by Waimarama Anderson and Leah Bell the following year, and the appointment of a sympathetic minister of internal affairs in Chris Finlayson, was Te Rā Maumahara established in 2016. Nor has the wish to remember the wars been uniform in te ao Māori, with iwi and hapū holding diverse perspectives on the past and a variety of reasons to remember or forget. And yet, to use Bruce Babington's words, the New Zealand Wars epic is 'the most resonant genre' in New Zealand fiction feature film. One after another filmmakers have undertaken the difficult task of making not only feature films but documentary, television drama and other kinds of screen stories of these wars. Given the difficulty involved in funding and producing historical film and of filming in historical locations, these efforts are testimony to an extraordinary cultural determination on the part of creative communities to portray this past. The films represent a huge financial commitment on the part of individuals and institutions, as well as the commitment of years of labour; their creators often look back on these productions as their best, if most demanding work. They are testimony to a long history of cultural engagement in which Māori and non-Māori have worked together on projects they may often have disagreed about, but where they nevertheless found ways to rearticulate and remake the past. There are many accounts here of Pākehā whose stories shifted in the making as they became more familiar with sources and with mana whenua; and conversely, there are accounts of Māori who came onto a film set and discovered a past they knew nothing about, or in which they found a new value as it was discussed and made its way on to the screen. The stories are many and diverse – good and bad but mostly mixed – and they each represent processes of negotiation, accommodation, participation and engagement between filmmakers, iwi and historians.

Some notes on sources and approaches

Archival records of some of the productions discussed here are held in the collection of Ngā Taonga Sound and Vision. Newspaper reports on the making of films and reviews offer some background to the productions and how audiences responded to them. I have tried as far as possible to interview people involved with the making of each production, or their descendants, and many people involved have been enormously generous with their time, their knowledge and their insights. As much as possible I have let them speak in their own words. Some films were made too long ago for families to remember much; others are too recent, or too difficult, for some of those involved to want to discuss them. Therefore, there are perspectives on these films that I have not been able to properly represent.

Scholarly work from several fields has informed my argument; I note only a sample below. Martin Blythe's *Naming the Other: Images of the Maori in New Zealand film and television*, Jonathan Dennis and Jan Bieringa's *Film in Aotearoa New Zealand*, Bruce Babington's *History of the New Zealand Fiction Feature Film* and Diane Pivac et al., *New Zealand Film: An illustrated history* scope out the broader territory of the history of New Zealand film, and include valuable discussions of some of the films analysed here. Studies of the screen industries – Trisha Dunleavy's *Ourselves in Primetime*, Dunleavy and Joyce's *New Zealand Film and Television*, Jo Smith's *Māori Television* and a series of articles by Mary Debrett – have been invaluable in charting out the industrial context, as have Roger Horrocks' various essays. As well as the body of international work on historical film, two collections on historical film made in New Zealand – *Making Film and Television Histories: Australia and New Zealand* and *New Zealand Cinema: Interpreting the past* – include studies of some of the films on the New Zealand Wars. Peter Limbrick's *Making Settler Cinemas* provides a comparative example of the contextual approach I have taken.[55] There are several rich and thoughtful pieces of graduate research relating to this field: Diane Pivac's honours dissertation on *The Te Kooti Trail*; Melissa Cross's master's thesis on the score of the 1940 *Rewi's Last Stand* and Gregory Wood's on James Cowan; and three PhD theses: Lisa Perrott's study of *The New Zealand Wars* documentary series, Lynette Read's study of Vincent Ward's aesthetic, and Cherie Lacey's psychoanalytic study of settler subjectivity in New Zealand historical films.[56]

Finally, a note of caution. It is extraordinarily easy, from the comfort of the present and in the position of the viewer, to cast a superior eye backwards and identify filmmakers' shortcomings rather than their achievements, especially as technical advances, aesthetic conventions and the revolutions of ideology and theory open up an ever-increasing distance from the screen stories and the filmmaking practices of earlier periods. The historian E.P. Thompson famously called such a stance 'the enormous condescension of posterity'. I have tried not to be that kind of scholar, and to resist easy judgement. In inquiring into these screen productions I have sought to keep several considerations in mind. The first is that filmmaking (especially in a small nation) is hard and expensive, and filmmakers are invariably involved in compromise as the films they hope to make turn into the films they are able to make. Indeed, I discuss many examples of these compromises in what follows. The second consideration relates to the ideologies and vocabularies of race relations and racism, which are subject to rigorous critical surveillance, but also to constant change as the meanings understood by one generation slip beneath the terminologies of the following one. In quoting from statements made in the past, I quote the language used then, but the reader should keep in mind that these vocabularies change and that the past speaks in its own terms: in short, the historical use of a particular phrase is not a definitive sign of racism. An ethical consideration arises from the fact that I asked filmmakers, performers, descendants, historians and others to talk to me about these films and the making of them. Those who agreed to do so have spoken openly and freely, and I have aimed to acknowledge this openness with respect. Sometimes they have not agreed with each other, and where this occurs I have tried to reflect differing perspectives without passing judgement.

HAYWARD IN THE BAY OF PLENTY
The silent *Rewi's Last Stand* and *The Te Kooti Trail*

As a young man in the early 1900s Rudall Hayward, already 'fascinated by what's been called our rough hewn story', devoured James Cowan's *The Adventures of Kimble Bent* and began to imagine the New Zealand past in moving images:

> I think that James Cowan had in his mind the idea that the younger generation would read this and be inspired by its story because it came right from the very heart of the country. That's what really started me thinking about New Zealand films. When I saw all round me American films dealing with the history of their West I considered that New Zealand had material equally as fascinating because when you look into it you find that the period of unrest in New Zealand when there was fighting going on between Maoris and Pakehas, all through that period of pioneering … a vast amount of material is available in the form of historical accounts which would make fascinating films.[1]

Hayward was descended from several generations of professional entertainers. His family emigrated from England to New Zealand when he was four and toured variety shows that included short films, sometimes locally made ones.[2] He grew up in and around theatres, watching films that brought romance, thrills, Cowboys and Indians and news from around the globe to the cities and small towns of the colony.

Hayward took to filmmaking at a time when production and distribution were not yet separate parts of the industry. He brought to it a robust energy, resourceful pragmatism and a trained eye for the box office and publicity. Working with minimal budgets he learned on the hoof to make films that were both economical and popular. His first two-reel film, *The Bloke from Freeman's Bay* (1921) 'made on less than a shoe string', he later admitted was 'terrible': his uncle offered to pay him to 'burn it to save the family name'. Hayward declined; instead he and a friend plastered Auckland with posters that were 'so much better than the film itself' that they had a crowd fighting to get in. Hayward called the fire brigade and the police, and then the newspaper, and next day published a public apology to 'the number of people who were crushed in the crowd outside the West End Theatre last night' – ensuring a fortnight's run in Auckland and full houses when he toured the country.[3] Luckily, his films improved.

From the first public screening of moving pictures in Auckland in 1896, films caught popular attention. The first local film, of troops departing for South Africa, was made in 1900. The following year the government commissioned the *Royal Visit of the Duke and Duchess of Cornwall to New Zealand*,

1901, including their welcome to Rotorua by 5000 Māori from all parts of the country. This was the beginning of a three-way relationship of filmmakers, Māori and Rotorua scenery: over the next 20 years three films were made of the Hinemoa legend alone, among a cluster of films by visiting and local filmmakers: Frenchman Gaston Méliès, American Alexander Markey, New Zealand-based Australian George Tarr, Australians Raymond Longford and Beaumont Smith, and New Zealanders Hayward, Ted Coubray and Charles Newnham.[4]

Rudall's uncle Henry Hayward opened his first picture theatre in 1909, and his company and Fullers became the two leading distributors; by 1912 Haywards owned 33 theatres. Films rapidly joined other forms of popular entertainment and became a weekly outing for a large proportion of the population. In 1915 there were 165 picture theatres in the country; by 1928 there were 612 theatres in the cities and towns, and 359 'country circuits' that took films to more remote areas.[5]

The silent-era westerns were regular fare in cinemas right around the country, from the smallest towns to the cities, through Hayward's youth. Their popularity is evident from the extra publicity often attached to them. As Jacquelyn Kilpatrick has shown, the 'celluloid Indian' was instrumental in creating an 'all-purpose, generic Indian' for consumption by a white population that seldom or never encountered actual Native Americans. Many used white actors in dark makeup for lead 'Indian' roles, rode roughshod over customary practice and combined the dress and practices of unrelated tribes with gay abandon. The silent westerns, in their reliance on the codes of melodrama, produced either 'noble or bloody savages' – seldom anything in between. Kilpatrick observes that although both negative and positive portrayals appeared in these stereotypical narratives – and in the early years the 'noble' dominated – it was the negative that ultimately won out.[6] Occasional exceptions toured New Zealand, including Native American director James Young Deer's *White Fawn's Devotion* (1910).[7] In 1926 the 'sixth annual Paramount Week' was celebrated, including 'some big attractions from the works of Zane Grey'. The same notice promotes the visit of 'ten North American Indians' featured in *The Vanishing Race*. The touring party attracted a lot of attention on its arrival from Sydney in January 1927 and during its tour of the country, including visits to marae in Rotorua and Ōtaki.[8]

In some respects Hayward's films reiterated the narratives of inevitable colonial expansion overcoming wild indigeneity that most early Hollywood westerns had laid down – 'genre memory' had established the forms in which colonial conflict was translated to film. The translation of 'Cowboys and Indians' into 'Pakehas and Maoris' was a logical progression for Hayward, but the move from one side of the Pacific to the other wrought changes, too. While his portrayals included motifs familiar to the filmgoers of the time – the Indian maiden who sacrifices herself for a white hero, the descent from a hilltop by hostile 'natives' on horseback as they prepare to lay siege to an ill-defended settlement, or a wild chase through rough country – there is an individuality and a sympathy for figures on both sides in his films that prevent them collapsing into stereotype. Hayward knew the movies, but he was always closely attentive to the local histories of colonial encounter – this too was important to him. In contrast to some of the foreign filmmakers who arrived to make films in Aotearoa, he always acknowledged the calibre of Māori performers. In his films Māori always played Māori. He later recalled with disgust the custom of 'browning up' imported white heroines: one of his first jobs on a film set had been to dye the legs and arms of an Australian actor brown so she could play a Māori woman, but, he recalled, 'acting against a background of Rotorua Maoris she was at a great disadvantage, and despite her undoubted talents, was never convincing'.[9]

Hayward's instinctive showmanship, combined with a genuine interest in making films about Aotearoa, translated into a talent for generating community involvement in his projects – an enormous asset in the early years of local filmmaking. It was a talent honed during his sequence of films on the New Zealand Wars, which drew on the cooperation of local townspeople and iwi – showing his increasing understanding of what Māori brought to films about the wars, and how he could work with Māori actors.

Telling the national story on film

The US westerns of the silent era have come under fire for their telling of a national past – whether for exploiting 'natives' as exotic box-office fodder or for purveying heroic stories of colonial expansion. There were elements of these imperatives in Hayward's filmmaking: the ordinary soldiers of *The Te Kooti Trail* nobly 'make the pathway safe' for the settlers yet to come, and bring about the inevitable defeat of the rebellious Te Kooti – themes that are well in tune with the more common fare of silent-era and early sound westerns. But Hayward's stories of colonial conflict, and his filmmaking practice, ran in many directions. The cultural engagements that took place as these histories were enacted shaped the stories the films told; and, as Bruce Babington observes, they are 'redolent … not only of heroic, sacrificial progress but of melancholy and nostalgia'.[10] An understanding of these films requires that we recognise the agency of the Māori casts, and Hayward's own complexity.

Hayward's first film feature, *My Lady of the Cave* (1922) adapted a newspaper serial about the aftermath of the wars.[11] He went on to make three New Zealand Wars films: two silent films, *Rewi's Last Stand* (1925; of which only most of the first reel and a plot summary survive), *The Te Kooti Trail* (1927), and a sound version of *Rewi's Last Stand* (1940). The second *Rewi* is less a remake than a different film, with a different scenario from the silent version. It has not survived in its entirety: the existing version is a recut, much shortened film, *The Last Stand* (1949) – made in order to fit into double-feature screenings in Britain. *The Te Kooti Trail* is therefore the only one of the three films that is now available in close to its original form: there is some decomposition in the copy restored in recent years by Ngā Taonga Sound and Vision, but it is almost complete. It is not the best known of the three, but it is, I think, the best film.

All three films attracted attention nationwide, but they were local events, too. Each had a definitively local character, and each was made using a production company formed for the purpose by Hayward and local residents – Maori War Films Ltd for the first *Rewi*, Whakatane Films for *The Te Kooti Trail* and Frontier Films for *The Last Stand*. Hayward brought in actors for some lead roles but most parts were played by locals. Cowan's histories were Hayward's main historical source for each film – indeed, he took his cues directly from Cowan – but he also drew on other written sources and on local knowledge. For each of the films on the wars he endeavoured to work with people who had taken part in the actual events portrayed in the film, or their relatives.

Hayward's New Zealand Wars films share some common themes. His socialist sympathies inform his affectionate treatment of ordinary soldiers – the Forest Rangers, the colonial troops of Te Kooti's War and the Māori soldiers of the Arawa Flying Column. These irregulars drink, fool around, form close bonds with each other and provide the comic relief, but in the heat of battle they attain nation-building stature. Honourable and skilful, they fight to protect Māori women and they respect a 'worthy foe'. Their manly egalitarianism is often contrasted with pompous imperial soldiers or dithering senior officers.

Another theme that runs through Hayward's war films is that, although they necessarily dramatise conflict, he avoids making that conflict explicitly racial. Enmity is mitigated by his depiction of interracial intimacies – friendships, alliance and love affairs – and by the historical events he chooses to portray. In marked contrast to D.W. Griffith's portrayal of miscegenation as degeneracy in *Birth of a Nation*, interracial marriage is idealised in Hayward's films, and Māori and Pākehā socialise amicably. The events he depicts include a 'scouting adventure' south of Auckland, the Battle of Ōrākau in the Waikato War, Te Kooti's siege of the Te Poronu mill in the Bay of Plenty, and the colonial hero Gilbert Mair's pursuit of Te Kooti outside Rotorua. The scouting adventure pits Māori against Pākehā in an atmosphere of tension – but the Battle of Ōrākau retained its standing in the Pākehā world as a byword for Māori heroism, and the belief endured that it had initiated 'mutual interracial respect'. At Te Poronu and Rotorua, colonial soldiers and Māori fought against Te Kooti – and alongside each other.

Rather, Hayward's concern was nationhood, and this helps explain why he limits portrayals of interracial conflict. Hayward shared Cowan's enthusiasm for the New Zealand past and especially for the 'Battling Sixties'.[12] All three of his films tell a national story with emblematic figures who embody national virtues and bring peace out of conflict. Each film was made at a pivotal moment of nationhood in New Zealand. The national ethos in which the first two films were released, in 1925 and 1927, was shaped by not-yet-distant memories of soldiers' experiences in World War One. A sense of Kiwi egalitarianism was still present in the minds of troops who had encountered the British hierarchy; and they still recalled the attitudes of white South Africans and Australians to indigenous peoples whom they encountered while overseas. Moreover, the calibre of both Māori and Pākehā troops in combat had been widely praised. New Zealand soldiers had returned home, in short, with a powerful and flattering sense of what made them distinctive not only as soldiers but as men. Cowan's official history, each film's main source, had also been written in the immediate aftermath of World War One.[13] Its closing peroration is not necessarily characteristic of Cowan's stance overall, but it is a compelling example of the way that the New Zealand Wars came to be interpreted, around this time, through the filter of World War One experience:

> *One thing only was needed to cement for ever the union of the races, and that opportunity the Great War brought. Maori soldiers fought and died by the side of their* **pakeha** *fellow-New Zealanders; descendants of Hone Heke's warriors, of Te Kooti's fierce followers, of the gallant Arawa, and the fighting Ngati-Porou suffered and achieved with their white compatriots on the shell-swept slopes of Gallipoli and in the trenches and red fields of France … So in the greatest of all wars the Maori of the young generation proved his warrior worth, and showed the world that the heroic spirit and the quality of endurance which won the grim defenders of Orakau a deathless fame have not deserted the sons of the ancient fighting-race.*[14]

By the time Hayward was beginning his third New Zealand Wars film, the country was addressing nationhood from two perspectives: as it prepared for the centennial of the Great War, World War Two was looming on the horizon. Hayward's films made two important contributions to the national effort: a shared history – and heroes.

'The Victorious Defeat': Preparations and negotiations

At the end of 1924 Hayward wrote to Cowan inviting him to be the historical advisor for a film entitled, at that point, 'The Victorious Defeat': 'I am an earnest reader of all your works, in fact I owe it to your admirable "Adventures of Kimble Bent" (read at Wanganui College some years ago) for the ambition to some day reproduce on the screen the stirring episodes of the Maori wars.' With his usual thriftiness and optimism, he offered Cowan a nominal £3 a week while on site and 100 shares 'which are now worth £50 but will ultimately be worth anything up to £250 and more if the film catches on'.[15]

Hayward's family connections and the commercial instincts of his uncle Henry, magnate of the family cinema chain, underwrote this desire to film New Zealand historical stories. Henry Hayward had 'read the story of Rewi's Last Stand and knew something about it … he did know it was the basis of an epic'; and he put up part of the money to back the film. Rudall recognised the potential in marketing the film to schools, 'which would be an important factor in getting the cost back'. Despite this, though, he could raise only a very tight budget of £1700.[16]

The Maori War Films Ltd prospectus signalled plans for 'The Victorious Defeat' first, and later a second film, 'On the Track of Te Kooti'. 'The Victorious Defeat' was to be based on 'the celebrated defence of Orakau Pa at Kihi Kihi, March 31st, 1864, by Rewi, chief of the Ngatimaniapotos, and his heroic band of Waikato Maoris'. It would be pitched not only to New Zealand but to the Australian, British and American markets, 'which should prove lucrative propositions'.[17]

The company's broader object was less commercial:

the promoters consider it desirable that some of the romantic and historical exploits of the wonderful Maori Race and the early pioneers, which are rapidly receding into the dim past, should be permanently and definitely preserved by film records, whilst we are yet near enough to obtain accurate and realistic representations. Indeed, the promoters consider that it is a duty to all who respect and love the chivalry, the courage, and honour of the Great Maori Race. We, the British people who have taken the place of the heroic type of Maori, and with our civilization have altered their character, and perhaps not entirely to their advantage or happiness – we at least owe them the accurate recording for all time by the indelible camera, of their great and wonderful struggle …[18]

This pitch appealed to the popular memory of the Battle of Ōrākau – especially the notion that it had established 'mutual respect' between Māori and Pākehā and had fostered a distinctive ideal of race relations – in a way that would have been widely recognised among the better educated Pākehā who were Hayward's potential investors.

Hayward also contacted cabinet minister Māui Pōmare to ask – in vain – if the government would lend out items in the national museum as props; and Peter Buck (Te Rangi Hīroa), who suggested he approach Te Puea Hērangi and try to make the film in conjunction with the newly established Tūrangawaewae marae at Ngāruawāhia. As part of her fundraising for the marae, Te Puea had formed a touring concert party; Buck may well have thought they could become Hayward's actors.

Cowan's response was swift and apparently positive, because Hayward wrote again a couple of weeks later to say that he had now arranged with Te Puea that '300 of her people' would participate in the film.[19] A third letter to Cowan the following March, though, revealed that negotiations with Te Puea had broken down, and Hayward had made a deal to make the film – now called *Rewi's Last Stand* – in Rotorua instead.[20]

Most of the early silent cinema in New Zealand had been shot in Rotorua, partly because the region offered dramatic scenery but also because the Te Arawa people who lived at the heart of the tourist industry and operated as guides to the thermal regions already had extensive experience in providing entertainment for European visitors, and these skills adapted readily to film acting. Te Arawa were the first iwi involved in the film industry: when Gaston Méliès visited Aotearoa in 1912 he produced his three features with Te Arawa performers.[21] The Māori star of Hayward's *Rewi*, the young Te Arawa woman Tina Hunt, was the daughter of a well-known guide and had been a guide herself. Rotorua was, in short, the easiest place for Hayward to make the film and, from a production perspective, the obvious place.

It tells us something about his approach to historical film, therefore, that Rotorua was not his first choice. In his initial approach to Te Puea he seems to have seen her as a representative of the iwi who had fought at Ōrākau: in fact, there were only a handful of Te Puea's Waikato people among the defenders of Ōrākau, and more from Ngāti Maniapoto, Ngāi Tūhoe, Ngāti Kahungunu, Ngāti Raukawa, Ngāti Kohera and Ngāti Tūwharetoa.[22] But Te Puea could provide a group of seasoned performers – and her people had at least been on the resistant side in the Waikato War. Hayward's later description of the negotiations with Te Puea reveals a mixture of cultural knowledge and misinformation about the defending iwi, overridden by a degree of impatience:

> We wanted to use the Waikato Maoris because, of course, the Waikatos figured largely in the original historical incident and I went to Princess Te Puea and told her that I wanted to use Waikato Maoris in the film. I didn't want to use Arawas from Rotorua and I pleaded with her to organise for me a group of Maoris who would be suitable to play the part of the heroic defenders of Orakau Pa. I went to Ngaruawahia and I spent two days waiting round and listening to the Maoris discussing what would happen and eventually Princess Te Puea came to light with a proposition in which she wanted £2000 in cash, a carved meeting house and a carved gateway. I had £1700 to make the entire film so contrary to the usual methods I didn't stop to bargain – which I should have done – I should have waited and bargained but I didn't …[23]

It is not surprising that Te Puea drove a hard bargain. In the mid-1920s she was leading an immense effort to establish Tūrangawaewae marae there. Her concert group had cultivated fine performers, but with an extensive marae complex to fund and build they could hardly afford to work for minimal return.[24] Hayward, though, was also scraping by with scarce resources and was not in a position to pay them properly. Not for the last time, impoverished Māori negotiated with an underfunded filmmaker.

Nor was it surprising that Te Puea was angry about Hayward's decamping to Rotorua. The Kīngitanga, as Hayward probably knew or discovered, had reason to object to Te Arawa people playing the defenders of Ōrākau. In 1864 Te Arawa had refused passage through their lands to East Coast people travelling to assist Waikato's defence against the government invasion. Waikato and its allies had attempted retribution in 1867, but it was still a sore point. But as Hayward recalls, 'I went to Rotorua and used the Arawas, and that was the most terrible sin of all. [Te Puea] never forgave me for twenty years.'[25]

The defenders of Ōrākau were played by veterans of the campaign against Te Kooti, who had served on the government side in the bush-fighting companies led by Gilbert Mair and George Preece. The *Star* reported that Manahi Tū-mātahi from Rotoiti, who had 'marched through the Urewera Country from end to end in the Arawa flying column chasing Te Kooti ... came proudly wearing his war-medal ... but the veteran soon was fittingly accoutred as a Kingite warrior'. Kepa Tāmati had also fought throughout Te Kooti's War: 'in the trenches Kepa played the part of a wounded warrior with all the realism of the actual thing'.[26]

Hayward's tight budget meant the film was always precarious, but the local production company operated well, organising ammunition and clothing, and digging extensive trenches to recreate Ōrākau pā. What they could not control was the weather, and on the first morning of the shoot:

> the weather changed suddenly and it came down in tremendous rain squalls. It washed away the trenches. The army of extras who were fully attired in their uniforms were getting so wet that they tore off their uniforms and cleared out and we were left standing in the middle of the drenched battlefield without a foot of film being shot and with all our money gone, and that was what we thought was the end of Rewi's Last Stand.[27]

The resilient Hayward and his 'stout hearted' supporters bounced back, only to be faced with a byproduct of the enormous local interest generated by the filming. Hayward had made a deal with a bus company to transport his extras to the site in return for the exclusive right to bring members of the public to watch the filming. Hearing of this deal, a rival bus company turned maverick and brought out 'half the population of Rotorua ... and parked themselves not behind the cameras but in front of them and so we had the tremendous problem of blotting out the hills in the distance, on which there were hundreds of people sitting round waiting for the battle to start'.[28] Community enthusiasm was not always a bonus.

By this time Hayward had considerable filmmaking experience, augmented by his work for the Australian pioneer Raymond Longford, and his connections in the developing industry meant he could work with other experienced people. Frank Stewart was the cinematographer for the first *Rewi*, backed by Ted Coubray: these were the country's most experienced cameramen.[29] Hayward's first wife Hilda, although she was not explicitly acknowledged, was regularly involved with casting and editing and other roles.

The first *Rewi's Last Stand*

Only the first reel and some fragments of the silent *Rewi's Last Stand* survive, but the film's press kit tells the rest of the story. Ken Gordon (Edmund Finney), a young English immigrant eager to escape his Auckland office job, joins the army as war looms in the Waikato. Before he leaves town he falls in love with a white girl, Cecily Wake (Nola Casselli), encounters a pompous retired imperial colonel, and fights with a devious officer who is also in love with Cecily. Luckily Ken's employer has advised him to join the Forest Rangers rather than the imperial army. Here Hayward points up the contrast between the British military hierarchy (and Old World class distinction) and the casual camaraderie of the locally raised irregular units. Ken's urban new-chum status brings him some teasing, but the puffery and arrogance of the other town-based imperials are shown up by the manly martial skills and expertise of these hardened bush fighters. Egalitarian to a man, they fight 'like the Maori'.

Two historical figures appear in a real-life setting, the Travellers' Rest, the Forest Rangers' famous watering hole and recruiting headquarters south of Auckland. Gustavus von Tempsky and Thomas McDonnell rise off the pages of Cowan in a mock fight and an expedition. Ken is keen to try his swordsmanship against a taiaha – and here Hayward draws on

Rewi's Last Stand (1925): The new chum among the Forest Rangers: Thomas McDonnell, armed with a taiaha, takes on Gustavus von Tempsky, wearing his Garibaldi shirt and wielding his famous sword. Young Ken (Edmund Finney, centre) absorbs this display of colonial masculinity.

All stills from *Rewi's Last Stand* preserved and made available by Ngā Taonga Sound and Vision. Courtesy of the Hayward Boak Collection

the reputation of the historical McDonnell, who liked to show off his ability with Māori weapons but conceded that he could never beat von Tempsky.[30] Equipped with a taiaha McDonnell quickly defeats Ken and his sword, whereupon McDonnell takes on von Tempsky in a set-piece fight. Their skills are put to a riskier test in the portrayal of a historical scouting expedition: here, the film cuts between McDonnell and von Tempsky creeping through the forest and the Māori who almost discover their hiding place.[31] These episodes configure irregular soldiers as emblematic colonial men: they are egalitarian, 'rough-hewn', but brave and highly accomplished; and they are 'becoming native'.

While on sentry duty, Ken rescues Takiri (Tina Hunt), a 'Māori maiden of high birth' from the opposing side, who has 'leapt into a torrent to prove her bravery' – the first in a series of defiant Māori heroines in films about the wars; her remarkable leap into water far below, in the surviving footage, was later repeated by the equally athletic Kura in *Utu*. The meeting between Ken and Takiri initiates an 'across the lines' relationship that provides the counterpoint to the story of racial enmity. They talk by the river after the rescue, then sit down side by side, absorbed in their growing intimacy. Warriors find them there and threaten to kill Ken, but Takiri intervenes and he is imprisoned instead. He later helps Takiri search for her little brother who is lost, and they come across Ōrākau pā in the process of construction. Ken is brought to Rewi Maniapoto and is again confined – 'bound up and thrown into a rua'. Drawing on Cowan's official history, the film shows preparations for the

Rewi's Last Stand (1925): Between the lines, Ken encounters Takiri (Tina Hunt) on a riverbank.

Rewi's Last Stand (1925): The chiefs debate whether to stay and fight at Ōrākau. Rewi Maniapoto, foreground at right, was played by 'Chief Abe', according to the publicity.

defence, and the chiefs debating whether to stay or to abandon the pā.

Here the sequential footage ends. The plot summary tells us that during the breakout from the besieged pā, Takiri frees Ken; they attempt to regain the British lines but Takiri is shot and dies in Ken's arms, and Ken is eventually reunited with Cecily.[32] This version of *Rewi's Last Stand* dramatises alliance across opposing lines, but the death of Takiri offers the alliance no future: only the Pākehā couple survives. The plot summary does not tell us how Ken's return from the dead Takiri to the living Cecily is handled, but reviews at the time show that it is the Pākehā love story rather than the interracial one that dominates. Only a few brief sequences remain that portray the battle and the breakout from the pā, but these events were apparently central to the film's portrayal of Māori heroism.

Hayward knew he could rely on public knowledge of the Battle of Ōrākau and respect for the defenders – the company

Rewi's Last Stand (1925): The cavalry charge at Ōrākau: waves of soldiers sweep across the camera in one of the more dramatic sequences of the surviving film.

prospectus and the film's publicity take these for granted. The defence and breakout are referred to in a heroic style that dates back to the influential editorial in the *Press* by James FitzGerald that praised the defenders' resilience.[33]

Further information about the missing footage can be garnered from reviews – they reveal how attentive Hayward was to the rendering of the battle, and give us a sense of how Ōrākau was understood in 1925. Several reviewers considered *Rewi's Last Stand* the first film of international quality produced in the country, and the audiences were enthusiastic. The Auckland papers were especially fulsome in their reports on the premiere at Haywards' Strand Theatre:

The theatre was filled to the doors with an expectant audience, and that there was no disappointment was evidenced by the applause at the conclusion of the screening. The picture was above the level of many imported films seen in Auckland, and parts of it were far above that standard. The commencement of the Battle of Orakau, in particular, was a veritable triumph, and need not fear comparison with the world's best. The director and all concerned are to be congratulated on the excellent manner in which the correct atmosphere was obtained. The acting of the Maoris at this point was especially deserving of praise. The heroism of the natives during the long-drawn siege was brought home vividly to the audience. The scornful answer of the Māori women to the offer of their freedom struck a particularly stirring note, and was effectively presented. The whole of the battle scenes provided a historically correct and dramatically effective portrayal of an epic struggle which all to whom their country's history is of interest would do well to see.

The large audiences which attended the theatre yesterday found their greatest expectations eclipsed. The picture is better in all respects than numerous imported films that have come to this city. Founded on the record of one of the most conspicuous occasions in the history of the Maori War it brings into this modern metropolis a page out of the stirring times of the 'sixties, when the Maoris fought for what was undoubtedly their own property. The most terrible engagement between the natives and the British troops took place at Orakau, where a mere handful of Maoris defied our soldiers for three days, the women fighting in the trenches with the men. That battle is depicted most sensationally in the film. These battle scenes are greater even than some taken in American country under the most modern and favourable conditions.[34]

Hayward was more critical in his own assessment of the film many years later. Crediting his 'old friends' for their assistance, he notes:

the photography was magnificent, but the story itself, with my inexperience, lack of dramatic experience … was fairly crude … it was my first feature production and it contained all sorts of then very modern photographic effects, soft focus, dissolves, transitions, very artistic lighting, all the tricks that I had learnt in Australia were put into it. Frank Stewart was the cameraman and he loyally carried out many of these ideas which in my inexperience I was determined to inject in my first production.[35]

Despite such excessive virtuosity the film impressed audiences and turned a profit in New Zealand. Sadly, the returns were eaten up in an unsuccessful effort to secure international release.[36]

The Te Kooti Trail (1927)

Two years later Hayward turned from Ōrākau to Te Kooti. Te Kooti's campaign and the colonial pursuit of him were still present in the national memory – and still resonated in local memory – but these were very different memories from those of Ōrākau. Many Pākehā recalled this war with a sharp frisson: the words 'Te Kooti' and 'Hauhau' could still summon fear in the night. For Māori, memories of the campaign and the pursuit differed: members of the Ringatū faith cherished the memory of Te Kooti, while others saw him in a distinctly negative light.

The Te Kooti Trail linked several incidents, some better known than others. The recipe was written for box office success, with all the ingredients of a western and of melodrama: a siege, fierce warriors, a chase on horseback and heroic efforts at rescue, a shootout, two romances and a plot against the fictional hero. Remarkably, Hayward managed to include a substantial amount of historical reenactment of episodes taken from Gilbert Mair and Cowan's accounts of the Te Kooti campaign. Historical fidelity, however, meant breaking cinematic convention by killing off his heroine.

Hayward's many skills were to the fore in this film: he was responsible for scenario, cinematography and direction. Once again he brought together an impressive team, including Hilda Hayward, who was likely the uncredited editor of *The Te Kooti Trail*.[37] The film's post production and editing are strikingly effective and technically adventurous, using techniques such as oval framing, and complex superimposition as one shot fades into another. The photography includes romantic scenes on the Whakatāne River, some superb closeups and dramatically filmed chases, including western-style wide shots and a shot of horses thundering towards the camera.

The story of the defence of Te Poronu mill outside Whakatāne had come to Cowan and then to Hayward through the well-known former soldier Gilbert Mair (who comes into the story). The original accounts, though, came from Māori participants; the only European involved was the French miller Jean Guerrin, who did not survive the attack.[38] In the early years of his campaign Te Kooti undertook a series of guerilla-style raids on small settlements, aimed at gaining ammunition, supplies and recruits for his band of followers. In 1869 he attacked Rauporoa pā and the small Te Poronu mill and redoubt nearby, just out of Whakatāne. The film portrays the attack on the mill only: the siege, its defence and the aftermath constitute the central drama. (The filming was as much a drawcard here as it had been in Rotorua: hundreds turned out to watch the filming of the siege from the surrounding hills.)[39]

The mill was defended by Guerrin, his wife Erihapeti and her sister Monika, and a handful of local Ngāti Pūkeko (Ngāti Awa) people – seven or eight men and women in all. They held the mill and redoubt for two days, but the mill defences were finally breached and the defenders overcome. Erihapeti and Monika were captured by Te Rangihīroa, one of Te Kooti's lieutenants, who spared their lives – in contravention of Te Kooti's orders. When he brought the sisters to Te Kooti, Monika refused to reveal the location of a buried cache of gunpowder. Angry at Te Rangihīroa, Te Kooti ordered him to take Erihapeti as a wife and to kill her sister Monika.

Meanwhile the armed constabulary at Tauranga had been told of the attack, and Mair was trying to persuade a reluctant senior officer to let him go and relieve the siege. Mair was given permission to raise help from Māori at Matatā, just north of Whakatāne. The rescuers arrived too late to prevent the fall of the mill and pā, but they fought Te Kooti's followers and covered the retreat of some of the defenders of the pā who had managed to escape.

After a series of complex conflicts that the film does not portray, *The Te Kooti Trail* concludes with a 'running engagement' carried out by Mair's Te Arawa contingent a year later; Cowan describes it as 'a truly brilliant action on the part of that most gallant young officer Lieutenant Gilbert Mair, a deed rewarded by a captaincy and the decoration of the New Zealand Cross'.[40] In February 1870 Mair realised that Te Kooti, who had showed signs of making for Tauranga, was in fact approaching Rotorua and the families of Mair's Te Arawa troops. Suspecting a surprise attack, the unit undertook a difficult journey that lasted a day and a half, ending with a full morning's run. They found Te Arawa chiefs on the point of negotiating with Te Kooti. Convinced that Te Kooti intended to slaughter his hosts, Mair stamped on the chiefs' white flag. He and his unit then went on another day-long run in pursuit of Te Kooti and his followers as they retreated. The fight concluded with the death of several of Te Kooti's leading warriors, including the bugler and 'butcher' Peka Makarini (Edward Baker McLean). This event 'not only saved the Arawa people at Ōhinemutu from massacre in the absence of most of their fighting-men, but deprived Te Kooti of some of his best warriors, and inflicted so severe a blow that he never again risked a battle in the open'.[41]

The film drew on Cowan's chapters on the Whakatāne raid and the pursuit outside Rotorua, and on Mair's account of the killing of Monika, which her sister Erihapeti had related to him in detail. A third written source that Hayward did not acknowledge – perhaps because its author was a known imposter – was George Hamilton-Browne's *With the Lost Legion in New Zealand* (1911).[42] This book, which purported to be a soldier's memoir of the Pai Mārire period of the wars, lent Hayward source material for the knockabout comedy of soldierly life in *The Te Kooti Trail*, but also its more sombre idea of the 'lost legion' that shapes one strand of the plot. Hamilton-Browne took this term from a Kipling poem that compares imperial soldiers in colonial India to the Roman Ninth Legion that marched north in Roman Britain and was never seen again; he used it to align colonial soldiers in New Zealand with the soldiers of Empire in general – casting them as heroic but uncelebrated figures: 'I have noticed no one ever gives the colonial irregular troops the least credit of having fought and suffered in the imperial cause.'[43] *With the Lost Legion* was dedicated to 'the memory of the officers and men of the Lost Legion whose bones lie buried in forgotten graves on the wild fern ranges and in the dense bush of New Zealand where they fell fighting for Queen and flag'.[44] Hayward in turn put this celebration of soldiers in the service of Empire to good use: he incorporated the scene painted in this dedication, several stories from Hamilton-Browne's *Lost Legion*, the term 'lost legion' itself and some lines from Kipling's poem into the fictional plot centred on the hero Eric Mantell and his soldier mates.

Hayward whetted public appetite for *The Te Kooti Trail* with a serialised version of the plot published in several newspapers, including the widely circulated *New Zealand Herald* and *Auckland Weekly News*.[45] Frank Bodle, a retired businessman living in Whakatāne, wrote the serial and co-wrote the film script, although the precise nature of his contribution is difficult to establish. The serial followed the film scenario closely, but it also provided historical background to the story, drawn extensively from Cowan's official history. Aimed at rousing public enthusiasm for the film, the serial is obviously designed too to educate audiences in advance about the historical events. Hayward's intention was not just to entertain but to inform, enrich and engage public memory of the colonial past.

Because *The Te Kooti Trail* has survived complete, it offers the best evidence that Hayward was seeking to craft a set of cultural memories on which New Zealand nationhood could be securely established. The selection of conflicts, in which Te Kooti's raids were primarily targeted at other Māori, deflects the spectre of racial opposition; and colonisation is portrayed largely as a story of affection, alliance and mutual protection between Māori and Pākehā. Even Te Kooti who – given his reputation at the time among some Māori and most Pākehā – might have been rendered simply as a bogeyman, is quite sympathetically portrayed, and the central villainy of the story is deflected instead onto another individual, Peka Makarini. There were many events in Te Kooti's War, such as the raid on Matawhero or the executions at Ngātapa, in which both sides committed far bloodier acts than those depicted in the film. Hayward avoids these, diminishing the bloodshed and avoiding the demonisation of either side. Instead he selected events from the historical record to produce from the conflict an ultimately harmonious national story, structured around the memory of heroes both Māori and Pākehā. He might have been following Ernest Renan's recipe for nationhood, in establishing shared memories of 'great men' (and women), and in 'forgetting many things'.[46]

Film as memorial

Explicit claims on memory underpin the nation-making story of *The Te Kooti Trail*. Hayward used his written sources to craft heroic stories, and at every opportunity he reminded his audiences of their duty to remember. But the film was shaped not only by the written record. It was set and shot in a community where the historical events were still very immediate; where they were, for some, an unresolved part of the past; and where people did not necessarily share the same views of the past or align themselves all on the same side. These divergences of memory were an accepted part of life, but they meant that the cultural memory the film drew on was not a unitary memory; it embodied instead a range of allegiances and interpretations.

One object of Hayward's active remembering was Gilbert Mair. Apart from Te Kooti himself, Mair was the film's best-known historical figure – still renowned in 1927 as an outstanding soldier who carried out remarkable feats of military endurance. For Hayward, as for Cowan, Mair embodied an admirable colonial masculinity, bush-hardened and athletic. Hayward had met and been rather star-struck by Mair, who was a charismatic figure even in his old age.[47] By 1927 Mair was seen as not only a military hero but a symbol of racial integration, having maintained a close relationship with Te Arawa throughout his life. When he died he was buried at Ōhinemutu alongside Te Arawa aristocracy; his body stopped at four Arawa marae on its journey there.[48] Mair died only four years before the film was made, and his monument at Ōhinemutu is the closing image of the film – the doubled memorial in stone and film recording the bond between Mair and Te Arawa. The *Auckland Star* review on the film's release immediately recognised the film as 'a tribute to Lieutenant Gilbert Mair, one of New Zealand's greatest heroes'.[49]

Mair is not the only hero of the film. In fact the film calls on viewers to remember a series of historical figures – individuals and groups. Although it closes on the obelisk that marks Mair's grave, the opening title directly echoes Cowan's plea for a memorial to a less well-remembered figure, the French miller: 'I only hope that this humble effort may awaken a greater public interest in the history of our dear country, and perhaps cause some suitable monument to be placed on the nameless grave of heroic Jean Guerrin.'[50]

Guerrin – married to Erihapeti, and shown interacting with affectionate ease with other Māori as well as in his heroic defence of the mill – is another racially integrated character whose bravery and self-sacrifice mark him as an unsung hero: coordinating the defence of the mill, he dies bravely defending the gateway as the attackers close in. Hayward takes care, though, to match Guerrin's (Pākehā) heroism and sacrifice with

ABOVE: *The Te Kooti Trail* (1927): A convivial cross-cultural tableau: dinner at Jean and Erihapeti Guerrin's. Jean (H. Redmond) and Erihapeti (Mere Kingi, seated left) with Monika (Tina Hunt, centre) entertain Gilbert Mair (Tom McDermott, seated centre) along with the film's comic trio, Jules, Eric and Barney. In the fashion of this period, Hayward tinted many scenes in *The Te Kooti Trail*: here, he lends warmth to the occasion with a pinkish red. ABOVE: *The Te Kooti Trail* (1927): Monika loads and Jean fires as they defend the mill.

that of Monika shortly after. Tina Hunt's heroines, Takiri and Monika, set up a pattern of Māori heroines who step outside the conventional trope of the 'woman in need of protection'. Although she asks, early in the film, if the troops will defend her if Te Kooti comes, in the end it is Monika who protects others, in the superbly rendered scene that is the emotional heart of the film. Hunt, here, has a far more fully developed role than in *Rewi's Last Stand*. Although the character of Monika has a romantic dimension, it is also developed through friendly exchanges with Guerrin, a comic scene where she teases the soldiers, and scenes during the siege where she works with Guerrin to load the guns as he fires on their attackers, and promises him that she will not reveal where the gunpowder is concealed. A series of close-ups make the most of Hunt's expressive range; these continue through the climactic scene in which she and Erihapeti face Te Kooti and she confronts him defiantly, refusing to give up the gunpowder that would enable him to prolong his campaign. With this refusal she knowingly chooses her own death.

Mair's written account of the event, which both Cowan and Hayward drew on, displayed his commitment to preserving and passing on Erihapeti's memory of her sister's death. He invited other artists to memorialise the story: 'This is the most pathetic incident of the Maori wars within my memory. I gladly put it on record in the hope that perchance it may inspire some New Zealand artist to make it the subject of a picture.'[51]

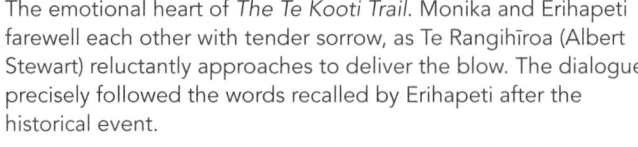

The emotional heart of *The Te Kooti Trail*. Monika and Erihapeti farewell each other with tender sorrow, as Te Rangihīroa (Albert Stewart) reluctantly approaches to deliver the blow. The dialogue precisely followed the words recalled by Erihapeti after the historical event.

Hayward's picture draws in exact detail on Mair's record of the sisters' last tender words to each other, as told to Mair by Erihapeti. The intertitles repeat these words in Māori and in English translation:

> Monika: E Peti [Erihapeti] tena e roa te whaka mamaetanga?
>   (O Betty, will the suffering be long?)
>
> Erihapeti: Kaore he poto noa iho (No, Sister, it will be quite brief).
>
> Monika: Mau te pupuri i oku ringaringa Kaimanawanui ai ehau
>   (Hold you my hands that I may have courage).[52]

Monika's unyielding determination and the grief of the sisters' last embrace – delivered with moving performances in this exchange – retain their dramatic power even today. The film's first audiences, expecting it to abide by the codes of melodrama, were taken by surprise. As Hayward later recalled:

> *I can remember the sensation it caused at the opening screening in Auckland on a morning matinee audience composed mostly of women. Last minute rescues were the orthodox format for films in that day, but when New Zealand history ran counter to this and the heroine was killed off half way through the film, the audience was shocked and groaned.*[53]

These three individuals – Mair, Guerrin and Monika – are explicitly marked as heroic figures who warrant a place in national memory. So, also, are two categories of participants in the events, paired to display the heroism of both Māori and Pākehā: colonial irregulars and 'friendly' Māori or kūpapa.

To shape the stories of these groups Hayward added fictional characters to the plot.

A story that pitches the admirable qualities of colonial masculinity is embodied in the fictional soldier hero Eric Mantell. The prologue, set in England, introduces Eric and links him to Hamilton-Browne's 'lost legion' and its association between the British and the Roman empires. A venerable rector tells the story of the 'lost' Roman Ninth Legion – 'a pretty mixed lot, sir,' says Eric. 'What happened to them?' The rector tells the story:

> *They went to an unknown death, but they achieved their object – the rebellion simmered down – Roman Britain was saved … It is these unknown deeds by men of lost and forgotten legions that build empires – they go out to the ends of the earth and make pathways with their dust!*

It is curious that Hayward took on Hamilton-Browne's reference to the cyclical patterns of history here without questioning it – since the Romans were the imperialists in that story, and the Britons the indigenes. This perhaps underlines his evident acceptance, in the 1920s, of the inherent value of empire.

As the film opens, Eric seems secure as the younger son of landed gentry and already an officer in the Hussars. But he is in love with the rector's penniless daughter and, to make matters worse, he is framed for theft by his unscrupulous brother and a conniving manservant; so he leaves Old World class iniquities behind and decamps for the colonies. When we next see Eric he is in New Zealand and has already undergone a remarkable transformation: his formal dress is discarded for the tartan waist shawl of the militia and, with his mates Jules and Barney (a 'mixed lot') he is meandering along a track, singing riotously, the stiff bearing of the officer of the Hussars abandoned for the lurch of the colonial private. Jules, the second Frenchman in the film, derives directly from Hamilton-Browne's *Lost Legion*;

The Te Kooti Trail (1927): Young Eric Mantell (Arthur Lord), fictional hero of the film. An officer of the Hussars, Eric is introduced with formal dress and bearing in the film's prologue.

The Te Kooti Trail (1927): A Frenchman, an Englishman and an Irishman walk along a colonial trail: Eric after arrival in New Zealand, flanked by comrades Jules (left) and Barney (right). Now a private in the colonial militia, he has adopted their waist shawl, Garibaldi shirt and relaxed air.

he wears his cooking pot as a hat like the French character in that book. Colonial military egalitarianism is fully established as Lieutenant Mair arrives on horseback: there are no salutes but friendly waves and handshakes instead, and Mair is quickly teased into descending from horseback to demonstrate the fleetness of foot that features later in the film, by racing the Irish Barney and beating him 'man to man'.

A more serious note is signalled beneath the foolery when Monika accosts the comic trio and teasingly mocks their soldierly pretensions, then asks if they will fight for her if Te Kooti comes. The soldiers' later pursuit of Te Kooti after her death reveals them as heroes beneath their comic exterior. Along with Mair and the fictional character of her lover, Taranahi, they promise to avenge her. Jules is mortally wounded in the bush fighting that follows, and Eric bravely refuses to leave him. A far cry now from the polite Hussar, dishevelled and smeared with colonial mud, Eric is a tough fighter, loyal to his friend and the imperial cause. The 'lost legion', the forgotten heroes of the expansion of empire, now make explicit claim on national memory as the dying Jules urges Eric to give up on the colony and return to England:

> Jules: … There is no honour – no glory in this – only ze grave in ze bush – where I go – lost – forgotten –
>
> Eric: They'll come from the crowded cities – to a cleaner brighter world – we're making the pathway safe –
>
> Jules: Will they think of us, Eric – these people to come?

But before his question can be answered Jules' eyes close, the screen fades to black, and he is consigned to the lonely bush grave, concealed to hide it from the 'marauding Hau Haus'. His question remains for the 'people to come', seated safely in the theatre, to ponder.

The second memorialised group, 'friendly' Māori, are represented extensively and idealistically by the Ngāti Pūkeko people including the defenders of the mill, the Matatā people who rally to help them, Mair's Arawa Contingent and especially Taranahi, who enlists in Mair's unit after Monika's death. Early shots of the peaceable coastal Ngāti Pūkeko show them harvesting their wheat fields and bringing their grain to the mill that has been gifted to them by Governor Grey. They live in amicable harmony with the miller Guerrin and the marriage of Erihapeti and Jean displays interracial intimacy in a happy domestic exchange.

The scenes of Te Kooti's attack, the siege and Monika's death that dramatise the conflict between Māori, and the joint heroism of Guerrin and Monika, establish the film as a narrative of conflict between extremism and peaceable coexistence rather than of racial conflict. Monika and Erihapeti are central to this emphasis. Indeed, the scene of Monika's death – the film's climax – is entirely structured around enmity among Māori: there are no Pākehā in the scene. This structure is maintained through the sequences involving the Arawa Contingent – the Māori troops led by Mair – in the Rotorua action. The famous race to the defence of Rotorua, the pursuit of Te Kooti and the death of his lieutenant Peka Makarini dramatise both the alliance between colonials and 'friendly' Māori, and the conflict among Māori.

The character of Taranahi extends the collaboration between Pākehā and 'friendly' Māori to the end of the film. As the attack on the mill looms, it is he who undertakes a desperate run to raise the alarm (matching Mair's long ride back to relieve the siege). When he returns he finds his beloved Monika dead, and his commitment to 'Utu! Utu!' is echoed by the colonial soldiers' determination on 'vengeance' – even if it is, in Mair's words, 'an ugly thing for a white man to speak of'. At the end of

ABOVE: *The Te Kooti Trail* (1927): Te Kooti's men dig in to lay siege to the mill: Jean Guerrin's rifle picks out any who raise their heads.
ABOVE RIGHT: *The Te Kooti Trail* (1927): Gilbert Mair, followed closely by Taranahi (Pātiti Warbrick) leads the Te Arawa Contingent in pursuit of Te Kooti. Hayward used green tinting to enhance the bush setting of this sequence.

the film Taranahi follows Mair in pursuit of Peka Makarini, is mortally wounded, and saves Mair's life with his last shot. Just as Guerrin's and Monika's deaths echo each other, Taranahi's death is paired with that of Jules, and his heroism with that of Mair – demonstrating that the nation has been built with the 'dust' of 'friendly' Māori as well as of colonial soldiers. The broader story of alliance between settler–soldiers and friendly Māori defending a peaceable coexistence against separatism and conflict unites them within the film as memorial.

It is notable that, while 'friendly' Māori troops are shown in comic scenes, the film almost entirely rejects the prevailing conventions of 'Hori humour' that deployed negative stereotypes of Māori. Hayward contemplated using this style of humour elsewhere, but in *The Te Kooti Trail* he appears to have specifically avoided it.[54] There is humour based on racial stereotypes in this film, but its targets are the two Frenchmen and the Irishman. In one scene Māori troops are shown laughing at Barney as he cadges their rum rations and imbibes 'courage'. And Monika makes 'the Englishman, the Irishman and the Frenchman' the butt of friendly joshing. In one brief exception at the end of the film, a plump Māori woman eyes up the equally plump Irishman Barney.

The analogy between soldiers who fought in the New Zealand Wars and in World War One would not have been lost on contemporary audiences: in both, men travelled to the other side of the world to fight; many died and lay in unmarked graves. Jules – whose nationality is perhaps no accident – becomes the 'unknown soldier' of the New Zealand Wars. Here Hayward

The Te Kooti Trail (1927): Heroes of the nation-to-come: Eric comforts the dying Frenchman Jules, and Gilbert Mair embraces the dying Taranahi. The two scenes, marking the significance of these heroic deaths, are linked by the affectionate pairings and the vivid colouration.

enlists the strong prevailing understanding of memory as a national duty, and he reinforces it at the end of the film with the shot of Mair's memorial.

In contrast to both of Hayward's *Rewi* films, Pākehā in *The Te Kooti Trail* are cast not as invaders but as agents of peace and protectors of Māori communities. Early intertitles explain that the mill was a gift from Grey; Guerrin has brought the expertise of milling to Ngāti Pūkeko; Mair is both friend and protector. These were, of course, historical events that Cowan had placed on record in the official history, but Hayward's choices normalise notions of 'gentle colonisation' and endorse at least one element of Te Kooti's prevailing reputation – as an extremist working against the greater goal of interracial harmony.

The Māori cast and another memorial agenda

As with the first *Rewi*, Hayward looked to cast people who had connections to the historical events – especially for the Māori characters. In *The Te Kooti Trail* there were many more parts for Māori than for Pākehā. Hayward drew from several iwi in the Bay of Plenty region – perhaps the most complex theatre of the wars, where all iwi were involved in one way or another – and so all the Māori he cast brought with them some connection to these wars.

In casting his romantic couple Hayward returned to Rotorua and to Te Arawa actors he had worked with before – Tina Hunt and Pātiti Warbrick. Both were from guiding families and were skilled and experienced cultural performers who had moved directly into film acting; their style was far more naturalistic than that of the Pākehā actors, whose more hammed-up performances probably derived from stage acting. Hunt is compelling in her comic encounters with the soldiers, in her intense seriousness in the battle scenes – where she easily outplays the actor playing Guerrin (H. Redmond) – and in her big scene, the defiance of Te Kooti that leads to her death. Hayward recalled Warbrick's performance:

> *Probably the most moving moment I ever had the good fortune to record on celluloid, was a brief scene in 'The Te Kooti Trail' when Patiti Warbrick as a young warrior, first discovers the body of his sweetheart, Monika, after she had been executed at the order of Te Kooti. What Warbrick succeeded in putting into this scene will remain unforgettable to all who saw it.*[55]

The Ngāti Pūkeko people, the defenders of the mill, the Te Arawa troops, Te Kooti's troops and several named roles were played by mostly Ngāti Awa locals from in and around Whakatāne. One mill defender, an elderly woman, was said to have been among the besieged at Rauporoa pā as a young woman. People leapt at the chance to be in a movie – especially a movie that put their history on the screen and sent it out into the world. For them, film was a means by which their own past might be wrapped up in the thrill and glamour of the cinema and exported globally. There was a more practical and pressing reason, too: employment. Ngāti Awa had lost land in the confiscations and this left them heavily reliant on work for pay – and in the 1920s jobs were scarce.[56]

There are some vestiges of the casting of the film. In August 1927 Hayward was still advertising for a 'refined Maori girl, tall, long hair, with good teeth and features and acting ability: age about 22';[57] but if this was a call for the part of Erihapeti, he in fact found Merewakana Kingi in a teashop in Whakatāne, where he approached her to ask if she would act in his film.[58] Her name – given as Mere in the credits – is a clue to the connections between Ngāti Awa people and the history portrayed: Merewakana is a transliteration of Mary

The Te Kooti Trail (1927): Barney, looking for some extra courage, begs rum from the Māori troops of the Te Arawa Contingent. The Irishman is the target of the humour.

Völkner, indicating that she was named after the missionary Carl Völkner, who was killed in 1865 by Kereopa Te Rau in the act that reignited the wars on the East Coast. According to her children, Mere Kingi had been educated at Völkner's mission at Ōpōtiki and would have been strongly opposed to Te Kooti; and there were no doubt others among the Ngāti Awa involved in the film who shared her opinion.[59]

Nevertheless – and despite the film's narrative of fierce opposition between the attackers from the mountains and the peaceable people on the coast – some Ngāti Awa people had joined Te Kooti. After his pardon, moreover, Te Kooti had spent his last years until his death in 1893 at nearby Ōhiwa, and was a familiar presence in Whakatāne. For many locals this later public memory overlaid memories of the raid, and

Hayward spotted schoolteacher Mere Kingi as she was having afternoon tea in Whakatāne. She had a great time playing the part of Erihapeti, and all her life remained proud of being in the film.

Photo courtesy of Pauline Butt

by 1927 Whakatāne Māori remembered him in the main with warm affection. Most importantly, Te Kooti's Ringatū faith had many adherents among Ngāti Awa and other iwi in the region. The part of Te Kooti's lieutenant Te Rangihīroa was played by town councillor and legal interpreter Albert Oliphant Stewart (credited as Arapeta Tuati), whose grandmother was related to Te Kooti. He was one of many Bay of Plenty people who were descended from iwi who had resisted the government, as well as iwi who had allied with it.

Hayward spotted another performer, Steve Hotene, in the street while he was in Whakatāne raising money for the film. He wrote home to Hilda: 'Met a wonderful Maori in the street last night who would make a great "Peka Makarini" six feet three in height with great glowering eyebrows and an ugly expression. He told me he knew "Peka" and all about him so I think I have found a good type.'[60]

The Arawa Contingent and Te Kooti's warriors were played by young Ngāti Awa men, who earned 10 shillings a day. They had 'lots of parties' at Tāneatua, where most of the film was shot. Many extras were needed for the siege of the little mill, for horseback and foot chases and scenes of manly conviviality. They practised getting shot, falling off horses and dying in what the *Sun* described as 'a regular epidemic of movieitis'. There were injuries: Tom Tunui took home blank cartridges and a shotgun to practise falling dead with a friend, but 'wads from the cartridge hit him over the right ear, making a long cut in the side of his head'. Paoi Roia, a 'rough-riding' actor, went to

The Te Kooti Trail (1927): Monika's heroism, as she defies Te Kooti and refuses to reveal the location of the hidden ammunition he seeks. Te Kooti pleads with her to tell and save her life. Seated beside him with evil intent is Peka Makarini (Steve Hotene). In a departure from his sources, Hayward made Peka rather than Te Kooti responsible for her execution.

hospital unconscious after a fall from a horse during filming of the chase through White Pine Bush. 'Outdoing Tom Mix' read the *Star* headline, in a reference to a popular Hollywood cowboy of the day; the writer pronounced earnestly that 'the accident was probably the result of the Maoris taking risks, in an endeavour to outdo the "rough-riders" of the American films'.[61] These young men were familiar with the codes of the westerns that screened in their local cinema, and their energetic performances reflected their knowledge of the genre.

In his use of Gilbert Mair's account of the capture of the sisters and Monika's death, Hayward made one substantial modification to the events as Erihapeti had related them to Mair. The film dramatises Monika's refusal to betray the location of the buried gunpowder, and Te Kooti's directive that the captain who had failed to kill the sisters after their capture, Te Rangihīroa, should now kill Monika and take the newly widowed Erihapeti for his wife. Hayward followed Erihapeti's account in precise detail, except that he transferred the reponsibility for this cruel field sentence from Te Kooti to his lieutenant, Peka Makarini.

This change – which stands in striking contrast to Hayward's efforts in the rest of the scene to maintain detailed historical accuracy – has generated debate about how Peka Makarini is identified in the intertitles as a 'half-caste' and is portrayed as malevolent and cruel. Some critics, alerted by the use of the term 'half-caste', have argued that the displacement of the film's cruellest act from Te Kooti to the 'half-caste' Peka betrays Hayward's suspicion of miscegenation and racial degeneration – a theme that is central to D.W. Griffith's *Birth of a Nation*

(1915), a film that Hayward greatly admired. In 1920s Aotearoa, however, 'half-caste' was a relatively neutral term. While many families (both Māori and Pākehā) opposed interracial marriages, and such couples often suffered discrimination, there was little in the way of a broader cultural anxiety about intermarriage between Pākehā and Māori; indeed, racial 'blending' with the longer-term aim of assimilating Māori into the dominant Pākehā population had for some time been widely perceived as a national good, in contrast to the anti-miscegenation culture of the United States that is echoed in *Birth of a Nation*.[62] *The Te Kooti Trail* portrays interracial marriage and affection as desirable and, as Bruce Babington observes, although Hayward admired Griffith, 'nothing is made of [Peka's] mixed race as Hayward steers clear of the fears played upon in *Birth of a Nation* ... It is as if Hayward, propelled by his admiration for Griffith into a region of unfamiliarly extreme attitudes, backs off, finding his mentor's beliefs less admirable than his aesthetics.'[63]

Apart from the transfer of responsibility for Monika's murder, the film's portrayal of Te Kooti and Peka Makarini is consistent with Cowan's. Cowan frequently described Peka as 'half-caste' but, in using that term, he made no connection between Peka's violence and his descent;[64] elsewhere he used the term to describe individuals he plainly admired, such as Pou-patate.[65] It is much more probable that it was Peka's actions, not his mixed descent, that marked him out for Hayward as an available villain. Rather, in the broader context of the film, if Peka's 'half-caste' descent was a factor in this change, it is likely that Hayward's attribution of the most terrible act of violence in the film to a figure who descended from both Māori and Pākeha was a means of avoiding the appearance of *racial* conflict.

There were other, more local and compelling reasons for shifting the blame to Peka. Diane Pivac and Babington have both argued that Hayward's concern was not Peka but Te Kooti. Hayward had reason to tread cautiously around Te Kooti's reputation, especially given that Ringatū elders, as we shall see, were keeping a close eye on how he portrayed the founder of their faith, and the fact that many Māori in the eastern Bay of Plenty, almost certainly including quite a few of his cast, belonged to the Ringatū faith.[66]

An exploration of this change and why Hayward may have made it gives us an appreciation of how subtly he structured his plot in order to negotiate between the demands of genre that were essential if his film was to appeal to a broad audience; the demands of the historical record that he sought to enshrine in national memory; and the demands of working in a community where historical events had an ongoing life. Deflecting the blame for killing Monika onto Peka underpins several elements of the film: its bicultural revenge/utu plot, its memorial to Mair – but also its memorial to Te Kooti.

Te Kooti was never caught: he was pardoned under the general amnesty in 1883. His reputation among the Pākehā who knew him locally softened, Māori affection for him grew; and so did the Ringatū faith.[67] As Cowan explained, it was not hard to see why Te Kooti took up arms – he had been unjustly treated. Peka Makarini, in contrast, never grew old and mellow, and his reputation for brutality never diminished, making him a more obvious choice for the villain. It was Mair who ran Peka down in 1870, leading Te Arawa troops in the 'running battle' portrayed in the last act of the film.[68] In first blaming Peka for Monika's death and then concluding with Mair's triumph over Peka, Hayward created a satisfactory revenge plot and with the same change effected a fitting memorial to the Pākehā–Māori hero. The revenge structure is set up in the scenes following Monika's death. Erihapeti laments, 'Had it not been for that

The Te Kooti Trail (1927): Taranahi distraught with grief over the body of his lover. This tableau frames the couple with two circles of comforting allies: an inner ring (Gilbert Mair, Eric, Jules and Erihapeti) and an outer (the Te Arawa troops and the Irish Barney). Once again, the arrangement of the scene emphasises cross-cultural affections and ties.

devil, Peka, Te Kooti would have spared her'; Taranahi vows 'Utu! Utu!'; and Mair vows vengeance: 'I swear that I shall never rest until I bring that bloody monster, Baker McLean, to justice!' With Peka as villain, vengeance can be served in a satisfying near-accord with both history and genre; and the career of Mair as friend, protector and leader of Māori loyal to the government can continue to be celebrated. There is historical support for the connection between the events. Paerau Warbrick, Monika and Erihapeti's great-great-nephew, notes that 'Gilbert Mair was indeed closely associated with my whānau. With Jean and Monika's death, Gilbert Mair took it to heart and that was why he was relentless in pursuing Te Kooti. There was the personal connection there'.[69]

In another reattribution, Hayward substitutes the fictional Taranahi for the soldier Te Warihi who 'finished [Peka] by putting a bullet through his head'.[70] Fatally wounded, Taranahi avenges Monika and protects Mair by killing Peka with his last shot. This heroic act endorses the commitment of 'friendly' Māori to their colonial allies: as Taranahi dies cradled in Mair's arms, he addresses Mair affectionately by his Māori name, Tawa. Utu is resolved in parallel with revenge, and just as important as Mair's heroism is the prominence of interracial alliance in putting paid to the barbarism Peka symbolises in the film – leaving Te Kooti and his historical reputation safely out of the circle of vengeance/utu.

Finally, the film is also a memorial to Te Kooti. This may seem surprising, but Hayward's desire for historical accuracy, his strong preference for filming on the historic location and with people closely connected to the conflict, and his search for a figure who could convincingly perform the part of Te Kooti combined to bring another powerful memory agenda to the set: that of Te Kooti's followers. Here we find the strongest traces of the direct influence of Māori people involved in the film, and the ways their involvement may have shaped its character and especially the depiction of Te Kooti.

Hayward did not record how he cast the 70-year-old Tūhoe chief Te Pairi Tūterangi from the Waimana valley in Te Urewera as Te Kooti, nor how and why Te Pairi agreed to take the part.[71] It was an inspired choice. Ngāi Tūhoe had sheltered Te Kooti through much of the war, and allegiance to him, consolidated by his visits through the region and the growth of Ringatū marae there in the 1870s and 1880s, was strong among Tūhoe people. Te Pairi himself was 12 when Te Kooti's War began. Along with

LEFT: Te Pairi Tūterangi, photographed c.1930.

1/2-030871-F, Alexander Turnbull Library, Wellington

RIGHT: *The Te Kooti Trail* (1927): A close-up of Te Pairi Tūterangi as Te Kooti, with 'piercing eyes'.

his uncle Te Whiu, he had joined Te Kooti and had served as his powder-boy, and he remained a close follower until Te Kooti's death in 1893;⁷² he therefore had knowledge of Te Kooti over many years.

A high-ranking chief who never learned English and who had actively protected Tūhoe culture against Pākehā influence, Te Pairi was a casting coup for Hayward for two other reasons as well.⁷³ First, he was a renowned exponent of whaikōrero – the best of his generation, according to Tūhoe scholar Pou Temara. Second, he was a devout member of the Ringatū faith. Not only was this Te Kooti's faith, but Ringatū rituals placed great emphasis on exact repetition and the training of memory.⁷⁴ Te Pairi brought to the film a capacity in performance, attention to detail, an intimate knowledge of Te Kooti's appearance, manner and gestures – and knowledge, perhaps eyewitness knowledge, of historical events.

Te Pairi's arrival in Whakatāne caused a stir: the *Auckland Star* reporter described him as 'the living image of the redoubtable Te Kooti, with his fierce, piercing eyes and pointed black beard'. He was 'one of the few real old-time rangatiras' and his decision to take the part had

> *caused considerable trouble among the elders of his tribe, who look upon these things as 'child's play' and not befitting a man of his rank and age. Four meetings were held up at Waimana, and strenuous efforts were made to influence the old man away from the idea of appearing in the film, but, like a true rangatira his only answer to the elders of the tribe was: 'I have given my word to the pakehas – I must go' … So the old fellow came down to Whakatane and suffered the indignity of having his grey hairs clipped and dyed to such a faithful representation of Te Kooti that it startles those who knew Maoridom's greatest warrior and strategist … Strangely enough, he followed Te Kooti as a boy of 12 carrying ammunition, and he knows Te Kooti's every mannerism and habit, and at a rehearsal startled the onlookers with his magnificent acting.*⁷⁵

Precise evidence of Te Pairi's contribution is fragmentary. He was said to be very insistent about details such as Te Kooti's gestures and expressions and the flax bridle on Te Kooti's horse, which had to be exactly replicated. Te Kooti's biographer Judith Binney notes that Te Pairi's hair was shaved close at the back and that he rode a white horse, like Te Kooti; and she suggests that the extreme closeup of his face with 'piercing eyes' early on in the film 'probably derived from Te Pairi's knowledge'.[76] One newspaper reported that he returned home 'the living image of Te Kooti' to 'great rejoicing and welcome'.[77] In an early scene of Te Kooti preaching to his followers, Te Pairi's gestures are very specific. He would have seen Te Kooti preach often and with this highly distinctive performance he was reproducing Te Kooti's style of preaching as closely as he could. Hayward commented later that Te Pairi 'had, from his close knowledge of Te Kooti's mannerisms and tactics, given a most convincing portrayal'.[78] According to one source Te Pairi was present during the events surrounding the siege of the mill and its aftermath, including the death of Monika. It is possible that he contributed to the staging of this scene in the film.

An early scene in which Te Kooti preaches to his followers was filmed at the meeting house Tānenui-a-rangi in Maungapōhatu – by 1927 the home of the community formed by Rua Kēnana. Hayward, his crew and Te Pairi travelled 100 miles, mostly over very remote bush roads. There was no road beyond Ruatāhuna, where they slept overnight. The following day they hired a local guide. The loquacious cameraman Ted Coubray recalled the trip on horseback that followed:

> our big tripod was strapped to pack-horse and other gear on the other side ... I was on horseback – talk about having a sore stern for some days after that! And we followed the track, it was only just a track – in rugged country up hill and down dale and we'd come to rivers, fairly fast flowing ones, but fortunately [they] were not in flood. And you could see the boulders and we'd go down, right down there to the water. The horses knew their job, they would slide down, use their back feet and slide down, I'd hold my breath, get to the bottom and we'd walk up the stream and then the leader ... he'd go up, I couldn't see him! But when you got near, you could see where you were able to struggle up a bank and push over country tracks and finally we seemed to be climbing for quite a while and then we sort of come down and we were told that we were getting near the camp, Rua's, and of course I was expecting to see a tough fellow, tattooed. And we got down to the gate, there's the great big fence, and a great big locked gate and there was a [...] and someone came down from the pa and asked our business ...[79]

Hayward made sure some useful publicity came out of this expedition: the *Auckland Star* reported that he had 'secured the first motion picture ever made of the Maungapohatu mountain village, and the "Prophet" Rua and his wives' and 'the entire village, including some of Te Kooti's original warriors, took part in the final scenes of the film "The Te Kooti Trail"'.[80] Tānenui-a-rangi did not date from the time of Te Kooti – it was built by Rua's community – but Hayward went to prodigious lengths to set the preaching scene in a precise historical location.[81] This suggests that someone in the production was committed to a close rendering of Te Kooti's preaching at Maungapōhatu – most probably Te Pairi, who had connections to Maungapōhatu and may even have been born there. Te Pairi was at first strongly opposed to Rua Kēnana and his departure from Te Kooti's teachings, but by the 1920s 'his stance towards Rua had softened greatly'.[82]

All this leaves open the question of why Te Pairi agreed to a portrayal in which Te Kooti was, if not the film's villain, certainly its antagonist. Te Pairi's own elders tried to dissuade him from

The Te Kooti Trail (1927): Te Kooti Arikirangi (Te Pairi Tūterangi) preaches to his flock. Te Pairi had followed Te Kooti through the late 1860s and 70s, and remained a member of the Haahi Ringatū. With his hair and beard trimmed to emulate Te Kooti and dressed in uniform, he is said to have resembled his former leader closely. It is likely he took great care in rendering Te Kooti's style of preaching. This scene was filmed on the porch of Tānenui-a-rangi at Maungapōhatu in Te Urewera.

taking the part, and there was heated debate about whether they would support the making of the film. Tūhoe communities were extremely impoverished throughout this period and it is likely that the fee for his performance was a factor. Pou Temara observes that Te Pairi probably didn't object to the portrayal of Te Kooti's part in the conflict precisely because Te Kooti was operating in wartime – the film's intertitles follow Cowan in characterising him as 'a great military genius'. Te Kooti was acting in accordance with the codes of Māori warfare, just as past leaders had done, and these codes would have been perfectly understood by Te Pairi.[83] More to the point perhaps, as Paerau Warbrick commented, Te Pairi 'loved the limelight … we all knew that'.[84]

We have no evidence, though, about where Te Pairi stood on another issue that arose during the filming and that resulted in the first case of film censorship in Aotearoa. In a remarkable story of Māori agency, Ringatū elders, armed with access to their Māori members of parliament and new censorship legislation, held up the release of the film until they were satisfied that it would not damage Te Kooti's mana. Early in the production an unidentified group of Ringatū elders – we do not know if Te Pairi was among them, although he may have been a source of their information – asked to see a copy of the film's scenario. A report in the *Sun* read: 'Trouble is anticipated with a section of the natives who still regard Te Kooti as a god.'[85] Hayward was conscious of this, and of the need to take care with Te Kooti's memory, but he did not supply the elders with the scenario. In August the press reported that 'a local Maori prophet of a certain religious sect, declared last Friday's storm to be a Divine protest agains the filming of the life of Te Kooti'.[86] By September 1927 the elders had hired lawyers to compel Hayward to release the scenario. When this, too, was unsuccessful they approached Āpirana Ngata, MP for Eastern Māori, who contacted Māui Pōmare, minister for internal affairs: these were formidable allies. Pōmare alerted the censor, who would not release the film until Ringatū representatives had travelled to Wellington for a screening. As a result, two intertitles and one scene were deleted. They have one element in common: Te Kooti's reputation as a prophet.

A surviving still of the deleted scene shows Peka Makarini concealed in darkness behind a screen, apparently raising a cross. This scene derives from Cowan's sceptical account of Te Kooti's rituals during his exile in the Chatham Islands, in which Peka purportedly covered wooden crosses with phosphorus and drew them up, glowing, behind an altar in a darkened church – thus gaining Te Kooti a reputation for working miracles.[87] The censor instructed Hayward to delete two intertitles and replace them with substitutes:

Part II. Sub-title referring to Te Kooti 'resorting to faked miracles' has been removed – please submit the working of another title omitting the reference.

Part II. Sub-title referring to Baker [Peka] as 'torture master' and 'stage manager of miracles' has been removed – please submit the working of a new title regarding Baker.[88]

A frame from the scene deleted from *The Te Kooti Trail* by the censor. Peka Makarini (Baker McLean) draws up a cross, apparently in an effort to trick Te Kooti's followers into thinking that they are witnessing a miracle. Ringatū elders objected strongly to this implication that Te Kooti had faked miracles.

Ngā Taonga Sound and Vision S261815

These instructions point to the accusation that Te Kooti had faked miracles as the grounds of the Ringatū elders' objections.

The elders had the necessary backing, through Ngata and Pōmare, to prevent the film's release unless aspersions on Te Kooti's mana as a prophet and religious leader were removed. Their concern was very precise: another intertitle that *was* approved is far from flattering of Te Kooti but does not threaten his standing as a prophet: 'Te Kooti in a looted uniform aped the British officer, and with quotations from a mission Bible, incited his followers to kill all white men.'[89] It is perhaps not incidental that apart from the one still (of Peka holding up the glowing cross), all the other material about Te Kooti that could be read as derogatory is in the intertitles, which did not require the presence of actors but could be created at a later stage, during the editing.[90]

Cowan was well aware of this issue, and how the politics stood. He wrote a piece in the *Auckland Star* noting that it was 'a very curious sign of the changing times that Government and Maoris alike should exhibit such tenderness for the reputation of Te Kooti, as is indicated in a report about the holding up of a film on an historical subject until it is approved by Tangata Maori'. He observed that this was a considerable shift since the 1880s:

> *But times have changed; and there is an opinion even in many pakeha minds that something can be said for Te Kooti after all. As for the Maoris ... he is reverenced as an 'atua' or deity today by a great section of Bay of Plenty and East Coast people ... and is not to be despised even in politics, for every Ringatu has a vote, and don't you forget it.*[91]

When the the censor delayed the premiere, the tensions between Hayward's historical perception of Te Kooti as primarily a military leader and the Ringatū elders' veneration of him in 1927 as a prophet became plain. Seeing the promotional possibilities, Hayward first spun the delay as a taster: 'Mr Hayward stated last evening that he thought it possible some sequences too realistic, and amendment might be found necessary.'[92] But the next day his frustration exploded at what he saw as undue concern given to Ringatū sensibilities:

> *'The superstitious Maoris still look on Te Kooti as something approaching a saint,'* continued the film producer. *'They are objecting to the part he plays in my picture, where he is shown in his true character as a misguided patriot.'* During the time the film was being made, it is stated that these Maoris did everything in their power to hinder the production, chiefly, it is thought, because they were piqued at not being invited to play parts.[93]

He snatched victory nevertheless, by glossing over the deletions and producing new flyers in true Hayward style:

> Held up by the NZ censor! And then released because it happened to be THE TRUTH!

Hayward may not originally have intended *The Te Kooti Trail* to be a memorial to Te Kooti as well as all its other heroic figures. His idea might have been more exclusively a story of imperial progress, nation formation and interracial alliance against extremism. But Te Pairi's performance and the censorship fracas suggest that the filming in the local area, Hayward's openness to local knowledge, his involvement of Te Pairi, and Ringatū access to official channels all created opportunities for Māori connected to this history to portray Te Kooti according to their memory and to shelter his legacy from a representation they could not endorse. Te Pairi showed his capacity to shape the film's representation of the prophet, and his performance endures as a sympathetic and respectful portrayal.

Aftermath

Reviewers responded enthusiastically to the film: 'Undoubtedly a success' said the *Herald*, and it went on to praise the action, the scenery and the Māori leads. The *Sun* review thought the film was long, and the English plot and prologue could be cut, but the New Zealand material 'should make the blood course through the veins of every New Zealander, whether he be white or brown'.[94] The Māori actors gave the best performances, especially Hunt, Warbrick and Te Pairi; the European performances were variable. The review opened with a reflection on Te Kooti's place in national memory, noting that the opinions of those who remembered him were divided: 'murderous rebel or sanctified saint according to which particular school of Maori thought one leans to'. It went on to note 'some hesitancy in the past' in addressing these events, but 'that time has passed. Surely, half a century later, we can dispassionately review a period of national adolescence, and make allowances for both factions.'[95]

The arrival of the talkies in the late 1920s dealt a poor hand to *The Te Kooti Trail*. Most people moved on from the silent films, which lost their place in collective memory. The 1940 sound version of *Rewi's Last Stand* was to last better than Hayward's silent films. But local pride in *The Te Kooti Trail* endured. People whose families were involved suggest that they appreciated having a film made about their own history, with their own people, in the local area. When the Whakatāne museum director arranged a fundraising screening in 1964, 600 people packed out the War Memorial Hall. Rudall and Ramai Hayward attended, along with surviving members of the cast and the descendants of others. Merewakana Kingi (Erihapeti) brought her children and all her grandchildren dressed in their best. She remained proud of her part in the film all her life.[96] A screening at a secondary school the next morning was so popular that the primary school children, who had been promised a programme of short films in the afternoon, demanded *The Te Kooti Trail* instead. The film production itself had become a local historical event. Young Jonathan Mane-Wheoki was at the War Memorial Hall screening in 1964:

> *I do know that the film made a very strong impression on me, that I was wide-eyed with astonishment at the vivid recreations onscreen of historic events, and very moved by them, and I was also struck by the immediacy of the film settings in local places that I knew well – the horse (and rider) galloping down Ohope Beach, for example, where the surfing clan now rode the waves! I do remember that the audience was deeply engrossed in the film, that there was an air of excitement and that the screening itself felt like an historic event of some magnitude. The Whakatane and District Historical Society was very active at that time and the screening of the film was a fund-raising event for their proposed museum …*
>
> *When I briefly took on the role of Assistant to the Director at the Robert McDougall Art Gallery in 1971–2 … I arranged for the film Te Kooti Trail to be screened … as part of a public events programme related to an exhibition of art from the colonial period.*[97]

From the 1990s on, the New Zealand Film Archive held screenings of the film by request on several Ngāti Awa marae. People recognised the film as representative of older colonial ideologies, but they valued it for another reason. Brad Haami noted that the Ngāti Awa actors' descendants 'all know each other anyway. The actors in the film, they were all cousins, so we're all related.'[98] The story itself was by then of relatively minor interest to the descendants. They accepted that the film was 'of its time' in its portrayal of Māori, and younger people found it 'a bit long and boring'.[99] But the people at these screenings enjoyed seeing the locality as it was in 1927; and they liked the fact that one of their stories had been recorded. The filmmaking was a special event that can be recalled with pleasure because it involved all those family members and it happened there: so now, the film is a reminder of the filmmaking.

But by far the most important memorial dimension of the film for the older people, according to Haami, was that it included the images of tīpuna who had passed on: there they were, alive and in their youth, 'their living image up on the screen'. It was this that generated the demand for screenings, including at family reunions. As Haami said, 'my grandmother used to cry when she saw her father up on the screen. They all used to cry when they saw their dads.'[100]

Conclusion

The effort Hayward made to represent events with accuracy, to produce the film at its historical location and to cast Māori actors who were descendants of the people involved in the historical events enabled him to present the film as 'History as it Really Happened', as one flyer ran. It seems likely that

Hayward's publicity was never half-hearted.

Preserved and made available by Ngā Taonga Sound and Vision MS325. Courtesy of the Hayward Boak Collection

dimensions of the film carry the kind of authenticity, in the attention to locality and detail, that would have registered with Bay of Plenty Māori audiences at the time as well as having an appeal to national audiences. The flipside of this historical embeddedness, for Hayward, was the caution he had to exercise around the portrayal of Te Kooti. The constraints of dealing with local people plainly frustrated him during the censorship incident. Despite these limitations on artistic freedom, Hayward persisted in his belief in the importance of what people who were connected to historical events, and especially Māori, could contribute to films made about them. Eleven years later, when he went on to remake *Rewi's Last Stand*, he made a renewed effort to produce the film in the Waikato, this time with descendants of the Māori participants.

HAYWARD IN THE WAIPĀ
Rewi's Last Stand in the sound era

On the second occasion I was determined to try and make the film more accurate ... —Rudall Hayward

As the centennial of the signing of the Treaty of Waitangi in 1840 approached, commemorative projects gathered pace. National pride swelled and progress was the catchword. When James Cowan included a chapter condemning the Waikato confiscations in *Settlers and Pioneers*, the book he was commissioned to write for a centennial series of histories, the editors took that chapter out.[1]

The newly established National Film Unit produced a documentary history, *One Hundred Crowded Years*, in which early scenes dramatise the debate among the chiefs at Waitangi, and Rev. Henry Williams' translation of the Treaty: the chiefs agree to cede sovereignty to the Crown, and brown hand shakes white in confirmation. The narrative turns to the settlers' sea journeys and arrival, their felling of bush and building of houses and farms. Then come rumours of war, signified by drumming, whooping and images of 'excited natives' amid swirling smoke. *One Hundred Crowded Years* offers no grounds for Māori discontent. A preacher's warning that 'no good ever came of fighting' is disregarded as the film's settler couple are driven off their farm, their hard labour put to the torch by hostile Māori. Crowded into a redoubt, the settler community puts up a robust defence and drives the rebels off into the bush. Wars done, we are off to discover gold.[2]

In contrast to this offering from the government, Rudall Hayward's *Rewi's Last Stand*, remade with sound for the centennial, stands out as a subtler treatment of history and far superior filmmaking. The National Film Unit's cinematography is inept by comparison, the acting stilted, the pace cumbersome and the editing clumsy.

With his keen eye for opportunity, and far from immune to the surge of national emotion, Hayward had been thinking towards the centennial from early 1937. When he first mooted a new *Rewi* he planned a remake of the 1925 film, reshooting a few scenes and adding sound effects and narration to the rest to bring it up to date for the centennial. He wrote to the newly formed Te Awamutu Historical Society, which he hoped to enlist in the project. Many people, he told them, had commented on the 'great historical value' of the silent *Rewi*:

> Since it was last screened a new generation of children has grown up and it had been suggested to me on many occasions that the historical sections of the film should be reissued with the addition of sound effects and a descriptive comment so that coming generations might have a visual impression of the heroism of the Maoris in this action.[3]

Hayward proposed to add further scenes of the historic battlefield as it was now, and a shot of 'the monument at Kihi Kihi' (on the site of the Battle of Ōrākau). He hoped to include 'a closeup scene' of any living Māori survivors, and 'school scenes and the Maori scholars' at the nearby Parawera School, 'indicating the progress of education and peaceful development reflected in the descendants of many of those who took part in the Orakau defence'.[4] He also planned:

> to re-photograph closeups of the conversation between Major Mair and the messenger from the Council of Chiefs in which the famous 'Ake! Ake!' reply of defiance was given. This could be done with my sound camera in a very simple fashion if suitable people could be found in your district to play the two roles, preferably descendants of the originals, so far as the Maoris are concerned.[5]

Hayward's timing was lucky: the society, in its first flush of industrious enthusiasm, was keen to help and replied straight away. The last of the Ōrākau defenders had recently died; his son, who was a member of the society, promised 'the assistance of as many Maoris as you require'.[6] Hayward was off to a good start: this time, he hoped, he might be able to make the film with descendants of the historical participants.

Hayward's ambitions grew as the year progressed: by May and June, the talk was of entirely 're-filming the epic story as a "talkie"'.[7] Hayward had screened his silent *Rewi* along with his most recent film and first talkie, *On the Friendly Road*, to the members of the society and to 'representatives of the Native Race', and he had formed a company, Frontier Films, with society members as directors and major shareholders.[8] With the assistance of two of these directors Hayward wrote a scenario that departed substantially from that of *Rewi* 1: a new film was under way. As the company prospectus announced in August: 'In the Picture will be scenes of Maori life and customs of the time and concerted Maori singing, Hakas, Poi Dances and games, features which should add greatly to the undoubted appeal of the main theme.'[9]

The Te Awamutu Historical Society itself, and the way it gathered historical knowledge, appears to have been instrumental in this change. In this conservative rural town peopled by the descendants of military settlers in confiscated territory, its formation marked an unusually reflective view on the colonial past by a small group of local citizens. Most were middle-class male Pākehā professionals or businessmen, but the first minutes recorded their pleasure at the presence of 'several members of the native race'. Close friends Raureti Te Huia (Ngāti Maniapoto) and local doctor James Roberton formed its nucleus. Raureti Te Huia's father Te Huia Raureti and his grandfather Raureti Paiaka were leading figures in the Ōrākau defence.[10] Te Huia Raureti was the 'last survivor' mentioned above, who had died in 1935. He was a relative of Rewi Maniapoto and one of the group of close affiliates who had formed a bodyguard around him during the breakout from Ōrākau. He was also James Cowan's most extensively quoted informant about Ōrākau, and was therefore already an important source of historical knowledge about the battle. By the 1930s Raureti Te Huia, following his father, was deeply versed in Ngāti Maniapoto history. Both Roberton and lawyer H.A. Swarbrick had also dedicated themselves to recording local Māori history: each left extensive archives.[11] Cowan was the society's first patron, and members modelled their recording of local history on his example. They instituted early bicultural research, often relying on Raureti Te Huia's knowledge and connections; for example, Raureti and either James Oliphant or H.A. Swarbrick carried out extended interviews with elderly Māori.[12]

There is irony in the fact that, through the Te Awamutu Historical Society – on the face of it a settler organisation in a settler town – Hayward had gained an entrée into more appropriate iwi connections with Ngāti Maniapoto and the defence of Ōrākau than he ever had in his first *Rewi*, when he approached Te Puea Hērangi.

Society members formed the nucleus of Frontier Films, and the shareholders initially provided capital of £2000. Raureti and Jim Roberton were the signatories to the appointment of the directors – lawyers Swarbrick and Oliphant, and stationer Gavin Gifford. The company's list of shareholders and shares tells a story: some of the local Pākehā, especially society members, bought 50 or more of the £1 shares, but Māori shareholders bought much smaller amounts. E. Thomson owned 35 shares – far more than any other shareholder who was identifiably Māori. J. Matetu bought 12; others bought one, five or 10. King Korokī owned 10, Te Puea five and – most strikingly – Raureti Te Huia, whose involvement was so central, bought only five shares. Tainui people may have been reserved in their support. It is more likely, though, that the relative investment of these two communities reflects their relative wealth in the long aftermath of the confiscations: Māori had little to spare and other claims on their resources. In hindsight they were wise to be cautious, as the film did not turn a profit.

Frontier Films helped in practical ways beyond the immediate value of raising funds. Women formed working bees to make the many soldiers' uniforms, and members ransacked their homes and sheds for props. Hayward had the assistance of a representative Māori committee 'in obtaining the necessary numbers of Maoris from this district to amply represent the Chieftains, notable characters, and warriors of those historic times'.[13]

Hayward had also – perhaps through Cowan – made contact with another important descendant, Te Rongonui Paerata. Rongonui's great-grandfather, grandfather and great-uncle, the Ngāti Kohera/Raukawa rangatira Te Paerata and his sons Hone Teri and Hītiri Te Paerata, were also among Rewi Maniapoto's close group of advisors through the Battle of Ōrākau. Te Rongonui's grandfather Hītiri Te Paerata had addressed parliament in 1888, where he gave a harrowing account of the siege and the breakout from the defenders' perspective. His sister Ahumai was famous for refusing the government offer of safe conduct for the women and children in the pā.[14] Hītiri and Ahumai survived the battle, but Hītiri told parliament: 'The whole of my tribe were slain; my father, brothers, and uncle all died. My sister Ahumai, she who said the men and women would all die together, was wounded in four places.'[15] Te Rongonui accompanied Hayward to Te Awamutu in early 1938.

The forebears of Te Rongonui Paerata and Raureti Te Huia had given two of the most important historical accounts of the battle – one to parliament and one directly to Cowan. Te Rongonui and Raureti both had chiefly status. And yet, whether it was because he had so little capital or for some other reason, Hayward mishandled his relationship with Te Rongonui: when he learned what he was to be paid, he was furious that a chief should be paid so little and left the production.[16]

Hayward had, however, smoothed things over with Te Puea Hērangi since their falling out over the first *Rewi*. As well as taking shares in Frontier Films, she offered the waka *Te Winika* and another canoe for use in the film. Scenes involving poi, haka and games were filmed at Tūrangawaewae: besides their potential to appeal to an international audience, these showcased Māori culture, and their performance on film for a wider audience supported Te Puea's long campaign to revitalise the communal life of Tainui people.

Not all Māori who had links to the battle supported the film. The minister of internal affairs received a letter in February 1938 from the Rewi Maniapoto Memorial Committee to say that the committee 'along with those Elders whose ancestors spilt blood in that Battle expresses strong disapproval of such an undertaking'. The writer, R. Amohanga, thought Pākehā would not appreciate the screening of the battle 'under the conditions which existed then'. The main objection, though, stated at the end of the letter, seems to have been that to represent the battle would represent things that were tapu. The minister advised that government had no power to prevent the film from appearing, and recommended a direct approach to Hayward – but there is no record of whether this happened.[17]

The *Te Awamutu Courier* found good copy in following the plans for the film. Its columns noted the value of 'an appreciation of the past', but the paper's sense of the past of the land concentrated on the settler era: 'not as some dim and distant past, but as the past of the land on which our shop, or house or cowshed stands; the land on which our grandfathers fought – on which they built their hopes for the future'. The paper praised the 'romantic and daring soldier of the bush', and added a section on 'Maori pride and greatness' at the end. It reported the filming in detail and included sketches of the leads as they arrived in town.[18] The *Auckland Star* interviewed Hayward in early December 1937 after a lucky discovery of 'an unopened tin of caps for muzzle-loading Enfield guns' in a Mt Eden factory, which could be 'fired off in the big battle scene'. Its report ranged from questions about whether 'our pioneer grandmammas, living in the bush during the Maori wars, [wore] crinolines' to 'What were their colloquialisms and their opinions of the whole war and settlement business? These are the kind of questions which send a film producer's hair prematurely grey.'[19]

Three new versions

The production of three distinct versions of the 'Rewi' story between 1937 and 1949 gives some clues as to the changes made during the process of making the film. This film took far longer to make than *Rewi 1* or *The Te Kooti Trail*. Hayward's first scenario for the new film, written with the help of Swarbrick and Oliphant from the Historical Society, was done by late 1937.[20]

The main parts were cast and initial filming had begun by 1 October. The big battle scenes – which required Hayward to bring together a large cast for a weekend shoot so the extras could return to work on Monday – were scheduled for early February 1938, but the weather turned against him: a long run of sunny weather broke, disrupting the first weekend's filming, and the cast – 500 people in all – had to be brought back at substantial cost the following weekend. Again the weather turned foul and filming was abandoned; by the third weekend, his cast was 'very diminished', along with his budget. To allay anxiety that the capital would run out before the film was done, Hayward edited and screened completed parts on 18 July 1938 for 'an audience of shareholders and prospective shareholders': the response was enthusiastic and more capital was raised.[21]

The following year Hayward repeated the publicity tactic he had used for *The Te Kooti Trail*: he collaborated with a writer to produce a story based on the film's scenario, this time not as a newspaper serial but as a novel. The book, *Rewi's Last Stand*, was published in April as the work of A.W. Reed; like the *Te Kooti Trail* serial it included historical information, in this case, about the prewar period and the progress of the war.[22]

On 12 August 1939, as another world war loomed, the film was (inaccurately) reported to be 'in the final stages of production', but by 8 November the directors were worried again: they 'resolved that Rudall Hayward be asked to consider cutting scenes out of the film and shortening the ending, in an effort to save money'. It is hard to establish whether the ending was in fact shortened in response to this request, but the end of filming was now in sight. Hayward gave a private screening for the shareholders at the Te Awamutu Regent Theatre on 26 February 1940, and another private screening in Wellington for the visit of John Grierson, the filmmaker who had driven the development of documentary film in Britain.[23] *Rewi's Last Stand* premiered in Auckland on 12 April 1940.[24] Unfortunately for the box office, the release coincided with national mourning for Prime Minister Michael Joseph Savage, who had died a fortnight earlier.

The film was finished in time for the centennial year. In 1940 the nationalist feeling of the centennial was boosted by the emotions of a country at war. For a second time Māori and Pākehā were leaving the country to fight side by side. This *Rewi's* narrative of unyielding Māori resistance, the sentiments of interracial affinity reiterated in the film, and the Pākehā soldiers' cheers in response to the bravery of the defending Māori at Ōrākau, acquired a new appeal as these events unfolded. But Taranaki and Waikato iwi did not share the national mood with quite such enthusiasm: they boycotted the centennial celebrations on 6 February 1940 in protest at the Crown's failure to honour the Treaty.[25]

Hayward was keen to get international release, the first for a New Zealand film, but had no success during wartime. So when he and Ramai went to work in England after the war, the British release of *Rewi's Last Stand* was on their agenda. The double-bill system, in which a main feature was shown following a cheaper feature of around an hour's length, provided their opportunity but also meant cutting the film to a little over half of its original length, reducing it from 112 to 64 minutes' running time. The film also had to be made palatable to a British audience. The footage removed during this cut is now lost, and there is no remaining print of the original sound *Rewi's Last Stand*. The excision of all this footage, and the consequent loss of the original structure of the film, was a poor investment. *The Last Stand*, as the British cut was entitled, did not do well there – and it is now all that remains of the film.

Hayward thus made or contributed to four versions in total: the silent *Rewi's Last Stand* (1925), the novelisation *Rewi's Last Stand* (1939), the full-length sound film *Rewi's Last Stand* (1940) and the cut-down *Last Stand* (1949). Only the novel and *The Last Stand* – a publicity device and a version savagely cut for British release – still exist intact.

*

Rewi's Last Stand (1940) was shaped by opportunities and circumstances as much as by Hayward's dissatisfaction with the limits of his earlier film. Sound, of course, brought it up to date, and it provided him with another collaborator, the composer Alfred Hill, a collector of Māori music who was so keen to be part of the film that he returned to New Zealand from Australia to work on the score.[26] Hayward, with his irrepressible resourcefulness, had overcome the punitive cost of purchasing sound equipment by building his own in collaboration with Jack Blaxendale. More importantly, the documentary elements of the film were reshaped by the fact that the film was now to be made on locations close to the site of Ōrākau and with local people, many of them playing their forebears. Hayward's satisfaction was apparent as he recalled settings in which the signs of their history were still evident:

We did the scenes of the Maori meeting before the battle in front of an old meeting house in this district. Just how accurate this background is can be judged by the fact that the carvings on the meetinghouse are unfinished. The men who were doing them went to Orakau to fight under Rewi and never came back to finish them![27]

Although he held to his intuitions about what would draw audiences, the local historians, both settlers and tangata whenua, also informed this film. Hayward worked on the script with Te Awamutu Historical Society stalwarts Swarbrick and Oliphant, both of whom were interviewing older Māori along with Raureti Te Huia. Moreover, filming in the Waikato, visiting and dealing with local people on a day-to-day basis meant Hayward was spending his working days on the land that had been fought over; and he was meeting the descendants of mana whenua who were still dispossessed of that land as well as the now well-to-do descendants of settlers. The spread of share ownership alone – with even the highest-ranking Māori purchasing only a few shares – was an indication of the continuing effects of the wars. All these circumstances fed into the film. Hayward's recollection of the whole experience was succinct – although, as he spoke about it many years later, he seemed not to realise that it was not 'the Waikatos' but other iwi in the Tainui confederation who were best represented both in the historical events and in his film: 'on the second occasion I was determined to try and make the film more accurate and to go to the Waikatos and to make it with the Waikatos, if it was possible'.[28]

Several elements of the film are a result of Hayward's familiarity with the people and the locality. First, the film's history was far more carefully located in the Waikato and the Waipā especially – in the detail of the battle itself but also in its rendering of the prewar culture and economy of the area.

Rewi's Last Stand/The Last Stand (1940): 'This is my home, and I'll fight here, at Ōrākau.' The chiefs debate whether to go, or to fight.

All stills from *Rewi's Last Stand/The Last Stand* preserved and made available by Ngā Taonga Sound and Vision. Courtesy of the Hayward Boak Collection

Second, there are signs that Hayward valued kinship and personal connection in casting the Māori roles, and he worked with a Māori committee. And third, he was now attentive to the descent of knowledge about historical events and, like Cowan, he was keen to reflect the knowledge that Māori sources brought.

A more local history

Filming in the Waipā meant the film was connected to its community through the past of place and the use of sites close to the historial events. Although some scenes were filmed in the Urewera 'to get shots of old thatched whares' and some were shot in Auckland, most of the scenes of the Waipā were filmed there or elsewhere in the Waikato. The river is the Waikato, and the pā was recreated at Aotearoa pā at Arohena, not far from Ōrākau itself. The replica of the pā followed the plan Cowan had drawn. Some scenes were filmed at Hairini and Rangiāowhia, sites of attacks in the weeks leading up to Ōrākau.[29] Hayward's efforts at authentication through places, objects and people were recognised in an *Evening Post* review:

> Search was made to obtain and record the actual words used on historic occasions. Many of the 'props' used are the actual weapons and garments used in the wars of that period in New Zealand. The canoe loaned by Princess Te Puia is the famous *Te Winaka* which was partly destroyed by von Tempsky in 1863 and since repaired. The players are largely descendants of the original participants re-enacting the deeds of their forefathers.[30]

The reshaping of the film engaged with the history of the locality in two related ways: in its documentary record of the Waikato War, and in the fictional romance Hayward now developed around new character types. 'As far as the history was concerned this time we tackled it from the point of view of what was happening in Te Awamutu and Kihikihi just prior to the Waikato War,' he later recalled, including the 'kind of cold war' of the months leading up to the war.[31] These were important developments.

The 'cold war' involved the tensions arising from the establishment of the Kīngitanga. Pōtatau Te Wherowhero had been crowned the first Māori king in 1858; he was succeeded on his death by his son Matutaera, later called Tāwhiao. Contention grew around the Kīngitanga movement, its resistance to land sales and its efforts to achieve Māori administrative authority. When George Grey was recalled to replace Thomas Gore Browne as governor in late 1861, the government response ramped up. Historians now are a great deal more suspicious of Grey than either Cowan or Hayward were. James Belich and Vincent O'Malley both observe that Grey talked peace but planned war: he set about the construction of the Great South Road from the beginning of 1862, even while he was ostensibly negotiating over Māori self-government.[32] Following Cowan, Hayward frames Grey as a wise and benevolent figure seeking to negotiate a way through the restless war fever emanating from the south. The missioner John Morgan – who was also an informer for Grey – is a similarly uncomplicated figure in the film.

Hayward spoke of this 'cold war' in relation to two places: Te Awamutu and Kihikihi. Te Awamutu was the site of Morgan's Anglican mission and school, and it was where John Gorst, a government official, had his administrative post and ran his newspaper *Te Pihoihoi Mokemoke i Runanga i te Tuanui*, an anti-Kingite propaganda machine. But Kihikihi was Rewi Maniapoto's own settlement and therefore a centre of the Ngāti Maniapoto leadership. Hayward is pointing out that by this second *Rewi* film he was much more aware of the local politics: some of this information he drew from Cowan but his local collaborators were another important source. The 'cold war' involved the local prewar activity on the government side and the information that was being fed back to the governor from Morgan and from Gorst; and, on the other side, the intertribal negotiations taking place among resistant iwi in the lead-up to the war. The film follows Cowan's own practice in repeatedly crossing battle lines, inviting viewer sympathy to track this shifting point of view.[33] Hayward dispensed with the silent *Rewi*'s Auckland-based prelude in order to situate the new film in this historical context.

Hayward was also drawing on a longer local history, in developing his romantic plot, than he had in the first *Rewi*. The rich agricultural potential of the Waipā meant that, well before the 1860s, Pākehā had moved into the area and married into local iwi: there were many established intermarried families, often with prosperous farms.[34] This was one form of the prevailing ideal of 'racial amalgamation' in the area. Another, related form of amalgamation was one of the colony's most successful mission enterprises. Reverend Morgan had established a 'half-caste school', and had introduced European crops and agricultural methods to the tangata whenua and their fertile land from the 1840s.[35] This opportunity for Māori economic independence in the colonial economy was successfully taken up and had created a buoyant, Māori-led trade: rich harvests were shipped along a regular route to Auckland and beyond, and the tangata whenua enjoyed a prosperity that many, even today, remember as a golden age. The downside was that the very wealth it created drew the envy of settlers.[36]

In the climate of uneasy affiliations in the prewar period, Morgan was spying on the Kīngitanga, and he left the mission not long after Gorst was expelled by the Kingites in 1863. Around the same time some of the mixed-race families were divided when some of their less trusted members were expelled from the area under Kīngitanga control while others were allowed to remain.[37] People of mixed descent played a variety of roles as a result of their ability to cross lines. Some were useful sources of knowledge and information for the Kīngitanga; others acted as spies or guides for government troops before and during the war. Other figures such as traders, who had a long history of living in Māori communities and who in the nature of their work dealt with many people, were involved with one or both sides, and these in-between figures came to be the object of some suspicion. But to the extent that in various ways they embodied the policy and practices of 'racial amalgamation', they also mitigated an explicitly racial opposition. Like William Satchell in his novel *The Greenstone Door*, Hayward saw the dramatic potential of these complex prewar alignments in the Waikato.

The interracial history of the Waipā fed into the characterisation of both heroine and hero in the romantic plot. In the silent *Rewi* and in *The Te Kooti Trail* the fictional heroes were 'new-chum' Englishmen: the development of their characters consisted in their becoming ideal colonial men as they cast off urban and English constraints. In the second *Rewi*, Hayward was interested in two kinds of hero. The first of these was more like the historical figures of McDonnell and Mair, who had featured in the earlier films. The native-born Pākehā was a more developed form of the new-world masculine ideal. Bob Beaumont, the male lead in this *Rewi*, incorporates elements of Thomas McDonnell's history that in the silent *Rewi* were attributed directly to McDonnell himself. Bob – called Ropata by the Māori characters – is a trader, as McDonnell's father was, and he incorporates McDonnell's own upbringing and expertise. Like McDonnell he has been brought up in Northland 'among the Ngapuhi', is an expert with the taiaha and speaks fluent Māori. He is trusted by Māori – which could not be said for McDonnell, but was true of some of the Pākehā in the Waipā at the time. This native-born, culturally and linguistically in-between hero first turns up in the script Hayward wrote in collaboration with Swarbrick and Oliphant through 1937.

In the silent *Rewi* the romance plot began and concluded with Ken's love for the white girl Cecily. His over-the-lines adventure with Takiri, who demonstrates her affection for him, is a relatively brief interruption to the more enduring

Rewi's Last Stand/The Last Stand (1940): Bob Beaumont (Leo Pilcher), also known as Ropata. Hayward's new fictional hero is native-born: here he arrives at the mission casually exchanging greetings in te reo Māori.

relationship he returns to. In the new *Rewi* the interracial romance takes priority. Cecily makes an appearance in Reed's 1939 novel, but now her love for Bob entirely escapes his notice as he pines for the heroine Ariana, somewhere behind the lines to the south. Cecily does not feature at all in the 1937 script or in the 1940 film. In replacing Takiri, the young woman from the defenders' village, with the 'half-caste' heroine Ariana, Hayward matched native-born Bob with another type of in-between figure – his second new type of hero. Ariana signals Hayward's increased familiarity with the Waipā, its intermarried families and its 'half-caste' school. She was derived from a historical figure from the Waikato who was the subject of a newspaper story in 1864. Cowan retold the story several times, including in *The Old Frontier*, his account of Waipā history (and one of Hayward's sources).[38]

The historical Ariana (or Hariana) was a 'pretty half-caste girl', child of a Māori woman and a long-departed Englishman. Cowan recorded that she had been living with a settler family and, when war broke out, was 'carried off by rebels'. Later she was wounded in the defence of Ōrākau but was protected by 'some brave fellow [who] stood over her and defended her life'.[39] Once the story – and her beauty – became known several soldiers came forward to claim credit and to make a bid for her affections. As Hayward noted, 'One was particularly persistent … [but] the young girl completely denied him. Well that didn't make good film material so I didn't use it but that was the basis for the character …'[40] Hayward connected his Ariana to Morgan's mission and his family: with her father gone and her mother dead, she has been brought up as the Morgans' adopted daughter. While her story gave Hayward his love interest, her descent and her connection to the mission situated the interracial legacy of prewar Waipā and the acute dilemmas it gave rise to during the war at the heart of the romantic plot. Hayward's belief in intermarriage as a national good – already signalled in the opening scroll of the film as it looks forward to the eventual 'blending of the races' – is evident in this character.

As a heroine of melodrama in a period of wartime, Ariana also signals something else: combining heroism, self-sacrifice, beauty and both Māori and Pākehā descent, she is an adaptation of the feminine symbol of the nation-to-be-protected – a persistent wartime trope and, curiously, a more conventional one than is evident in either Takiri or Monika. Nevertheless, she is also more than this, and her decision in the film to transfer her allegiance to her Ngāti Maniapoto relatives ensures she is as much agent as sacrificial victim. Indeed, Ariana's allegiances consitute the film's central dilemma.

The early sections of the film establish a network of crosscultural ties and connections, linking these central characters to both cultures. Bob's first words are a familiar greeting in Māori to the young warriors who are observing the missionaries' departure with suspicion. As the Europeans leave the Waikato after fond farewells to Morgan's Māori flock, Bob remarks on the peace and productivity Morgan has created and expresses confidence that they will survive: 'The seed is too widespread now. The roots have gone too deep,' he says – referring to Morgan's agricultural and spiritual introductions to the area. Ariana is keen to leave with the departing missionaries, but Bob has news that the Ngāti Maniapoto are claiming 'half-castes', so he arranges to smuggle her out of the mission rolled in a mattress, as they depart for Auckland. Their mutual attraction provides a flirtatious interlude on the journey, but they are surprised by the warrior Tama Te Heuheu leading a tauā or war party to retrieve Ariana. At this point viewers learn of Bob's upbringing. Confronted by Tama, he proposes they fight with the taiaha.

'What know you of Māori weapons?' asks Tama. 'I spent my boyhood in the Far North, amongst your ancient friends, the Ngapuhi', says Bob … 'Yes, I am a Ngapuhi. We opened our veins … our blood ran as one.' And although he loses the fight, his skill with the taiaha demonstrates his facility in both cultures. In return for Bob's life, Ariana agrees to return with Tama and his warriors.

The course of the film now divides between opposing sides of the war. Bob carries on to Auckland, enlists with the very unimperial Forest Rangers and accepts a dangerous mission back to the Waikato as a dispatch rider, in the hope that he will

Rewi's Last Stand/The Last Stand (1940): Bob and Tama Te Heuheu (Hēnare Toka) fight for Ariana. Bob's taiaha skills are better than anyone expects, making for a thrilling contest, but Tama is victorious.

Rewi's Last Stand/The Last Stand (1940): Knockabout comedy among the Forest Rangers, as Old Ben (Stanley Knight) and Bob break in Bob's new boots. The task requires quite a bit of rum.

find Ariana. Here, as Babington observes, Bob's standing as a trusted insider is put firmly in question, raising the question of betrayal of trust.⁴¹ Now, when he finds Ariana near her Ngāti Maniapoto village, she refuses to leave.

Much of the war is dealt with in documentary-style narration, with arrows moving on a map to show the path of the military advance. Rewi's decision to 'make a final stand' is announced in voiceover. When the dramatised action resumes it is with the Māori side. Rewi relates his dream foretelling the defeat at Ōrākau to his followers, as others declare their willingness to die in the defence of the land.⁴² As the drama intensifies, Bob is among the troops besieging Ōrākau. He sees Ariana across the trenches, among the defenders. He already suspects that his new comrade, the old sailor and soldier Ben, is her father: this further consolidates her connections to both sides of the conflict – and Bob's ambivalent alignment with both sides. A brutal bombardment is followed by images of the wounded, including children, lying in the trenches. The defenders run out of water and ammunition and suffer agonies of thirst. Growing more and more desperate, they nevertheless refuse the offers of surrender and finally break out in a group. Many are killed or wounded during the retreat. Ariana's lover Bob and her father Ben search for her and find her wounded. The film's two interracial romances – old Ben and Ariana's mother, Bob and Ariana – converge as Ariana is reunited with Bob and, apparently at the point of death, realises that Ben is her father.

To turn from Bob's narrative arc to Ariana's, however, is to see the fictional romance diminish in significance throughout the film. Ariana's history derives from the 'half-castes' kept with Ngāti Maniapoto during the war. Martin Blythe and Bruce Babington have both discussed Ariana's mixed descent and the centrality of her dilemma of allegiance to the film's theme of nationhood. She must choose whether to align with her paternal or her maternal descent, and she is challenged at several points.⁴³ Her shifting alignment invites viewer sympathies in ways that bear closer attention, and her story opens up new themes in Hayward's work. Let's roll back the film, then, and see it through her story.

In the opening scenes Ariana is assisting the Morgans as they pack up to leave. She is a child of the mission: she speaks and is spoken to as one of the family, and her white European-style dress confirms that she has been brought up as a family member. Bob's arrival with the news that 'the Maniapotos' are claiming 'half-castes' centres the tension on her escape rolled up in the mattress on the Morgan's drey. But on the journey north, when Ariana emerges from her hiding place and she and Bob walk into the bush, Tama Te Heu Heu arrives in pursuit to seize her back. Bob fights and loses, and Ariana protects him by agreeing to go with Tama. Later, in her grandfather's village, she protests her love for the Morgans – but now her grandfather reminds her of her chiefly descent and her responsibilities. From this point on she adopts this responsibility, takes part in the stick games and dances, and then the defence of Ōrākau, and wears Māori dress until the end of the film.

Bob rides south hoping to find and rescue her, but when he is almost caught it is she who rescues him, hurrying him away in a canoe and concealing him. She now has a second chance to 'escape' but this time she declines: 'Māori women fight with their men … I can't change what is in me,' she protests – asserting her changed affiliation and prefiguring Ahumai's famous declaration during the Ōrākau negotiation. Bob must leave her behind. Later, in the prelude to the battle, he and old Ben seek her out again. Primed for sympathy with the defenders by

Rewi's Last Stand/The Last Stand (1940): Bob and Ariana (Ramai Te Miha): romance by the riverside. Here Ariana still wears the costume of a mission daughter. ABOVE RIGHT: Bob finds Ariana once more as he travels south, but puts himself in danger. He hopes to help her escape 'the Maniapotos' but she has made her choice. Here, it is Ariana who helps Bob escape along the river.

their brave refusal to surrender, Bob and Ben soon realise that Ariana is inside the pā. With this, their emotional allegiance is drawn across the lines: from this point they are at odds with the attack they are involved in.

The question of Ariana's identity and allegiance is larger and more central than the story of the romance; by the end of the film Bob and Ben's concern – and that of viewers – is oriented to a figure on the resistant side of the conflict. Now it is not so much that Ariana must be with her white adopted family, but that Ben needs to be brought back to Ariana, to acknowledge *his* place and his regret at having left Ariana's mother. If we read Ariana as the central figure around whom the other characters' – and viewers' – sympathy circulates, then the film's claim on viewers' emotions brings sympathy to the defenders' side of the lines. Not for the last time in New Zealand Wars stories, the woman who crosses the lines charts the film's ambiguous allegiances, and crosscultural affiliations are confirmed through romance.

Kinship, continuity and knowledge in performance

As he tried but failed to do in the first *Rewi* and achieved with more success in *The Te Kooti Trail*, Hayward was again determined to embed the film in the history it portrayed by casting descendants or relatives of the participants where he could – particularly for the Māori parts. The film was on a larger scale and demanded a larger cast than the silent films. Some Pākehā were recruited locally, including several who were descendants of soldier–settlers. Serving members of an Auckland regiment travelled down to take part. Named Pākehā parts were drawn from experienced or professional performers: actor Leo Pilcher played the male lead Bob, and Stanley Knight, star of Hayward's previous feature *On the Friendly Road*, returned to play old Ben. H.A. Swarbrick of the Te Awamutu Historical Society played the smaller but prominent part of William Mair, the government negotiator. The production company's supply of 'the necessary number of Maoris' represented iwi who had defended Ōrākau – Ngāti Maniapoto, Ngāti Raukawa, Ngāti Hauā, Ngāti Toa and Ngāti Tūwharetoa.[44] Some young men were recruited from the Waikeria Borstal; according to one onlooker they were under guard but showed no sign of wanting to escape from such 'a day of exceptional fun'.

There were three prominent Māori roles. Raureti Te Huia himself played the part of Rewi Maniapoto. According to Pei Te Hurinui Jones, this part was given a great deal of consideration because of Rewi's mana: deciding factors included that Raureti was from Paretekawa, the same subtribe as Rewi, was a kinsman, and bore some physical resemblance to Rewi.[45] Given that, by 1938, there were no living survivors of the battle, Raureti would have been more knowledgeable about the history of the defence than almost anyone else – about Rewi's telling of his prophetic dream, the debates about strategy among the defenders, and the famous offer and refusal of surrender – and he would definitely have known Rewi personally. The seriousness with which he took on the role is suggested by the fact that in the film he carried a mere given to his grandfather by Te Kooti.[46] There is a pattern to the casting of Te Pairi as Te Kooti and later Raureti as Rewi – two senior and knowledgeable kaumātua in these important roles – that supports the view that Hayward looked to these performers not only for their ability to give a convincing portrayal but for their personal knowledge of and intimate connection to the figures they played. They may also have been strategic allies for Hayward as he dealt with local communities.[47]

The role of the fictional character Tama Te Heu Heu changed more than any other between the 1937 script and the film – probably because Te Rongonui Paerata left the film and the part of Hītiri Te Paerata which he was to play seems to have been partially absorbed into that of Tama. In the film the role combines three historical incidents, all anchoring motifs of Ōrākau heroism. The first directly connected the original actor to the role: Te Rongonui's grandfather Hītiri had crept out of the besieged pā and through the government lines at night to get water for the wounded, going right through the soldiers' lines. Hītiri recalled: 'Perhaps they knew what I wanted the water for, because they did not fire on me.'[48] The scene was filmed with Te Rongonui enacting his grandfather's foray. Although Te Rongonui insisted footage showing him was removed when he left the production, Hayward left his performance in for this scene and some of the rest of the battle sequence. In the script this act is attributed to Hītiri, but at some point the roles of Hītiri and Tama merged.[49]

A second incident was also related by Hītiri: the story of the warrior who, in the retreat after the breakout, kept turning and aiming in order to delay the soldiers' pursuit of a wounded girl, but did not fire; she finally 'hobbled on towards the river and safety'. Hītiri's testimony revealed that the warrior's gun was unloaded: 'He had not a charge left when he knelt down and kept the troops off with his levelled *tupara*.'[50] The third incident, similar to the second, was a story of another warrior shot and killed as he covered a retreat with an unloaded gun.[51]

Rewi's Last Stand/The Last Stand (1940): The night-time foray across the lines to fetch water for the wounded. Te Rongonui Paerata performed his grandfather Hītiri Te Paerata's action in this sequence. Although Rongonui left the production, Hayward retained this footage in which he featured, perhaps in recognition of the connection between Rongonui and his tipuna. ABOVE RIGHT: *Rewi's Last Stand/The Last Stand* (1940): Tama Te Heuheu (played here by Hēnare Toka) covers Ariana's defeat, turning an empty rifle on the pursuit. The character is fictional but the incident was based on one recorded at Ōrākau.

Hēnare Toka, who replaced Rongonui, also contributed his expertise with the taiaha: he trained Leo Pilcher (Bob) for three months. The taiaha fight is one of the film's set-piece highlights.[52]

Ramai Te Miha (Ngāti Kahungunu, Ngāi Tahu), a professional photographer and singer, was persuaded to audition for the lead part of Ariana. In the end she did more than act: she sang several songs that were written for the film (they were lost in the 1949 cut), spent at least some time behind the camera, and drew the posters.[53] As she recalled later, referring to her own experience but also that of others who were involved in Hayward's films:

Well I always helped you know, with Rudall's films, you know he would get them to help, in the making of the films ... I was a photographer, I had my own ... photographic studio in Devonport, when he came and asked me to act in Rewi's Last Stand, *but it wasn't long before he had me behind a camera, and ... people he worked with, he taught them.*[54]

By the late 1930s Hayward's first marriage was dissolving, although Hilda Hayward contributed her usual (unacknowledged) expertise – including editing the film.[55] In 1943 Hayward divorced Hilda to marry Ramai, and they made films together until his death.

Rewi's Last Stand/The Last Stand (1940): The Forest Rangers, in Garibaldi shirts and armed with bowie knives, attack Ōrākau.

Ōrākau and the negotiation

Although this *Rewi* gave more screen time to the prewar Waipā, its climax was still going to be Ōrākau, as the title proclaimed. In the publicity material sent out to theatre owners, Hayward included a copy of FitzGerald's 1864 *Press* editorial about Ōrākau. His rendering of the battle was shaped by the long reach of FitzGerald's prose as well as Cowan's account, which was especially striking for the emphasis it gave to the defending side.[56] The idea of Ōrākau as a 'last stand' was FitzGerald's, although it was never very accurate: the Kīngitanga retained control over the Rohe Pōtae until the early 1880s. The 'last stand' took hold of the national imagination nevertheless, and Hayward was tapping into a well-established myth of Ōrākau. Desperation, nobility in extremity and unyielding courage against overwhelming odds, but also – among Pākehā – the notion of 'mutual respect' defined the battle in the national imagination. Cowan's description – 'The splendid devotion and fearlessness displayed by the Maori heroes of that retreat aroused the admiration of their enemies' – is a characteristic response.[57] Hayward would have known that he could draw on wide public recognition of the Battle of Ōrākau.

But if Pākehā tended to recall a narrative of Māori heroism at Ōrākau, Tainui people and their allies held a more complex set of memories. They remembered the heroism but they also remembered the battle as a brutal slaughter. The brutality related to the shelling of the pā, the use of grenades, the fighting in the pā and the pursuit as the defenders broke out; about half escaped across the Pūniu and half – many of them women and children – were killed or too badly wounded to escape. Memories of colonial ruthlessness in this phase of the war extended also – and with profound bitterness – to the attack on Rangiāowhia, which had been occupied by unarmed women, children and elderly men. Despite the insistence of some Pākehā such as FitzGerald, these elements of the battle had little anchorage in broader national memory, which maintained the narrative of 'mutual respect' and emphasised the defenders' heroism rather than the nature of the attack. If Pākehā and Māori cultural memory both held this battle so close, but divided so sharply over what it meant, how was it to be translated to film? Assessing Hayward's response to this question is complicated by the fact that we have only the 1937 script and the 1949 *Last Stand* as evidence – the latter cut tailored to avoid offending British audiences.

Rewi's Last Stand/The Last Stand (1940): Hayward's script direction calls this set the 'Pit of Agony', reflecting the defenders' sufferings from grenade wounds and thirst. Māori women feature prominently among the defenders.

Rewi's Last Stand/The Last Stand (1940): The defenders' haka as they face the enemy troops.

In the script there is greater emphasis on the suffering in the trenches than in the cut-down *The Last Stand*. Hayward's shorthand for the scenes in the defenders' trenches was 'the Pit of Agony', a phrase he uses several times as the script cuts back and forth to these scenes. His notes include 'FLASH OF "PIT OF AGONY" Wounded being attended by Maori women – the dugout is crowded with wounded warriors – two women are covering up a shallow grave'; 'E.S. FLASH OF TRENCH – WITH MANY WOUNDED Through the smoke – many warriors line the bottom of the trench – some are dead and others writhing in agony'.[58] Unlike *The Last Stand*, though, the 1937 script ends with the evacuation of the pā; it does not include *The Last Stand*'s sequences of Tama covering Ariana's retreat, or of Bob and Ben meeting other troops and later finding the wounded Ariana.

The 1937 script and Melissa Cross's evidence from the score suggest that in the film as it was released in 1940, to a greater extent than in the remaining *Last Stand*, Hayward portrayed Māori heroism, Pākehā respect for the defenders, and what the defenders faced: the slaughter as the pā was shelled, the suffering of the wounded and the thirst as water ran out. The score suggests there was more in the film about the attack as the pā was evacuated, and the cavalry charge on the defenders retreating on foot. In reviews, the battle sequence was one of the most highly praised sections of the film. Hayward was at pains to underscore its historical fidelity as documentary, though not without a little sleight of hand. To reinforce viewers' sense that they are watching history on screen, he shows the pages of Cowan's official history being turned, and this segues into a still of a page that gives a quick summary of the action – making it look like a page from Cowan's history (although it is not).[59] From what we can see from the script and the remaining footage, the spirit of Cowan's account is faithfully rendered in the attacks and counter-attacks, the bombardment, casualties and suffering of the wounded. Hayward took care, too, to include some of the haka and chants that Cowan had documented. When reinforcements arrive too late to give assistance to the defenders, the script directs that one of their haka should be 'The great Taupo war-song – "Uhi mai te waero"', and another 'the Kingite composition "He kau ra, he kau ra!" or "Awhea to ure ka riri"'.[60]

The battle scene was heavily reduced in the 1949 British version – precisely, it seems, because of how it portrayed the British attack. Melissa Cross's evidence, derived from the cues in Alfred Hill's score, shows that lost scenes included 'Māori digging trenches ... a sequence of Ariana and the young boy Rimi in the trenches ... Māori praying before the battle ... explosions and Māori suffering ... a re-ordering of the shots around Rewi's words of defiance ... and shots from the final massacre'.[61]

One scene from the Ōrākau sequence lost in the 1949 cut suggests the kind of nuance that was present in the 1940 film. Cowan described the moment when the advancing troops are first spotted by the defenders who have been building the pā. Most of the pā builders are outside the pā at prayers: the lay reader Wi Karamoa 'was praying to Jesus Christ to guard and uphold us, and protect us against the anger of the pakeha ... and the people were bowed with their hands over their eyes, so'. Tupotahi, one of Cowan's informants, was the first to see the glinting of the troops' bayonets in the distance as they approached, and he sounded the alarm after the prayer was finished.[62] Hayward's script followed Cowan's account closely, although he replaces Tupotahi with another character. A still that survives from the 1940 film shows defenders outside the pā with their heads bowed in prayer. This sequence, which showed that British troops had attacked a Christian community, was cut for the British release.

The nature of Hayward's use of historical record and iwi memories is evident in another incident that was already the object of historical debate: the very well-known negotiation between William Mair, the government interpreter, and the defenders.[63] Mair was commissioned to offer terms of surrender: he made two offers, both of which were refused. First he offered terms of surrender to all the defenders; a refusal came back from Rewi. Second, an offer was then made to allow the women and children to come out; this offer was refused by Ahumai Te Paerata. At the time of the fiftieth anniversary of the battle, in 1914, there was a debate about who had said exactly what during the negotiation, and various competing versions appeared. Mair's version of these statements had entered the national consciousness as an emblem of the heroism of the defenders, and the wording now became a point of contention. Cowan had been involved in this discussion and, in *The New Zealand Wars*, he sets out the separate versions. He points out that the defenders' accounts differed from Mair's, that there were several versions among the defenders and they differed from each other. Hayward – working in the Waipā, drawing from Cowan's several versions, speaking with people with allegiances to the various accounts of the battle and the negotiations, and working with Raureti Te Huia – had to decide which account to follow.

The best known of the declarations, and the one where there was most heated disagreement over the wording, was Rewi's refusal to surrender. In *The New Zealand Wars* Cowan gives Mair's version of this as: 'E hoa, ka whawhai tonu ahau ki a koe, ake, ake!' ('Friend, I shall fight against you for ever, for ever!') Another common version was 'Ka whawhai tonu matou, ake, ake, ake!' ('We shall fight you for ever, for ever!'). Cowan records that Ngāti Maniapoto survivors recalled Raureti Paiaka delivering Rewi's message. According to Paiaka's son Te Huia:

> *Rewi cried, 'Kaore e mau te rongo – ake, ake, ake!' ('Peace shall never be made – never, never!') Raureti returned to the outer parapet, stood up on the firing-step a few yards from Mair, and delivered this decision, and all the people shouted with one voice, 'Kaore e mau te rongo – ake, ake, ake!' Rewi came out to the north-west angle when the final decision had been made, and stood in the trench a few yards in rear of Raureti. 'As to the reported words, 'Ka whawhai tonu matou, ake, ake, ake!' says Te Huia, 'I did not hear them uttered.'*[64]

Reed in the novel uses 'Ka whawhai tonu matou, ake, ake, ake!',[65] but the film (and the script) charts a more convoluted path.

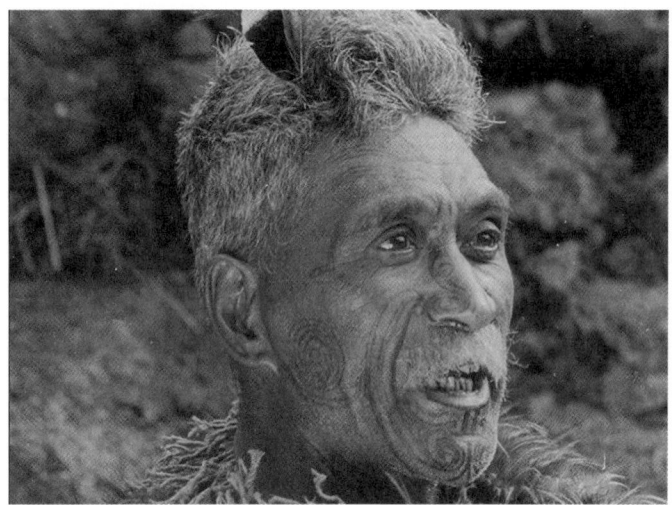

Rewi's Last Stand/The Last Stand (1940): The negotiation at Ōrākau: Rewi Maniapoto (Raureti Te Huia) and William Mair (H.A. Swarbrick). Raureti drew on a Ngāti Maniapoto account of this event as he delivered the refusal to surrender: 'Haere hokitia, kaore e mau te rongo – ake, ake, ake!' [Go away, peace shall never be made, never, never, never!']

When William Mair makes the offer of surrender in the film his words are those recorded by Mair, but the defenders' replies are not: they follow Te Huia's Ngāti Maniapoto account. Rewi says: 'Haere hokitia, kaore e mau te rongo – ake, ake, ake! (Go away again, peace shall never be made, never, never!) Raureti Te Huia was probably the author of the colloquial 'Haere hokitia' (go away again) added at the beginning here (it is not in the script). The rest of the refusal follows the words his father had conveyed to Cowan. In electing to follow this version, Hayward was acknowledging where he was, and acknowledging the continuity of kinship – in the literal whakapapa and in the genealogy of knowledge – between the four Maniapoto men said to have spoken these words: Rewi Maniapoto, who first spoke them; his relative Raureti Paiaka, who relayed them in the negotiation according to the Ngāti Maniapoto account; Te Huia Raureti, who heard them spoken by the father he was about to lose, and who conveyed them to Cowan and also, no doubt, to his son Raureti Te Huia; and Raureti Te Huia himself, now a guardian of this knowledge and playing the part of Rewi. Even if Raureti was not directly consulted when this part of the script was written – although it is most probable that he was – Hayward's collaborators Swarbrick and Oliphant would certainly have had their own commitments to Te Huia's version of what was said.

Hayward was mediating between his sources. But he was also mediating between his sources and his audiences. He gives precedence to this Ngāti Maniapoto version of Rewi's refusal in the Māori words, but rather than translating them directly into English, he gives Pākehā audiences the phrases that were familiar to them. As the words of defiance come across the lines, Bob takes on the role of translator. Everywhere else in the film Bob's Māori is accurate, but here he mistranslates the refusal, producing instead Mair's words that had entered the Pākehā mythology of the battle: 'Friend, I shall fight against you for ever, for ever!' It is probably not coincidental that the translation begins with the word 'friend'. 'Hoa' is a broad term and the English 'friend' is too narrow here, but it serves Hayward's desire to sustain the idea of enduring interracial friendship.

Hayward's complicated shuttling between this Maniapoto account and the words familiar to the national public is part of a larger mediation between tangata whenua and Pākehā understandings of what Ōrākau meant: whether the emphasis was on an expression of ongoing resistance ('peace shall never be made'), or respectful recognition of the worthy foe ('e hoa' translated as 'friend'); whether it was brutal dispossession or an occasion on which Pākehā acknowledged Māori heroism, and a foundation was laid for mutual interracial regard. The myth of mutual respect seems to be endorsed by what happens next in the film: old Ben responds by raising a cheer from the ranks ('Let's give 'em a cheer boys!') and, after Ahumai has rejected the offer to allow the women and children to come out, he again registers his respect: 'Well, what do *we* know about courage?' Respect is further reiterated at the highest rank: behind the British lines General Cameron pronounces: 'General, this country is a grave of glory. What glory can there be in killing men like these?'

Nevertheless, even the reduced 1949 cut, tailored not to offend its British audience, continues on to scenes that were far harder to portray positively, showing the thirst of the defenders

Rewi's Last Stand/The Last Stand (1940): 'Let's give 'em a cheer, boys!' Old Ben leads the colonial troops as they contribute to the story of 'mutual respect' at Ōrākau.

as the water runs out, the shelling of women and children, the wounded in the pā, the bayoneting and the breakout, narrowing to follow the wounded Ariana, protected by Tama, as she limps away in retreat.[66]

Was Hayward trying to have it both ways – to show the battle as the emblem of Māori resistance in the face of overwhelming imperial odds and an occasion of terrible suffering and death, but also as the crucible of the interracial respect that would take Māori and Pākehā into two world wars as allies, not foes? There is a sense of this in the careful line he walks in scripting the negotiation scene. A second possibility – that does not rule out the first – was that he found it hard to resolve these questions himself as he confronted the dilemmas of representing this 'difficult past'.

The end

Hayward's ambivalence is also apparent in the ending – or endings: the script, the novel and *The Last Stand* all end differently from each other. These variants pose some questions about what happened between the authorships of Reed and Hayward, and between the script and the completed film. In the film it appears that Ariana dies of her battle injuries (like so many of the women at Ōrākau), although she does not actually die on screen, leaving a degree of uncertainty. The film ends as Bob and Ben find her wounded after the battle, and Bob unites father and daughter. The script ends earlier, with the evacuation of the pā, and Ariana leaving with Tama, both of them resolved to prepare for whatever comes.

In the novel, in sharp contrast, a fully recovered Ariana is looking forward to a prosperous future: Bob and Ben have been awarded blocks of land on their return from war, and Ben donates his to the young couple as a wedding present. Ariana, in her enthusiasm over this land that has been confiscated and is now in their private ownership, betrays no disquiet about the origin of their sudden wealth – despite her earlier shift in affiliation to her maternal side.[67] In this way, the end of the novel returns to the beginning and Morgan's departure from the Waipā: Bob plans to continue Morgan's work alongside Ariana; they will 'take up our fifty acres at once and start out to cultivate this land once more', resuming the prewar work of productive cultivation. The novel allows the loss of land to pass with only a brief comment that 'to the Maori it was a peace that had been bought with honour' – as if the old cultivation and the new were connected by a smooth continuity.[68] But this private ownership by the interracial couple echoes exactly the paths by which Māori land loss was effected as the nineteenth century wore on: through confiscation and individualisation of title, and often through the transfer of title through intermarriage.[69] For Tainui people, the details of such a 'happy ending' must have encapsulated a cruel irony as they lived with the long-term consequences of land loss.

The novel's ending added another small interracial episode: Ariana's nephew Rimi, whose father was killed at Ōrākau, is taken up by the Forest Rangers and appears kitted out as one of them, proudly marching up and down with a toy Bowie knife and a gun. But Tama Te Heu Heu – a prisoner at large in the rangers' camp – takes him away and brings him back stripped to the waist and armed with a taiaha, which Rimi proceeds to wield with equal enthusiasm.

The happy contemplation of the new farmer, Ariana's forgetful joy at the acquisition of confiscated land, and Rimi's implausible ability to move in both worlds and bear no grudges so soon after being orphaned, appear in neither the script nor in *The Last Stand*. There is no indication in Hill's score that they appeared in the 1940 film. The conclusion of the novel is so much in contrast to the script and *The Last Stand* as we have it, that it recasts the emphasis of the entire plot. There is an important distinction, though, between two elements of this variation. The first is that the film ends as tragedy in the aftermath of the battle, with Ariana's possible or probable death. In 1962 Hayward described her as dying at the end, and she is plainly severely wounded.[70] Tama enacts the historical incident of the defending warrior, turning with his now-empty gun to cover Ariana's retreat, and dies a hero.[71]

After the breakout from the pā Bob and Ben search for Ariana and find her lying wounded. In a scene of high melodrama she greets Bob, who matches up the two coins that she and Ben are wearing to show they are father and daughter. In the 1949 film there is just time for Ariana to tell Ben her mother's name and to be reunited with her father before the film ends. Ariana's apparent death is nevertheless inconclusive. Seeing her wound, Ben looks across at Bob and shakes his head. Her eyes close as if she is on the point of death, but they open again for the closing shot. It is a strangely ambiguous finale and we cannot be certain of exactly how the 1940 film ended. Ramai's view, in contrast to Rudall's, was that Ariana's fate was left deliberately unclear. The 1940 reviews noted with approval the 'fitting note of progress' and the 'attractive romance of fusion of Maori and Pakeha', which sounds more like a response to a happy ending than a story of doomed love.[72] A romantic ending for Bob and Ariana would have had box-office appeal: its narrative of successful racial 'fusion' was in tune with the centennial celebrations, and suitable for a nation seeking unity in time of war.

The other difference between *The Last Stand* and the novel was whether Ariana, if she recovered, went on to happily assume joint ownership of a confiscated Waikato farm, as she does only in the novel. The two most senior figures in the Kīngitanga, King Korokī and Te Puea, were among Hayward's shareholders – and Te Puea was a driving force in the long battle to reclaim confiscated land.[73] Some settlers might have welcomed the glossing over of the raupatu, but it is harder to imagine Raureti Te Huia viewing it without comment. Swarbrick and Oliphant were both researching Tainui history in collaboration with Raureti. Ramai herself had distant connections to Waikato, and she and Hayward later went on to make films on race relations together – but frustratingly, there is no record of her involvement or her opinion on this matter. Hayward had by now spent an extended period in the Waikato, with people from several iwi who had been involved in the defence. He must have been aware of the impact of the confiscations on Tainui people.

Rewi's Last Stand/The Last Stand (1940): A wounded, perhaps dying Ariana is united with Old Ben, who acknowledges her as his daughter.

Hayward was also in contact with Cowan. He would probably have known that Cowan had his own centennial project in 1939, having been commissioned to write one of the series of centennial histories, *Settlers and Pioneers*.[74] As Chris Hilliard has shown, Cowan wrote a chapter on the Waikato War that slated the government for its conduct of the war and its punishment of Tainui afterwards: 'the revenge for acts of so-called rebellion in Waikato was wholesale dispossession and eviction'. Cowan called the raupatu 'a tragedy, the ruin of a people'. He felt very strongly about the widespread ignorance of the Waikato's history, writing to the series editor that he had written forcibly to try to overcome it.[75] The editors thought otherwise, and deleted the chapter.

Whatever the immediate and underlying reasons for the differences between the novel's ending and that of the film, the discrepancy itself may point more broadly to irresolvable problems for a Pākehā history-maker – whether Cowan or Hayward – mythologising Ōrākau as a site where 'interracial respect' was forged, and from which the 'blended race' looked forward to a harmonious future, as the film's scrolling prologue signalled. Was Ōrākau a heroic defence in which both sides displayed nobility, laying the ground for mutual respect, future reconciliation and eventual happy conjugality – making it a fitting subject for the centennial? Or did the desperation of the defenders, the carnage, the killing of women and children, the invasion of the Waikato itself and the long aftermath of the land loss make it complex indeed to engage fully with the historical traces and the divergent cultural memories of this event? If, as Ernest Renan had claimed, nationality rests in part on the agreement to forget many things then, at some point – and despite the film's voiceover narrative of pioneer progress and the depictions of colonial admiration of the defenders – Hayward appears to have been unable to ignore the bitter realities of Ōrākau.

Reception and aftermath

The film gained an early boost after the private screening in February 1940 attended by John Grierson, the doyen of documentary film and then Canadian film commissioner, who had been brought to New Zealand to undertake a survey of the film industry. Grierson's speeches, widely reported, emphasised the contribution to citizenship of national film industries that 'dramatise[d] all aspects of national life'; he argued that the country should be 'producing its own film men and its own film style'.[76] In this context Grierson's praise for *Rewi* was a gift from above:

> Mr Grierson said that it was more important that New Zealanders should have produced that film than that they should see a hundred films from Hollywood … because in the film they had just seen the nation had expressed itself. It was a good film, and he was surprised how near to producing a Cecil B. de Mille spectacle Mr Hayward had come with the resources at his disposal. The speaker said he realised the difficulties of creating a number of the scenes in 'Rewi's Last Stand'.[77]

Grierson's belief in documentary's social and civic purpose immediately attached itself to the reception of the sound *Rewi*. It also endorsed the film's standing as national history – which would have pleased Hayward.

The premiere at the Strand in Auckland drew a large and enthusiastic crowd. The *Star* praised the 'excellent standard' of the film and found that it brought 'a fitting note of progress to mark this Centenary year'. The portrayals of colonists and Māori, the story of the defence of Ōrākau, that 'attractive romance of the fusion of Maori and pakeha', the faithful rendition of dress and customs and the 'glorious bush, river and moorland scenery', the excitements of the 'canoe chase, and duels with the taiaha' all attracted plaudits.[78] The *Star* noted *Rewi*'s popularity as it entered its second week:

> Many Aucklanders who had expected little from the film, 'seeing that it was only a local affair', have been pleasurably surprised at its quality. Not only is it a film Aucklanders should see, because of its historical and educational aspect; it is one that they can enjoy to the full because of its high entertainment value.[79]

Other reviews remarked on the unexpectedly high quality of the film, its excitement, the acting – especially that of Ramai

Te Miha – and its contribution to a shared appreciation of New Zealand history. The *Evening Post* valued the film's 'authenticity' – the care taken with 'costume and custom', the use of the waka *Te Winika*, the 'actual words used on the historic occasions' and the inclusion of descendants as the actors. Describing it as 'a saga of Maori chivalry, courage, and endurance', it noted the portrayal of the defence 'by 300 Maori men and women, who, greatly outnumbered and fighting a hopeless battle, nevertheless carried themselves so gallantly that the British general marvelled at their qualities'.[80]

A few weeks later Cowan linked the defence of Ōrākau to the lead-up to the Battle of Britain: in the light of Churchill's rousing speech of 19 May 1940, he recalled Rewi's speech to the assembled chiefs at Ōrākau as they debate whether to stay and fight : 'Listen to me, chiefs of the council and all the tribes. It was we who sought this battle, therefore then should we retreat? This is our land. If we are to die, let us die in battle. If we are to live, let us survive on the field of battle!' Cowan noted that white New Zealanders must look to the Māori for 'such inspiring declarations'.[81]

The film circulated around small-town and suburban cinemas for the next couple of years. When the Haywards took it to England, the creation of the cut that was released as *The Last Stand* in 1949 was a protracted process. It involved attempts to persuade British distributors to release a film made on a smaller budget than most of their productions, and now beginning to look out of date, especially in its technical aspects.[82] The cut which reduced its length by half meant that much of Alfred Hill's fine score was lost and the rest was savaged.[83] Ramai and Rudall's later reflections show that they were highly aware of how the colonial war story would be received in postwar Britain. The cut had to address the problem of selling a film in which the Māori defenders were the heroes and the British were the outnumbering attackers, to British audiences who had only narrowly averted an enemy invasion.[84] Hayward later recalled that the film was poorly received because 'with all those British troops surrounding a handful of Maoris it was like Rorke's Drift in reverse – an unsporting kind of thing'.[85]

It was another logistical exercise to extract the shortened and neglected film from its British distributors and return it to New Zealand.[86] When Hayward finally retrieved it, *The Last Stand* was re-released in cinemas in the 1950s. (H.A. Swarbrick took his grandchildren to see it, proudly explaining its part in the family history.)[87] Hayward deposited the negatives and sound tracks with the National Film Library, and 16mm prints of the film were made and circulated to schools where they were reported as 'being widely used' in 1963. The film was shown in 1964 as part of the centenary commemorations of the Battle of Ōrākau.[88] The New Zealand Broadcasting Corporation purchased it in 1970, and it was the first New Zealand film to be shown on television.[89]

The film circulated almost in a vacuum: because of the cost of making sound films and the competition from better-funded overseas films, this period saw very few New Zealand films made, and except for the National Film Unit's documentary or newsreel material, no other sound film that was historical. As a result, *The Last Stand* was 'the' New Zealand history film for many years; *The Te Kooti Trail*, although it was a better film and had survived more or less intact, suffered from its silence. People still recall seeing *Rewi* at school or at rescreenings in the 1960s, before the new wave of New Zealand cinema meant that it ceased to be a novelty and began to look outdated. The film's prominence helped to consolidate Hayward's nuanced and ambivalent narrative of Ōrākau for several generations.

Even though the version circulating was the heavily cut film with the harsher battle scenes removed, it put events at Ōrākau in question. People remember it for Rewi's heroic defiance, and many still recite his 'Ake! Ake! Ake!' when the film is mentioned.

The visiting American film scholar Robert Sklar, writing in the literary review *Landfall* in 1971 at a time when the western was beginning its revisionist phase, contrasted Hayward's New Zealand Wars films with the ideological perspectives of Hollywood of the same era:

> *Until recently the American Indians were pictured in films as ruthless and treacherous antagonists, a people fighting against white encroachment but hardly ever shown as representing a life or culture of their own. In Rudall Hayward's handling of New Zealand's conflict the Maoris are treated with dignity and indeed their sense of the land precedes and even shapes that of the Europeans. Most historical films demean our sense of history; Rewi's Last Stand is one of the few I know which can enhance our feeling for the past.*[90]

John O'Shea came to a similar conclusion: he noted that if the white troops 'are handled with the near slapstick earthiness that marks John Ford's depiction of US Cavalry forces, Hayward clearly avoids the carelessness with which Hollywood allowed its Injuns to bite the dust. Though Maoris are seen to be slaughtered, they are shown to be brave, fighting against overpowering odds, intelligent, and, above all, chivalrous.'[91]

Merata Mita – only the third Māori film director, after Ramai Hayward and Barry Barclay – wrote in 1992 that she preferred Hayward's films to much of the work from later Pākehā directors. She described *Rewi's Last Stand* as 'an engaging, high-spirited film' that 'approached its Maori theme and story with respect for Maori courage and integrity'. According to her, 'The outrage that Hayward, and other historians since, felt about the injustice of the British advance is clearly evident in the film.' Mita viewed Hayward's work as 'sadly neglected.'[92] Not everyone agreed: the anonymous Māori reviewer in *Te Iwi o Aotearoa*, after *The Last Stand* screened on television in 1990, thought the film reflected the unconscious racism prevalent in Aotearoa at the time it was made.[93]

The Last Stand's melodrama is more heavy-handed than that of *The Te Kooti Trail*, and this is partly what makes it less engaging to today's audiences than the earlier film. The heavy cutting and the odd ending have muddied the film's narrative arc. Tainui people today who view the film are not overly impressed: one kuia dismissed its emphasis on 'that silly little girl', and Tainui historian Tom Roa laughed as he recounted how, at a marae screening where everyone gathered to watch the film, 'one by one we all fell asleep, including me!'[94]

Ramai was Aotearoa's first Māori director. She and Rudall made several films together locally and in Britain and China, mostly documentaries, including some on Māori subjects. Their next feature film was *To Love a Maori*, in 1972 – which, as the name suggests, also dealt with a cross-cultural love affair, this time as a 'social problem' film. Rudall said in 1973, reflecting on a life in filmmaking:

> *New Zealand filmmakers get no official backing, the big theatre chains have done nothing. There's little hope for upcoming young filmmakers, they'll either have to make a box-office certainty or work with television. I have had to wait fifty years to make a moderate box-office success in New Zealand with* To Love A Maori, *and then because it's timely and encouraging to Maoris – I would have liked to have done a lot more.*[95]

Conclusion

In taking these incidents from the New Zealand Wars into film, and using his considerable flair as a publicist to ensure that they became national events, Hayward, like Cowan, was an influential figure in mitigating Pākehā memory loss of the New Zealand Wars through the first half of the twentieth century, at a time when the world wars were overtaking them in making strong claims on public memory. *The Last Stand*, despite the diminished form in which it survived, gained the status of a New Zealand cinema classic.

In taking up Ōrākau, Te Kooti, Gilbert Mair and Rewi Maniapoto, Hayward chose to represent people and events that were already well known and defined in the public memory. But his treatment of these figures and events was searching and thoughtful, and developed in complexity over his career. As in Cowan's writings, ideologies of advancing civilisation do inform Hayward's narratives. The advantages of colonisation are not fundamentally in question: Māori are shown to benefit from the patronage of 'good Pākehā' like Jean Guerrin, Governor Grey and Reverend Morgan, and from the wealth and productivity of European culture. But Hayward rendered the Māori resistance to colonial invasion not just with sympathy but with recognition of colonial injustice. He increasingly explored the intricacies of colonial encounters during the wars with detailed reference to both written and and oral history. Ramai Hayward recalled years later, 'It was Pākehā and Māori who made the film.'[96] Mindful always of the box office, he was also driven by a desire to foster a public sense of the distinctiveness, excitement *and* the complexity of the New Zealand past at a time when drama seemed to attach itself only to Hollywood.

In the final analysis, though, it is the evidence of ambivalence that, in so confident and flamboyant an individual as Hayward, offers the best clue to the complexity of the past that he sought to convey, and its significance for the worlds of 1925, 1927, 1940 and 1949, into which he launched his film histories.

WARS IN THE LIVING ROOM

The Killing of Kane and *The Governor*

> … *at school we were given the white man's version of New Zealand history, and this was a programme which inverted that and gave us a broader-based idea of what had actually happened.* —Michael Noonan

If you talk to anyone who was in New Zealand in 1977, chances are they will remember a television series called *The Governor* that screened that year. Director Tony Isaac and scriptwriter Michael Noonan, employees of the newly arrived TV One, parleyed their way into getting state funding for a drama-documentary that set its critical sights on national memory of the 'Good Governor' George Grey and, in the process, targeted the myth of racial harmony. In the still short history of New Zealand television no commissioned drama had ever had a million-dollar budget before – nor would it happen again for quite some time. Prime Minister Robert Muldoon was appalled that it overran a budget that, to him, seemed far too large in the first place. In *The Governor*'s aftermath, an inquiry was held into the funding of public television, with the result that nothing on its scale was approved for the following 20 years. Nevertheless, while the series screened the country stopped to watch as a story of the colonial past unfolded – a story that didn't look at all like the colonial progress that the school textbook *Our Nation's Story* was still telling. *The Governor* was a national rite of passage – and that had something to do with the coming of age of television, and something to do with the beginning of a seismic shift in thinking about how New Zealand's past had shaped its present.

The early 1960s marked the centenaries of the Taranaki and Waikato wars. Although local Pākehā plans for commemorations were beginning to include Māori – some more than others – popular memory among the Pākehā residents of these flourishing dairy regions recalled a century of prosperity. Postwar affluence in the still largely Pākehā cities and towns nurtured a sense of comfort, and the prevailing public image of Māori was still of happy brown citizens of an enlightened modern nation.[1] But behind the scenes at the celebratory events there was discontent among Māori, and many from the Waikato stayed away from the commemoration of Ōrākau in 1964. There was, as Keith Aberdein reflected, 'a rolling thunder out over those hills'.[2] The thunder sounded from several directions.

Through the 1960s and 70s an increasingly well-educated generation was coming of age in a time of relative affluence. Māori–Pākehā relations were shifting as Māori migrated to the cities, making them more visible in the population. Young Māori were becoming better educated and far more vocal, and were gaining the sympathy of left-leaning Pākehā and generating anxiety in more conservative camps. The National government of 1975–84, and Muldoon himself – a combative and often vituperative leader – provoked protest from a range of social movements. But the tectonic plates were moving anyway. Māori, workers and women were all asserting their rights – cultural as well as political and economic. Industrial unrest resulted in major strikes, many of which also involved Māori. Second-wave feminism gave rise to the articulation of Māori feminism, and several young, political Māori women emerged as prominent figures. Donna Awatere's *Maori Sovereignty* (1984), published first in the feminist magazine *Broadsheet*, signalled the connections between these movements.

Public debate moved out of the newspapers and the House of Representatives and onto the streets as public protest came to mark divisions of authority and generation. Sporting contact with South Africa provoked angry debate. The New Zealand Rugby Football Union defied the international anti-apartheid boycott and continued sporting contact with South Africa, and Muldoon would support its decision to bring the South African team to New Zealand in 1981. Involvement in the Vietnam War, as Aotearoa followed the United States and Australia into Indochina, divided the country along broadly similar lines. These international issues went on to turn the spotlight back onto colonial legacies in Aotearoa: land, the Treaty of Waitangi, language and culture.

The issue of land rights simmered throughout the 1970s, with political activism supported by a growing scholarship on historic and ongoing injustices. The activist group Ngā Tamatoa was formed; and they and other activists pointed to systematic breaches of the Treaty of Waitangi and demanded that it be given the backing of the law. Whina Cooper led the great hīkoi from Te Hapua in Northland to parliament to protest land loss – forging cross-tribal unity in the fight for action over land. The Waitangi Tribunal was established in 1975, although it was another 10 years before it was empowered to consider historic grievances. In Auckland Ngāti Whātua occupied their historic land at Bastion Point for 506 days before a huge police operation evicted them. As well as redress on the matter of land, activists wanted action on other matters of social justice such as protection of tikanga Māori and te reo, in which fluency and knowledge were dropping as older kaumātua and kuia died. Younger Māori entered tertiary education at an increasing rate and gained greater access to professions, including media. These changes strengthened the public presence and influence of Māori, and the issues that concerned them slowly, if unevenly, began to impinge on Pākehā consciousness. Aotearoa's 'racial harmony' began to be thought of as a myth rather than a fact.[3]

Television

Television had arrived late in New Zealand, beginning in 1960. Not until the late 1960s did the New Zealand Broadcasting Corporation (NZBC) begin funding local drama – investing initially and rather sporadically in one-off plays. *Pukemanu* (1971–72), a drama series set in a timber town, was the notable exception to this pattern. Among its cast and crew were many whose paths converge in this book: director Tony Isaac, writer Keith Aberdein, script editor Michael Noonan and actors Don Selwyn, Geoff Murphy, Bruno Lawrence, Tama Poata and Peter Vere Jones. *Pukemanu* was very popular, despite the warning to the writers not to include Māori characters because 'we don't have any Māori actors', as one executive airily informed Noonan, and despite some criticism because, as Noonan recalled, 'people back then still wanted to see Māori only in the position where they were doing pretty songs and poi dances and things, and didn't like to see them in a real life position'. The 'Charlie's Rock' episode, which featured a Māori-centred plot, in fact rated exceptionally well.[4] Through their work on *Pukemanu*, Isaac and Noonan developed a working relationship with Don Selwyn, one of the 'nonexistent' Māori actors, and Selwyn went on to be a central figure in *The Governor*.

While Māori were still scarce in the industry both off and on screen, the underlying commitment of many to the mandated 'cultural requirement' of public broadcasting gave rise to one remarkable documentary series. In 1974 director Barry Barclay (Ngāti Apa) and Pākehā journalist–historian Michael King's six-part series *Tangata Whenua* screened in the Sunday evening slot that was reserved for prestige programming.[5] It offered a rich portrayal of Māori history and contemporary life and was distinctive in letting Māori speak for themselves and on their own terms. *Tangata Whenua* is remembered by Māori viewers who seldom saw themselves represented on screen in this way, and by Pākehā viewers, many of whom were gaining an unprecedented insight into te ao Māori. In the episode on Waikato, King interviews a kaumātua as they walk across the site of Rangiriri, talking about what happened there; it then switches to narration about the emergence of the Kīngitanga and its attempts to reestablish Waikato in its whenua after the wars. Another episode focused on Te Kooti – but as a prophet and founder of Ringatū rather than as a guerilla leader. Also in 1974 Geoff Murphy adapted Māori myth to make the first te reo drama, the television play *Uenuku*.[6] Political documentary and protest movement converged with Geoff Stevens' *Te Matakite o Aotearoa: The Maori Land March*, which documented the 1975 hīkoi from Northland to Wellington, and screened later that year.

The NZBC was dissolved in 1974 and replaced by the Broadcasting Commission of New Zealand (BCNZ) – which, for television, meant a two-channel structure and a newly competitive environment for local drama production. This, Trisha Dunleavy argues, proved to be a creative spur as it converged with a broader climate of cultural self-discovery.[7] The second television channel arrived in 1975; like the first it was publicly owned, although the era of increasing reliance on commercial funding was on its way. But in the late 1970s the channels still competed with each other on quality, rather than profits:

> the early two-channel phase (1975–77) continues to be remembered by the in-house producers, directors and writers who were directly part of it, as an era of unrivalled opportunity and expansion for TV production in which local programming was finally able to flourish, the result being a higher, more sustained schedule for the full range of locally produced TV forms.[8]

Michael Scott-Smith, head of drama at the newly created TV One, recalls: 'we seriously had a sense of cultural requirement. It wasn't a joke … I think my great boast was at the end of the first year of Television One we had made more drama on air than the NZBC had made in the previous ten years prior to that.'[9]

The circumstances of New Zealand television from the 1970s gave it a degree of public reach that did not diminish until the 1990s. By the end of the 1960s most households owned – or more likely rented – a television set. In the days of the two-channel system, TV One was the recognised 'quality' channel, with a larger market share. Because there was no alternative yet to real-time viewing, audiences watched at the same time and discussed programmes over the following days. This created a single community of viewers with a shared public memory. It became a national community in 1973 when national, rather than regional broadcasts became the norm.[10] In Aotearoa the limited choice of two channels lasted longer than in larger overseas markets, so this shared community of viewers persisted later than in countries where the more rapid proliferation of free and pay channels competed for viewers and fractured audiences.

Even after the arrival and takeup of video recorders in the 1980s, which allowed viewers to shift their viewing time, the habit of watching close to the time of screening persisted, as did the established culture of discussing popular programmes. Even in the late 1990s when the *New Zealand Wars* documentary series screened, TV One was still a forum that could define national debate because it had such a hold on public attention. As a result, high-profile local series such as *Tangata Whenua*, *The Governor* and, later, *The New Zealand Wars* are still remembered by people who watched them when they first screened. All three series helped to effect change in a generation's understanding of the past.

From the mid-1970s TV One employed a small production staff, most of them from the old NZBC era, to create local documentaries and drama. Aspiring filmmakers boosted their income by doing contract work in television drama – so there was a degree of flow between the public and the independent sectors. This did not always foster warm feelings between those employed by television, who were government servants with secure permanent jobs, and the fledgling independents, who were also often dependent on government grants but whose creators and crews – in a contrast not lost on them – lived a hand-to-mouth existence from one production to the next. The flow between the sectors and the relatively lax levels of accountability in the state sector did, nevertheless, contribute to an environment where there were some extraordinary creative opportunities – including what became *The Governor*.

Over the same period, the country's written history was changing. Burrowing into colonial and imperial archives, the first generation of university-trained New Zealand historians retrieved evidence that was to underpin changing historical perspectives on the wars. And even before their work appeared, a more overtly political and more accessible style of history had begun to reach broader audiences thanks to journalist Dick Scott's revelations – to Pākehā, that is – about what had occurred at Parihaka.[11] Historical novels – especially Errol Braithwaite's trilogy – positioned the wars in Taranaki and the Waikato as traumatic events for both Māori and Pākehā, written against the larger context of Aotearoa's involvement in another colonial war, Vietnam.[12] Even popular history and historical fiction, though, could not compete with the screens that were now invading the nation's living rooms. *The Governor* did not come out of the blue. Nor was it the first television drama to take up a New Zealand Wars story; that honour goes to a less well-recalled one-off production called *The Killing of Kane*.

The Killing of Kane, 1971

In 1971, with Vietnam very much on the public agenda, the population sat down in its armchairs to watch this country's first television production shot in colour, commissioned by the NZBC from the young playwright Warren Dibble. (They watched in black and white, because although colour production had arrived, colour broadcasting had not.) The play screened just four years after the publication of Braithwaite's novel *The Evil Day*, which featured a fanatical and cruel Tītokowaru. *The Killing of Kane* told another kind of story about Tītokowaru's War, both more even-handed and more ambivalent. A docudrama about the attack on the government redoubt at Turuturumōkai in July 1868 and then the death of the defecting soldier Charles Kane (a story told in James Cowan's *The Adventures of Kimble Bent*), it was shot near the historical location outside Hāwera in southern Taranaki, and drew on several strands of historical knowledge.

The origins of the script lay in the bedroom. Some years earlier as he was about to leave for his OE, Dibble's girlfriend Kiri told him she was pregnant and, despite his friends' attempts to dissuade him, they married. The couple moved to Kiri's home town of Hāwera in Taranaki so they could bring up their child near her whānau, and spent upwards of a decade there.[13] Through her mother, Kiri was related to Tītokowaru.

It was a life-changing event for Dibble, a young Pākehā from Auckland. Two dimensions of life in Hāwera proved especially fertile. The first – perfect for a would-be author – was the town's highly active cultural life, including an intense commitment to drama: 'it was the centre of one-act plays, which were very big in those days … it was bigger than the footy'. A stock genre for radio, one-act plays were making the transition to television. The year Hāwera won the national one-act play competition, 'everyone knocked off work'.[14] Dibble set to work writing.

Second, he began to absorb the local side of a story of which very few Pākehā knew anything at all in 1970. Knowledge of the past came from all kinds of sources. He met archaeologists working at the site of Tītokowaru's pā at Te Ngutu o te Manu. Alastair Buist, a local doctor, was excavating the pā of North Taranaki and had published a monograph in 1964. A combined centennial occasion for Turuturumōkai and Te Ngutu o te Manu had been held in 1968, and had perhaps prompted local stories. Kiri's Pākehā stepfather Leo Carr was fascinated by local history and Dibble began reading writers such as Elsdon Best, Keith Sinclair and James Cowan. But these books were less important to him than the stories he was hearing from local, mostly Māori people: 'the daily contact and the slow absorption of casual gossip … it would just come up and usually in humour, in mockery'. Dibble had happened upon a Māori world that was entirely new to him:

> *Interspersed and between all that was the deep history of the Māori, coming from the land, because it was all around, it wasn't coming from books and stuff, you met people who were telling you little bits … as far as I was concerned I walked into this mosaic, it was like a kaleidoscope of bits and pieces.*[15]

His marriage took him into this world, so while he had much to learn, he had plenty of opportunities to learn it:

> *I used to travel with Oriwa Haddon … he gave me all the stuff on Tītokowaru … His father, Tahupōtiki Haddon … although he was a Methodist minister … he combined that sort of spillover that came from Parihaka, the mixture, when you had the Hauhau and the Māori culture sort of blending … A lot of paths led indirectly into this. In Hawera, a lot of people were talking about von Tempsky's sword … in the pub …*[16]

Dibble had already written a successful short drama for television, and on the back of this success was commissioned to write a script for New Zealand television's first foray into colour production. He was given a free hand: 'Do anything you like, big cast, bigger the better … they hadn't any idea what I was going to do …' He found himself wanting to kick back against what he saw as a patronising Pākehā tendency to regard Māori with sentimentality and the idea that 'the Maoris are lovely, they just want to go back to their past'. Fascinated by that contradiction and by the fact that 'it's not just always between good and evil', he wrote a play that paid serious respect to tikanga and, in mining Cowan's *Kimble Bent*, he included one thoughtful and one arrogant Pākehā and a charismatic Tītokowaru. The play also included practices calculated to unsettle that annoying sentimentality: 'I liked the scene where the heart was [chopped out] … that sort of cut through a lot … I thought people should realise, they're not all *nice* people.'[17]

Like others drawn to the Tītokowaru story, Dibble was interested in figures who moved between the two cultures and, especially, Kimble Bent's well-documented adaptation to another world – which of course echoed Dibble's own experience at the time. This provided the basis for a contrast between Dibble's two Pākehā characters: Bent who adapts, and the second defector, Charles Kane, who does not.

The Killing of Kane opens with a scene-setting sequence that quotes directly from a letter sent by Tītokowaru to the encroaching settlers on 5 December 1868.[18] The opening shot – a slow pan across a skyline ending on the distinctive cone of Taranaki, which locates the land as the central question of the play – is followed by a closeup of water running over rocks. A letter is then read out in voiceover as a Māori man carrying a taiaha but dressed in formal European suit and hat walks along a ridgeline, followed by a small girl:

> Tēnā koe, tēnā koe, tēnā koe.
> I want to ask you this question. Who does England belong to, and who does the land you are now standing on belong to? I will tell you. The heavens and earth were created in the beginning. Then was man created and also all things that are in the world after their several kinds. If you believe that God created them all, it is well. So far, we agree.

The man and child pause, and as the man turns to the camera, his almost clerical appearance is disrupted when we see he is

The Killing of Kane (1971): Taranaki in silhouette in the opening scene.

All frames from *The Killing of Kane* courtesy of TVNZ Television Archive, Ngā Taonga Sound and Vision

blind in one eye, apparently as the result of a wound. The letter writer, now identified as this man, continues:

> But you were made a Pākehā, and England was named for your country. We are Māoris, with New Zealand for our country. Between you and us is a great ocean. Why did you come? We did not cross over to you. Away with you from our country to your own country. Away with you from this town. Enough.
>
> Signed, Tītokowaru.

Now there is a cut to the letter's recipient and reader, Tītokowaru's adversary Lieutenant Colonel Thomas McDonnell. McDonnell turns to the camera and, briefly, acts as a narrator to provide

The Killing of Kane (1971): 'But you were made a Pākehā, and England was named for your country. We are Māoris, with New Zealand for our country. Between you and us is a great ocean. Why did you come? We did not cross over to you. Away with you from our country to your own country.' Tītokowaru's letter in voiceover opens the film. Napi Waaka as Riwha Tītokowaru.

historical background, filling viewers in on Tītokowaru ('best chief the Hauhaus ever had'), the religious beliefs of the 'Hauhaus', and the importance of land in the events to follow. McDonnell's exposition is intercut with a series of quick scene-setting vignettes in which the perspectives of the settlers – from land-hunger to missionary zeal – dramatise the grounds for conflict.

Later in the play McDonnell reads and interprets a second and more ominous letter in which Tītokowaru threatens that if the colonists continue 'going on the roads' they will be killed and eaten: 'we have begun to eat human flesh. My throat is continually open for the flesh of man.'[19]

With the context established, the play moves between the resistant Taranaki iwi and the colonial camps, drawing on Cowan's oral history of Kimble Bent to distinguish two characters who have separately defected from the colonial troops to the Māori camp. Kimble Bent (Peter Vere Jones) remains loyal to Tītokowaru throughout, but Charles Kane (Alan Jervis) is killed when he attempts to betray Tītokowaru and defect back to the colonial side. Bent and Kane take contrasting approaches to their situation in a Māori world. Bent, in a new turn in the remaking of the Pākehā male, proceeds with cautious humility, claiming no special privileges and seeking to understand the world he has entered; Kane, arrogant and superior, makes repeated cultural blunders and is increasingly at odds with his Māori hosts.

The two main actions of the play deal with historical events: the attack on the redoubt at Turuturumōkai near Hāwera, and Charles Kane's ill-fated attempt to defect back to the colonial side by trading information about Tītokowaru in return for immunity. As well as Cowan's Kimble Bent, Dibble is drawing on his Māori sources here, too. The ritual selection of the tekau mā rua, the war party for the attack on the Turuturumōkai redoubt, is derived from Bent's account to Cowan. But the attack itself, which Bent did not participate in, must have derived from Māori sources – probably Oriwa Haddon, who learned about them from his father. Taketake, a leader of one of the attacking parties, had given a lengthy account to Tahupōtiki Haddon, including the following extracts:

> *Previous to the night chosen by Titokowaru our spies, men and women, mostly women, were continually in and round the redoubt. They reported the weakness of structure, number of men*

and method of guard. All this was laid before Tītokowaru and taken into consideration by him in planning the procedure and method of attack …

With my party was a pakeha 'Kaina' (Kane), a renegade deserter. While we crouched in the fern he complained of the cold and kept moving about. We were afraid lest he be heard by the sentry. Some of our young men threatened to tomahawk him. He persisted to grumble about the long wait. Our young men became suspicious of him and thought he was trying to convey a warning to the sentry. They pulled him down into the fern and would have tomahawked him had not the sentry heard the scuffle and fired …

Later I saw [Kane] approach the dead body of a soldier and attempt to drag it towards the gate. This afterwards we learnt was the body of the kapene (captain – Captain Ross). Kaina cut out the heart of his dead countryman. I took no notice at the time. On returning to Te Ngutu-o-te-Manu after the fight Kaina, unknown to us, in an endeavour to win favour with Tītokowaru, presented him with the captain's heart, thus claiming that he had killed the first man.[20]

The Killing of Kane (1971): Charles Kane (Alan Jervis) and Kimble Bent (Peter Vere Jones) argue over what it means to be Europeans in a Māori community. With permission from Peter Vere Jones and Alan Jervis

The spies scouting out the redoubt, Kane's risky behaviour before the attack, and the attempt to perform the whāngai hau (cutting out the heart of the first enemy killed as a ritual offering) are all elements of the attack that are dramatised in *The Killing of Kane*. Only Māori witnessed the prelude to and aftermath of the attack – with the exception of Kane himself, and he was killed soon after. The play invites us to respond to them on Ngā Ruahine terms: to recognise Kane's arrogance and how he jeopardises the attack; and that his presentation of the captain's heart to Tītokowaru is clumsy and misplaced as well as dishonest.

Another theme is the question of how Pākehā might live in a Māori context. Kane and Bent both served under Tītokowaru. Kane is an example of how not to assimilate – he refuses to adapt to the Māori world he lives in. Bent provides the alternative: he makes fruitless attempts to enlighten Kane ('it's the way they do it Kane, everything's shared, even the work'), to confront him ('when you came over to us … what did you expect, you'd be made a rangatira?'), and to persuade him to understand the ways and beliefs of the people they are living among. The production pays a great deal of attention to cultural perspective: how can Pākehā see these events as Māori saw them? How might Pākehā conduct themselves among Māori?

The irrepressible Reverend Napi Waaka (Ngāti Pikiao), recently arrived in Hāwera, took the role of Tītokowaru. Dibble counted him as a friend and respected his knowledge, but confessed he had hoped for a somewhat less 'amiable-looking' Tītokowaru. His annotation of a newspaper photograph of Waaka as Tītokowaru reads 'Physically miscast: Titokowaru was lean, hungry, and had only one eye … but Napi was a friend of mine, and he had the right spirit, *and* the knowledge. He was a Maori scholar, as well as a methodist minister.'[21]

The NZBC director Chris Thomson took the production to Hāwera to shoot on the historical location; when this proved a problem because 'Taranaki is full of telephone poles', they built the set of the redoubt on the brow of the hill. As a *Listener* feature on the production noted, 'Ironically, that is where the redoubt *should* have been in the first place. The heavy Pakeha casualties at Turuturu-mokai were caused partly by the fact that the redoubt could be fired into from the hill, and Titokowaru's men did just that.' The designer, Cedric Leeming, used historical photographs and drew on the knowledge of local people.[22]

The Killing of Kane walked a fine line in audience sympathy: while portraying some quite bloodcurdling practices, Thomson plainly sought to represent events involving Māori on Māori terms. Much of this is a result of the level of cultural advice he invited, and took, during the production. The Reverend Napi Waaka was instrumental in facilitating the production and especially the involvement of some of the mana whenua. He was from Rotorua but, through his work in Taranaki as minister, he was involved in establishing the legendary Patea Maori Club and other cultural activities. 'I realised how much the people had suffered,' he said, when he began finding out about the history of Taranaki.[23] This recognition gave him a strong sense of the importance of telling that history. He made efforts to involve local descendants in the production and was involved in training the Māori cast in cultural performance, in which he had extensive experience. He worked alongside Taranaki advisors Bob and June Jackson. Three Taranaki Māori clubs were involved in the production, and Napi Waaka worked closely with them on posture, stance and ritual performance as well as on the use of te reo. The obvious care taken in portraying cultural performance, the time given to it, and the use of te reo Māori, both translated and untranslated, are striking features of the production. Some of the cast brought their own taiaha for use in the production, and refused to use anything else.[24] Napi Waaka – a fluent speaker of te reo who did not learn English until the age of 10 – was especially concerned 'to make sure what was represented as Māori was genuine'; he recalled in 2012 that Thomson had given the cast every opportunity to use their knowledge and expertise, 'to be ourselves'.[25] Peter Vere Jones, who played Kimble Bent, recalled the very positive engagement among Māori who worked on the production. But he also recalled that it was 'scary at times': in the local context, they were only one generation away from the people directly involved and he was conscious of that.[26]

Not everyone connected to the history was pleased about the production. For some mana whenua the stakes were high. Te Rau Oriwa Davis (Ngāti Ruanui, Ngāruahine, Nga Raurukitahi, Ngapuhinuitonu) was a teenager at the time, and she recalls everyone talking about it when auditions were advertised. One of her aunts got a part (and had funny stories to tell about it), but there was a lot of debate and a range of opinion expressed within her whānau, who descend from Tītokowaru. She points out that 'Napi Waaka was not tangata whenua of Ngāti Ruanui/Ngāruahine kawa tikanga – or the holder of things whakapapa/kōrero of Riiwha Tītokowaru'. Acknowledging his good intentions in seeking to make

Taranaki whānui history better understood, she nevertheless remembered that her mother was not impressed with him taking on the role: 'my mother's rebellion was removing her tamariki out from Reverend Napi Waaka's pastoral care', and she recalls others doing so too.²⁷

Te Rau Oriwa Davis explained that for many of the mana whenua in the 1970s, the time was not yet right for talking publically about the events the programme dramatised: 'our history was still raw'. It was still, she recalled, 'on the cusp of the old world', and there were some things 'you kept to family', especially when it came to talking about the tupuna (Tītokowaru). She grew up hearing the stories of what had happened on their land, as the adults told them in te reo in the evenings, including stories of the atrocities that had occurred during the Taranaki Wars. Even for the children, she recalled, 'the mauri of energies on the land were still there then. The mauri of the whenua has weakened since' with modernisation, she said, but for her mother's generation Tītokowaru's deeds in his lifetime were often 'called up' when whānau met. The phrase they often used was 'Kaua e kōrero. Ka nohopuku. Ka haramai e wā. In other words, don't say a thing, be still, there'll come a time.' In 1971, even though there were efforts to involve local people in the production of The Killing of Kane, many people she knew thought it was too soon, and that they had no say about it. Some of her whānau and hapū did get involved: 'they were more concerned about how the tupuna was going to be portrayed, and what the effect would be for the descendants in the years ahead.'²⁸

Alexander Fry, in the Listener feature, drew several conclusions from his visit to the production site. One was that the battles themselves were of great interest, and especially the 'Maoris' remarkable flexibility and military skill [which] gave them

The Killing of Kane (1971): Tītokowaru (Napi Waaka) performs the karakia as warriors depart to attack the redoubt at Turuturumōkai.

most of the victories. Titokowaru himself perfected methods of fortification which made his positions all but impregnable to European artillery.' This view was not yet historical orthodoxy. Fry also thought that in New Zealand history 'perhaps only the wars of last century provide such inherently dramatic material' for television production, reflecting as they did 'the interaction of widely differing cultures and outlooks'. He anticipated more to come: he noted that a documentary on Hone Heke (now lost) was to screen a week later. And finally, Fry appreciated the dynamic of the production itself. It had ended with a feast in which the Māori cast cooked an unfortunate pig that had provided the 'human' heart for the drama. 'There is material for another film,' Fry concluded, in the Māori and Pākehā in

Von Tempsky (1974). The film was screened on television but is now lost. Here George Harris (in hat) talks with editor Dermot McNeilage on the set in the Wairarapa.

Photo courtesy of Peter Janes

Bruno Lawrence plays the title role in *Von Tempsky*, complete with bullet wound to the forehead.

Photo courtesy of Peter Janes

the production 're-enacting a bitter incident in an unjust war, then feasting together before going happily off in their several directions to see how they will look on TV'.[29]

Three years later, George Harris wrote, directed and produced a half-hour documentary called *Von Tempsky*, starring Bruno Lawrence. This made Harris the first Māori director of a film about the wars, but in the world of television at the time he was 'reticent' about his Māori descent. The documentary was filmed in Kapiti, Wellington and Otago, but now appears to have been lost.[30]

The Governor, 1977

After the television restructuring of 1974, Michael Scott-Smith of TV One was asked to develop a weekly soap opera. He put the idea to Tony Isaac and Michael Noonan, who replied with a counter-offer: they would develop the soap – which became *Close to Home* – if they could make a drama-documentary series on the career of Governor George Grey. They were granted $1.3 million, which seemed astronomical at the time, to create a series involving numerous locations and sets – the largest-scale production the country had yet seen. The budget overrun – which is disputed – sent Prime Minister Muldoon into public outrage, although many took the view that the real source of his anger was the programme's stance on colonial history rather than its bottom line.[31]

The series followed George Grey's two terms as governor of New Zealand in 1845–53 and 1861–68. Probably the most influential figure in shaping New Zealand's colonisation, Grey was governor during most years of the New Zealand Wars – his first term coincided with the latter part of the Northern War, and he became governor again in late 1861 at the time of the fallout from the First Taranaki War, remaining through the Waikato War and the East Coast War. *The Governor* opened his career up for scrutiny through the medium that had the widest public reach at the time. As Grey had played such a determining role in the conflicts, the wars were always going to be important events in the drama.

Grey was a governor of extraordinary ability. He became fluent in te reo Māori, learned a lot about Māori, and supported the development of Māori economies. He was genuinely interested in the process of colonisation, and at times attempted to stall the efforts of the more land-hungry politicians. Even by 1847 his abilities had begun to earn him the title of 'Good Governor Grey', an epithet William Pember Reeves took up and used as the title of his chapter on Grey in *The Land of the Long White Cloud: Ao Tea Roa* (1898). But even Reeves, in a paragraph beginning with Grey's 'knightly virtues', went on to list the more dubious elements of Grey's character:

> *Naturally fond of devious ways and unexpected moves, he learned to keep his own counsel and to mask his intention; he never even seemed frank … so far as persons went, his antipathies were stronger than his affections, and led him to play with principles and allies. Those who considered themselves his natural friends were never astonished to find him operating against their flank to the delight of the common enemy.*[32]

Reeves was not the only one to be fascinated by Grey's character. Historian Keith Sinclair found similar delight in recounting the murky depths of such a complex figure; he began his sketch like this:

> *George Grey was one of the most distinguished men ever to live in New Zealand. To those who have studied it, his conduct is a never-failing source of astonishment. Such a mixture of greatness and pettiness, breadth of intellect, and dishonesty, is rarely met with. Twice Governor, and later politician and premier, he ruled New Zealand, as in later years he ruled his cabinet, with a despotism not less firm because it was generally shrouded by the meshes of his guile …*[33]

Little of this complexity, and none of the deviousness, had entered Cowan's official history: there – and in Hayward's screen portrayals which drew on Cowan – the 'good governor' held sway. In *The Te Kooti Trail* Grey's gift of a flour mill to the Ngāti Pūkeko stands as a sign of colonial benevolence; in *The Last Stand* there is nothing suspect about Grey's intentions in the Waikato. And although by the 1960s most historians were in agreement about the shadiness of Grey, their views did not reach much beyond those who read New Zealand history. In the public eye Grey remained, in general, a respected figure, consistent with the generally comfortable exceptionalism that, until the mid-century, shaped most of Pākehā New Zealand's ideas about its colonial past.

This public respect was challenged by *The Governor*. The series secured the English actor Corin Redgrave, a member of the English stage aristocracy known for his strongly left-wing views, for the part of Grey. Isaac and Noonan actively went beyond published histories that relied primarily on European-derived archives. Their determination to introduce iwi perspectives on Grey's career and his influence brought new knowledge to the public assessment of this influential figure and the events surrounding him. Isaac had long wanted to make television that involved Māori communities in the production. Noonan recalls going into the early stages of the research with a view of Grey more or less in line with the postive public view – but when 'we did the research we found that the story was a lot more complicated'. The story that resulted had evolved some distance from the one they began with, and Noonan found himself altered in the process: 'it radically changed me … it's a bit like … you can have no opinion about something, and you read material or you study something and you say, *wow*, and it hits you in the face'.[34]

Englishman Keith Aberdein had attended a Quaker boarding school in Ireland – an experience that equipped him with a sceptical view of English colonialism.[35] When he arrived in New Zealand as a young man he first went to university to study law, but abandoned that to work on roading gangs, often alongside Māori men – and it was there that he discovered another side to living in Aotearoa. He later turned to journalism and then to writing for television, including on *Pukemanu*. He was brought in as co-writer on *The Governor* and in the end scripted all except the first episode, which he co-wrote with Noonan.

Don Selwyn, who also worked with Isaac and Noonan on *Pukemanu*, became increasingly important over the period of *The Governor*'s production. Selwyn was already involved in his long project of developing the expertise of Māori performers.[36] The New Zealand Opera Company production of *Porgy and Bess* in 1965 had drawn together an exceptional Māori cast including Selwyn, George Hēnare and Wī Kuki Kaa, who went on to form the Maori Theatre Trust – an incubator for Māori drama – in the late 1960s.[37] Aberdein believes that by the mid-1970s the depth of Māori acting expertise was substantially greater than that of Pākehā, and points to the evidence for this in *The Governor*:

> *almost without exception … nothing made in either the film or television in that early period in which there is a Māori actor involved, however inexperienced, they are never embarassing, where there are some really embarassing Pākehā performances, my own included at times … I don't want to sound like a patronising shit about it, [but among the Māori actors] there is a much richer stepping over into the craft of acting … a 'yes, I will step up to this part because actually, it's about my blood' … whereas some of the Pākehā performances in* The Governor *are absolutely dreadful, unfixable, people who were so way out of their depth, unfairly cast because we were floundering to fill the roles.*[38]

Noonan and Aberdein both emphasised the importance of Selwyn's role in liaising with iwi to cast the Māori parts and bring iwi knowledge to the production. In the early phases some

Māori were cautious about sharing their history: 'That had to be developed. We had liaison through people like Don Selwyn and … in the end [we had] fulsome cooperation.'³⁹ The Māori queen Dame Te Ātairangikaahu was consulted early in the process. Noonan says that, especially for Episode 4, which deals with the creation of the Kīngitanga and includes scenes that are set entirely in a Māori context, they had her permission to proceed:

> *If in fact the programme had not been authorised to do it by the Queen, it would have been difficult. But because the Queen saw what our overall perspective was, in the programme, she said go for it. It was like that, really. Do it, don't have any hesitation. And so, we were very lucky.*⁴⁰

The Governor, alone of the major productions relating to the New Zealand Wars, was not filmed on historical locations, but mostly on sets built in the hills around Lower Hutt. Its connections with iwi were created instead by a series of hui around the country arranged by Don Selwyn that he, Napi Waaka, Keith Aberdein and Tony Isaac attended. The aim was that 'everybody was comfortable with doing it, and lo and behold they were …'⁴¹ The casting of Māori parts involved discussions about which actors would be appropriate to play the Māori leaders. Often there was discussion about iwi affiliations in making these decisions. Some casting was straightforward. George Hēnare's style and range of performance suited him to the provocative, teasing nature of Hōne Heke Pōkai as well as the more sombre dramatic elements of Heke's story. Hēnare's primary whakapapa was to Ngāti Porou but his father's Ngāti Hine origins made him acceptable to Ngāpuhi elders:

> *Other people had been suggested for the role and, unbeknownst to me, the elders had said 'no no no, it's got to be somebody from this area', which I wasn't. I'm actually Ngāti Porou but my dad is from Ngāpuhi, and Ngāti Hine, and so when my name came into the mix they said, 'yes, he's the one, he's a direct descendant of Hōne Heke' – which I didn't know.*⁴²

Other roles yielded surprises and some discussion. At a hui in Northland, Napi Waaka was suddenly asked if he would take the role of the Ngāpuhi chief Tāmati Waka Nene. There were some objections on the grounds that Waaka was from Rotorua, but it was agreed he was the best actor for the role – before he mentioned that he, too, had whakapapa links to Ngāpuhi and to Te Ruki Kawiti.⁴³

Because the series took its documentary role very seriously it was crucial that historical figures – especially Māori – were performed in a manner appropriate to their historical significance. Sometimes an actor from another iwi might be suggested. Noonan recalls that there was no suitable actor from Ngāti Toa for the part of Te Rauparaha, 'but we had a perfect person [Tamahina Tinirau] for the role, so negotiations had to take place'.⁴⁴ The decision that Selwyn himself – from Ngāti Kurī and Te Aupōuri in the north – would play the important role of Ngāti Hauā rangatira Wiremu Tāmihana from the Waikato was the outcome of a long negotiation in the face of Selwyn's own reluctance. Aberdein's account of this process reveals the multifaceted and central role Selwyn played in connecting the series to the Māori past – and the high level at which these decisions were made. It was Dame Te Ātairangikaahu who had the final say about this role:

> *Don resisted right till the end, he did not want to play Tāmihana, he did not want to be in it, he kept saying no to Tony … though Tony had absolutely no doubt that he'd always wanted Don to play Tāmihana. I think, it's hard to know [why Selwyn was reluctant] because … 'let this cup pass from me', I think it came with many poisons, it was a big undertaking, he'd had enough*

*to do, and he was going to carry a big can anyway, particularly with his people, if things went badly wrong culturally in any way, and so he had enough of a burden. But I don't think he was being falsely modest, I think the cultural hesitation was real and … Don was just capable of having hoped that the Māori Queen would say 'no you can't do it', which would have let him off the hook. But that was never going to happen I don't think, and he probably knew it was never going to happen, but he went through the protocol and that was good.*⁴⁵

Selwyn spoke in a radio interview at the time about the integration of actors in the roles they played:

*this is a secret really that if you're playing Wiremu Tāmihana that's who you're playing … if you're playing Hone Heke that's who you're playing, that's who you are. Now in a Māori sense there are various attitudes, a lot of apprehension about playing re-enacting roles about tīpuna. If it's done with the integrity and the good will and it's representative in its real true sense then I don't think there's any fear, it's only when you abuse that privilege that one can expect any repercussions as it were.*⁴⁶

Keri Kaa recalls Selwyn asking her and her brother Wī Kuki to audition. They were amused because some of their lighter-skinned relatives didn't get parts:

Engari ko māua Wī Kuki ngā mea pangopango kei te uru atu ko māua! Hei kata mā māua nē. Nō te mea i a mātou e tamariki ana koinā te whakatoi o ēnā hawhe-kāke ki a māua – mangumangu taipō, kī atu engari, engari ngā mangumangu taipō kua uru atu ki roto.

(And as for me and Wī Kuki, the blackest ones around, we were accepted. That was hilarious to us both because when we were kids it was those same half-caste kids who tormented us – spooks, that's what they would say, but it was the spooks who got the parts.)⁴⁷

They were from Ngāti Porou, and both played the parts of Tainui people: Keri Kaa played Wikitoria, wife of Tāmihana, and Wī Kuki Kaa played Rewi Maniapoto.

At these consultative hui Selwyn and Waaka also asked about the events that were dramatised in the series, so that iwi accounts could be incorporated into the production through narrative, dialogue, staging and emphasis. An important result of this process was that the series included a relatively high number of scenes in Māori settings among Māori, as well as interactions between Māori and Pākehā. In this way it rendered the complexity of the implications of colonisation for Māori, the ensuing political debates within te ao Māori, and the political and then military responses to government. Again, Noonan and Isaac saw Selwyn as indispensable to the process:

*we wanted to have direct access [to] Māori contributors, so we negotiated with people … Don Selwyn … gave us access to principal people all over the country, particularly the crucial people who had taken part in the Treaty, the Ngāpuhi, and of course all the people who had been involved in what became known later as the Land Wars, and that was actually quite a lot of hard work …*⁴⁸

One example is the scene of the coronation of King Pōtatau Te Wherowhero: it reveals the sharing of knowledge, the sense of legacy and the spiritual connection involved in the recreation of these important historical events. Keri Kaa talked about the way the staging and performance of this scene were informed by descendants of Wiremu Tāmihana:

Mōhio koe, ka haere mai te whānau a Wiremu Tāmihana me te koroua rā a Hēnare Tūwhāngai. Ka kōrero mai rāua mō ngā kōrero e mōhiotia e rāua e pā ana ki te karaunatanga o te Kīngi, it tērā, tērā hui tuatahi, hui tapu! Whakamārama mai rāua ki a mātou, kāore hoki mātou i te mōhio! I konei a mea, i korā a mea, ko ngā tamariki i runga hoiho e tūtū ana i konā, ko mea i konei, pēnei te āhua o te Paipera, ērā taonga, kawea mai e ngā koroua rā. Ka kī atu a Don Selwyn ki a rāua: Would you two like to be in it? Oo, ka rawe tērā pātai ki ēnā koroua! Tīkina ngā kākahu, tomo mai rāua ki roto. Mena ka āta titiro, kei reira rāua. Ki a rāua, he mea wehi tērā nō te mea ki a rāua i reira ngā tīpuna i te rā i mahia e mātou tērā mahi! Āhua wehi!

(You know, the family of Wiremu Tāmihana and the old man Hēnare Tūwhāngai [of Ngāti Maniapoto] came onto the set one day. They shared with us the kōrero that they knew regarding the first coronation of the Māori king, at that first gathering, that sacred occasion. They both explained everything to us, information that we never knew about. Here stood this one, and there was that one, the children were on horseback and stood there, that one was positioned here, this is what the Bible was like, those sacred treasures, they knew it all and carried them. Don Selwyn said to them: 'Would you two like to be in it?' Oh, that request was much appreciated by the koroua. Wardrobe was fetched and they were incorporated into the scene. If you look carefully, you will see them there. In their opinion, this was an awesome rendition because they were sure that the ancestors joined with us on the day that we filmed that piece. It was spine-tingling!)[49]

Noonan had been told that the making of 'He Iwi Kotahi Tatou' played a restorative role for Tāmihana's descendants. He was visibly moved as he recalled this:

his people had sort of disappeared ... this is what I've [heard]... I'm giving you this secondhand ... they sort of disappeared, and with the programme they found their heritage which had been lost and forgotten, and it gave them their mana back.[50]

Keri Kaa found she sometimes had to explain tikanga Māori to non-Māori actors, and this briefly created some tension with her brother. The incident she relates illustrates how new the role of Māori cultural advisor was at that time in the industry, not only to Pākehā but to Māori. Selwyn had been hired initially to provide cultural advice, and others had increasingly taken on the role, but mostly in an informal way. Wī Kuki Kaa, with more background in the media world, had come to see cultural knowledge as specialist expertise that should be recompensed:

Ka haere mai a Wī Kuki ki a au ka kōhete mai kī mai ki a au: 'Kāre i te pai to mahi ki a au!' Tana whakamārama mai te ako ēnā kūare. Kī mai ia: 'Kāre tātou i te utua!' ... 'Koinei taku mahi! Ko māua ko Don koia tā māua oranga kei te hokona e koe mō te kore noa iho!'

(Wī Kuki came to me moaning and said to me: 'I don't like what you are doing! ... We don't get paid for that! ... That's my job! That how Don and I earn our livelihood, and you're just giving it away for nothing!')

She later came to recognise that this was his livelihood, and agreed with him.[51]

Selwyn's expansive personality and humour brought another dimension to the production. Many of the Pākehā involved found themselves absorbed into the Māori world for the first time simply by being in his company and being taken along for the ride. And Māori found themselves hauled into acting because Selwyn convinced them they could do it. Waihoroi Shortland recalled that a lot of casting was done at Debretts Hotel, 'where we all used to drink'. Keri Kaa described Selwyn's instinct for picking talent: 'he would say, I know a fulla, I met him in the pub, then he'd turn up with this fulla who would've had no acting experience and he'd convince you, he'd convince the poor fellow, you're gonna be this character'.[52]

The Governor (1977): Hōne Heke (George Hēnare), no longer buoyant, confronts the full implications of European settlement in Episode 1, 'The Reverend Traitor'.

With the permission of George Hēnare All stills from *The Governor* from the TVNZ Television Archive, Stills Collection, Ngā Taonga Sound and Vision. Courtesy of the Arthur Wrigley Collection

Episodes

Departing from a strictly chronological structure, the creators instead organised each of the six episodes of *The Governor* around entanglements with a series of contestatory figures, so that the political and personal dramas of Grey's two terms as governor unfold through interactions and negotiations. Aberdein saw this as a practical strategy to deal with the overburden of historical detail that could encumber and confuse the story. The structure also sharpened the series' emphasis on the complicated and autocratic elements of Grey's character, and on penetrating the aura of farsighted paternal benevolence that still dominated public memory. Not everyone liked this:

Richard Campion's review criticised the structure for a failure to convey 'the main thrust of an exceptional man of vision succumbing to the pressures, both within and without, of the ancient, muddled, self-serving world'.[53] But this was the point – to underplay the 'man of vision' and to emphasise instead the complex web of relationships he created. As Dunleavy and Joyce observe, the adversarial structure effected a shift in point of view: 'it allowed the series to narrate episodes not from the usual perspective of the central character, Grey, but from the viewpoint of each of the … figures with whom Grey conflicted'.[54] Three episodes concern Grey's involvement with colonial war; and partly perhaps because they involved faster-paced action, they were also the most popular with critics and in letters to the editor. This chapter discusses these three episodes.

In Episode 1, 'The Reverend Traitor', Grey's adversary is the missionary Henry Williams (Grant Tilly), whose influence Grey undermines by informing the Colonial Office in London of the extent of Williams' land purchases. In its focus on the Northern War and the war in Wellington of the mid-1840s, the episode also charts Grey's manoeuvering against Hōne Heke Pōkai and Te Rauparaha. This configuration of adversaries positions Grey from the outset as a canny double-dealer. Other characters drawn in include Bishop Selwyn and Grey's wife Eliza, whose disapproval of her husband's unscrupulous dealings operates as a persistent commentary.

But dissent with the colonial process is signalled well before Grey appears – in the opening scene, which depicts the signing of the Treaty of Waitangi. 'Kahore, kahore' are the first spoken words of Episode 1 as a succession of rangatira declare their refusal to sign the Treaty. The dialogue in this opening sequence is primarily in Māori, with Henry Williams translating. Williams speaks in favour of the Treaty, and Hōne Heke is the first to be persuaded to sign. Smiling as he corrects governor William Hobson's clumsy Māori, Heke reiterates the governor's statement – 'He iwi kotahi tatou. Now, we are one people. Yes Governor, that's good, very good. How do you do, Kawana?' – and leans to shake the governor's hand. Heke's theatrical wit, his cross-cultural fluency and his initial optimism about the world to come are thus established. So is his mana in the north: other chiefs follow his lead and sign. Now the episode's dynamic is set up: proceeding from a Māori perspective, it will turn on a struggle over mana.

A jump forward four years to the early stirrings of the Northern War marks Heke's disillusion with the Treaty as he recognises that sovereignty and chiefly mana are under threat. He challenges Hobson's successor, Robert FitzRoy, by repeatedly felling the flagpole at Kororāreka. In keeping with Heke's reputation for theatre there is an air of comedy as the pole pitches down, time after time, against a clear blue northern sky. George Hēnare's Heke moves from challenging good humour to angry eloquence and then prescient melancholy as he comes to understand the full implications of colonial settlement.

As the defences at Ruapekapeka are being constructed, Grey arrives to replace FitzRoy. Heke – who is more politically astute than Williams – warns that Grey will undermine them both. In the lead-up to the attack on the pā, Williams explains earnestly to Grey that the Māori do not fight on the Sabbath, so Grey attacks while the defenders are holding their Sunday morning

The Governor (1977), Episode 1, 'The Reverend Traitor': TOP: The flagpole falls to Hōne Heke; BELOW: Grey's troops enter Ruapekapeka on a Sunday; with the defenders at prayer, the pā is lightly defended.

service, against a soundtrack of Māori hymn-singing – and the pā falls.[55] (This narrative is consistent with the views of historians at the time; it is now more widely thought that Heke and Kawiti evacuated the pā as a deliberate strategy.)[56] Grey then turns to eroding missionary influence: 'He has beaten me in battle, he is destroying you by stealth … he understands the meaning of mana,' Heke tells Williams.

When the action shifts to the Wellington War, the contest is played out once again as Grey captures Te Rauparaha, attacking his chiefly authority too. Heke, Te Rauparaha and Williams offered different kinds of resistance; all began with mana; and all are defeated by cunning rather than by force.

Episode 1 concludes with a celebration of Grey's five years in office. The name 'Good Governor Grey' – the attribution that the series will contest – is already in use. But Grey is conscious of his wife's reservations: 'At what cost?' she asks as he is praised for bringing peace. There is a cut to another kind of gathering: Heke's tangi, with Williams looking on. A voiceover provides broader context as Heke's body is carried away for burial:

> Henry Williams and Hōne Heke Pōkai had already seen some of the sacrifices George Grey was prepared to make in order to achieve his vision. Although the archdeacon was finally reinstated, the missionaries never again exerted the influence they had before the coming of Grey. In time the Māoris would rise to fight the causes that had carried the dead Ngāpuhi chief into rebellion, but for the moment the governor wielded undisputed power. The mana was his.

In this first episode, then, the series laid down a challenge to Grey's mana – taking on his public reputation as a benevolent founding father, and replacing it with a more devious political creature. In this respect it followed the prevailing view of historians in the 1970s, but ran ahead of the generally more positive public memory of Grey. The first episode garnered measured praise from critics: 'it was gripping, and it was long,' Warwick Roger said of the 90-minute opening episode.[57] Yet there was no great outcry at the damage to Grey's reputation per se; the greatest public objection in the first three episodes was to a naked Eliza Grey appearing in prime time in the second episode. Public memory of Grey may have been positive, but apparently it was neither deep nor especially loyal: few reviewers or letter-writers much cared that the programme slated a long-dead politician. When the first data came in, 86 per cent of the viewing audience had watched *The Governor* – the strongest audience in TV One's previous two years – and the ratings remained high through the series, despite some feeling that Episodes Two and Three (the naked Lady Grey aside) lost pace.[58] Reviewers later praised Episodes Four and Five, which dealt with the emergence of the Kīngitanga and the Waikato War, more highly.

Episode 4, 'He Iwi Kotahi Tatou/Now We Are One People' deals with the background to conflict in the 1860s. Grey's adversary in this episode is Wiremu Tāmihana Tarapīpipi (Don Selwyn), the Ngāti Hauā leader widely regarded as the leading conciliator through the 1850s, who came to be the kingmaker. If the series as a whole works by contrasting Grey with his adversaries, then this episode shifts the focus. In a concentrated duplication of the series' overall structure, it makes Tāmihana the central character and explains the change in his political actions through a sequence of encounters and events that also serve to map out the cultural-political landscape of the 1850s. He is a substantially more sympathetic central figure than Grey.

Episode 4 begins with a prologue set in the 1830s, in the darkness of an intertribal night attack by Tāmihana's father, Te Waharoa, on an enemy village. Tāmihana is introduced as he refuses his father's injunction to eat the body of an enemy. We next see him being baptised, and then announcing his plans to build a church and create a peaceful community. Most of the episode takes place through the late 1850s, concentrating on Tāmihana's efforts to maintain his commitment to peace in the face of competing pressures, and his attempts to stave off government and settler pressure on land.

The episode is framed by two sets of paired encounters: at the beginning and again at the end, Tāmihana confronts Rewi Maniapoto and George Grey, who make opposing demands on him. Rewi Maniapoto first appears with a band of warriors on horseback, come to challenge Tāmihana's dedication to peace. 'You will soon have no land left to dig', he says – implying that Tāmihana's men are no longer warriors but carpenters. He throws down a taiaha, which Tāmihana breaks, replying that God was a carpenter. In setting up this opposition – peacemaker and firebrand, moderate and extremist – the series was conforming to long-standing stereotypes of these two men that dated back to the war itself, and that originated, as Vincent O'Malley argues, with John Gorst, Grey's civil commissioner in Te Awamutu in the early 1860s.[59]

Grey arrives soon after, more quietly but no less threateningly. They talk and eat together in the soft firelight of Tāmihana's kitchen; Grey holds Tāmihana's baby and the other children come in to meet him. Tāmihana challenges the governor's position on land, while they test each other out in a game of draughts. In these scenes the writers' use of history can best be described as 'free and indirect': they draw phrases from recorded speeches or letters by these figures, and the characters represent positions the historical figures are known to have argued, but the meetings themselves are not based on documented events.

The Governor (1977): Wiremu Tāmihana (Don Selwyn) and George Grey (Corin Redgrave): a fictional game of draughts provides the setting for the clash of intellects and political perspectives between these historical figures in Episode 4, 'He Iwi Ko Tahi Tatou'.

With the permission of Aubrey Selwyn and the estate of Corin Redgrave

The episode dramatises Tāmihana's evolving change of mind, and the underpinning arguments for the Kīngitanga, through a sequence of experiences as his initial resistance to the rising idea of a Māori king is overcome. Following documented encounters, he is shown being treated rudely by drunken Pākehā, being refused a meeting with the governor when he goes to Auckland to discuss land, and finding two Māori men fighting each other in a return to the law of utu because, despite British sovereignty, the justice system will not adjudicate between Māori, leaving them with neither the old means of settling disputes nor a new one. In the meantime, scenes from the Waitara dramatise the background of land loss through the late 1850s and the growing crisis that gives

LEFT: *The Governor* (1977): 'Remember we were once Ngāti Toa, Raukawa, Ngāpuhi, Tūhoe, Maniapoto? We are Māoris now, and you Mr McLean with your gold in your hand, you are the threat that has made these tribes one people.' Ruiha (Makuini Menehira) confronts Donald McLean and provides Episode 4 with its ironic title, 'He Iwi Ko Tahi Tatou' [Now We Are One People].

With the permission of Makuini Menehira Wright

OPPOSITE: *The Governor* (1977): Rewi Maniapoto (Wī Kuki Kaa) during the debates over the creation of the Kīngitanga in Episode 4, 'He Iwi Ko Tahi Tatou'. With the permission of Sylvia Kaa

rise to kotahitanga – a pantribal landholding movement. The repeated use of close-up reaction shots focuses our attention on Tāmihana's state of mind. In this focus on his thinking and his response to competing pressures and shifting circumstances, the episode portrays him according to his prevailing historical reputation, as a careful and judicious statesman – a thinking man attempting to play a mediating role, and a devout Christian working to bring about peace with justice.

The title of Episode 4 was carried through from Governor Hobson's phrase at the Treaty signing in Episode 1 – 'He iwi kotahi tatou' – but here it is turned around to take on a new, ironic meaning. Ruiha (Makuini Menehira), Grey's interpreter, spells this out when she confronts Donald McLean, chief land purchase commissioner and driver of the government's policy on land purchase since Grey's first term. Once, she tells him, Māori thought of themselves only as belonging to iwi. But 'we are Maoris now, and you Mr McLean with your gold in your hand, you are the threat that has made these tribes one people'.

This episode bears the signs of the two strands of sources for the series. It reflects the creators' use of academic histories, most notably Sinclair's account of the origins of the wars of the 1860s. Sinclair discusses the increasingly underhand way in which land was being purchased through the 1850s, largely driven by McLean, and the growing resistance of iwi to the pressure to sell. This resistance led to kotahitanga. Sinclair also discusses the role played by the rising generation of Māori leaders, including Tāmihana, and the reasons for Tāmihana's support for a Māori king – causes that are systematically enacted in the vignettes in Episode 4.[60]

The second main source used in the series is the knowledge derived from consultations with iwi. In Episode Four a series of scenes takes place mostly or entirely among Māori, including two that represent the great pantribal rūnanga held to debate the kingship. Filmed in a dimly lit wharenui, these scenes reenact debates among chiefs including Te Wherowhero, Waka Nene and Rewi Maniapoto. Here, the series showed its commitment

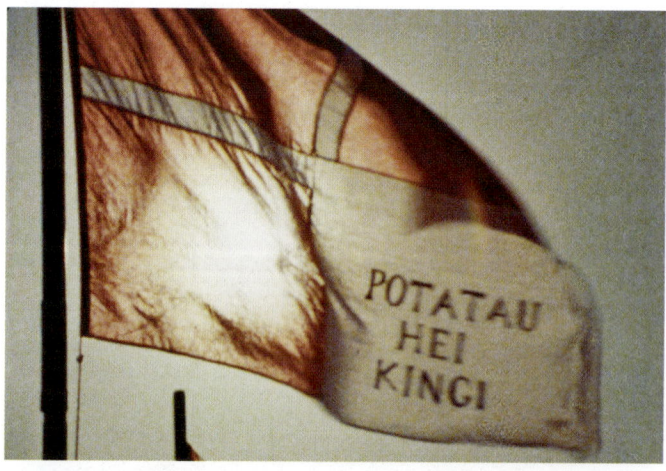

The Governor (1977): The sun shines on the newly created Kīngitanga. Kīngi Pōtatau Te Wherowhero (Bill Tawhai) and Wiremu Tāmihana (Don Selwyn), stand among the people after the coronation of the first Māori king. This scene was staged according to the information provided by Wiremu Tāmihana's descendants. Episode 4, 'He Iwi Ko Tahi Tatou'.

With the permission of Taylor Tawhai and Aubrey Selwyn

to portraying the events that were most important for iwi, and to drawing on knowledge provided by iwi – in the case of this episode, from Tainui sources.

One of these scenes is a public hui where McLean confidently assumes that because of their old enmities, Tāmihana and Pōtatau Te Wherowhero will never settle their differences.[61] Despite McLean's assurance, though, Tāmihana gives Te Wherowhero his support: they hongi and sit down together. The crowning of Te Wherowhero, the climax of the episode, is lit with Tāmihana and the king standing against the sun, its aura around them, and the flag inscribed with 'Potatau hei kingi' illuminated as it flaps in the wind. The people at the hui shout out: 'Ae! Ae! Pōtatau! Pōtatau hei Kīngi!' This was the scene that, according to Keri Kaa, was staged with reference to the knowledge of Tāmihana's descendants, who also appeared onscreen. It is still, as Keri Kaa described it, 'spine-tingling'.

The episode concludes with Waikato under pressure to support Wiremu Kīngi in Taranaki as the tensions over land flare into open conflict. Two fictional encounters render the state of relations as the writers saw them. By the time Grey returns for his second term as governor, and he and Tāmihana meet once again at the end of the episode, the warmth between them has gone. Grey delivers his well-known statement that he won't fight the king with a sword, but 'will dig around him till he falls of his own accord'. This meeting is followed by the second encounter with Rewi, who arrives to charge Tāmihana bitterly with weakening Waikato Māori by delaying the fight. In response to Tāmihana's claim that 'you are only a handful of tribes, no more', Rewi picks up the episode's refrain: 'We will not even be that, unless we fight as one people.' You cannot win, replies Tāmihana, and Rewi responds, 'If it is so it is because we waited too long to fight … We listened to you, Tarapīpipi, and we lost our land.' Just as Heke's optimism in Episode 1 proved to be misplaced, so has Tāmihana's in Episode 4. British troops cross the Mangatāwhiri Stream in the act that began the Waikato War, and the concluding voiceover proclaims: 'The Pakeha Wars had begun.'

If the series had not nailed its colours to the mast in Episode 1, it most surely did so in Episode 4. It posed the problem of colonial conflict from the perspective of Māori, and centred not on the better-known Rewi but on the Tainui leader who had been most reluctant to embark on conflict. The narrative exposed Grey's reluctant complicity with the land-grabbing agenda, even as he proclaimed himself sympathetic to Māori. Noonan says:

… the time you got to Episode 4, you were watching something that had never been considered in a broad base by anybody as far as I can see, including historians. I remember having a battle with Professor Beaglehole in the paper [because] he wrote a review of an episode of it, where he said that we had … twisted history, and I replied to him by saying that the points that he was [objecting to] could be verified if he only read the material, it was all there.[62]

A large proportion of the dialogue of 'Now We Are One People' was in Māori. Noonan recalls the debates over how the episode would be scripted:

This is how Episode 4 happened. We were trying to work out how to deal with it. We knew that it was really the episode from a Maori perspective, had to be from a Maori perspective and we were trying to work [it] out. We're lying on a hillside outside Tony Isaac's home, Keith Aberdein, myself, Tony Isaac, and we're trying to run around how we could possibly do it … By that stage we knew that we could probably get access to all the people that we needed to, and authorisation, and permission and so on, and blessing, of course, and we were thinking we'll have to have it in English …[63]

None of them found this satisfactory though, so, assisted by a quantity of beer they kept talking until they decided they would do the whole episode in Māori. In the end they didn't quite achieve that, but Māori is the predominant language, and the language spoken in all the Māori scenes in the episode; 'and that was the programme of the year of course … it won awards, and quite rightly'.[64] Reflecting on this episode in 2010, Noonan was frank about the creators' perspective:

Now here is where the programme becomes complicated. Its sympathy lies with Māori. It doesn't all the time, but in the end it does, and particularly in [Episode] 4 … the whole emphasis is that Māori are being preyed upon badly, that land is being confiscated just for the benefit of the Pākehā and so on. That is something that is really crucial to the programme, that we did have a bias … We didn't know it was biased when we wrote it, we didn't know it was biased when we considered it, but I think in reflection it was biased, that we really did want to uncover some stories that had been hidden, or had been deceitfully redesigned.[65]

In the next episode, 'The Lame Seagull', Grey's adversary is General Duncan Cameron, played in a standout performance by Martyn Sanderson. The episode covers the course of the Waikato War, and centres on Cameron's growing disaffection with Grey and with the war. He begins as a stiff-necked Scot, convinced that his purpose is to deal with armed rebellion and ensure peace. Over the course of the episode his belief crumbles as a series of incidents present him – and viewers – with the uncomfortable realisation that the war is not about rebellion; it is about land. In a brief prologue Grey and Cameron ride through an abandoned village south of Auckland, where one

Keith Aberdein found the inspiration for writing the character of General Duncan Cameron in this photograph, in which Cameron stands against the wheel with his hands in his pockets.

PAColl-3396-1, Alexander Turnbull Library, Wellington

old man appears. Grey tells him he should go to be with his people, but the old man shouts angrily that he will not leave his whenua. This is the first in a series of incidents that confront Cameron with the gap between the overt and the underlying purpose of the war.

Aberdein described the difficulty he had, at first, in understanding Cameron. The character as it was developed derived from a photograph:

it wasn't that there wasn't much information, we knew roughly what Cameron had done in terms of the military up and down the country, but finding the character was very very hard … [I] couldn't get a handle on who this man might be and how he might interact with Grey's character … It was based ultimately, we found, there's a photograph … with Cameron and his troops lining up to have their photograph taken, and it looks like one of those old-fashioned school photographs … And there's Cameron down the front with his men, and you just went, aah, a man who would do that, you can start to make some character assumptions about, the fact that he stood down there with the blokes and had his picture taken, no, not out the front, he was just in amongst them down to one side, I mean in amongst them, no sense of separation – [no] 'these are my men and I order them around' – so it went from there and it was only that photograph …[66]

The episode echoes this affinity with ordinary soldiering in a subplot that follows three soldiers – a fresh recruit (Tanner), another young soldier (Landis) and an older, more experienced sergeant. Like Cameron himself, these soldiers embody the ambivalent and changing perspectives of troops engaged in the war and the ways in which they are altered by the experience. They begin confident in their military superiority and disregard for the humanity of the Māori, but over the course of the campaign they change. Landis exemplifies this transition: early in the episode he rapes a Māori woman in a defeated village, bringing Cameron's fury down on him; but later he will not fire on a defender at Ōrākau. Where Episode 4 charted diverse and developing Māori perspectives, Episode 5 turned the camera on the other side to show how the Europeans were changing.

Sanderson portrays Cameron as a man who, initially convinced that a soldier does not think – 'we leave that to politicians' – is driven to thought by the course of the Waikato War. At Rangiriri the defending chief Tioriori laughs at Cameron's advice that if the Waikato put down their weapons they will not lose their land: 'You say that, but we know the Pākehā lies.' Cameron returns to tell a sick and indecisive Grey that he has taken Ngāruawāhia and that Tāmihana has sent his mere as a sign that he will negotiate; now, he assumes, the war can end. But Grey responds that it's complicated: parliament wants land on which to settle troops, to defray the costs of the war.

The troops, too, believe the war is done. But the episode cuts again to Grey, in conflict with Alfred Domett and the premier, William Fox – politicians eager for the confiscations to proceed more quickly. The war rolls on. The episode moves to an event that was not part of the broader public memory of the war, but that Tainui still recalled with bitter intensity: the attack on the undefended village of Rangiāowhia. As the soldiers ride in they

The Governor (1977): The young Tanner (Barry Emslie) goes into battle for the first time, in Episode 5, 'The Lame Seagull'.

With the permission of Barry Emslie

find women sitting around a fire; they attack and the women flee. Amid scenes of panic the soldiers set fire to whare and a figure in flames runs from one. Cameron arrives to find a girl dead from sword wounds: shocked, he shouts for a ceasefire. Here the disquiet that some soldiers felt about the war is concentrated in the figure of Cameron.

The next scene is a meeting between Cameron and Tāmihana: two of Grey's adversaries are pitted against each other – only to find common ground. Tāmihana reiterates Tioriori's claim that there will not be peace 'until the Pākehā has our land', and again

The Governor (1977): Troops attack the undefended village of Rangiāowhia in one of the most bitterly remembered events of the Waikato War. Women and children run in fear as the whare burn. Episode 5, 'The Lame Seagull'.

The Governor (1977): Wiremu Tāmihana (Don Selwyn, above left) and Duncan Cameron (Martyn Sanderson) were on opposite sides in the Waikato War, but both came to distrust Grey and the colonial enterprise. A fictional encounter in Episode 5 brings them together. With the permission of Aubrey Selwyn and Wanjiku Sanderson

Cameron refutes this: 'I don't believe these battles are being fought for land.' But neither of them can understand why Grey has not come to make peace terms, since Tāmihana has sent his mere. After their meeting Tāmihana sends a letter to Cameron, protesting at the pack rape of the young woman; the two are further aligned as a furious Cameron tells his men: 'I start to wonder, who is the savage?'

The action moves now to two of the best known battles of the wars, Ōrākau and Gate Pā, and picks up incidents that they were remembered for (some echoed those in *The Last Stand*). At Ōrākau Cameron takes a pragmatic military decision to mount a guard near the only water source and to bombard through the night: 'If they can't sleep and they can't drink, we may still force a surrender.' But Landis – showing his better side – does not fire when he sees a woman creeping out to get water at night. When Cameron confronts him, Landis replies that he could hear children crying in the pā – a justification that Cameron accepts.

As in *The Last Stand*, the negotiation over surrender at Ōrākau is a centrepiece. The negotiator William Mair approaches the lines to propose a surrender, and in contrast to most historical accounts, Rewi himself walks forward to refuse, using these words: 'E hoa, ka whawhai tonu matou ki a koe, ake, ake, ake.' Other defenders echo his words, and Ahumai then stands to deliver her refusal of the offer to let the women and children go. Later, the breakout from the pā is filmed through fog: Cameron and Carey watch as the hurrying defenders flee carrying children on their backs. Here the generals briefly seem to will them to escape, since they give no orders – they only wonder why nobody moves to attack. But, says Cameron, 'Von Tempsky will'; and then shots of the retreating backs of the defenders are intercut with an extended scene of the cavalry charging and women and children being cut down as they run.

If Rangiāowhia was news to many Pākehā viewers, most had still heard of Ōrākau. Here, like Hayward, *The Governor*'s creators negotiated the overburden of legend: the series shows the unequal slaughter – predominantly of women and children – and the brave defiance of the defenders, but simultaneously marks the respect of the troops for the defenders. What viewers saw on screen was the thundering cavalry bearing down on thirsty, starving people who had run out of ammunition, and the killing of many women and children – despite Cameron's apparent distaste for all of this.

Gate Pā, or Pukehinahina, was another battle with legendary elements that are given attention here: the code of conduct drawn up before the battle by the chief Rāwiri Puhirake and found later on the body of a dead warrior, and the story of the woman from the pā who went out after the battle to bring water to dying colonial troops. The ordinary soldiers echo Cameron's disillusion as they discuss the code of conduct and the honourable character of their opponents. Landis, who had earlier defended his actions with 'No sir, it wasn't rape, sir', now asks, 'Why are we fighting 'em?' *The Governor* does not, however, elaborate on the fact of the British defeat at Gate Pā

TOP: *The Governor* (1977) Episode 5, 'The Lame Seagull': William Mair and Rewi Maniapoto (Wī Kuki Kaa) negotiate across the trenches at Ōrākau, as the defenders hold their rifles ready. With the permission of Sylvia Kaa   CENTRE: The breakout from Ōrākau. Women carrying children are among the defenders who cluster together as they hurry through the fog and smoke in the attempt to reach the Pūniu River. BOTTOM: The wounded girl: cavalry thunders by as the wounded fall during the breakout. *The Governor* confronted viewers with the deaths of women and children, as well as showing its ordinary soldiers allowing some to pass through the lines unhurt.

– this would not fully become part of the historiography for another decade.

The conclusion of the episode charts the final disintegration of Cameron's relationship with Grey. Inspecting the troops for the last time, Cameron asks his sergeant what he plans to do after the war. 'Thought I'd stay on, sir, get some land.' Cameron responds wearily. 'Like Tanner and the others. Well, if you do, remember what it took to get it.' At the end, Grey enters parliament triumphantly claiming that war was over, but the voiceover contradicts him: 'Grey was wrong …'

Aftermath

As the series reached completion its budget overrun hit the headlines. It had been dogged by persistent rain, and a summer storm had demolished some of the sets; and, as the first production of its scale in Aotearoa, it was inventing the process as it went. There was conflict in Avalon, TV One's Lower Hutt studios: those who were not involved grumbled that *The Governor* had monopolised the best equipment and crew and most of the funding; and as an exhausted crew returned from yet another long, muddy day hauling equipment around the hills above Lower Hutt, they were lambasted for traipsing mud through the building. Internal relations soured when Muldoon accused TV One of wasting public money, and in September 1977, a month before the series screened, he initiated an inquiry by the Public Expenditure Committee into its costs.

Before the series went to air most papers gave it some introductory publicity – reporting on the history and on curiosities such as how the moko artists worked (with felt pens and artificial skin). Hugh Nevill interviewed creators and crew and wrote a four-page feature for the *Listener*, in which Aberdein declared it was time the schoolbook view of 'Grey the great peacemaker' was overturned: 'Going on believing that kind of stuff may have something to do with our not being able to come to terms with the bi-racial situation here.' If Māori had only fought 'as one people' rather than tribally, he said, they might have won and New Zealand might have been the better for it.[67] Isaac discussed how he had approached the dramatising of history – drawing on letters and speeches, but using them in fictional conversations and meetings. One problem they had encountered in the research for the series, Nevill reported, was 'the sheer sloppiness of historians'. This comment was unattributed but provoked some return fire: D.A. Hamer, professor of history at Victora, defended the strength of historical work on Grey; and Keith Sinclair responded with a two-page article evaluating Grey's career that began with a broadside for Aberdein, aimed mainly at the popular historical novel Aberdein had written to accompany the series ('Arduous months of research has produced a revelation: Grey was an active heterosexual!').[68]

The Governor went on to win the 1978 Feltex Award for best programme of the year, and Episode 4 – Māori dialogue notwithstanding – won the award for best script. Most critics shared this positive view of the series as the episodes rolled out, although some waxed and waned through the course of it. The most common complaint was that the episodes did not present events in chronological order, which viewers found confusing; and at times – in the second and third episodes especially – they found it over-long and a bit dull. The wars in Episodes 1, 4 and 5 provided pace and action that most critics liked, and in general they were full of praise for Sanderson's performance as Cameron. Most commented on the value of informing viewers about the country's past. The greatest controversy remained Eliza Grey's nakedness in Episode 2: some thought it unnecessary; others, that it was not sexy enough. Richard Campion, comparing the politics of funding in film and television, wondered what reaction *Sleeping Dogs* – the first of the new wave of New Zealand films, released at the same time as *The Governor* aired – would have got had it been made for television. Satirising Muldoon's attacks on *The Governor*, he wrote: 'It's a travesty! New Zealand Prime Ministers don't behave like that … Who authorised the use of NZ Air Force helicopters? TO HUNT DOWN THE GOOD GUYS! … Disgusting sex … gratuitous violence … motorcars destroyed – vicious waste of public money. A HALF-A-MILLION for ONE FILM!'[69]

None of the major papers gave any space to Māori reviewers, although several critics commented on the Māori perspectives on the wars in Episode 4. Few reviewers commented on the frequent use of te reo Māori. While 'Ariel' of the *Otago Daily Times* thought the reliance on te reo in that episode might turn viewers off, Graeme Douglas for the *Herald* noted 'a good blend of Maori with sub-titles and Maoris speaking English without lapsing into … caricature … Fraught with dangers though it was, Isaac's blend seemed to work without being either confusing or annoying.' Like others, Douglas had found episodes 2 and 3 'a bit of a bore':

> But last night's programme [Episode 4], dealing as it did with the rise of Maori nationalism as their land was gradually bought or stolen, was the first sign that the series was there to 'help the average New Zealander know more about his history' … The raising of the Maori King Movement, the beginnings of the land squabbles and the duplicity of the settlers and Governor Grey all provided ammunition for a fine tale.[70]

The Governor provoked letters to editors as it screened, but not as many as Helen Brew's film on natural birth, shown at the same time, or the hot current affairs issue of the day, the Security Intelligence Service bill. History buffs grumbled about historical detail and the use of the provocative phrase 'The Pakeha Wars' to replace the then-customary 'Maori Wars'. But the praise generally outweighed the objections. Several viewers wrote to contest Muldoon's attack on the cost of the series; they pointed out how much American history New Zealanders had seen on screen and how little of our own; that the quality of the series had amply justified the expense; and that they were willing to sacrifice a few lightweight entertainments for another historical epic.

Most people involved with the production saw the underlying source of the prime minister's anger as the use of government money to fund what seemed to be a radical revision of Grey's governance and, by extension, a critique of the colonial foundations of New Zealand society. The series washed its hands of a beneficent 'Land of the Long White Cloud' – a perspective that historians had already abandoned; it pointed instead to an often self-serving and deceptive colonial strategy and a colonial world that was rife with unresolved moral and political questions. It posed a more immediate problem in lending force to contemporary Māori claims about land rights and historical injustice, as Ngāti Whātua's occupation of Bastion Point entered its tenth month.

A *Star Weekender* review canvassed opinion on the cultural and political impact of the series as it screened. The series had generated a lot of interest in the past, and especially in the battles – the phrase 'the Pakeha Wars' had achieved its intended effect of making people think again. Sir Dove-Myer Robinson, Auckland's mayor, was anxious that it might inflame young Māori. Keith Sinclair restated, as in his *Listener* article, that the series was one-sided and anti-Pākehā and gave too little attention to issues other than land; but he nevertheless appreciated that it had popularised history effectively. Ranginui Walker, chair of the Auckland District Maori Council at the time, was more fulsome in his praise:

> *Maori children have been excited by the series because for the first time it has shown the Maoris as the goodies, says Dr Walker. …*
>
> *Up to now we have been living under the myth of harmonious relations between Maori and Pakeha. This is a fine ideal but it shouldn't blur the reality of history.*
>
> *Many people now understand why the Bastion Pt protestors are camped on Crown land and why groups like Nga Tamatoa exist.*[71]

Barry Shaw, reviewing for the *Auckland Star*, reflected on the series' imperfections. He didn't like the flouting of chronology, and he thought *The Governor* would be hard to sell overseas. But he reflected a prevailing view among reviewers and letters to the editor that the series, in being 'made first and foremost for us … it was about New Zealand, and New Zealanders, brown and white', was fulfilling one of the most important expectations the country had of television: to show us ourselves. (Here he directly echoed Grierson's view of the function of documentary.) His conclusion was consistent with Walker's:

> *But outside of any advances in the television field, there is one gigantic credit – Prime Minister please note – that 'The Governor' can properly claim.*
>
> *It has made Maori matter.*
>
> *If Pakehas now have a better understanding for the Maori point of view; if the Maori, particularly the younger generations, now have a new pride in their race, it stems from 'The Governor.'*
>
> *Now, do you measure that in dollars?*[72]

The Governor screened twice on TV One. It was widely anticipated, viewed and discussed. Its viewing history since is another story. Because it was broadcast before the arrival of video recorders, until recently it has not been viewed outside of its real-time screening. Copyright difficulties prevented it being rescreened later, so from the end of the 1970s it remained in TVNZ's archives, viewed only by those sufficiently motivated to make the trip to Avalon and request a viewing. Since 2009 the episodes discussed in this chapter, as well as *The Killing of Kane*, have been progressively cleared for online streaming on the NZ On Screen website – giving them a new life in the digital era.[73]

*

The Governor's revisionist stance on the wars and on Māori history in general was not universally adopted; although, as Russell Campbell notes, in the TVNZ series *Landmarks* that went to air in 1981 'the burden of blame for the outbreak of racial conflict shifts to the Pakeha colonists'.[74] But *The Governor* may have made its mark on later documentary in more circuitous ways, as the political documentaries discussed in the next chapter suggest.

The Killing of Kane and *The Governor* also had an impact on the small film and television production industry of the time by bringing together performers and crews who, in this early phase of television production, were learning on the job. As Barry Barclay and Michael King had done in *Tangata Whenua*, their creators actively sought to work in ways that expressed Māori knowledge and engaged with Māori worlds. Some brought expertise to the productions; others gained experience that they took into later work. In the fledgling industry many people found themselves extending their skills. Conditions

The NZBC in Hāwera: cast and crew on the set of *The Killing of Kane*. Around the camera crane (top), Geoff Murphy at left, Wayne Williams and Leo Shelton on the crane, Derek Williams with cigarette, and Chris Thomson directing in the white hat.

Photos courtesy of Peter Janes

were rudimentary: the young camera-crane contractors working on *The Killing of Kane* had nowhere to stay 'so we moved into their set, which was a redoubt, a military redoubt, it had a whole lot of tents in it, we moved in there, that's where we lived, and we hung washing and stuff … it made it look lived in,' said Geoff Murphy, who took up residence on the set with his mate, cameraman Alun Bollinger. They hired themselves and their crane out to *The Governor*, too.[75]

The Governor gave Māori actors the opportunity to perform in prominent screen roles. For George Hēnare, whose previous work had been mostly in live theatre, it provided experience in screen acting.[76] *Kane* and *The Governor* gave Māori training in other capacities too. Both productions placed a high value on Māori consultation – a role that hardly had a name at that stage. Although earlier productions such as Hayward's had had Māori advisors, these television productions of the 1970s were early approaches to a conception of partnership – something that probably would not have occurred to Hayward. Selwyn essentially shaped the role of Māori cultural advisor through *The Governor*, but although it was a large and demanding role it was as yet relatively informal – and, as Aberdein noted, he was poorly remunerated for it. He went on to take this role in later productions, although the relationships were not always so smooth as the industry developed and the role was formalised.

Another crew member who developed a career as a result of his work on *The Governor* was James Belich, who became fascinated by the trenches he was digging, guided by a historical drawing of Ruapekapeka, as chapter 5 explains .[77] *The Governor* challenged prevailing conceptions of the wars and put Māori perspectives back into the public understanding of their purpose and what was at stake. Belich went on to challenge received views of military strategies and to question historical understandings of their outcomes; 20 years later he would bring the wars back to television.

Indeed, Belich later questioned some elements of *The Governor's* interpretation of the past. In the wake of his analysis, which emphasised the depth of Māori strategy during the course of the wars and the level of Māori agency in the conduct of warfare and politics, the series' tendency to situate Māori as victims of a relentless war machine came to seem too simplistic, and it underplayed Māori victories such as Gate Pā. The series was provocative in its moment – in its vocabulary ('the Pakeha Wars'), in its portrayal of scheming land-hungry politicians, in showing the carnage at Rangiāowhia and Ōrākau, and in taking up the points of view of Māori leaders and attending to the politics internal to te ao Māori. But while it challenged some prevailing views, it accepted others, such as the characterisations of fiery Rewi and peaceable Tāmihana, and land as prime cause. Belich and others would go on to question these perspectives, arguing that sovereignty was equally significant and indeed encompassed the issue of land.

Pictures (1981)

This turmoil of the 1970s and the revisiting of colonial history is also evident in Michael Black's *Pictures* (1981), a period drama he co-wrote with Robert Lord, produced by John O'Shea. The historical and photographic inspiration for *Pictures* was a journey made by Dunedin-based photographer Alfred Burton that resulted in *Through the King Country with a Camera: A photographer's diary* (1885). Burton accompanied surveyor John Rochfort through the King Country in the 1880s, more than a decade after the wars and as the King Country was 'opening up'. *Pictures* loosely follows Alfred Burton's expedition and shows him becoming increasingly disenchanted with the colony in the aftermath of the wars. The main action of the film, though, is preceded by an entirely fictional wartime episode in which Alfred's brother and partner Walter takes a series of pictures of prisoners shackled and shuffling through the rain after an unidentified battle, not long before they are to be shot. When he returns to Dunedin, local businessmen react with disgust and anger at these images and tell him he must not exhibit them. Walter is disillusioned and sinks into alcoholism as a result.

Many critics took *Pictures* as a serious engagement with 'authentic' history; the publicity pointed to the use of antique furnishings and the attention to detail in recreating the period. But Sandra Coney's review ran against the trend in calling the film's use of history 'a breathtaking act of artistic dishonesty' that 'distorted history to Pakeha advantage'. She argued that it built on its appearance of authenticity to create inauthentic colonial men – the film's conscience-stricken Burtons, she said, were implausible colonists.[78] In a recent, more extended analysis Cherie Lacey has argued that *Pictures* projects a twentieth-century depth of unease about the effects of colonialism back onto the nineteenth-century Burtons. Lacey, too, argues that the film's relationship to history was fundamentally dishonest, especially given that Walter Burton's 'prisoner photographs', which precipitate the story arcs of both Burtons and are the moral centre of the film, never actually existed – and nor does the brothers' disquiet about colonialism appear to have any historical basis. In her study of the draft versions of the screenplay, Lacey discovers that 'all references to the wars were increasingly omitted', and she argues that 'the film [took] flight from any uncomfortable history'.[79] The film's preoccupation is with the effects of colonialism on the colonisers – on Pākehā as Pākehā – but the effect of this is that Māori are left almost entirely out of the picture, and the characterisation and the schematic stances towards racism are highly stereotyped. Given O'Shea's work with Māori over the years, it is surprising that the film never moves beyond clichéd interactions between Māori and Pākehā, and that there seems to have been so little Māori involvement in the making of the film. One marae from the Whanganui is credited, and there is one named Māori character, Ngatai, who serves largely as a litmus test for Pākehā racism. As a result, perhaps, the film always seems artificial as it manoeuvres to show up its characters' moralities. Peter Vere Jones, who played Walter Burton, recalled that the shoot was extremely difficult, and that there was 'very strong feeling' among the Māori involved.[80]

Pictures was released internationally in 1981, but did not show in New Zealand until mid-1983. Its makers wanted to avoid releasing it at the same time as another film about the colonial past: they were keen to represent *Pictures* as a more serious, thoughtful film than what O'Shea dismissed as the 'Cowboys and Indians version of the Land Wars' in the other film.[81] But in both the short and long term the other film proved more successful with audiences, and more searching and disquieting in its engagement with the past. That film was *Utu*.

4 THE PŪHĀ WESTERN
Utu

Utu was something that was really – exciting – at the time. Everybody wanted to work on it. There were a lot of films being made because we actually for a moment could raise money to make a film of the vision and scope of Utu. So Geoff had a work he'd held close to his heart, and it was exciting, exciting. —Gaylene Preston[1]

Utu was the one, I saw it here at home in Rotorua. I went along and Zac Wallace was there after the movie and aah, it blew me away, and I was like, oh wow, front and centre. —Cliff Curtis[2]

Geoff Murphy's *Utu* arrived on New Zealand screens in 1983 proclaiming: '100 years ago is today. The past is the present. The future is now.' *Utu* was wild, comic, disquieting and movingly tragic. With all its explosive action it was the most sophisticated film the country had yet produced, and most critics had no idea what to make of it. Audiences loved it, and it went on to claim its place in the pantheon of New Zealand cinema, garnering deeper critical recognition along the way. Its restoration and re-release as *Utu Redux* in 2013 generated a warm reunion akin to Whakatāne's welcome home to *The Te Kooti Trail* in 1964. Cast and crew flocked to the Wellington premiere to reminisce. The fans on opening night were vocal, cheering and hooting at the action and lamenting as old friends now gone appeared on screen.[3]

Utu was set in the same late phase of the wars as *The Te Kooti Trail*. Fifty-five years after Hayward had ventured into Whakatāne, the Te Kooti story – or something that borrows from it, with additions from other stories and some disguising – was taken up again by a filmmaker who, in the context of a present that had moved a long way from Hayward's interwar perspective on colonial conflict, and shaped by the emerging revisionist era of westerns, saw another kind of significance in this past. There are continuities between these films despite the technological and artistic developments that make *Utu* a much more accessible film now; and they demonstrate the changes that took place in cultural memories of the New Zealand Wars between 1927 and 1983.

Both films display a degree of sympathy for the resistance, although the balance is very much in favour of the colonial project in *The Te Kooti Trail*: in the earlier film, settlers, colonial soldiers and 'friendly' Māori unite in defence against Te Kooti's men who descend on the settlement. *Utu*, in contrast, opens as colonial troops massacre a peaceful village, announcing the perfidy of the military command and providing a provocation that justifies revenge. In both films the leader of the resistance becomes increasingly ruthless, although Hayward and Murphy alike drew back from fully representing documented levels of historical violence, on both sides. Both films are greatly interested in how Pākehā and the Māori who are allied with them forge relationships with each other, and these connections seem to prefigure nationhood – the Pākehā who makes Māori friends and the Māori who makes Pākehā friends are marked as the creators of the future – although *Utu* conveys this with far more ambivalence than the earlier film. Each film includes an interracial love affair, and each has a doomed Māori heroine. Perhaps the most striking parallel between the two films is that the 'big scene' in each is derived from a story told by Gilbert Mair about Te Kooti's War: in each, Mair recorded the story and it was then retold by James Cowan.[4] But Hayward and Murphy were drawn to different stories from Te Kooti's War, and the colonial past that Murphy put before his audiences did not anticipate the harmonious future implicit in *The Te Kooti Trail*. Between 1927 and 1983, thinking about race, nation and empire had become a great deal more ambivalent.

Utu in its time

Before turning to *Utu* we need to set the scene. This involves tracking developments in filmmaking and in its funding in a politically charged period, and the convergence of a network of people who went on to become central players in *Utu* and in the cultural politics of its production. *Utu* was the brilliant child of two related circumstances: the emergence in the 1970s and 80s of a remarkable generation of independent filmmakers and film professionals intent on creating a national film industry; and the brief existence of a tax shelter that guaranteed returns on investment in New Zealand-made films.[5] The newly created Film Commission was supportive of local cinema and, importantly, in its early years gave directors a relatively free rein.

Funding was, as ever, an issue. By 1981, Murphy recalled, 'the investment community knew for a fact there was no risk in investing in New Zealand films: *you will lose your money*'.[6] But Robert Muldoon's interventionist government had created a tax shelter originally designed to foster investment in primary industries: it was Film Commission director Don Blakeney, later *Utu*'s producer, who recognised the potential for diverting this income stream into filmmaking.[7] The discovery – and the fact that Murphy's *Goodbye Pork Pie* had just been a runaway success – enabled a budget of a little over $3 million for *Utu*, easily the largest budget to date for a New Zealand film. It was a strange convergence of forces peculiar to the world of film, therefore, that saw corporate tax dealings support the creation of a serious and complex antiwar film. The backers' tax incentive to spend extended to the funding of a documentary about the making of the film – Gaylene Preston's *Making Utu* – which now gives us an unusual insight into the processes and the culture of the making of the film in this broader context. Preston was on the set with the express purpose of observing, and was interested in 'the Māori–Pākehā shoreline'.

Still, that $3 million was a very tight budget for what Murphy hoped to achieve, so the production had to 'solve its problems by the use of intelligence', as he later put it. The extras in the wide shots of massed troops crossing the high-country plateau were schoolchildren wearing their own black clothes with masking-tape webbing across their 'uniforms' and cardboard hats they had made themselves, and the cavalry in long shot were local pony-club girls having the time of their lives.[8] The inventive, resourceful character of this production, and its incorporation of enthusiastic local input, was reminiscent of Hayward's production style.

The tax loophole in the early 1980s enabled a historical epic on the scale of *Utu* to be made without the international funding that supported but also constrained later productions. In this moment Murphy had a creative liberty that was later closed off: with entirely New Zealand funding he could make a defiantly local film without international stars or crew. *Utu*, despite its affectionate references to spaghetti westerns and the aesthetics and honour codes of Japanese cinema, put its dialogue with local audiences first.

In the wider context, the film was made during a time of great social, political and cultural change that included a reassessment of the colonial past. Murphy had been planning *Utu* throughout the tumults of the 1970s, as the country fought over a colonial war in Vietnam and the hīkoi of 1975 protested the alienation of Māori land. He was developing the script in earnest with Keith Aberdein at the beginning of the 1980s, when ongoing opposition to sporting contact with South Africa erupted in the protests against the 1981 Springbok Tour.

Political documentary

The growing expertise in filmmaking and the increasing attention to political documentary through this period meant that film was a medium deployed in radical politics and, as a result, a medium in which radical political movements were recorded. Three documentaries offer insight into the broader cultural–political context of *Utu*, and Merata Mita, Gerd Pohlmann and Leon Narbey, who worked as a collective to develop a practice of politically engaged documentary, were central to the making of all three. These films help to situate *Utu* thematically in its present, but they also informed the making of *Utu* more directly, as people who had appeared in or contributed to the documentaries went on to work on *Utu*.

Bastion Point – Day 507 (1980) documented the last day of the occupation of Bastion Point, the headland in Auckland that had been occupied by the tangata whenua, Ngāti Whātua, for 506 days in 1977–78. The occupation, along with the 1975

Bastion Point – Day 507 (1980): Zac Wallace is arrested, here flanked by two police officers, one Māori, one Pākehā.

Frame enlargement from *Bastion Point – Day 507*, preserved and made available by Ngā Taonga Sound and Vision. Courtesy of Gerd Pohlmann, Merata Mita Estate and Zac Wallace, Hawke Whānau and Leon Narbey

hīkoi, was instrumental in raising awareness of Māori land issues in the broader population. The documentary debates the strategy of the occupation, but – using mostly footage from the day of the eviction – its main action is the arrival of police to evict the occupiers, and the non-violent resistance they offered. As Mita later described it:

> This film is the total opposite of how a television documentary is made. It has a partisan viewpoint, is short on commentary and emphasises the overkill aspect of the combined police/military operation. It is a style of documentary that I have never deviated from because it best expresses a Māori approach to film making.[9]

year-long stalemate on the Māngere Bridge construction site. Filming began during the strike's early optimism and unity, and continued through arguments between the strike committee and the national union and the drifting away of many members, to the final compromised settlement. *The Bridge* provided *Utu* with its lead: the film's narrator was Anzac Wallace, whom the filmmakers quickly recognised as a charismatic central figure for the documentary. Gerd Pohlmann recalls that he first met Wallace at Bastion Point on the day of the eviction, 1978. 'He was passionate and vocal about Māori issues and soon became a friend of mine and Merata's. He worked as a labourer on the Mangere Bridge … When the Mangere Bridge dispute started, Zac became chairman of the disputes committee.'[11] The camera returns repeatedly to Wallace as he delivers speeches, sings at meetings and argues with the national organisers. Murphy first saw Zac Wallace in footage for *The Bridge*, and when Mita brought him in during casting, he had no doubt:

> *I'd never met a guy before that you could see anger in his eyes even when he was smiling, I thought shit we've got our man here, and the only question was whether he could … keep the lid on it and not explode during the shoot, you know, because he was a very violent man … but he was doing his best to break the recidivist cycle, he wanted to stay out of jail, and the two of us got on really well.*[12]

The third and most widely-seen of these documentaries, *Patu!*, documented the campaign against the 1981 rugby tour by the South African Springboks. It reveals a kind of civil war breaking out in New Zealand streets. The tour, the Muldoon government's refusal to intervene to prevent it, and the enthusiasm of many New Zealanders for flouting the international boycott against sporting contact with South Africa's apartheid regime brought attention not only to New

The Bridge: A Story of Men in Dispute (1982): Zac Wallace was the local union leader of the long-running Māngere Bridge strike. The film centres on Wallace's charismatic screen presence, and he narrates the film. Gerd Pohlmann screened *The Bridge* for some of the cast and crew during the shoot of *Utu*, because he wanted them to learn about Wallace's 'working-class battles and politics and remarkable leadership qualities'.

Frame enlargement from *The Bridge: A Story of Men in Dispute,* preserved and made available by Ngā Taonga Sound and Vision. Courtesy of Gerd Pohlmann, Merata Mita Estate and Zac Wallace

The film was 'partisan', but Leon Narbey recalled that the mood of the time enabled the filmmakers to draw on support from many quarters, including personnel inside television and radio who provided footage and voice reports, and access to equipment.[10]

The Bridge: A story of men in dispute (1982) tracked the longest strike the country had experienced – the two and a half-

FAR LEFT: *Patu!* (1983): Protesters against the Springbok Tour carry a banner echoing the famous cry from Ōrākau. LEFT: *Patu!* (1983): Tom Poata confronts police and rugby supporters with one of the film's most powerful speeches.

All frame enlargements from *Patu!* (1983), preserved and made available by Ngā Taonga Sound and Vision. Courtesy of the Merata Mita Estate

Zealand connections with South Africa but to the issue of racial justice in Aotearoa.[13] At no time before had the idea that Aotearoa was *not* necessarily a world leader in race relations been so forcefully thrust on Pākehā attention, and as the tour protests continued, the emphasis of the campaign shifted to incorporate a wider and more conflicted perspective. This changing position is articulated in *Patu!* in a direct-to-camera statement by Canon Hone Kaa (brother of Wī Kuki and Keri Kaa). Until now the campaign had been about racism in South Africa, he says; now it had to confront racism at home. The film's trajectory echoes this statement, moving from the early prominence of Pākehā protest leaders to the increasing presence of Māori speakers and their rising authority in redirecting anti-tour sentiment towards home.[14]

Almost all the main personnel of *Utu* had to some degree been involved with anti-tour protests. Martyn Sanderson (*The Governor*'s Cameron and *Utu*'s vicar) did some of the filming for *Patu!* Tom (Tama) Poata (Puni in *Utu*), a long-time unionist and veteran of earlier anti-apartheid protests, confronted police in a memorable standoff in *Patu!*[15] Keith Aberdein, who through the period of the tour was working on the script of *Utu* with Murphy, recalls the feel of the time:

> *I remember marching with Geoff through Wellington … coming down through MacAlister Park, suddenly about twelve of them, most I knew, youngish Māori at the front doing a haka for real in front of the Red Squad … and thinking this is for real, this is what this is all about, and thinking perhaps now it would be all right to die now that we're going to get the shit beaten out of us … the tour sat in our consciousnesses in the creation of* Utu *quite large …*[16]

Despite its prominence and the intensity that surrounded it over much of a year, the tour was not an isolated event: there was – as these documentaries taken together indicate – a broader political sensibility at work that was helping to make colonial conflict 'the kind of territory' it seemed right to be in, as Murphy noted much later. *Utu* is an artefact of that sensibility:

Patu! (1983): A Māori officer's sombre expression in this closeup suggests the internal conflicts that policing the Springbok Tour represented for some Māori.

as they were making *Utu*, many people involved were already part of a network with a political and political-film history in common.[17]

All three documentaries declare a strongly political stance. They produce images of the power of government in footage of lines of police convoys of heavy vehicles: they emphasise the weight of the force ranged against protestors or strikers. All, to varying degrees, chart alliances between Māori and Pākehā and the emergence of Māori leadership, but also internal divisions within groups and the ways that difficult historical events pit people against each other, disrupt loyalties and confront certainties. Māori as well as Pākehā police remove protestors from Bastion Point and face anti-tour protestors. Māori as well as Pākehā assert their right to watch a game of rugby. All the films are records of defeated resistance, more or less, but each of them also charts longer-term trends: the emergent visibility and increasing authority of Māori through these political protest movements; and the formation of a new cultural–political consciousness.

The late 1970s and early 80s was a period of highly engaged alliance between Pākehā and Māori. *Patu!* itself was testimony to this alliance: several Pākehā filmmakers supported the decision that Mita, a Māori woman, would be the film's director. Vanguard Films (Rod Prosser, Russell Campbell and Alister Barry) provided about a third of the footage; they agreed to contribute it to *Patu!*, as Gerd Pohlmann recalls, 'and that Merata, as an emerging Maori filmmaker, should be trusted to put it together'. The alliance that made *Patu!* was never plain sailing.[18] Just as in the actual protests, Māori–Pākehā relationships were being forged but also tested as they shifted from passionate but also sometimes naïve affiliations to something more fractured and at times suspicious.

Murphy's idea and the script of *Utu* were under way before the events these films documented. But the 1981 era brought many people to *Utu* with an intensity of purpose that could not fail to inform the performances the actors produced, the commitment to *Utu*'s commentary on the nation's past, and its practices of crosscultural collaboration. Preston made the point that Murphy's conception of the film predated the tour – 'the film was the film. He had a vision for that well before 81'. She went on to say: 'The people you have on screen are all people who are on the same side in 81, they were among the protestors. It is full of activists, Pākehā and Māori … The Māori and Pākehā making that film together have a lot more in common because of the 1981 experience.'[19]

ABOVE: *Making Utu* (1983): 'What's manifest in this film is what's happening today. We have that, we have Māori fighting Māori, we have Māori fighting Pākehā, we have Pākehā fighting Pākehā and it's very hard to draw the line in New Zealand along the terms of racial conflict, cause it's a lot more than that, it goes a lot deeper than that.' Merata Mita, director of *Patu!* and casting director of *Utu*, connects *Utu*'s past with its present. With the permission of Hepi Mita

ABOVE RIGHT: *Utu: Redux* (2013): 'The people you see on the screen are all people who are on the same side in 81, they were among the protesters. It is full of activists, Pākehā and Māori …' Merata Mita (as Matu) and Tom Poata (as Puni), veterans of *Patu!*, reconvene in *Utu*. Except where noted, all frame enlargements have been created from *Utu: Redux* by the author

The personnel included Māori crew as well as cast and advisors. Murphy had appointed Mita casting director for *Utu*, and also asked her to be the Māori advisor. Despite her experience, Mita was convinced that many Māori would not accept a woman in this role; she suggested Joe Malcolm instead.[20] In the end both of them were closely involved in the cultural advice. In his memoir Murphy discusses his decision to hire as many Māori crew as he could, and to send strong signals about their roles:

> *The political climate was such, at that time, that I felt it would be important to position the film* Utu *as a racially balanced film. … This was not easy, as the film industry was predominantly white in 1982, and had done a pretty good job of shutting Māori out until this time.*

Lee Tamahori had been a boom-swinger on several films including *Pork Pie*. Murphy's account of promoting him to first assistant director offers a revealing insight into the canny mix of political strategy, eye for talent and the commitment (which he deftly downplays here) that he brought to the process:

> [Tamahori] was also a smart bugger, smart enough to use that front seat [which boom-swinging entailed] to learn a hell of a lot about how a film set runs. I believed he could do it. But most of all I wanted him because his name was Tamahori, and to any casual observer the first assistant is like the site foreman on a shoot, and consequently very high-profile. It was a power position, and I needed that name to give the film credibility amongst Māori.[21]

The cultural politics of *Utu*'s post-tour moment had a profound impact on the culture of the film's production. The following example of how things worked on the shoot illustrates the dynamics of the cultural transition as seasoned film personnel readjusted. The production of *Utu* was a sign of the times but it was also a site that, with its Māori personnel and the active support they had from Murphy, drove change:

> It [involvement in political films] drew people together, and it definitely affected the attitudes of people, I do remember a huge row blowing up in the middle of the shoot and it was to do with Merata's moko. They were drawing Merata's moko on down in the makeup caravan and she was saying 'that's wrong', and the makeup people were saying 'well we're the makeup people, we'll decide what the makeup is thank you very much, you're just the actress' … and so she called on Joe Malcolm who was the Māori advisor, who was on set at the time. And he came down and had a look and said 'no, definitely wrong, change it' [laughs], and they were going 'rrr rrr' you know and eventually a delegation came to me, and I'm in the middle of directing a bloody scene, what was going on, 'they're arguing about Merata's moko'. I said, 'What the fuck're you arguing about?' [laughs again] and I said, 'Look, this guy, this Joe Malcolm, [more seriously] he's the Māori advisor. I expect you to pay as much attention to him in his specialty as you would to Graeme Cowley who's the lighting cameraman and he's an expert on that aspect of filmmaking. And so you've got to really take notice of what he says. So, just do what he says, that's it, just because he's a Māori doesn't mean he's second-rate, you know.'[22]

TOP: *Making Utu* (1983): First assistant director Lee Tamahori and a crew member register relief and delight as a grand piano falls from a window and splinters into pieces. All frame enlargements from *Making Utu*, Gaylene Preston Productions

ABOVE: *Making Utu* (1983): Joe Malcolm, Māori advisor, talks to Geoff Murphy about the shooting of Hēnare's tangi: how can the film create the feeling of a real tangi, and what is appropriate to photograph? The discussion rolls on through several conversations, including with Merata Mita, Lee Tamahori, and the kuia performing in the scene. With the permission of Joe Malcolm

Murphy remembered shooting *Utu*'s tangi, a scene that required heavy rain. Reluctant to have the special effects crew drenching the kuia in the scene with firehoses, he suggested they could stand under a shelter as the rain descended. This sparked a debate involving Joe Malcolm, Lee Tamahori and Murphy as they worked out how to balance care of the old people against the cultural and historical integrity of the film. The scene had no precise historical basis; the measure of integrity had to do with taking cultural advice and 'getting it right'. While Malcolm's knowledge is the recognised authority, there is no sense here that the Pākehā have one opinion and the Māori another:

> And Joe Malcolm was there, and he made this noise with his tongue, t-t-t, and I knew there was a problem and I said 'what's wrong with that, Joe'. And he said, 'they would not stand under that shelter'. I said, 'where would they stand?' 'Out in the rain, at a tangi' … I said 'oh shit', so I said 'well maybe we can damp them down and spritz them a wee bit and put a curtain of rain in front of them,' so we did this, and Lee Tamahori, who was the first assistant, was going 'who the hell would know the bloody difference?' [laughs] I said, 'Lee, we are obliged to get it right … although we're not making an historical documentary or anything, when you see a group of Indians sitting in a teepee going "ugh, paleface, many moons, across running water", and they all look like Italians, you know it's wrong, and you don't know anything about Indian culture [laughs]. You know, we can tell from here … So let's get it right. If we get it right, the Inuits in Canada will be going "looks right to me"'. That was my argument about the moko and all, 'just get it right' … But it was interesting, those arguments were going on and Lee, Lee was arguing for the Pākehā side of things and he's Māori, it wasn't that clear-cut.[23]

Another incident made it apparent that not all Māori arrived with the same cultural background. Murphy recalled how both Malcolm and Mita recoiled at footage showing Wallace as Te Wheke eating the eyeballs of the vicar he had just decapitated. Wallace had chewed them, instead of swallowing them whole according to tikanga, and this horrified them – 'so, rather than offend our Māori audience, which I hoped would be huge, I never used it'.[24]

A more sustained example of how the cultural expertise and advice – and the cultural authority – operated in the production relates to the direction of *Utu*'s last and most important scene, which hung on Wī Kuki Kaa's performance as Wiremu and especially his final speech. Kaa was a well established professional actor who had worked for over a decade in Australia, largely because there were few roles for him in Aotearoa; he had returned previously to deliver a powerful performance as Rewi in *The Governor*. He came from an eminent Ngāti Porou family, Māori was his first language, he was a skilled orator, and the power of his screen presence was widely recognised. Discussing his relationship with Kaa and Kaa's contribution to the film, Murphy recalls: 'When Wī came onto the set in the first instance, we flew him in from Australia, and everyone was a bit scared of him [laughs] … he kind of is intimidating.' At first Murphy found Kaa reluctant to accept his directing. He became concerned about whether Kaa would deliver in the final scene, given that the film would hang on this performance. There was a frank discussion at this point, and it resulted in a strong relationship between them. 'The agreement that you have with the actor is that he has to trust you, and the opposite is true too, you have to trust him,' Murphy said. His trust in Kaa, and in Malcolm, resulted in a striking transfer of directorial authority for Kaa's final speech.[25] As the final drafts were written, Murphy handed over responsibility for Wiremu's speech to Kaa himself, both the short English section and the longer Māori part that is also translated in subtitles.²⁶ There was some debate over Kaa's initial drafting of the English-language section of the speech, which was at first too long and expository for Murphy and which Kaa shortened; but the Māori segment was entirely given over to Kaa. Murphy did not understand the Māori words, which were only translated later, but trusted Kaa and Malcolm:

> *in the English script [of the Māori-language segment] it's my roughing out sort of, of what he had to say. I don't think the script, the printed script [included] stuff like 'when this gun fires it can be heard in the seventh heaven' you know, none of that stuff, that was all Wī, I didn't even know what he was saying until Joe Malcolm translated it for me, you know … Wī'd say something in Māori, and I'd turn to Joe and say 'is that ok?' [laughs] and Joe'd say 'yep'. I didn't care what he said, if Joe said it was ok it was ok, you know [laughs] and Joe would translate it … and go 'yeah that's appropriate for this scene' … so Joe was directing it to a certain extent, which, if you're going to involve other cultures … you have to give them that power, you have to share the power with them, you just are obliged to, you know.*²⁷

Kaa loved westerns, especially because of the parallels between Native American and Māori experience, and according to Sylvia Kaa, both he and Zac Wallace were 'completely happy in roles that had to do with them, that were relevant for them'. Kaa's own Ngāti Porou descent equipped him to understand the complexity of kūpapa, and gave this history a powerful personal resonance for him: 'Wī Kuki's own village, in his own personal history, in his whakapapa in the nineteenth century, they had both: they had the Te Kooti supporters and they had the kūpapa in the same village in Rangitukia.'²⁸

Local cultures

Once again the film's location played its part. Murphy lived on a communally owned property at Waimārama in Hawke's Bay, and had travelled between there and Wellington where he moved in a music scene that morphed over time into a film scene.²⁹ In 1974 they made the first fully Māori-language television drama, *Uenuku*, in which Murphy gained experience working closely with Māori. Hawke's Bay was the southern boundary of the wars that took place in the late 1860s to early 1870s, and it was still a landscape in which memory of colonial conflict persisted, but unevenly. The *Utu* locations around Te Hāroto and Te Pōhue had been associated with Pai Mārire resistance in the 1860s. The Napier–Taupō road, where much of the film was shot, bisected territory that Te Kooti's troops, and the colonial troops who pursued them, criss-crossed in their movements around the central North Island. During the shoot of *Making Utu*, Preston found nobody prepared to talk about land: it was

> *the real tapu subject … the Māori owners, some of them were loyalists, in the wars, you know, they were on different sides. So who lived where and how they'd all worked was very fresh for the Māori and … well, they were positive they weren't going to talk to me about it … and Pākehā owners wouldn't talk about it because they kind of were unconscious [of it].*³⁰

In events reminiscent of local responses to *The Te Kooti Trail*, rumours circulated about the making of a film. The documentary crew inadvertently generated concern when it began filming before Joe Malcolm had spoken to the elders at Te Hāroto. A newspaper report quoted how a local couple, the Hills, reacted to the news: 'So of course, we were up in arms, because we're both members of the Ringatu Church, which Te

Kooti founded. It was supposed to show Te Kooti as a rebel – and we don't think of him as a rebel.' The filmmakers were asked to a meeting at the Te Hāroto marae, after which local people agreed to support the filmmaking, and some acted in the film. Despite the Te Hāroto marae's support, though, rumours of Ringatū resistance continued, just as they had in the Bay of Plenty in 1927: some Ringatū people were reported as saying that 'Murphy will mis-use the concept of utu and make an exploitative, inaccurate movie – a thinly disguised portrayal of Te Kooti,' and there were intimations of court action, complaints and the placing of tapu. Just as in 1927, though, no names are mentioned in this report, and the reporter appears to have had this information second-hand.[31]

Making Utu shows something of how this relationship with local people played out on set. One sequence follows discussions about how to represent the tangi, where Murphy, Mita and Malcolm talk with local people and with one kuia in particular, all of whom have parts in the film, about the waiata that is sung, the way that the body will be carried, and whether and how it can be shown on screen. As Preston recalls it, these conversations happened while cast, crew and equipment, whose costs 'tick along on a very, very fast meter', stood by waiting. *Making Utu*'s record of these discussions – which were attentive and unrushed – is telling. Preston puts them in context:

> [Murphy] wasn't just having discussions with actors, he was having discussions that were to do with the cultural interface … in 1982, Māori weren't as vocal in mixed company as they are now … they're media-savvy [now] … but they weren't then, and so there's a very shy conversation going on, and it's really important in that situation for Pākehā to listen intently.[32]

The casting of Māori extras was done locally by Lee Tamahori and Chris Short. There were two groups to cast: the armed constabulary unit who fought on the side of the Crown, and the resistance fighters who followed Te Wheke. Te Wheke's followers had to be fit but a bit edgy, and the constabulary – the commandos – had to look like toughened bush fighters:

> Lee and Shorty and them went off to … some rugby club in Napier … they got most of the extras from this one club, they were a Rastafarian-looking lot … yeah, so they came back with them, and then for Scott's commandos, those guys, I said now these jokers have to be bloody good horsemen … so they went up to Te Hāroto and they got young fellas from up there, Te Hāroto was, you know Billy Bush the All Black was from there, and some of his relations were these guys, young Bushes, and yeah, they had a real different look about them, they were all dressed in military uniform … riding the horses and shooting underneath them and all that stuff … they were great. And that input was fantastic, I don't know how, without that cooperation I don't know where we would have gone …[33]

The aura of resistance of Te Wheke's warriors in the film was defined as much by a more recent anticolonial figure as by their knowledge of colonial history. Bob Marley's tour of Aotearoa in 1979 had left a legacy of Rastafarianism, especially around the East Coast. Dreadlocks and radical cool migrated onto the screen. Connie Hill from Te Hāroto, who had initially objected to the film, saw how the filmmaking had sparked the young people's interest in their past: 'Before they were not interested. Now they want to know. This is a positive thing that the film has done for us.'[34] In *Making Utu*, cast and crew, including these young extras, speak to the camera about their renewed appreciation of history, land and the Treaty.

In such a setting, and given the personnel who worked together on *Utu*, it is not surprising that there was a reflectiveness about the culture of the production. Like *The Governor*, *Utu* is now regarded as a training ground for Māori filmmakers

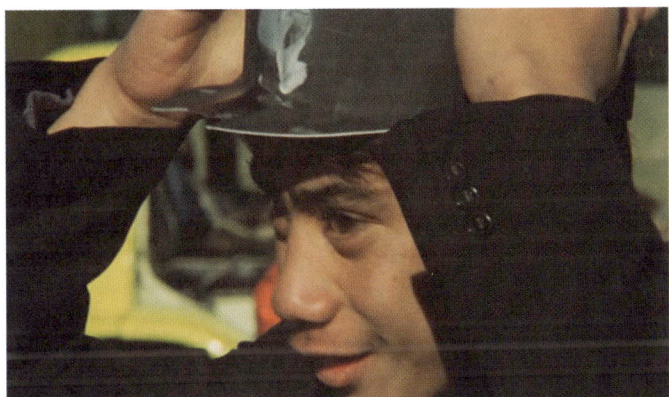

Making Utu (1983): The massed troops crossing the plateau consisted of a few closeups of seasoned veterans, and long shots of extras drawn from Napier schools and pony clubs. Here a soldier tries on his cardboard cap.

Making Utu (1983): 'This is Te Wheke's land, eh. He knows it, that's why he came here. We've got them on our terms here, they're in our country and bush. It's like if we're fighting them out in the town like Te Puna, that's how we got caught eh, we're on their ground. But we're on our ground now.' A young actor demonstrates the excitement many Māori felt in seeing the story through Te Wheke's eyes.

who went on to make Māori-directed films. Despite Murphy's emphasis on the practical strategy behind his decisions, it is evident that the presence of Māori crew as well as performers, and the importance he attached to Mita and Malcolm's cultural advice, meant that the production itself was a site of cultural change, aiming for a bicultural practice as well as prompting those involved to reconsider the past. The excitement carried into personal relationships too: Murphy and Merata Mita's own cross-cultural romance began during the production.

Utu's story

The plot of *Utu* is complex. The film begins as soldiers, led by the arrogant English Colonel Elliot, descend on a peaceful kāinga; they kill the people and torch the village. When a small group of soldiers follows up the main body a day later, one of them, Te Wheke (Anzac Wallace), expects to see his family – this is his village. Distraught with grief, he sees no option but to 'kill the Pākehā' in utu: he shoots one of his fellow soldiers and sends another to the colonel with a message: 'I will catch up with him sooner or later.'

We are next introduced to Lieutenant Scott (Kelly Johnston), just returned from fighting Boers in South Africa and keen to try the bush-fighting methods he saw there. Naively confident, he strikes up a conversation with the more reticent corporal Wiremu (Wī Kuki Kaa).

Te Wheke attacks a church and beheads its vicar. Soldiers move settlers out of their farms, but Williamson (Bruno Lawrence) refuses to leave – instead he boards up his house in preparation for an attack. Te Wheke and his men arrive and demand ammunition, and in the ensuing shootout Williamson's wife Emily falls from a balcony and is killed. From this point

Williamson is a crazed but knowing anarchic presence, looking to hunt down Te Wheke but equally at odds with the English commander. Scott, meantime, befriends another soldier, Hēnare (Faenza Reuben), and first encounters the young woman Kura (Tania Bristowe), whose allegiance is ambiguous. Scott and Hēnare train the Māori troops in bush-fighting tactics, despite the colonel's scepticism about such colonial methods. Hēnare is killed just as he contemplates defecting to Te Wheke and Scott is wounded in the fight. More defections follow, but Wiremu holds to the government side. Called back by the colonel, Scott is set to guard a prisoner – who turns out to be Kura. She charms then tricks him and escapes into the night. When the troops arrive en masse in the little town of Te Puna to regroup for the pursuit of Te Wheke, she comes back to retrieve him and keep him out of harm's way – she knows that Te Wheke is poised for a surprise attack. Williamson, however, witnesses the arrival of the attackers, raises the alarm and foils the attack. Many of Te Wheke's men are killed and he retreats into the mountains with the troops in pursuit. As his situation becomes more desperate Te Wheke increasingly turns on his own followers – he kills his wounded lieutenant Puni (Tom Poata), and then Kura, who he believes has betrayed him. Finally the troops surround his camp and capture him – and during this fight Wiremu surreptitiously shoots the colonel. In the final scene, as Te Wheke is tried and sentenced to death, Williamson, Scott and Kura's aunt Matu (Merata Mita) all advance their claims to be executioner. But Wiremu now declares that he is Te Wheke's brother, and on the grounds that only if he kills Te Wheke will the bloodshed cease, overrules them.

As several reviewers noted, *Utu* echoed Sergio Leone's spaghetti westerns with their structural sophistication, enigmatic characterisation and lyrical use of landscape. (Murphy's joking title on some of the early drafts, 'Puha Western', makes this debt explicit.) He also drew, visually and thematically, on Kurosawa's *Seven Samurai* and *Throne of Blood* – for the stylised appearance of the antihero Te Wheke and for the film's misted, epic landscapes. In an echo of Kurosawa's adaptation of Shakespeare's *Macbeth* in *Throne of Blood*, the character and the narrative trajectory of Te Wheke makes explicit reference to *Macbeth*. These echoes enrich the film's exploration of violence, retribution and justice, and their effects on both perpetrators and victims. Looking at first like a revenge tragedy, the film finally moves away from revenge to the Māori concept of utu – the restoration of balance and the resolution of conflict – as Wiremu's killing of Te Wheke brings an end to the violence.

The destination: 'A Bush Court Martial'

The history of *Utu* itself begins at the end of the film. Into a turbulent present where Aotearoa was enmeshed in debate over race, colonisation, violence and justice, Murphy brought a story from Te Kooti's War – Cowan's 'A Bush Court Martial'. In the late 1860s and early 70s when imperial involvement had ceased and resistant fighters were opposed by colonial fighters and, increasingly, Māori troops, the conflict was no longer between empire and Māori: it was between peoples of the colonial world – colonisers and indigenes – where some of the latter formed alliances with some of the former. On the East Coast, in the Bay of Plenty and in Te Urewera, long-standing tensions among iwi were reignited as some iwi or hapū resisted colonial expansion and others allied themselves with the Crown. Te Arawa, most of whom were allied with the Crown, had fought other iwi from the Bay of Plenty; some Ngāti Awa joined Te Kooti but others opposed him; Ngāi Tūhoe protected Te Kooti but were driven by colonial tactics to distance themselves from him and deal with the Crown. Ngāti Porou and Ngāti Kahungunu from this region were divided – notable kūpapa leaders and troops came from these iwi as well as from Whanganui. Many people were descended from iwi and hapū on both sides, resulting in a spectacularly complex pattern of alliance and opposition in this region.[35]

Te Kooti's skill at guerilla warfare using raid-and-retreat strategies from the safety of steep bush country in Te Urewera and other parts of the central North Island provoked the formation of two Arawa contingents, under the leadership of the bilingual native-born captains Gilbert Mair and George Preece. These troops pursued Te Kooti across the region for nearly two years, never quite catching up with him, although his followers suffered heavy losses. One incident late in this campaign was the basis for Cowan's 'A Bush Court Martial'.

Gilbert Mair told the story to Cowan as the two travelled through Te Urewera visiting sites of former conflict in 1921. Cowan retold it briefly in his official history, where he described how Mair and Preece and their Arawa contingents surrounded and attacked a camp at the Waipaoa River near Waikaremoana in August 1871.[36] Te Kooti escaped as he always did but one of his lieutenants, Wī Heretaunga, was wounded and captured. When Mair bent to see to his wounds, Heretaunga drew a knife and attempted to stab him; Mair was saved only by the action of his sergeant, Hōhepa Rokoroko. Heretaunga's action outraged the Arawa troops and prompted women prisoners to give evidence about his role in killings at Poverty Bay and Mōhaka, and his recent murder of his own wife. Cowan's account in the official history concludes succinctly: 'It was decided, therefore, that the prisoner should be shot, and this summary execution was carried out.'[37] In the *Auckland Star* in 1926, Cowan again wrote about the incident, this time elaborating on the court martial and execution of Wī Heretaunga in an eight-page story, republished in 1934 in *Tales of the Maori Bush*.[38]

The story briefly tells of the pursuit of Te Kooti – how the soldiers sighted smoke, discovered the camp and carried out the attack, during which some of the fugitives were captured. Cowan's writing lends itself to a cinematic imagining:

The snow lay deep on the mountains and the clearing, and as the evening breeze increased in strength masses came swishing down from the tree branches like small avalanches. In the bush camp great fires were burning, and the blaze lit up as clearly as daylight a wild savage scene. The shawl-kilted Arawa moved about the camp or sat in groups talking …[39]

He describes Heretaunga's attempt to knife Mair, and lists his past crimes. He then turns to the heart of the story: how several soldiers claim the right to be Heretaunga's executioner, and the cultural logic at work in deciding who will be awarded the privilege. Hōhepa Rokoroko makes his claim on the grounds that he had saved Mair from being stabbed; Nīkora te Tuhi asserts his right since Heretaunga had killed his brother; but the last person to step forward is Kepa Te Ahuru, who argues that, since Heretaunga held high rank in the Urewera and Wairoa iwi, if an Arawa soldier killed him it would disrupt efforts to bring about peace, and start another feud, whereas Te Ahuru himself was from Tūhoe and, moreover, he was Wī Heretaunga's nephew: 'If I shoot him no more will be said about it, for it will be agreed that I, a chief of Tuhoe, have a perfect right to remove a man who has disgraced us by his many evil deeds.'[40] His claim was accepted.

Wī Heretaunga, who until this point had been abusing the troops and reminding them of his part in the killings at Mōhaka and Gisborne, is said to have now displayed 'a softening expression of composure and relief' and asked for a smoke. Te Ahuru borrowed Mair's carbine – a gift from a Scottish nobleman in return for Mair's kindness to his nephew – and began to walk up and down. He addressed Heretaunga:

> *You should be content and may consider yourself fortunate that you are to die by the hands of a chief of equal rank, your own nephew who will send you like a chieftain to the Night. But for me you would have been slain by those plebeian people the Arawa.*
>
> *So spoke Kepa Te Ahuru, punctuating his speech by jumping in the air, his eyes glaring in the* pukana *grimace, his tongue protruding. He told the prisoner that he would be honoured by being killed with the Captain's carbine. Wi Heretaunga smoked quietly, plucky and defiant to the end. At last Te Ahuru advanced slowly and, placing the muzzle of the carbine close to Wi's body, pressed the trigger and the prisoner fell back shot through the heart.*[41]

In 2013 on the re-release of *Utu*, Murphy described coming across the story in the late 1960s while he was reading around the subject of the colonial past, looking for historical material that would translate well to the screen. It 'felt like the end of a movie' and besides, 'I thought this was the territory we should be in anyway,' he said.[42] He was no doubt referring to colonial conflict more broadly, but the 'territory' of the film was the time and place of 'A Bush Court Martial'.

Where Cowan's interest in the story had been in the fittingness of Wī Heretaunga's having been executed by his nephew, the incident as it was made over in *Utu* centred on other themes. Murphy worked on and off for a dozen years crafting a backstory for the scene that 'felt like the end of a movie'. One early draft included Te Kooti as a separate named character. A lieutenant, called Te Paku in the draft, is captured and enacts Heretaunga's role in the final 'bush court martial' scene. Sometime around 1980 Murphy recruited Keith Aberdein to assist with the writing and they worked on the script together over a period of about 18 months. By 19 June 1981 the fourth draft had much of the shape of the script which went into production. By now the names 'Te Kooti' and 'Te Paku' had disappeared, and the resistance leader and the lieutenant on trial had become one: 'Te Wheke' (The Octopus).[43] This change enhanced the film's narrative and emotional clarity – and it may also have avoided two difficulties associated with historical fiction: the general one of how to steer a path between reference to documented historical events and fictional interpolations, and the more specific one of answering to descendants and local communities who have a stake in how their history is told.

The final drafts are informed by familiarity with historical events, and historical reference is woven through the film, but the film consistently avoids too precise a reflection of any single individual or action. Events surrounding the character of Te Wheke draw from historical accounts of Te Kooti (in his turn from fighting with the Crown to against it, his guerilla campaigns and increasingly ruthless leadership, and the retreat through mountainous bush in the late stages of the campaign), Wī Heretaunga (in the capture and the events of the final scene taken from 'A Bush Court Martial'), and the Ngāti Rangiwehiwehi warrior Kereopa Te Rau (another who began by fighting with the Crown, but after the killing of his family changed allegiance, and who was responsible for the killing of the missionary Völkner. The deleted scene in which Te Wheke scoops out the reverend's eyes and eats them was based on Kereopa's actions at Ōpōtiki.) Gilbert Mair, channelled through Cowan's 'A Bush Court Martial' and the official history, was one

Utu: Redux (2013): The Reverend Johns (Martyn Sanderson) faces a very frightening Te Wheke. This scene was based on the death of Reverend Völkner at Ōpōtiki.

Courtesy of Geoff Murphy and the New Zealand Film Commission

source, just as he had been for *The Te Kooti Trail*; and as an exemplar of the 'go-between' soldier figure he was a model for the young Lieutenant Scott – as was his fellow captain George Preece, perhaps. Scott's commandos are broadly modelled on the Arawa contingents, and Kepa Te Ahuru provided some of the raw material for Wiremu's role in the final scene of *Utu*. But with the exception of the deleted eye-eating incident, none of these echoes is clearcut. Aberdein, with the experience of dealing in historical reconstruction in *The Governor* behind him, recalls that although there had been a lot of talk and enthusiasm for making a film based on Te Kooti, he wanted to avoid making too precise a connection with identifiable historical events or people. Murphy's recollection of this process attends more to the kind of relationship the film had to the historical past: he notes that the intention was not 'to represent history in any sort of real way … we were trying to create a creative space in which history could be commented on'.[44]

Rudall Hayward, taking up another cluster of events from Te Kooti's War, had retrieved a story of Māori–Pākehā alliance against a common enemy. In Mair he saw a model of the adaptive colonial, the Pākehā who 'loved the Māori race' and led Māori troops in a bush war against extremism. Much had altered by the time Murphy drew on these events, and his take on them differed in several ways. Te Wheke, a fully developed tragic hero, has a great deal more screentime and claims far greater sympathy than Hayward's Te Kooti. Scott has some of Mair's bush-fighting abilities but, unlike Hayward's heroically competent Mair, he has as many inadequacies as masculine competencies: although he is the film's 'good Pākehā', he stumbles his way towards understanding his position in the colonial world, informed and protected by the far more knowing Māori – Hēnare, Kura and Wiremu. Hayward's Taranahi is a romantic lead, but in the end the Māori soldier is sidekick to the white captain. *Utu* reverses this structure, finally bringing Wiremu to the centre of the frame and moving Scott to the background. And *Utu*, child of its time, is far more interested in colonialism's complicated ongoing story. What does it take to live in the colonial world? it asks. What sacrifices does it demand?

The beginning, and the end

Te Wheke's demand for utu is set in motion by the massacre at the beginning of the film and his discovery of the village smouldering in fire and ash, the people dead. 'Why? They were our friends,' says one of his fellow soldiers — but Te Wheke lifts his comrade's white hand to compare it with his own brown skin, and shoots him.

The film begins – and proceeds –not only as a western structured around revenge but as Shakespearean tragedy, inflected with Japanese codes of honour.[45] Te Wheke's trajectory explicitly echoes *Macbeth*: he is a hero drawn into increasingly extreme and bloody actions and an increasingly extreme condition of mind, on the way to his tragic end. Like *Macbeth*, *Utu* begins with soldiers travelling (even to the 'fog and filthy air' of the play's opening) and learning something that leads one of them to understand that his future is determined. In this belief he sets his course on a lethal path. The opening graphics emblazon the word 'Utu' across the screen, with an accompanying burst of orchestral volume.

Anzac Wallace's Te Wheke is a frightening, unpredictable figure, but he is also an initially sympathetic hero whose anguish strikes home and whose moral dilemma is entirely comprehensible: 'What else can a warrior do?' A story of violence unfolds, and the film tracks between the resistant and colonial forces, developing sympathies with characters on both sides and with those who change sides. Te Wheke's early forays – the killing of two clergymen and the attack on the Williamson house that results in the death of Emily – summon the might of the colonial state against him. As his retaliation grows more ruthless and his treatment of his own followers more bloody, he becomes less and less sympathetic – and in this the film echoes Cowan's interpretation of Te Kooti's leadership. The colonial army, stocked with English, native-born Europeans and kūpapa, pursues him with increasing determination; and so does Williamson, the settler he has widowed. Into the mix is added the New Zealand-born Scott and his bush-fighting unit – and here is where the film begins to relocate its centre of sympathy. Scott is quickly at odds with the vicious, hierarchical English colonel; and he forms relationships with Hēnare, Kura and Wiremu, all of whom are ambiguously aligned somewhere between resistant and colonial forces.

By the final scene, the adaptation of 'A Bush Court Martial' is sustained by a narrative that has been building quietly throughout the film. Wiremu reveals himself to be Te Wheke's brother. Dismissing the other claims, he makes his own on the grounds that only he can effect utu in its full sense, not of vengeance but of resolution. In developing the move from 'utu' conceived of as revenge tragedy to 'utu' understood as the resolution of conflict – through the recognition of Te Wheke's mana and the strength of the bond between Te Wheke and Wiremu – Murphy deepened and complicated the Mair/Cowan narrative that had now travelled from its genesis in 1871, through Cowan's version for the official history, then for a popular readership in the 1920s and 30s, to become a story for the 1980s.

The final scene, beautifully crafted, lit and filmed, deserves its reputation as one of the most enduringly powerful scenes in New Zealand cinema. In maintaining the substance but shifting the tenor of Cowan's story, it reconfigures both the revenge and the tragedy. The Pākehā (Scott and Williamson) and the other Māori (Matu and Te Wheke) all yield place without protest to Wiremu's assumption of authority and his decision to bring about utu rather than to tolerate revenge. The colonial soldiers have pursued Te Wheke far into the bush and the mountains; now they are on his ground – and, as it turns out, Wiremu's. The firelight encloses them in a circle of common understanding as, formally and one by one, the speakers state their case, and colonial military law gives way to the laws of utu.[46] Here too, *Utu* charts a transition that echoes the political documentaries discussed earlier: its Pākehā characters step back and fall silent, and a character who has until this point said little, steps forward to bring about resolution. Murphy and Aberdein's pleasure in this turn is apparent in a direction in the script that persisted through several drafts:

> *Wiremu has decided it is time for him to speak. Quite a decision in view of the fact that up to this point he has been so taciturn and that he plans to talk from now until the end of the movie.*[47]

With a growing sense of mutual recognition, the characters move into alignment. As much is conveyed by what they don't say as by what they do – the calm attentiveness of the listeners as each character speaks, and their tacit assent to Wiremu's right to execute his brother and the reason for it: peace, albeit at a heavy price. If anyone else carries out the execution the fighting will go on; 'and besides, Pākehā have killed enough Māori, and Māori have killed enough Pākehā'.

Te Wheke's end fits the tragic mode: finally brought to account, he accepts his death. The resolution for Wiremu is a more complex tragedy: he brings about the end of resistance by killing his brother. A slow, intimate two-shot of their hongi at the end frames Wiremu and Te Wheke as trusting brothers rather than enemies. If the film's better Pākehā learn to take on something Māori in order to live with Māori, it is Wiremu's tragedy that he must sacrifice something of himself – personified here in Te Wheke but demonstrated in Wiremu's reticence throughout the film – in order to live with Pākehā. The film's persistent question – whose side are you on? – is at the heart of this second tragic conclusion.

Two themes, in parallel and in tension with each other, have built through the film and converged as the film reaches its conclusion in the figure of Wiremu: that of interracial affection and love on the one hand, and ambiguity and unease on the other. At the centre of the first are Scott's friendships with Hēnare and Wiremu and his love affair with Kura; at the centre of the second is Williamson's uneasy mistrust.

What colonial conflict tears apart, love and friendship seek to reunite, as with so many of the films in this book. Māori women were often present at the scene of battles and even more often at sites of invasion – unlike European women. Like Hayward's Takiri and Ariana, Kura moves across the lines and negotiates her allegiance, but she is a more assertive character than her predecessors. If Monika echoes the confident young women of the 1920s, Kura is very much of the 1980s: forthright, mocking, physically tough and sexually forthright. 'Are you chasing me or not?' she shouts to Hēnare, challenging his allegiance to the colonial forces. She easily outmanoeuvres Scott: escaping after her capture and then breaking back in through the lines to draw him out of the way of the attack on Te Puna, she once again organises him with ease. In *Utu* (as in *The*

Utu: Redux (2013): Kura (Tania Bristowe) crosses the lines. In the first image, her challenge to Hēnare – 'Are you chasing me or not?' – is more than a romantic invitation. Within days, Hēnare defects to Te Wheke. In the lower image, Scott (Kelly Johnson) knows less than he thinks; Kura is keeping him out of the attack she knows is coming.

OPPOSITE: *Utu: Redux* (2013): The dying girl. In the opening scenes, a horse flashes past the body of a young girl as colonial troops launch an unprovoked attack on a kāinga. We have seen her in closeup moments before; her mother calls to her as the attack begins but neither survive.

Te Kooti Trail) it is Māori women – Kura and then Matu – who directly challenge Te Wheke and reject the cruelty of a vengeful resistance; they become the voice of the film's disquiet about violence as a response to violence.[48] Just as Monika is killed for her continued loyalty to the government side, Te Wheke kills Kura when he suspects her of having warned the troops at Te Puna.

Like Takiri, Monika and Ariana, Kura occupies the point of cultural crossing in these films, embodying the desire for a bicultural solution. As in the earlier films it is unfulfilled, but perhaps for other reasons. M. Elise Marubbio discusses the trope of 'killing the Indian maiden' in North American film: the pattern in which the Indian maiden loyal to (usually) a white hero sacrifices herself for his sake.[49] Kura has the requisite bravery to save Scott, but she could hardly be described as self-sacrificial – so why must she die in *Utu*? Her death has less to do with fidelity to any historical source than with the contemporary moment of *Utu's* making: 1982 was no time for an easy romantic solution to the roiling problems of race and colonialism.

Scott's brief friendship with Hēnare is replaced by a deeper alliance with Wiremu. At first he takes Wiremu for granted as a ready ear but finds he gets provocative, unexpected responses. Their growing affinity is embodied in nonverbal exchanges; Scott begins to see the war in an altered light. Williamson joins them in an alliance towards the end of the film.

But Williamson (whose name links him to Wiremu) has been associated with the film's second and opposing theme of interracial relations, which centres on mistrust and suspicion. Here again the contrast with *The Te Kooti Trail* is telling: where the earlier film makes a great deal of the strong loyalties and ties of affection between 'good Pākehā' and 'friendly Māori'

Utu: Redux (2013): Bell tents in the vast expanse of Te Urewera: cutting away from a scene of busy military activity, we see the camp as tiny, isolated, precarious.

BELOW: *Utu: Redux* (2013): Soldiers on horseback burn Te Wheke's village in a scene that echoes historical attacks such as those on Rangiāowhia and Pōkaikai.

– an affiliation that Cowan and Hayward celebrated as the foundation of nationhood – the crosscultural relationships in *Utu* are on much less stable ground. Right from the opening scenes, *Utu*'s ambiguities are set up in a sequence of rapid reversals. The opening shot of the fort, showing Māori and Pākehā soldiers busy in their soldierly activity, pulls back to a wide shot revealing it as an isolated, tenuous position in the vastness of the forest. Then there is a cut to the kāinga where the clucking hens, the women's and children's dress and the child's name 'Wikitoria' are all signs of European influence and affiliation … but suddenly a bugle sounds and the women and children fall under a savage military attack. Next, a trio of Pākehā soldiers make their way nervously through unfamiliar bush, shadowed by mist and whatever might be lurking behind it. They start at a shot – but it turns out to be one of their own, Te Wheke, who appears as a rescuer, showing the way to safety ('we are in my country now'). But now Te Wheke finds his own unit has attacked his village and slaughtered his people; his fellow soldiers find that Te Wheke is their ally no longer. In these brief scenes, trust and allegiances shift dizzyingly back and forth and certainties falter.

From this disturbed beginning, crosscultural dealings are ambiguous, uneasy and seldom quite what they seem. Williamson deals trustingly with a Māori trader, speaking to him in Māori; but the trader, as he offers him a carved lizard, tells Williamson that when the lizard smiles, 'death is not far away'. Williamson hesitates, but accepts – and later passes the smiling lizard on as a gift to his beloved Emily. Even when Te Wheke arrives to demand ammunition, Williamson maintains his confidence in his dealings with Māori. Not until the death of Emily and the destruction of his household does he understand that such robust faith in his place in the colonial world is awry.

From this point he is pathologically, comically mistrustful, issuing warnings that no one believes (although they should). In a countercurrent to Scott's interracial friendships and love affair, trust between Māori and Pākehā is destabilised through Williamson.

The underlying rumble of unease and misplaced trust is an unsettling dimension of the film: it confronted post-1981 audiences with an imagined past that echoed the interracial uncertainties that the Springbok Tour had exposed. With the exceptions of the naively likeable Scott, the anarchic Williamson and the bold Emily, its Pākehā characters are in the main not very appealing, especially in their attitudes and behaviour towards Māori, whose rationale for resistance is made obvious. The Māori characters frequently provide a countering point of view: 'He thinks it's his land!' Te Wheke shouts mockingly to his followers as Williamson warns him off the property.

Wiremu comments repeatedly on the uncertainty of allegiance. Indeed, the Scott–Wiremu alliance may be forged in the campaign against Te Wheke, but it is grounded as much in their shared opposition to the colonel and the contemptuous racism he represents. In their first conversation, Wiremu's sly suggestion that the earl who gave Scott his gun was 'just like the colonel, ne?' provokes Scott to respond 'Yes, quite. No, not actually. He was nothing like him. He was quite a decent chap.' As the troops arrive at Williamson's farm after Te Wheke's attack, Williamson asks just who he can trust:

Williamson: How can you tell they're not his men?
Wiremu: I can tell.
Williamson: How can we tell you're not one of them?
Wiremu: You can't.

Utu: Redux (2013): Who can you trust?

TOP: The carved lizard comes with a warning, but in the first image Williamson (Bruno Lawrence) is still confident that the trader is a friend. CENTRE: After his house has been torched and his wife killed, a now-suspicious Williamson challenges Wiremu (Wī Kuki Kaa) 'How can we tell you're not one of them?'. Wiremu's reply – 'You can't' – is far from reassuring. BOTTOM: At the back of the church, two 'parishioners' know something the minister doesn't.

As the friendship between Wiremu and Scott grows, Wiremu prompts Scott to rethink his own position and Wiremu's: whose side are they on? is the enduring question. 'Same side as you sir. I was born here too', is Wiremu's elusive answer as they ride to Te Puna. A chess game between Wiremu and the colonel is another example of the film's ambiguous handling of Wiremu. Relaxed and confident as he plays, the colonel is surprised to find himself in check: Wiremu has closed in unnoticed. Wiremu's game is prophetic as, at the end of the film, he sacrifices first the colonel, and then Te Wheke – a piece from each side – to reach checkmate. This gives the final scene an underlying tone distinct from that in 'A Bush Court Martial' which, despite the kinship between Heretaunga and Te Ahuru, maintained a tidy separation of Māori into 'loyal' and 'rebellious'.

For most of the film Wiremu has the appearance of a minor character, sidekick to Scott as protagonist: he moves from margin to centre frame only at the final revelation. *Utu* plays on audience expectations that it will be the white officer Scott or the white rogue male Williamson who brings about the resolution; the film's references to *Macbeth* may prime savvy viewers to anticipate that Williamson (widowed by Te Wheke's attack on his home and resolute in his pursuit of Te Wheke thereafter)

TOP: *Utu: Redux* (2013): Lit by the fires around the bush campsite, the constabulary, both Māori and Pākehā, watch as Te Wheke's trial begins. The scene echoes the setting and the drama of James Cowan's 'A Bush Court Martial'.

BOTTOM: *Utu: Redux* (2013): Wiremu (Wī Kuki Kaa) accords Te Wheke the respect of a warrior's death.

Utu: Redux (2013): Tears at the beginning and the end of the film link its dual tragedies. LEFT: The face of Te Wheke, as he is precipitated into his campaign of utu: finding his village a smoking ruin and his people dead, he shoots one of his fellow soldiers. 'I cannot live this life. I would rather die.' RIGHT: The face of Wiremu, as he kills his brother and ends Te Wheke's campaign.

is lining up to be the avenging Macduff of the story. But – as Wiremu's unexpected checkmate has perhaps intimated – this plot is to be resolved by Māori. If Murphy had reshaped 'A Bush Court Martial' and given it a backstory, its resolution on Māori terms was the core element of what he took through to the film's dénouement. And in fact, as Kenneth Marc Harris explains, the film persistently undermines its candidates for a Western-style 'white-hat' hero. Scott's heroic credentials are repeatedly deflated, and nor can Williamson, undermined by his own excesses, claim heroic stature.[50] Finally, *Utu*'s Macduff turns out to be Wiremu, whose identity and therefore his capacity for resolution become apparent only at the point where he puts that capacity into effect. Just as Macduff is revealed, late, to be 'not of woman born' and therefore capable of finishing off Macbeth, Wiremu is revealed as Te Wheke's brother and therefore capable of ending the conflict. As the Pākehā step back and fall silent, he steps forward and speaks up – and from this point he is the dominant figure.

Wiremu voices the desire of everyone involved for the fighting to end, and it is here especially that he seems to embody the post-1981 moment. His speech – towards which the entire film has been heading – realigns the film's central drama. The tragedy that has been building, *Macbeth*-like, around Te Wheke as an increasingly desperate and ruthless flawed hero, has until now concealed the second tragedy: the first concerns the price of resistance, but the second centres on the price of alliance with the Crown. The resistance drama has hurtled to its tragic conclusion in fast-paced action; now the quieter but enduring tragedy of surviving in the colonial world is spelled out as Wiremu farewells his brother, leans towards him in a hongi, and fires the shot that kills him. In the final close-up the two tragedies converge: the tear on Wiremu's face might remind us of the parallel image from the precipitating moment of Te Wheke's campaign, as he stands in the smoking village with tear-stained face.

Where *The Te Kooti Trail* situates 'friendly' Māori and Māori-affiliated Pākehā at the centre of the film and the centre of the nation-building enterprise, *Utu* replaces these affectionate founding bonds with a more complicated and far more discomforting set of relationships. The creation of friendships involves negotiation, changing perspectives and unlearning assumptions, against a background of ambiguities, shifting affiliations and, for Māori, the higher price of sacrifice.

So the film shifts from an action drama between resistant Māori and colonial forces, to revealing the rifts among Māori through the late phases of the wars, as well as telling a shadow story about the fracturing of contemporary Aotearoa and especially the ruptures over the tour. It enacts alliances and divisions along racial issues but also across racial lines, contending for a change in the way that these issues, both historical and contemporary, are understood.

Reception

The press were interested in *Utu* right through its production. Partly this was because they connected its subject to the contemporary unrest, and partly because of the spectacular box-office success of *Goodbye Pork Pie* ('Pork Pie man to make epic on Maori Wars', was the headline in the Rotorua *Daily Post*). What would its director do next? The interest was also a result of well-crafted publicity: the makers of *Utu* let no opportunity slip, capitalising on the edgy appeal of Zac Wallace's jail time – he featured in many promotional stories – and the uneasiness of race relations post-1981.[51] Months before the shoot, Murphy (easily Hayward's equal as a showman) was throwing out tasters: 'However we do it *Utu* is bound to be controversial as the plot is set around a racial conflict many wish to forget. Some people are going to hate it. Some are going to love it. I'm just going to shoot it.'[52] Preston's *Making Utu* was timed to air on TV2 in January 1983, a fortnight before the film was released.

Several reporters had access to the set. They described Murphy's Kiwi style of filmmaking, and the views of local Māori, including the young Rastas who played Te Wheke's followers and who, like Wallace, were a popular choice for newspaper images. The scene in which Te Wheke ate the vicar's eyes had been deleted after Malcolm and Mita's concern over the way it was done, but it was useful publicity anyway. Some reporters bought the story that it was removed because it was far too gory for public viewing: 'Viewing the rushes, the crew agreed the scene was quite horrendous. As retching rent the air, Mr Murphy decided that New Zealand was not ready for such virtuosity.'[53] While the film was in production, commentators worried that it might exacerbate racial tension after the tour. What stance would it take? Would it inflame existing tensions? An expectation that it would contribute to contemporary debate is implied in a report that Hiwi Tauroa, the race relations conciliator, had previewed the film during production and thought 'it would probably make people of both races sit back and think and then discuss matters raised'.[54]

Reviews fell into several categories. New Zealand reviewers ranged from expert to amateur: many still thought of the western as a debased popular genre, and most underestimated *Utu*'s complexity and sophistication. Murphy's reputation, after the larrikin masculinity of *Pork Pie*, may have led them to look only for action and comedy. Some reviewers assumed an air of superiority and dished out faint praise: the *Nelson*

Evening Mail's David Manning gave a considered analysis but claimed it was often 'tedious': perhaps older Māori would find it emotionally stirring, he thought, but most viewers would be unmoved. 'Utu – entertaining yet rotten at the core', was the title of Nicholas Reid's sketchy review in the *Auckland Star*; he missed the wit and summed the film up as 'a diverting show once you recognise it as hokum'. Marc Knowles was more even-handed, but concluded the film was 'an interesting step, but as things turn out … no great leap forward'. David Lawrence for the *New Zealand Herald* found it 'fairly realistic drama relieved with fairly funny humour'; he praised the score, setting and acting, but labelled it pretentious and 'full of sound and fury, signifying not much' (he was one of several critics who drew on this line from *Macbeth*).[55] The film's use of western generic codes drew fire: to read the reviews now is to realise that Sergio Leone's films had not yet achieved the critical respect they enjoy today, at least not in Aotearoa.

There were positive local reviews, too. Bob Williams in the *Evening Standard* liked the performances and the film's exploration of historical complexity. Erica Short watched the film at a premiere screening in Napier: she disliked its western elements but rated it 'a superb piece of film-making', and she told readers, 'if you do not go to see Utu you will be at risk of overlooking a cultural benchmark'. She agreed with the person she overheard saying 'the best bits were the Maori bits', and she loved 'hearing Maori spoken as a living language'. Rob White for the *Christchurch Star* gave a balanced and careful review in which he recognised the strength of the film's appeal as either adventure or something more philosophical – either way, 'New Zealanders can be honestly proud' of it. Aline Sandilands' longer review for the *Otago Daily Times* was assured in its praise of Wallace ('breathtaking'), Lawrence ('eminently watchable'), and the photography and score. Rejecting earlier reviews that 'criticised Utu for being a Maori western – a somewhat general put-down which means very little,' she concluded that *Utu* was 'a film that's made with dedication, commitment, even passion. It's a film to be proud of.' She hoped, forlornly, that Murphy would not head to Hollywood: 'his would be the biggest loss of all'.[56] Bill Gosden's review was astute and, even while it contained criticisms, very enthusiastic.[57]

Māori critics were divided. The fact that *Utu* was released at a time when there was a rising demand for Māori to make their own films shaped several of their responses. Wī Kuki Kaa himself, after the film's release, reportedly endorsed it as 'the ultimate beginning' rather than the ultimate film; he hoped to see Māori more centrally involved in future filmmaking;[58] but Sylvia Kaa recalls now that 'he talked so much about the film. He loved that film.'[59] Ripeka Evans, writing for *Broadsheet*, condemned the film at length for what she saw as its 'white myths of Maori savagery', and pronounced it 'a racist and sexist Cowboys and Indians style film … Utu proves that whites will make films for whites, and only Maori can make films for Maori.' Protestors at the Napier premiere objected to a film they thought would be a '"white man's version" of Maori history'. Keith Aberdein recalled that Murphy 'took some flak for *Utu*' as younger Māori started saying, 'hey you buggers, stop making our stories'; he recalled Murphy's response that 'they were our stories too.'[60] These critiques echoed a wider national disquiet. Around this time Michael King was criticised for writing Māori history, as a move for Māori authority on these subjects gained ground.

In a substantial opinion piece for the *Dominion* a fortnight after the film's release, Witi Ihimaera wrote:

Utu in 1870 is Waitangi in 1983. It is New Zealand under stress today. It is one of only three New Zealand films in our history which might truly be said to have arrived at the right time to reflect the kind of people we are, where we've come from, where we seem to be heading, and how. It is a watershed film, and it stands alongside Rudall Hayward's sound version of Rewi's Last Stand *and Roger Donaldson's* Sleeping Dogs *in its exploration of the dimensions of the New Zealand Way.*

Ihimaera was unhappy with the generic western influences; he was happier with sequences he saw as 'pure Kurosawa', including the final scene, which he discusses at length. He was ambivalent about both Te Wheke and Wiremu – he wondered whether there were apologist elements to them – but he found it valuable that the film explored the 'shifting loyalties and sympathies' of Māori as both 'rebels' and 'loyalists', and that it cast these ambiguities as tragedy. Like other Māori critics he concluded the film was 'still a pakeha view of pakeha history in New Zealand. We still have to make our own film about ourselves and the reality of the Maori experience in Aotearoa.'[61]

Stephen (Tipene) O'Regan, although he saw some of the colonial roles as stereotypical, was more positive: he criticised some earlier reviews for failing to confront history with competence and confidence. More than any other contemporary critic O'Regan saw *Utu* as both product of and contribution to its cultural moment:

Perhaps its most important commentary on [Maori–Pakeha] relations lies in its treatment of the ambivalence with which Maoris and Pakehas view each other. The film constantly teases our stereotypes of each other to the point where it is difficult to say which is the Pakeha 'side' and which the Maori. Both the story itself and the recurring humour combine to provoke our awareness of ourselves and our own attitudes. At another level they combine to irritate our simple conceptions of New Zealand history and, in particular, the phase of guerilla war which followed the Land Wars of the later 19th century.

O'Regan was one of few critics to understand the character of Wiremu, and Kaa's qualifications for a role:

… almost designed for his bicultural and bilingual depth. He portrays as few actors could the ambivalences and contradictions of the Maori experience. In his own life he knows them, understands their presence. His grasp of the nature of Maoriness informs his performance.[62]

Writing for the journal of the Post Primary Teachers' Association, O'Regan – then a teachers' college lecturer – concluded that *Utu* would be a valuable teaching film for secondary school history, particularly if teachers screened it alongside Hayward's films for comparison.

Although international audiences watched a different and poorer cut (as noted below), reviews from the United States and France gave the film higher praise than New Zealand critics had. The influential French festival director Pierre-Henri Deleau thought highly of it, and the countercultural magazine *Actuel* ran a long feature review.[63] Many regional American newspapers carried enthusiastic reviews. But *New Yorker* reviewer Pauline Kael, the queen of US film reviewing at the time, produced the pièce de résistance – and no one associated with *Utu* has ever forgotten it. Her long assessment was lavish in its praise, and – unlike any other contemporary reviewer – she took the film's use of the western seriously. Making reference to the *Te Maori* exhibition that opened in New York on almost the same day as *Utu*'s release there, she linked the film closely to its historical setting and offered an astute analysis:

Mimicry goes on at so many levels in this horror comedy of colonialism that the viewer may be laughing, exhilarated by

The poster for *Utu: Redux*, restored, re-edited and re-released in 2013. Courtesy of Geoff Murphy and Graeme Cowley

constant discovery, yet be a little discombobulated and scared … I doubt if any other director has treated the conventions of this colonial-epic form with Murphy's off-hand audacity … Murphy and his co-writer, Keith Aberdein, skewer your expectations, and you think, Of course, it's richer this way.

Kael commented frequently on Murphy's direction and how it encouraged an open viewer response:

Probably what Murphy does that makes a viewer respond so freely is that he distances us – very slightly – and makes comedy out of the distancing. (He's a joshing, razzing director.) And because we're not asked to respond in the banal ways that action-adventure movies usually impose on us – there's no one we could conceivably root for – we're free to respond to much more. We're turned loose inside this epic, and the freedom is strange and pleasurable.[64]

Aftermath: four codas

There were, in the end, three versions of *Utu*, although only one has been discussed here. The producers recut the film for the international release, and reordered the narrative so that it was structured as a series of flashbacks cut into the trial scene. The resulting film was confusing (as several international reviews pointed out), and the altered plotting, by beginning with the end of Te Wheke's story, tipped the sympathy away from the lead character from the outset. This second cut has often been referred to as the 'director's cut' – perversely, as Murphy had nothing to do with it.

The third *Utu* is a much more recent production: *Utu: Redux* (2013). After its initial theatrical release the film was released on video and DVD in both the original and 'director's cuts'; it became a staple of university film courses and part of the canon of New Zealand cinema. It screened several times on television. But while its reputation rose, the quality of the print had declined. One of the television screenings shocked the film's cinematographer, Graeme Cowley, who found himself watching a film he didn't recognise. When he realised it was a seriously faded version of the 'director's cut' he contacted Murphy and *Utu*'s editor Mike Horton, and they raised funds for restoration of the original film. Luckily, as Murphy noted, it had been shot on Fuji film: it was new at the time, and they selected it because it had a reputation for being 'good with greens'. The quality of the original had held up, although it was no easy task to put it together again after the 'director's cut'. The restoration was a substantial project involving Murphy, Cowley and Horton and the skilled assistance – much given gratis, in a mark of industry respect for the film – of the post-production company Park Road Post. The film was reedited – it became nine minutes tighter in the process – and Murphy considers this version the best of the three. Its resurrection as *Utu: Redux* drew people who had been involved in the film, and many from its first audiences, back to watch the new film: *Utu* had itself become an artefact of cultural memory, a marker of a historical moment that people wanted to share in recalling.

*

Like *The Governor*, *Utu* provided opportunities for Māori to develop filmmaking experience. Merata Mita, already a filmmaker, learned about feature film and went on to make *Mauri* (1988). Lee Tamahori, promoted from boom operator to first assistant director on *Utu*, went on to direct *Once Were Warriors* (1994) and other films in Hollywood and back in Aotearoa (*Mahana* was released in 2016). Zac Wallace starred in *Mauri*, but sadly, neither he nor Tania Bristowe stayed in

Making Utu (1983): As the troops file out across the tussock, Preston and Bollinger turn their lens on Zac Wallace joking around, sending Tom Poata into fits of laughter: 'Well I reckon we should first of all get your other bullet, eh? Get your third bullet, we got a chance! I've only got two left!'

the industry. Wī Kuki Kaa's well-established career continued, mostly overseas and mostly playing brown people who were not Māori – but he returned for *River Queen*. Tom Poata wrote the screenplay for *Ngāti* (1987), and played Sam in *Wild Horses* (1984).[65]

*

One dimension of the aftermath of *Utu* changed the landscape for historical film in New Zealand. Preston's remarks on what made *Utu* possible at all are highly pertinent here:

I think what changed the film far more than 81 was the tax environment that meant you could sit in your little hut in

Waimārama and you could have that kind of vision and believe that a film like that could actually be made, because there was a way of financing it, without having to fill it with American stars. I mean that's the brilliant moment, to me as a filmmaker, the brilliant moment of Utu *... but it's also a very sad moment because I know what happened next.*⁶⁶

What happened next was that the tax shelter, which had been discovered and exploited by international production companies to a degree that could not be sustained, was not simply adjusted to keep out opportunistic overseas interests but was removed altogether by 1984.⁶⁷ Once it was gone, the possibilities of a national film culture changed: smaller-scale dramas were feasible, but large-scale historical film could only be made with an international budget, and with the kinds of constraints that international financing placed on production. *Utu* was the child of an important moment, but it was born of economic circumstances that have not recurred since.

*

Utu lives on in the hearts and minds of New Zealanders. In 2016 TVNZ's *Marae* programme ran a story on Zac Wallace who had come home at last after years in Australia, partly as a result of the premiere of *Utu Redux* in 2013. The story is absorbing in itself, but the responses it generated were especially telling – and moving. They revealed how deeply Wallace's role in *Utu* affected people, especially Māori, who saw the film in 1983 or who have watched it since, and how Wallace went on from *Utu* to gain a voice among Māori. The story attracted an astounding 643 comments, including the following.

I take my hat off to you Zac you've been there done that and you yourself know what it's like to survive. Kia ora mate atua koe e taiki e manaaki koe amene.

I love the movie Utu and still have a copy which I watched a few months ago ... I always wondered what happened to Zac Wallace ... Thank you bro for sharing your story and your long suffering hurt with us ... Welcome back home!! Much Aroha xxxx.

I can stop wondering as to whatever happened to Zac Wallace. He was the epitome of a fearful Maori renegade in UTU.

I went to the premiere. I was like 15 years old. I will never forget it, I dropped my jaffas on the wooden floor, lols. I said 'Oh No', they rolled on the wooden floor for ages & the whole cinema cracked up laughing. It was right before the start of the movie, lols ... You scared the Beegesus outta me, all of us I think. Your imbuement of Te Wheke was stunningly gripping.

Loved you when visiting my high school Otahuhu College ... was prob the only time school had meaning for me ... Had your paper clipping in my friendship book for many many years. Welcome home warrior – you have been missed. Arohanui xx.

I remember telling my dad I watched and loved the movie 'Utu'. Our teacher took us to the picture theatre in Kaikohe when the movie first came out.

Always had my own copy of Utu ... made sure my two watched it and they loved it too.

DOCUMENTARY ADVENTURES
The New Zealand Wars

I don't think anyone, except a handful of people, and they would be those who were involved with the making of New Zealand Wars, *expected it to rate in any way.* —Whai Ngata

On the 8.05 unit to Upper Hutt the pakeha conductor is intently quizzing the Maori train driver about Maori military strategy. —Paul Diamond

In 1998 TV One screened a five-part documentary series called *The New Zealand Wars*. Historian narrator James Belich pitched the wars as ripping yarns, hooking Māori and Pākehā viewers into stories that many now knew nothing about, and provoking angry responses from a vocal few. 'Great guns! It's our history – and we're hooked' ran one headline; 'a puerile and slanted commentary' wrote a less enchanted viewer.[1] The series' startling success on first release led to further television screenings on TV One and more recently on Māori Television, and a long public afterlife through DVD sales, high-school and university history classes, art galleries, museums and online streaming.

The series' origin story exemplifies the interconnected character of screen and written history. At the end of his third year of a degree in which he had studied no New Zealand history, Belich's interest was flagging and he wasn't sure he would go back to do his honours year. Then, in the summer of 1976–77 when he got that labouring job on the set of *The Governor*:

> one of the first things we did was build what I discovered was the pā at Ruapekapeka, and so my first encounter with the New Zealand Wars was to actually build, to physically dig one of these pā and I was quite amazed … they were just different from my expectations. It was very much a trench with a firing step – and they were working from reasonably accurate historical charts – and it was much more of an earthwork than a hill fort and so I was quite amazed by this and started reading … James Cowan's New Zealand Wars *and became interested in the New Zealand Wars as a consequence of that work. So it was actually TV labouring, rather than history, that got me into the New Zealand Wars …*[2]

He went back to university, wrote his honours dissertation on the New Zealand Wars and an MA on Tītokowaru's War, and continued to Oxford where he did a PhD tracing the history of the conflicts within the context of Victorian racial ideologies. The PhD was revised for publication as *The New Zealand Wars and the Victorian Interpretation of Racial Conflict* (1986), and Belich then turned back to the subject of his MA in another book, *I Shall Not Die: Tītokowaru's War, New Zealand 1868–1869* (1989). Both books sold well and attracted public attention through reviews and debate. There were discussions about making a documentary:

Some people were talking about it as a possibility after they'd read the thesis, but then it kind of died. I did the book ... I put in some sort of proposal to TV, but there was absolutely no response, and so although I was interested in doing a TV series and a few other people were ... basically TVNZ wasn't interested.[3]

Around this time, television producer Colin McRae happened upon Ken Burns' American series, *The Civil War*. Fascinated by the way the series had been made, he began turning over ideas about how some of its techniques – panning and zooming across historical images to generate a sense of a living past, voiceover narration of letters and diaries, the multiple voices reflecting many perspectives on the war, and the music of the era – might be applied in relation to the New Zealand past. He now approached Belich, and they assembled a production team for a proposed series. Whai Ngata, manager of Māori broadcasting at TVNZ, put McRae in touch with Tainui Stephens, who would become the director of *The New Zealand Wars*.[4]

The 1990s: deregulation, the Treaty and biculturalism

In 1989 government undertook a radical deregulation of broadcasting as part of the neoliberal reforms of government departments initiated by the fourth Labour government. In the process, as Trisha Dunleavy and Hester Joyce explain, most of TVNZ's inhouse production systems, including for drama and documentary, were dismantled and replaced by a system of commissioning through competitive bidding by independent production companies. The change broadened the field of talent and ideas and promoted creative competition. A funding body for local programming was set up, the Broadcasting Commission (which quickly changed its name to NZ On Air). The system had inherent internal tensions. On the one hand, NZ On Air's remit was to support programming that would 'reflect and develop New Zealand culture' and 'the commercially fragile areas of drama, documentary and comedy', and 'to ensure the production of specialised programmes for children and specified minorities'. On the other hand it had to 'reconcile the level of funding invested in a given TV project with the size of the audience anticipated for it as a completed programme': that is, it had to keep its eye on the balance sheet.[5] This dual responsibility to cultural development and ratings had implications for the selection process, but also for the production process if bids were to succeed.

Inhouse production of drama and documentary ceased, and the independent companies competed for programming slots from the networks and funding from NZ On Air. As Roger Horrocks shows, there was a dramatic increase in the production of both drama and documentary between 1988 and 1996.[6] The proliferation of creativity was nevertheless hobbled by a decision-making process controlled at key points by network executives required to deliver ratings. Dunleavy and Joyce explain:

Although it remained possible for producers to simply 'pitch' a good idea to a commissioning executive, production would most often be a schedule-driven process, initiated by the channel programmers. After identifying the gaps for new local programmes, networks would communicate these to the production sector, as the first phase of programme creation.[7]

From there, producers would put tailored proposals to network executives for approval, and only once the broadcaster's commitment was secured could proposals be assessed for NZ

On Air funding. That is, 'the commercial requirements of the broadcaster would need to be reconciled with the cultural objectives of NZoA'. The network would retain editorial authority through to the relatively late stage of the rough cut.[8]

Despite the ostensible commitment to freeing up the creatives, this was a very risk-averse funding environment, and it narrowed at one point of decision-making – broadcaster approval – so that it was concentrated in very few hands. The network programmers wanted ratings certainty, and anything novel was something untested: as McRae put it, 'broadcasters generally put on television tonight what worked last night'.[9] What this meant in practice was that a limited range of documentary styles emerged. Roger Horrocks points out that the appeal to a broad audience, accessibility, a personal story and an emotionally engaging tone were the ingredients of the low-risk programming that could be made on minimal budgets: this was already a departure from the visionary aims of documentary as 'a vehicle for the delivery of cultural rights'.[10] Yet in 1995–96, Horrocks argues, the emphasis on commercial programming increased and broadcasters were far more reluctant to commission documentaries.[11] Mary Debrett notes that in 1998, the same year that *The New Zealand Wars* screened, 'there were ten documentaries fronted by well-known personalities. Seven of these were comedians.'[12] She argues that the process worked against diversity:

> *Several producers also noted it was common knowledge that broadcasters regarded Maori faces as an audience turnoff, an awareness that served as a disincentive to filmmakers to explore Maori subjects ...[but] when NZOA imposed a minimum Maori content requirement, Maori and Pacific Islanders tended to be represented as sports heroes, offered as role models for at-risk youth, or as criminals sharing regrets ...*[13]

It could hardly have been more different than the early experimental, financially unconstrained (many would say undisciplined) environment that had produced *The Killing of Kane*, *The Governor* and *Tangata Whenua*, all of which had been leaps into the unknown; the last two were initiated by their creators, and all were made possible by the willingness of the broadcaster to extend a high level of trust in the judgement of the creators.

In this unlikely climate McRae and Belich built a case for a high-end documentary series with many Māori faces. Whai Ngata's support at TVNZ was pivotal: as associate producer on the series and an influential insider he became an informal kaitiaki for the production team, ensuring that doors were opened and helping with iwi liaison. McRae presented *The Civil War* to TVNZ as a successful translation of history to the screen,[14] but he believes that TVNZ was more persuaded by some unexpected competition: it became known that TV3 would put in a proposal for a series on the wars at the same time. At this point it became apparent that a slice of NZ On Air's budget would likely go to a New Zealand Wars series, and it would go either to TNVZ or TV3: now, TVNZ was very interested. NZ On Air granted both initial proposals $20,000 to develop a full proposal, and in the end the McRae/Belich proposal was the successful one. They were granted $1,246,000 in June 1994 – the largest NZ On Air grant given that year.[15] It was an outcome distinctly against the run of play.

Since *Utu*'s release in 1983, no substantial documentary or fiction feature on the subject of the country's colonial conflicts had appeared. One series called *Pounamu* profiling Māori leaders including Te Kooti Arikirangi, Te Whiti o Rongomai, Tohu Kākahi and Te Ruki Kawiti, among others, screened as part of the 150th anniversay of the Treaty in 1990. Shown as part of the Sunday morning Marae slot, however, it received little publicity.[16] In this 15-year gap, in the wake of the fervent years around 1981, the bicultural landscape had changed dramatically. From 1985 the Waitangi Tribunal was able to investigate historic claims going back to 1840. This amendment created the tribunal we now know, and opened the way for hundreds of claims by iwi throughout the country, a substantial if incomplete return of wealth to iwi, and formal acknowledgements of historic injustices. Many of these claims related to land confiscated as a result of colonial conflict.[17] In 1987, Claudia Orange's history *The Treaty of Waitangi* appeared: a scholarly book that sold remarkably well to general readers – even more so than Belich's history of the wars. Its initial success prompted more accessible editions – an illustrated and a shortened edition, and then books on the Treaty by other scholars.[18] The books were used in schools, and Orange's analysis of the Treaty made its way into government policy and practice as well as gaining a high public profile. Over the 1980s and 90s, the Treaty's status shifted from historical curiosity to being recognised as the nation's founding document.

Political and legal changes were accompanied by broader cultural shifts. The Patea Maori Club's song 'Poi E', a sensation in 1982, opened up some mainstream space for Māori and Pasifika artists. Efforts to stem the erosion of te reo Māori included the Kōhanga Reo ('language nest') movement that emerged in the early 1980s. Māori became an official language of Aotearoa in 1987, and Māori words became more common in everyday New Zealand English – even as the number of first-language speakers of te reo was dropping.[19] Recognition of Māori as tangata whenua gained traction in Pākehā worlds. In a series of incremental shifts, Māori were ceasing to be ceremonial add-ons to public life and were becoming a fundamental part of its fabric.

The Waitangi Tribunal generated a lot of activity: government institutions, research units investigating historical claims for iwi and Crown, and an expanding field of legal activity and expertise. Some Pākehā, watching the development of Treaty history and judgments, saw the process of redress as long overdue, and some altered their ideas of justice for land claimants as the changes unfolded. Others, though, were horrified at what they saw as a 'grievance industry' pouring an endless stream of money into Māori hands. They resented the language of partnership and the introduction of te reo Māori into the institutions they dealt with in their daily lives. Terms for these responses emerged – 'Treaty backlash' or 'Treaty fatigue'.

Nevertheless, over this period most Pākehā came to think of themselves as a Pacific people rather than a far-flung European outpost: 'Anchor me,' sang Don McGlashan and the Muttonbirds in 1994, 'in the middle of your deep blue sea.' The question here centred on the terms of belonging: through the 1980s and 90s, just how Pākehā 'belonged' came under scrutiny. John Newton argues that the more frequent use of 'Pākehā' as a self-descriptor signifies a willingness to embrace an identity in relation to Māori.[20] But the shift was contentious, and while 'Pākehā' became the norm for most younger people, for some – mostly older and more conservative people – the word was a flashpoint.

Despite growing familiarity with the Treaty as the tribunal produced reports on historic and contemporary claims, public knowledge about the wars – the origin of many of the historic claims – did not grow at the same rate. Most of the historical scholarship was corralled into the Treaty process and specialised historiographic debate; it was not designed for and did not extend to a wider audience. Belich's *I Shall Not Die*, a popular history of Tītokowaru's War aimed at secondary school students, was an effort to bridge this gap. It sold reasonably well but did not have the reach he was hoping for. School teachers told him: 'Kids don't read books. Write a 30-page pamphlet.'[21] Maurice Shadbolt's fictional trilogy based on the historical figures of Hōne Heke, Kimble Bent and Te Kooti was published between 1986 and 1993. Like Belich, Shadbolt avoided pathos: both writers recognised that it was easier to engage readers with excitement than with laments. Shadbolt's novels sold relatively well, but New Zealand fiction had a limited readership.

In contrast to this limited purchase of the wars on national memory, there was growing public interest in the commemoration of the world wars: more and more people attended Anzac Day ceremonies and there was intensive media coverage on the day. In this context it is not surprising that the strong reviews and sales of Belich's *New Zealand Wars* did not result in acceptance of the first proposals for a documentary. Nineteenth-century battles did not translate into late twentieth-century ratings, the television executives told him.

But as it turned out, they did.

Book

Belich wrote his doctorate in England using archival sources in the Public Records Office in London – mostly the reports and communications of empire and colony, parliamentary records and newspapers – and with a focus on the period when imperial troops were in New Zealand. His book, *The New Zealand Wars and the Victorian Interpretation of Racial Conflict* (1986), extended his thesis to include the later 'self-reliant period' – the late 1860s and beyond. *The New Zealand Wars*, although it was challenged on certain points,[22] was an ingenious and compelling book, and it transformed historical understanding of the wars.

Belich argued that the British and colonial campaigns in New Zealand were carried out largely in the light of a racial ideology that assumed that Māori were not capable of offering effective resistance to the British army. The British planned and fought their campaigns accordingly, and their military reports – and, in turn, the wider public view – reflected this belief that Māori were a primitive people who would inevitably be overcome by a more innovative civilisation and its industrial technologies. Belich argued that the British suffered defeats as a result of these ideological blinkers, and that they sometimes then reported defeats as victories since they were unable to comprehend or acknowledge defeat. In a broader sense, he was also making the case – as Cowan, Sinclair, Ward and others had done earlier, although most Pākehā had forgotten it by the 1980s – that the wars were pivotal events in New Zealand history.

Belich declared upfront that this was a revisionist history. It differed from earlier 'sympathetic' histories, such as Dick Scott's *Ask That Mountain*, in its methods – Belich used official sources to demonstrate the ideological limitations of government and military – and in its arguments. In crediting Māori resistance with agency and effectiveness, Belich questioned the perception of Māori as victims that Scott, despite his sympathies, had tended to consolidate, and that *The Governor*, a decade earlier, had also taken for granted – although *Utu*, with its canny antihero Te Wheke, had not. Belich argued that a series of Māori generals had out-strategised and out-engineered the British; and that leaders like Kawiti and Tītokowaru had used their knowledge of the foreigners against them, anticipating their moves and outwitting them more often than had been acknowledged.

Although he did not put it in these terms, Belich's argument was a revision of the conception of Māori masculinity: he replaced the stereotype of the 'savage' Māori warrior with a clever fighter who, through rapid innovation in military intelligence and engineering, could often defeat a larger and better-armed force. Drawing on British plans of defensive fortifications made in the aftermath of battles, he argued that Māori engineers had developed what he termed 'the modern pā' in response to the arrival of more and more effective firepower. First muskets and cannons, then guns with longer range and greater accuracy, had prompted Māori defenders to design sophisticated earthworks and stronger bunkers.

Book to television

Once McRae and Belich had secured funding for a documentary series, the academic history derived largely from British archives now migrated to a different medium, different sources and different sites. A single-author text became a multi-authored one as many people – especially Māori from iwi affected by the wars and often descendants of participants in the wars – contributed to the narrative. A history based on documents was informed by oral history and pictorial archives. A written text acquired image and sound. A story linked to places only by words was now narrated from the very landscapes that had been at stake, and with the collaboration of the mana whenua of those places. Belich himself became familiar with places and people he had only read about. Television, in short, changed the history.

The core production crew consisted of a small group who multi-tasked in the 'Kiwi way', all hands to the deck: Belich was scriptwriter and narrator, McRae was producer but also undertook a massive search for historical images, Stephen Ellis was the designer, and Tainui Stephens (Te Rārawa), a classically trained musician, was director and responsible for sound design. Like McRae, Stephens had seen *The Civil War* and was impressed by its style of telling history, but he was cautious when he attended the first meeting. He had reservations about New Zealand productions modelled on international ones – he saw them as a failure of imagination. He also expected that, as had happened several times already, he would be 'the troubleshooter, the interpreter, the fixer-upper … in those relationships with Pākehā … and I was getting tired of that and I was interested in my own career'. But the team kicked off on a positive note:

> What impressed me about the meeting was them, both Colin and [Belich], acknowledging that they didn't know stuff, and that they were comfortable in their ignorance, and willing to learn, and sincerely, because the kaupapa, the cause was something that was important and they felt passionate about and so I felt … very comfortable about embarking on all that because I could quickly see that as a director, and it was going to be well resourced for the time, a new experience for me [laughs] – let's go for it!²³

The production team was committed to a very high standard and determined to do the history justice. They are still proud of the series' achievements.

In the process of reconstituting the book as a script, the historical account was shaped into five episodes, organised around five distinct phases of conflict. The scripts were drafted by Belich, and workshopped with script editor Marcia Russell.

The series begins in 1916: it places New Zealand's involvement in World War One alongside the last conflict of the New Zealand Wars – the police invasion of Rua Kēnana's settlement at Maungapōhatu. The camera moves from a misty Urewera landscape superimposed on a photograph of Rua Kēnana, to Belich's opening piece to camera. 'The main body of the New Zealand Wars took place between 1843 and 1872,'

Belich begins, in the expository mode that would become familiar to television viewers over the next five weeks:

My generation didn't learn much about them at school. What we did learn was a sanitised version, supporting New Zealand's reputation as a paradise of racial harmony. Yet the New Zealand Wars raged across the whole of the North Island for almost 30 years, with heroism and massacre on both sides ... They were New Zealand's great civil war, the grand clash of its two peoples.

The series started out as it meant to go on – with provocative and attention-grabbing revisionism. The message was articulated in the title of the first episode: 'The War that Britain Lost'. Most New Zealanders' knowledge about the Northern War of 1845–46 went little further than the theatrical flair of Hōne Heke's flagpole felling. The episode set that action in context, charting Heke's increasing unease about the implications of the Treaty of Waitangi and the good faith of the incoming Europeans. The attack on the flagstaff is shown to be less a kind of youthful prank than a well-articulated symbolic challenge: if the British could not protect their own flag, what did their sovereignty amount to?

The story of the war that followed was designed to upset the expectations of viewers. Heke, whose prevailing reputation marked him as flamboyantly rebellious – indeed, this is how *The Governor* had portrayed him – is characterised instead as a politically astute leader who is prescient about the longer-term implications of Pākehā settlement. Belich then brings in Te Ruki Kawiti, whom most Pākehā knew nothing at all about. Here a theme unfolds as Belich argues that, although Heke and Kawiti defeated the British in open battle at Puketutu, they recognised that this kind of battle against the British with their superior firepower would ultimately be ineffective, so they moved to devise other means of military opposition.

The New Zealand Wars (1998): Images of Māori leaders, such as this photograph of Wiremu Tāmihana Tarapīpipi Te Waharoa, accompany a narrative that showed them to be statesmen and strategists.

lexander Turnbull Library, Wellington, 1/2-053942-F. All frame enlargements from The New Zealand Wars, Landmark Productions, courtesy of Colin McRae

Belich explains Kawiti's innovations in two modern pā, Ōhaeawai and Ruapekapeka. He argues that the British underestimated the strength of Kawiti's defences at Ōhaeawai – exactly as Kawiti had planned. Waves of soldiers were launched at a deceptively strong pekerangi or palisade, defended by a garrison who emerged from the protection of underground bunkers to deliver devastating volleys of fire at the oncoming redcoats. Drawing viewers into the drama not only of triumphing underdogs but of historical debate, Belich argues that although the British blamed the defeat on an incompetent officer, their problem was not their own failure but the brilliance of their opposition – something they could not yet comprehend. Kawiti, he argues, was anticipating European developments in trench warfare by about 70 years.[24] Ōhaeawai was followed by further developments at Ruapekapeka, where a system of deep rua provided protection from bombardment.

Episode 1 posed the series' first decisive reversal of popular belief – and of some historical opinion. Māori were not, Belich argued, a naïve people with only hopelessly primitive means of resisting a technologically advanced invading force – in fact, it was the Māori who displayed the adaptiveness in these conflicts. Morever, Kawiti's talents encompassed both the engineering and the psychology of warfare. And – another unexpected conclusion – Māori came out ahead on points in the Northern War: they lost no land, and the British retreated to Auckland.

The war stories made for exciting television, but the historical argument driving the series – unpicking Victorian ideologies of race and showing how their residues continued into contemporary belief right up to viewers in the present day – was at least as provocative. A week later, when audiences had had time to digest this first onslaught on their ideas about the national history, and to discuss these military innovations with friends and workmates, Episode 2 added another feather in the cap of Māori achievement: politics.

The episode title, 'Kings and Empires', seemed at first glance a reference to Britain's expansion across the globe in the nineteenth century. But – echoing the expectation-and-ambush dynamic of the previous episode – the empire at the centre of the narrative turns out to be Te Rauparaha's, and the king is Pōtatau Te Wherowhero.

> In 1840, the lands as far as the eye could see were all part of an empire. The empire was not British, but Māori. Its emperor was the great Ngāti Toa chief Te Rauparaha, poet, warrior and the greatest empire builder of Māori history. Along with his formidable lieutenant Te Rangihaeata he fought for Māori independence in the face of settlers from another empire, Queen Victoria's Britain. Governors FitzRoy and Grey represented that other empire and the colonising attitudes which ultimately sentenced New Zealand to a quarter century of war.

The episode begins with the Wellington War: it follows Te Rauparaha, as the expansive imperialist of the period, in the course of his and Te Rangihaeata's conflicts over the New Zealand Company's land purchases. It then moves to the genesis of the Kīngitanga, where settlers put pressure on the government to purchase land in fertile Taranaki, provoking resistance from the growing landholding movement, and the return of the series' next politician – Wiremu Kīngi Te Rangitāke – to Taranaki. Tensions build in Taranaki and spread to allied iwi in Waikato and beyond, leading to the great hui that finally established Pōtatau Te Wherowhero as the Māori king in 1858. The episode continues the narrative of Māori strategy: it shows how Te Rauparaha expands his domain from the natural fortress of Kāpiti and how, when war breaks out in Taranaki, the British are defeated by the same strategy of apparently weak defences at Te Kohia and Puketakauere pā. Another innovation – the Māori practice of building provocative but expendable pā on sites that demanded attack, only to abandon them once the enemy had wasted manpower and resources on them – drove colonists from the countryside into New Plymouth, where many died of disease.

A narrative of statesmanship now entered the fray. Settler hunger for Taranaki land and a good harbour is stalled: 'between them and Waitara stood the Ati Awa chief Wiremu Kīngi Te Rangitāke' (Belich rolls out this name with emphasis: here is someone to be reckoned with). Kīngi negotiates with Governor Gore Brown over Waitara, but in the end reluctantly goes to war. Wiremu Tāmihana Tarapīpipi comes into the story, and from the start it's obvious he is a statesman. Rewi Maniapoto and the first two Māori kings, Pōtatau and Tāwhiao, make their appearance in this context of the emergence of a pan-Māori politics. Announcing the arrival of the Kīngitanga, Belich argues: 'What we have here I think is something quite close to the birth of a Māori people as against a collection of disunited tribes. This was as important to Māori politics as Kawiti's modern pā were to Māori warfare.'

By the end of the episode, more of the early European victories are shown up as paper victories, and the significance of Māori military and political achievements has been spelled out. Other historians – notably Sinclair – had already discussed these political developments, and the fourth episode of *The Governor* had portrayed the emergence of the Kīngitanga in a serious and sympathetic light, as had Barclay and King's *Tangata Whenua*. The points Belich makes were not completely novel, but they now acquired a compelling narrative impact.

The title of the third episode, 'The Invasion of the Waikato', made Belich's perspective on the Waikato War evident to any viewers who might still have been unsure exactly what General Cameron's advance south had been about. This episode placed less weight on upsetting viewer expectations – unless viewers had been expecting Governor Grey's historical reputation to retain its former gloss. It deals with Grey's efforts to quell the Kīngitanga, Cameron's part in that endeavour, and the Māori leaders, King Tāwhiao, Wiremu Tāmihana and Rewi Maniapoto, who resisted the British advance south. Belich made much of Grey's standing as the most devious among these figures, a man of secrets and lies who was quite capable of suing for peace while planning war, and not above sending misinformation to London in order to bring more troops to New Zealand. Cameron, Tāwhiao, Tāmihana and Rewi register as more honourable, straightforward historical figures. Belich revisits the historical reputations of Cameron (who had at times been considered overcautious; given his opponents, we are told, he had good reason to be careful) and Rewi, whose 'last stand' is examined toward the end of the episode. Oddly, the episode appears to steer away from the still contentious attack on Rangiāowhia, especially by comparison with the emphasis on this incident in *The Governor*.

Episode 4 takes up the story of the Taranaki warrior prophets, and the turn in the course of the wars that saw the rise of Pai Mārire and greater ferocity on both sides. Most of the second half of the episode deals with Tītokowaru, long a favourite subject for Belich and an exemplar of his arguments about Māori strategic innovation. Tītokowaru strikes terror into the troops and the settlers and confuses, deceives and entraps attacking armies, enabling his initially small force to inflict a resounding defeat on a well-trained and well-equipped force many times its size.

Episode 5, 'The East Coast Wars', dealt with the most confusing wars of all – in fact so complex are they that Belich's *New Zealand Wars* book set a large proportion of them aside as being outside its scope. It is a sequence of wars in which as many Māori fought with government as on the side of the resistance, meaning large iwi like Ngāti Porou were embroiled in civil war. The wars concluded with the police invasion of Maungapōhatu in 1916 – and the series now ends where it began.

In carving out five 50-minute episodes from a 400-page book, the script inevitably had to be selective. The series presented a broad overview of the wars, from the Wairau to Maungapōhatu, first shot to last. It covered every major theatre of war. Economies of time were made by concentrating selectively on some battles in each region, and shaping each episode according to themes that expressed Belich's major arguments about the wars and the ways they had been remembered. So, for example, the first war in Taranaki is given more attention than the second, and the decisive Māori victory at Puketakauere demonstrates evolving Māori strategy. The years leading up to the Waikato War and the long progression to the first major engagements are dealt with quite quickly. The Waikato episode (Episode 3) elaborates on the series of defences as the troops moved south, then on how a myth emerged around Ōrākau as a 'last stand'. Belich points out the atypical character of the pā there, and that it was not the 'last stand' of legend but was in fact followed by a protracted stand-off as Māori controlled the Rohe Pōtae, the King Country to the south of Ōrākau, until the early 1880s.

The New Zealand Wars (1998): The historian narrator, speaking from the landscape. Standing on the site of Ruapekapeka pā, James Belich explains Kawiti's strategy.

Telling the story

Belich projected a large onscreen personality and he attracted viewer attention. He was making a deliberately provocative case, arguing that the ways we had remembered our past, and therefore the ways we should understand our present, needed reassessing. It was almost inevitable, therefore, that Belich's own persona became a central component of the production, and that he would have much to say. He was declarative and intellectual: he drew viewers into the historical arguments by setting up received wisdom and then chopping it down. Emphasising points with his hands, Belich sliced the air to push home his points. The hands gained a minor celebrity of their own, and his onscreen and voiceover presence quickly became synonymous with the series. As he trounced implausible or self-serving versions of the past, he marched across rural landscapes rather than sitting in front of academic bookshelves: this was an active, outdoor screen persona. The story of the summer job digging trenches on the set of *The Governor* – a story that Belich told at the end of the final episode – pitched him less as a remote academic figure, and more as an accessible, if well-informed, bloke next door.[25]

Distinctive as it was, and made more personal through the shift to television, Belich's voice was by no means the only one heard in the series – he was joined by an array of other voices and perspectives, from past and present. This was a deliberate strategy to balance Belich's Pākehā voice with Māori voices; and it also echoed Ken Burns' use of multiple voices from the archives and present-day commentators.

Voices from the past came in through historical individuals who had been caught up in the events, a strategy *The Civil War* had used very effectively. Belich undertook further research for this purpose, using diaries, letters and other kinds of documents:

I wanted to give the series more intimacy than the book ... it was a different audience. So I deliberately did things like try to interweave the stories of that woman warrior Hēni Pore in the Waikato War and the young British ensign, Spenser Percival Nicols. I went to quite a bit of trouble to ... find their diaries ... I did a bit of extra research myself, and so I did put a bit of effort into having sort of two interlocutors.[26]

These more intimate records allowed the documentary to offer contrasting perspectives from both sides of certain events. The narrated words of eyewitnesses augmented the main narrative with a multivocal set of stories and a variation in perspective, both literal and ideological.

The series used voice actors to read from these historical records. A few of these performances drew adverse comment from the public; and the way they came to be performed gives an insight into the cultural moment of the series' creation. The voice-acting was all done over the course of a weekend. In the process, some of the English historical figures who articulated views that now seem patronising or racist were rendered in a caricatured performance.[27] Although the instruction had been for all the voice-acting to be 'done straight' – performed as voices from their own time and within the terms and understandings of that time – it seems to have become almost impossible at the moment of performance for the actor to render these views without parodic inflection.

Voices from the present join those from the past. We hear the accounts of Gate Pā written by Hēni Te Kiri Karamū and Ensign Nicols, and of Hori Ngātai, another historical figure; and we also hear from Ngātai's descendant, Kihi Ngātai, who reflects on what it must have been like awaiting the attack.

Indeed, present-day voices from iwi involved in the conflicts became a distinctive feature of the series' narrative.[28] The team

The battle of Pukehinahina (Gate Pā) is told by voices from both sides. Hēni Te Kiri Karamū (Hēni Porei) took water to the wounded and dying Captain Booth after the battle.

The original image is held by the Alexander Turnbull Library, Wellington, 1/2-041822-G

travelled to every location and, with few exceptions, filmed on the site of the conflicts, sometimes in very remote places. There were dozens of marae meetings with the people connected to these places – echoing James Cowan's horseback travels through the North Island 70 years earlier, and *The Governor's* series of hui. Belich recalls these meetings and the way that they shaped the series' perspectives on the past:

> *one thing that became clear is that, you know sometimes Pākehā like myself think ... the notion that Māori are more sort of steeped in their history is a bit of a cliché, but when you actually look at some of these rural marae, the memory of the loss of*

*the land down the road, or of the 27 people that got killed over there, is very, very strong, in a way that, probably ... a southern European – I'm of southern European descent – could kind of understand ... so we did engage with those local communities, and I think the series derived indirect benefits from that.*²⁹

Stephens, McRae and Ngata arranged hui to discuss each conflict that the series covered, 'sometimes just to meet people, sometimes to do actual shooting. So we talked things through with those who we believed were the representatives of the relevant groups.'³⁰ Belich's account of these meetings suggests that his own ethnic identity as 'Ngāti Tarara' (Croatian) situated him as not-quite-Pākehā but from a community with long historic connections with Māori, especially in the north. He relates how he, as a historian, approached negotiation with communities: aware that local people often had knowledge they might contribute, he invited engagement but reserved the production team's right to make their own assessments:

*I'd do my [mihi] in Croatian, and I would say, basically, listen here's the story we're going to tell, about this particular region at this particular time, now, we want to hear your responses to that, but I'm not going to accept what you tell me any more than I do other sources, but here's a chance for the story to be retold ... I made it very clear that although we sought Māori participation, editorial control remained with us.*³¹

Belich's *New Zealand Wars* book was already quite widely known at the marae they visited. Many Māori had read it and others knew of it.³² Belich recalled that, with very few exceptions, 'once they got a sense of where I was coming from, the level of Māori support was enormous'.³³ Tainui Stephens remembers another dimension of these meetings: the crosscultural working of the production team through these negotiations:

*what I also felt very quickly and enjoyed was that when we moved into the Māori dimension they were open to roles being Māori roles, so that he was my teina, I was his tuakana when we were in that Māori world, with whatever we had to deal with, and there were things along the way. When we came out of that Māori world, he was back to being my tuakana ... a simple mechanism, to do something simple to show respect and being able to communicate that ...*³⁴

He commented on the change in what he could expect from his Pākehā colleagues:

*when we were in Māori circles, and there were some testing moments once or twice when people got the wrong idea about what we were doing or whatever, I can sit back, same with Vince [Ward], and listen to my colleague on the marae and not have to roll my eyes, because they are intelligent and they don't patronise and they are who they are, and those are the Pākehā I work with now ...*³⁵

The hui were not only consultations; they were a search for people who came to speak on screen about events they had whānau connections with. These came to be a feature in each episode. Each one is different – which seems to indicate that the speakers had some say over how they would speak. Some were delivered in te reo Māori and subtitled. They are delivered on the whenua involved. Jacob Hakaraia speaks to the camera from the churchyard on the site of the Battle of Ōhaeawai; Bill Wiremu speaks from the hilltop at Kororāreka and then, at the end of the episode, stands with pride at the site of Ruapekapeka as he tells Ngāpuhi's story. Rovina Maniapoto Anderson stands by the Pūniu River as she talks about the Waikato War. Tom Ngātai speaks on a Taranaki hillside. In most of these interviews the camera sits back, adopting the deliberately unintrusive style developed in *Tangata Whenua*; and the place around the speaker acquires an implicit significance.

The New Zealand Wars (1998): Bill Wiremu (Ngāpuhi) speaks about why Heke and Kawiti cut down the flagstaff at Kororāreka. With the permission of Bill Wiremu

The New Zealand Wars (1998): Tom Ngātai (Ngāruahine) speaks about his tupuna Tītokowaru. With the permission of Sydney Ngātai

Whenua

The other, inseparable dimension of the onsite filming of local speakers was the sites themselves: the land that was at stake. Hayden White has argued that images, rather than simply illustrating a text, may conduct 'a discourse in [their] own right'[36] and frequently go beyond the capacity of narrative, especially in their summons to a collective emotional response. The approach to landscape as whenua in *The New Zealand Wars* is a good example of how this can happen. The images of land were designed to elicit emotions, to connect landscape with its past and its people and to provide a 'discourse in its own right', with a strong Māori inflection.

Besides, the images of the landscapes were a story in themselves: in some, the traces of their histories were still visible, but many had since changed ownership, and use, in the aftermath of the wars. In portraying the land, the series reiterated the values associated with whenua by repeatedly showing images of the awa and maunga – the rivers and mountains – of the iwi involved in that place. This had the effect of creating visual references that gathered meaning through their accumulated association with events or people. The first episode's opening footage of Te Urewera was already associated for some viewers with the government invasion of Maungapōhatu. Like much of the filmed landscape to come, the opening sequence confronts viewers with the relationship between past and present and shapes their responses through sound. Images of the bush in mist gesture to the pastness of the bush 'as it was'; historical photographs of the invasion add narrative elements; and images of bush and pasture mark changes. A superimposed photograph of Rua Kēnana embeds his image in the landscape.

The New Zealand Wars (1998): ABOVE: '… the mood of that, the scope of that, the majesty of that was something I wanted …' Tainui Stephens talks about capturing the meaning of whenua in this image of Taranaki. ABOVE: Tītokowaru and Taranaki: the carved and painted panel of the one-eyed chief superimposed on the mountain.

Such visual connections between land as the past, land bearing all the signs of the present, and archival images of the chiefly figures associated with the defence of the land are repeated through the series. In Episode 3 on the Waikato War, the Waikato River is the repeated motif: aerial footage follows it southward. A carved taniwha stands for the connection to iwi in this episode. Spectacular footage of Mt Taranaki appears as a motif in the story of the First Taranaki War; in Episode 2 the image is reiterated, identifying it as the whenua of the Taranaki tribes. Tainui Stephens set out to address Māori viewers through the images of this maunga. One remarkable shot of Taranaki in intense late-afternoon light opens and closes Episode 4. It was, he said:

> a no-brainer to have Taranaki as central to that part of the history, everyone gets it, but further, with Taranaki, and you go by what shots you get, you pray for things and we were happy to get the shots that we got, by god we were … to get that [shot] we were blessed. One of the things about Taranaki, I remember being told by someone, it's like, when you grow there and live there, it's a presence in your everyday life, so when you're away there's an emptiness inside you that can only be filled again once you come back and see it, and so the mood of that, the scope of that, the majesty of that was something I wanted …[37]

In Episode 4, which deals with the Taranaki prophets and centres increasingly on Tītokowaru, the footage of the mountain acquires a more precise set of meanings. At the first mention of Tītokowaru, one of the very few known images of him – an image on a wooden panel, painted in a style that mimics a carved image – is superimposed on the wide shot of the mountain. This visual association is repeated until, by the end of the episode, a strong metonymic connection is built up between the mountain and Tītokowaru. Viewers have been pulled into the landscape and confronted with its past and the mountain is now associated with the struggle of invasion and resistance. Outlined against the sky – and accompanied, in the opening credits, with the defiant sound of a ngeri (chant) – it also signifies the mana whenua of the tribes of the Taranaki region.

The filming on historical sites introduced another kind of story about the changes between the occupation of land at the time of the wars and its present-day ownership and uses. Belich speaks to camera among a busy swirl of shoppers and workers on a rainy day in Manners Mall, Wellington, where fortifications once stood – pointing up the contrast between then and now. He speaks from the Hutt golf course, where a closeup of a golfball marks the changes since it was the site of the Battle of Boulcott's Farm; and from many a former pā site now turned to pasture.

Occasionally the current use of the land is organised to create a visual narrative. On a beach that was once a part of Te Rauparaha's broad empire, people sit and enjoy the day. Girls play, throwing sand at each other, then settle down to build a sandcastle. The episode cuts to other scenes and events, then returns to the beach. The sandcastle grows, and a closeup shows the girls' hands putting in sticks to make palisades. On the next piece to camera from this spot the girls have gone and Belich relates the story of Te Rauparaha's capture by Grey's soldiers, on this same beach: as we hear of how the Ngāti Toa empire was undermined, in comes the tide, the waves lap at the base of the sand pā and it begins to crumble into the water. A little everyday narrative, an ordinary day on an ordinary beach, charts the passing of time in past and present, and the fall of an empire.

The extreme familiarity of these ordinary places is disrupted by the insistent reminder of their history; the forgotten, other past more familiar to iwi than to Pākehā returns, with its history

The New Zealand Wars (1998): Familiar cityscapes are often compared to past images: here soldiers work on the Great South Road, built to invade the Waikato; James Belich stands beside its contemporary incarnation as traffic rushes by.

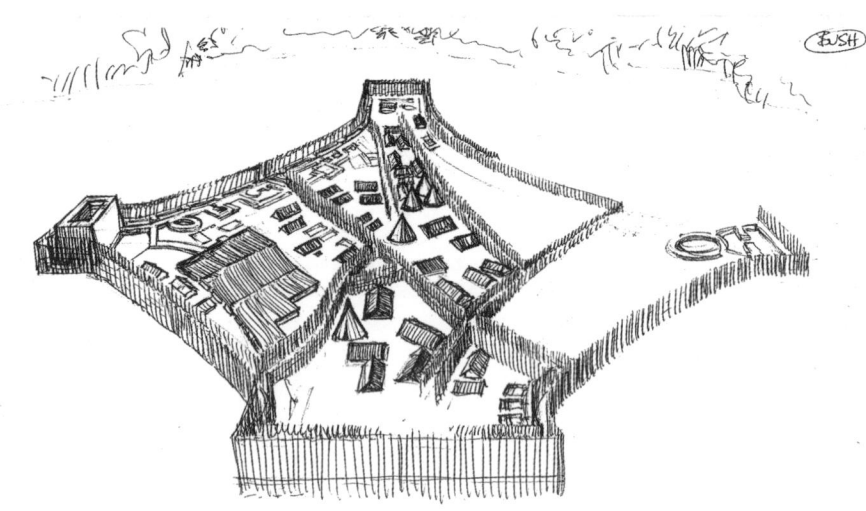

TAURANGA IKA.

TOWARDS COLONIALS

The New Zealand Wars (1998): The series' animated graphics brought viewers into the action, 'flying' them from one side to another, inside and out to illustrate the design of the modern pā. Stephen Ellis's drawings of Tītokowaru's pā Tauranga Ika; graphic by Animation Research. In the second drawing, Ellis shows the view 'towards colonials', shaping the point of view of the defenders.

Stephen Ellis and Landmark Productions

of conflict and appropriation, to haunt the present. Images of the present landscape with all the effects of settlement apparent are cut back into the story of the past.

The series made extensive use of archival images. Producer Colin McRae's image research for the series was a mammoth task that earned him the title of the Alexander Turnbull Library's first 1000-item customer. Many of the drawings and watercolours were the work of soldiers. In Episode 4, for example, Mt Taranaki is reproduced over and over again in a series of sketches and watercolours, its form often neatly replicated by the cone-shaped bell tents of the invading military. Systematically, historical images and present-day footage are juxtaposed: images of nineteenth-century paintings cut back to the narration to camera against the background of the site of conflict.

Another technique the series employs to unsettle the apparent neutrality of landscape is panning and zooming across these historical images to create dynamic 'scenes'– a practice adapted from *The Civil War*. The American series created these sequences from photographs, but *The New Zealand Wars* applies the technique to historical paintings of battle, with quick cuts that pull viewers into the landscape, fighting for it on one side or the other. A parallel technique uses present-day footage to give the sense of being in the midst of fighting – jumpy, swinging hand-held closeups and medium shots of ground, grass and trees: we are denied the detachment of the distant view. The quick, percussive soundtrack and the ominous pūrerehua (bullroarer) enhance the disorientation.

Many viewers were struck by the graphic animations created for the series by Animation Research led by Ian Taylor (Ngāti Kahungnunu, Ngāpuhi), based on Stephen Ellis's drawings. The series' argument about the technological inventiveness of the modern pā is vividly illustrated in innovative graphics that take viewers on a swooping aerial tour of the design of the fortifications, showing how each pā was constructed and how its defences worked. In combination with the narration – as Belich explains how underground rua allowed defenders to wait out bombardments, or that weak-looking defences were actually lethal traps – the agile graphics draw the audience into and around the pā, demonstrating those innovative elements. What was less obvious but just as effective was the animation's capacity to draw viewers into all sides of these battles, but especially into the view from behind the palisades. Audiences – Māori and Pākehā alike – were invited to occupy the perspective of the defender.

Sounds

The distinctive soundscape for the series articulated the clash and interplay of cultures, and gave a strong Māori 'feel' to the series. Tainui Stephens worked on the sound with veteran guitarist and producer Wiremu Karaitiana (Billy Kristian), whose musical and production experience encompassed both popular and Māori traditional music.

Like the letters, diaries and other records narrated in voiceover, the sound drew on the musical traditions of both cultures. It used European military music, especially for the martial sound of drumbeats and brass, as well as popular songs, shanties and rhymes set to music. In this respect the soundscape again adapted strategies used in *The Civil War*, although there was little similarity between the two scores. *The Civil War* maintains an elegiac tone, whereas *The New Zealand Wars* soundscape is much more lively, often percussive, and lament is almost entirely kept for the waiata that close each episode.

In several episodes a ngeri accompanies the opening credits. Technically the ngeri is a short haka without weapons, but here it is represented aurally only, as a cry or challenge. It opens the episodes in a way similar to the ritual of encounter on a marae: a challenge is laid down, situating the viewer as manuhiri before the kōrero of the episode gets under way. Each episode closes with a moving waiata tangi or lament, composed and sung by Whirimako Black. In this way sound builds a Māori structure into the episode: sound frames echo the story of each episode and intimate that the overall narrative of the series was, in the end, a journey from defiant resistance to loss.

The use of Māori vocals and taonga pūoro, and the extent to which they shape the series' character, demonstrates the extent to which the series was an authorial collaboration between Belich and Stephens.[38] These sounds must have made emotional claims on Pākehā viewers, but, as Lisa Perrott shows, they enabled the series to speak even more directly to older Māori. One elderly woman in Perrott's study on the series spoke about her response to the soundscape:

the soundtrack … I think that's the one that got me the most … and the ngeri, when I heard the ngeri … Waikato's famous ngeri being sung. Right away that's showing their mana in who they stand for, the Kingitanga. Oh yes, that's real Waikato … when you hear it, it sends goose pimples up your back. When you feel that up your back, well you know that documentary … the wairua's there … See that's where a lot of the history's kept … it's in the waiatas … it's in those ngeris. That's why I was glad when I heard the sound of the ngeri, in the background … because that's where the actual korero was … in those ngeris.[39]

Stephens' work on the soundscape was undertaken with a strong sense of its potential to make precise connections to iwi and hapū traditions. His discussion of the sound revealed the density of cultural and personal resonances he drew on. The opening waiata for Episode 1 (about the Northern War), for example, sung by Sir James Hēnare, was placed at the beginning because it came from the north. But Stephens' own personal connections – he is from Te Rārawa in the north – were important too. When I asked him what parts of the series he was pleased with it was sound he thought of, and this waiata:

James Hēnare singing his waiata in the very beginning. Specifically that one because he was an important old man to me, and I knew that waiata was one that he was first taught by his kuia, and was a general kind of waiata, it wasn't specific, it was safe to use, basically, it was safe to use … and I wanted to have acknowledgement in terms of Māori whakaaro, because we'd been setting up the veterans, the old fellows who'd fought and there were some lovely photos, so to have that snatch of waiata, from an old soldier like Sir James …[40]

Similarly, while the melody of the waiata in the closing credits was the same in each episode, the words were altered in the final episode to reflect the specificity of place and Whirimako Black's own iwi connections, 'because it's finishing at Maungapōhatu, so as she is a Tūhoe woman, it's appropriate for that song to have a Tūhoe angle …'[41]

The credits and section breaks were also defined by Māori instrumentation and visual design. Ellis's visual motif of the opening credits was two opposing tūpara or double-barrelled guns – one with a plain wood stock and the other carved. Each account of a battle began with a frame of a tokotoko (the carved stick held by a speaker) planted in the landscape, signalling to viewers that a kōrero about this place was about to begin. In these ways the Pākehā historian narrator was balanced not only by the iwi speakers but by Māori sound and visual elements

The New Zealand Wars (1998): Section breaks: the tokotoko in the landscape marks the opening of the kōrero about each place – here, Te Pōrere, with Ngāruahoe in the background. Accompanied by Māori instrumentation, these frames incorporated Māori performative elements into the series' design.

which give the series Māori performative elements. These elements spoke more eloquently to some viewers than to others.

As Stephens pointed out, he did not have an entirely free hand as a result of the editorial control of the TVNZ network executive. When the rough cut went to TVNZ, the executive made some editorial calls, including one that Stephens has never been happy with. In the series as it went to air, Belich first speaks to the camera from Albert Park, former site of the barracks in Auckland. The original version of this opening address was shot at Ruapekapeka, but the executive:

> *didn't like the original piece to camera that I'd shot up at Ruapekapeka, which is a longer piece to camera, moodier … and Tom didn't like it. Jamie was kinda neutral about it, I think they had an issue too about the length of it. Because part of the thing for me … in whaikōrero you're establishing yourself as a presence and I wanted him to be seen in long shot and to just make a visual sort of impact, his own tihei mauriora … So what I was forced to do in the end was a fairly standard piece to camera …*[42]

The change from Ruapekapeka to Albert Park, the move from long shot to medium shot, and the length of the introductory piece mark differences between Pākehā and Māori habitual modes of address – and of listening.

Audiences

These dimensions of the series were part of a broader sense, on the part of its makers, that they were creating something unusually significant and that it 'had to be done right'. They were looking for a way of addressing both their Māori and their Pākehā audiences – conscious that they were speaking to people with differing knowledge and perspectives; and that they were trying to effect changes in these audiences' cultural memory about the colonial past. They sought to persuade Pākehā viewers that the wars mattered and that they should be properly understood. They sought to give full acknowledgement to what many Māori viewers already knew: that the wars had had a profound and ongoing impact. And above all, they were trying to reach a younger generation of Māori who might know little of the wars except as stories of their tūpuna's defeat and failure, or as stories about figures of terror. Belich spoke with great satisfaction about some of the reactions to the series:

> there are some wonderful stories about people trying to turn the TV programme off in the pub and half the Mongrel Mob rushing over and saying don't do that … Young Māori kids would come up and say, great, and wouldn't quite know how to articulate it. And just the sense that, you know, Māori aren't nincompoops, and that they are capable of innovation and of great intelligence is a quite important lesson for Māori young people to learn …[43]

Tainui Stephens talked about the series' impact among young Māori:

> One of the responses we were most proud of – and it happened a number of times – was of a young lad from East Cape, who was … dropping out of school and just not interested in stuff, saw the series and was blown away, and turned his life around by getting into it and discovering the stories, and doing very well as a result, and we were buzzed out, that was just, it was a perfect example of what we wanted to try and achieve … that sense of pride that was generated was what we wanted …

> The responses I have had have unfailingly been the excitement of the stories, and feeling the wairua, and just enjoyment of it all, appreciation of it all. It's unfailingly been that, unfailingly …

> Sometimes it's expressed in different ways, from Pākehā perhaps, but Māori who understand being Māori all get it, they all get it …[44]

Lisa Perrott's audience research gives us valuable insight into how people responded. She screened Episode 3, 'The Waikato War', for several focus groups, including Tainui kaumātua, Māori youth, older Pākehā and academic historians. She describes how the Māori groups often responded in ways that were, as she puts it, 'visceral' – a thrill of pride, a desire to stand up and do a haka, goosebumps – and often these were responses to sound or landscape elements in the series. She noted the sense of pride among the Māori youth in response to the revelations of Māori achievement during the wars.[45]

Stephens recalled three main kinds of Pākehā response: the 'belligerent' ones who objected to content or style; those who were prompted to research their own family connections; and 'by far the biggest response is from Pakeha who really enjoyed the programme, and what links them is a sense of gratitude'.[46] There were challenges to elements of the series' interpretation of military history – several military historians objected to the assertion that Māori invented modern trench warfare – which Belich defended with some vigour.[47] Ngāti Hauā journalist Paul Diamond assessed the immediate impact and responses of the series for the *Evening Post*; he observed that the conductor and the train driver on the 8.05 to Upper Hutt were discussing it intently, and that the talkback shows were running hot and the ratings were high. Diamond canvassed the spirited letters to the editor; and he interviewed historians and Treaty minister Doug Graham. Some had reservations. All were enthusiastic about the way the programme was engaging audiences in historical debate and inviting a deeper understanding of the colonial past.⁴⁸ One dimension of the positive responses was an almost relieved appreciation of the high production quality and an implicit gratitude that, amid the rise and rise of reality television, audiences were for once assumed to be intelligent.

For Belich, the response illustrated the reach of television in comparison with historical writing. But he was cautious about assuming too much:

> I thought the book The New Zealand Wars had been quite successful ... so you sort of thought that New Zealanders knew about it, but when the TV series came out, you discovered that the book was complete news to 99 per cent of New Zealanders, so I think it's possible for the likes of us to delude ourselves into believing we're reaching a wide audience when it's just the people we talk to. It's hard to measure but I think [the series] raised an alternative view, which still survives, and although it hasn't taken over from the old one, it's out there and it's competing, and I think that's a reasonably important achievement, which I'm reasonably proud of. But the notion that it's swept the board is an illusion I've never had.⁴⁹

His caution was realistic, but the series unquestionably intervened in public memory of the New Zealand Wars. When it went to air it gained strong first-night ratings well above the network's expectations, and they remained high through the five episodes. By the time it ended it had been viewed by two million people, rating highly with both Māori and Pākehā audiences, but especially with Māori.⁵⁰ Viewers responded vigorously, most with immense enthusiasm.⁵¹ Margo White noted:

> Even TVNZ must have been surprised. [It] wrote, in its company email newsletter: 'These sorts of ratings break what seems to be the unwritten rule of New Zealand newspaper critiques, namely that the success of a TVNZ show is usually inversely proportional to the amount of critical acclaim it receives.'⁵²

McRae has a clear recollection of TVNZ's 'surprise'. The night the first episode was to go to air, one of the senior programmers conveyed his opinion that the series hadn't much chance of rating well. McRae's confidence in The New Zealand Wars was met with a dismissive reply:

> And in the morning the phone rang, and it was one of their programming people, ringing me to tell me how well it had done, and 'oh we've just opened the champagne here' ... I'm sitting at home drinking my Nescafé, they were cock-a-hoop with the ratings ... I don't think anyone was saying we're celebrating because this is a terrifically worthy and valuable addition to our history.⁵³

When he went back some years later to suggest a series on what happened after the wars, the enthusiasm had waned and once again TVNZ was 'not interested'.

The New Zealand Wars screened in June and July of 1998. Despite the increasing choice of programming, with more channels and the arrival of cable, at that point TV One still held its place, as Belich puts it, as 'the national marae'. Realtime viewing of primetime programming was still customary, and audiences went on to discuss their night's viewing the following day. Like The Governor, The New Zealand Wars generated widespread discussion and the series gained a high public profile. Its iconoclastic message, like that of The Governor, was aired, debated and argued out in living rooms, workplace tearooms and pubs. The historian narrator became a historian celebrity, recognisable partly because of his enthusiastic style, but despite a few detractors ('James Bellicose', one critic called him), the more common response was genuine fascination with unfamiliar perspectives on the national past.

Not everyone loved it, by any means, and the backlash, though in the minority, was vociferous. Some people wanted to know, 'Why were the Maoris always the good guys and the English always the bad guys?'[54] Diana Wichtel, writing for the *Listener*, puzzled over how the series had pulled off those ratings. She thought it had struck its moment:

> Despite the inevitable redneck backlash, the times are right for a post-colonial analysis of the New Zealand Wars. As Belich points out colourfully, they 'left deep wounds concealed but not healed by the scabs of legend!' This is a past that's still bleeding into the present. Some of the most moving moments are the interviews with some of the Maori warriors' descendants, who recall these distant events as if they were yesterday.

And it probably didn't hurt that the first episode had a lot about sex, guns and the general nineteenth-century equivalent of rock'n'roll. Wichtel also thought that the series' perspective was distinctive, and local:

> Belich's true achievement is to have invented a local history utterly devoid of cultural cringe ... 'Real wars, like real history, were supposed to happen overseas,' he says. 'Yet the New Zealand Wars raged across the whole North Island for almost 30 years, with heroism and massacre on both sides!' Our wars are as good as your wars.[55]

The documentary stood out in part because high-quality history programming was so scarce at the time. Mary Debrett suggests the series was 'arguably [NZ On Air's] best delivery of its legislated goals, to reflect and develop New Zealand culture'. She lists several distinctive features that set it apart from other programming of its time: its formal production style; that it tackled the controversial subject of Māori/Pākehā relations; its grounding in academic research; its comparatively high budget – and its popularity. 'One can only speculate as to why the series was so popular, but it seems reasonable to suggest that this signalled an appetite for cultural and social analysis that television had neglected.'[56]

The decision to emphasise excitement and vigour rather than lament, and an appeal to Pākehā guilt, sat well with many New Zealand viewers. Belich's appearance as an outdoor kind of historian – who looked as though he could still pick up the spade he'd wielded on the set of *The Governor* – may have softened the series' message for just the constituency who might be most suspicious of its stance, or of too much display of erudition. The 'ripping yarns' tone – the term was often used by commentators – reached and engaged large sectors of the audience. And the central argument of the series – that Māori were innovative, adaptable engineers and fighters who responded intelligently to the technologies and the sheer size of the forces arraigned against them – made covert appeal to two elements of middle New Zealand identity: Belich's adaptable pā builders seemed to anticipate the mythical Kiwi capacity with a piece of number-eight wire; and they were, he argued, Davids who nimbly out-strategised the Goliaths invading their territory. If much of the series' appeal was to those already sympathetic to Māori historical perspectives, these elements hooked in some of the more reluctant sectors of the viewing public: the number-eight wire expert and the underdog were amenable tropes. Indeed the series' appeal to such tropes, well established in the lexicon of 'middle New Zealand' masculinity, may well have helped to deflect some of the less palatable elements of the series for this part of the viewing audience.[57]

The fact that the series rated so highly, against industry expectations, is one measure of its reach and impact. Less obvious, but with more underlying impact, is that the availability of the series to schools and universities continues to inform history teaching. Many schools still do not include the New Zealand Wars in the curriculum. But for those history teachers who do cover the subject, the series is a highly inviting resource that engages students while it informs, and showcases the process of historical debate. The series still has a vigorous afterlife: in November and December 2017, the Māoriland Hub at Ōtaki held a number of screenings accompanied by talks and discussions with speakers, including Belich and Stephens.[58]

The series contributed substantially to a shift in how the wars were understood, and what events and historical figures were recognised as important. It drew attention to stories that marked the agency of Māori resistance, both military and political, and that highlighted intellectual rather than physical dimensions of resistance. So whereas, in the Northern War, Hōne Heke the 'rebel' had formerly been the well-known figure, Kawiti the strategist and engineer came to be better known, and Heke's own political insight was better recognised. Te Rauparaha came to be seen as a politician as well as a war leader. In the Waikato the statesmen Wiremu Tāmihana and King Tāwhiao came to the fore alongside Rewi Maniapoto. Tītokowaru was brought back into the public eye: Belich argued for him as a better strategist than Te Kooti, who had formerly attracted greater attention as a guerilla fighter and a figure of fear for Pākehā. The series therefore created something of a tidal shift in what came to be seen as the 'big' stories of the wars. Some of the next generation of screen dramas drew on figures and events that Belich had reinterpreted and for which, through the cut and thrust of its documentary narrative, the series had demonstrated the dramatic potential.

Tainui Stephens, when asked if he had a favourite episode, conveyed in his answer something of the depth of what it meant to make the series, and to make it in a way that was unusually satisfying to him as a Māori person working in the screen industry. As he traversed the series, the range and depth of feeling involved in creating it became apparent:

[Episode] One, because of the links to the North. Two, because of my pride in the whole Te Rauparaha thing and what Raukawa have done. Three because I think it's possibly the best structured narrative. Four because of the power of Tītokowaru and the old man Tom Ngātai. And Five because of the guerilla warfare thing, the whole Te Kooti thing. There's no favourite episode, they all mean different things … as a whole. Oh, I'm so proud of it, absolutely, absolutely. But maybe One, because of just being parochial and northern. And Sir James's voice. I knew that old man, I was there when he sang that song. I remember going out to Ruapekapeka and seeing Auntie Mabel Waititi had turned up. She died not so long ago in her nineties, first cousin to Sir James and she just wanted to be up there when I started filming. We'd been to see her anyway, and her support was great. So that, I guess because I'm northern, that sort of stuff is more special.[59]

TELEVISION HISTORIES IN UNCERTAIN TIMES
Greenstone, *Von Tempsky's Ghost* and *Frontier of Dreams*

These are our stories, our people. Our children need to learn about them. —Mike King

I do think that the only way that we can make, certainly, historic shows with integrity is to keep the foreign money out of it, because that never comes without codicils. —Greg McGee

Three productions screened on TV One in the years following *The New Zealand Wars*: the drama series *Greenstone* (1999), a one-off documentary *Von Tempsky's Ghost* (2002), and *Frontier of Dreams* (2005), a survey history that included segments on colonial conflict. In these three productions we have examples across the range of history television: a saga that raids history for good stories, a documentary with military reenactments that follows the career of a colourful individual, and a documentary survey with talking heads.

All three were bidding for their funding in the deregulated environment where the network programmer ruled (the 2003 Television New Zealand Act brought in a charter outlining a public service requirement, but its modest assistance came too late for these productions). As some of the productions' creators saw it, what programmers wanted was a proven format rather than anything unfamiliar: 'They only wanted what they'd seen before, and if they didn't know about it you didn't get anywhere,' said John Milligan. Greg McGee said of the dynamic between creators and programmers:

> This cynicism isn't unearned, you know ... In the end, still, there's someone in the network who has the power. And you know, you can go in there, and pitch several really exciting innovative projects and they say no no no, and you think, oh well, this is the next two years of our fucking company, you know, and so you always say, well what are you looking for? What kind of thing ... and whatever they say, you say ah! I've got one of those, yeah ...[1]

Programming as public service seemed to have slid beneath programming as product, as the uneasy balance between NZ On Air's underfunded public service mandate and TVNZ's requirement to return profit tilted, perhaps inevitably, towards the latter. Creative personnel had little option but to adapt or get out, and many went. Creatives, and the independent production companies, worked from commission to commission. In this environment the imperatives to make fundable programming were doubly pressing: there was no point in conceiving ideas that programmers would not look at. The costs entailed in historical drama made it risky; and despite the strong ratings of *The New Zealand Wars*, historical documentary was still under pressure to entertain as much as educate.

The creators of *The Governor*, working in drama-documentary, had adopted the conventions of heritage drama: detailed recreations of period interiors and costuming, and measured performances that attempted to render nineteenth-century manners, gestures and ways of speaking, both European and Māori. The style carried cultural value for audiences in the late 1970s: *The Governor* was screened in the primetime, high-status Sunday evening slot, uninterrupted by advertising.

There was no more historical drama on this scale until the mid-1990s when Mike Lattin, head of drama at TVNZ, proposed costume drama as the genre of choice for a big new historical series. The theatricality of costume drama, with its racy, populist edge, opened up a broader potential market. The prospect of an exotic setting – 'a Māori story' – favoured the potential for international co-production, which was now a necessity if the series was to be made, given the gap between the costs of historical drama and available local funding. The historical references in costume drama were loose and allusive; it gestured to broad themes and to the glamour of costuming and sets, rather than attempting to explain historical events by drawing viewers into identifying with historical figures. Its emphasis was less on drama as a vehicle for history and more on history as a vehicle for drama – or, increasingly in the new funding environment, as a vehicle for marketable product.

Greenstone

The idea for *Greenstone* (1999) was initiated when Lattin signalled his interest in a historical epic. Robin Scholes, co-director of one of the most successful independent production companies at the time, Communicado, took the cue. Scholes' record in making New Zealand-oriented and Māori drama had included Lee Tamahori's *Once Were Warriors* (1994), which, despite predictions that Māori stories would not sell, had done exceptionally well in New Zealand and internationally.

Communicado now embarked on the international co-production negotiations necessary to fund a historical drama series. There was substantial financial risk involved even in the initial development, Scholes recalls.[2] As an example of network-initiated programming, this series illustrates the complexities involved in making a New Zealand historical drama in the deregulated environment and, especially, the effects of working with international co-production. Those involved with the production of *Greenstone* have differing views on how it evolved.

A great deal had changed since the idealistic 'make it up as you go' energy of the 1970s, when *The Governor*'s creators managed to secure full state funding and set about questioning cherished national myths. Although the fallout after *The Governor* was spectacular, during the production its makers had been able to maintain what would now be seen as a remarkable degree of creative authority, unencumbered by anxiety about ratings and market appeal, or by network editorial control. The context in which *Greenstone* was produced differed from this in many respects. Communicado's co-production with the BBC was the first major foray of its type for New Zealand television production. It meant negotiating a balance between international and local markets. International investors – the BBC was joined by Australian company Beyond International – came in alongside the local investment of TVNZ and NZ On Air (which granted $3,200,000 in August 1996). The plan was to recoup investment through international sales. Scholes notes that then – as now – it was 'really hard to raise money internationally for New Zealand based stories'. Through *Greenstone*, the first venture on anything like this scale, she 'learnt a lot about creating stories for an international market from a New Zealand base'.[3]

During the initial development stage Scholes approached Greg McGee and Dean Parker, playwrights who had written extensively for television; Don Selwyn, whom she had worked with on *Warriors* and regarded as an important mentor; and script advisor Waihoroi Shortland. McGee, who is credited for devising the series, recalls that the initial brief was broad: 'TVNZ wants an epic … it could have been anything at that early stage, what it became was a kind of bodice-ripper, it could have been anything and we … signed and away we went …'.[4] McGee and Parker worked on the initial concept stage, roughing out a season's episodes.

The concept was pitched to the BBC producer Michael Wearing; he accepted it and the script went into full development. A condition of BBC involvement in co-productions was that they would appoint the senior writer and director. Scholes accepted this as part of the co-production deal; she saw its value as enhancing the potential for international sales: 'We used UK cast and a UK director and writer, because we wanted the story to be told from a UK perspective.'[5] McGee and Parker continued as co-writers with responsibility for the New Zealand side of the series, and Selwyn and Shortland as Māori advisors. Scholes wanted their ongoing involvement 'to ensure that New Zealand voices, especially Māori voices, were at the table'. Wearing and his development executives introduced the practice of a 'story room', Scholes notes, in which 'key writers sit down and plot the whole story and story arcs of each of the core characters, episode by episode', before individual writers wrote separate episodes. Scholes liked this approach which, she says, has now become the norm; McGee and Parker viewed its effects less positively.[6]

The BBC eventually withdrew for reasons unrelated to *Greenstone* – another colonial history series, *Rhodes*, had done poorly[7] – but its involvement had already made an imprint on the series. Although the English director left, the writer, Stephen Lowe, remained: he was also a playwright and had adapted Stendahl for television and written British dramas on the theme of class, set in Britain. McGee and Parker were unhappy with Lowe's involvement. It is not entirely obvious now how the series developed from the initial concept stage to the screen, but a comparison between the early documentation and the final story suggests some of the tensions that appear to have played out among the various people involved – the New Zealand writers, the English writer and the Māori advisors.

The initial concept development was written as a potboiler: McGee and Parker had obviously taken the 'costume' cue and approached it as a tongue-in-cheek bodice-ripper rather than heritage drama, in line with Scholes' idea for the series. Their tone was mock-heroic as they sketched out the episodes, and at this stage there is some fun going on as they camp up the drafting-out of historical types. This flavour is evident in one of the opening passages of the concept:

> *It is the age of steam, of iron foundries; of high-minded slaughter and deceitful good manners; of boundless ambition and knowing one's station. It is the age of a British Empire that stretches to the southernmost of the South Seas.*
>
> *Young Sam Markham, cribbed and confined in Nottingham, bridling at his appointed station in life, sets off to the heart of this world, London, in hot pursuit of a merchant deal. There is a visitor there, from the colonies, wishing to purchase a large number of weapons. Since Sam's father makes the deadliest guns in England, Sam is intent upon beating off all rivals and clinching the sale.*
>
> *It will be a sale that will change his life forever.*

For into this world of mills and palaces and fortunes and bankruptcies and romance and hypocrisy has appeared the strangest of the strange: the mellifluously eloquent and exotically tattooed Maori Chief Te Manahau and his lustrous daughter Marama. They have arrived ostensibly to meet, on equal terms, the young, mischievous Queen Victoria. And this they will do. But they have another task: purchasing guns. And when Sam bursts in upon them with his deadly samples, the exquisite Marama wins his heart and he glimpses in her and her father that brave, Byronic and boundless new world he craves.[8]

The concept planning portrayed the colonial world as a wild, opportunistic free-for-all in which Māori and settlers with varying agendas, pushed and pulled to the new world, jostled for advantage. McGee and Parker, who already had a more than fair knowledge of New Zealand history, made free with it, romping from the Musket Wars of the 1820s to land-hungry settlement to New Zealand Wars in a few short years of compressed dramatic time. The on-the-make world of nineteenth-century Auckland, complete with boom and bust cycles and colonial profiteering, echoes its counterpart of the late 1980s and 1990s.

The Northern English protagonist Sam, in the later episodes of the initial concept, becomes increasingly unscrupulous as he involves himself in the world of colonial finance: he fans the flames of conflict in the Waikato War in order to benefit from the ensuing land confiscations. Any initial sympathy the viewer might feel for him gives way as he becomes a rapacious profiteer (parts of his career echo that of the colonial lawyer and banker Thomas Russell). The chief Te Manahau, modelled on Hongi Hika, is a similarly unscrupulous figure who turns his access to the settlers and their guns to his own advantage as he raids his enemies, settles old scores and expands his domain.

Greenstone (1999): Simone Kessell as Marama. Her first appearance in an early scene signals the 'exotic' flavour of the series. All frame enlargements from Greenstone Comunicado

News of the series appeared in magazines and newspapers in 1996, as the production moved from the concept to the writing stage, the BBC came in and Lowe became the senior writer. Tensions inside the story room were becoming part of the narrative. The *New Zealand Herald* quoted Wearing in terms not calculated to appeal to local readers:

'One doesn't want to be imperialistic – bloody Poms and all that,' laughs Wearing, who is head of drama serials at the Beeb, and executive producer on projects such as Pride and Prejudice. *'But frankly, what Greg and Dean had done about the English scene at the time was a bit approximate. Stephen has a great sense of social history as well as being a dramatist. We hope that getting them in a room together to collaborate had the seeds of perfection. There's been a lot of crosscultural bonding.'*[9]

'Crosscultural bonding' was a shortlived description for the feeling around the table. After the BBC withdrew, Lowe stayed on and wrote five of the eventual eight episodes; McGee and Parker wrote the others.[10] Chris Bailey replaced the BBC director, who in the end had only a brief involvement. Bailey, too, recalled the involvement of the BBC as a difficulty for the series – if Wearing had thought the New Zealanders' writing of the English scene was rough, he felt that Lowe had taken too little care with New Zealand history:

> the English writer, Stephen Lowe ... he got here and I think he was reinventing history, and I seem to remember it happening quite quickly, his reinvention of history happened as a fast process ... It felt to me like our history was being – juggled – for the sake of a protagonist's story, who was English, who wasn't actually necessarily a representative of this country's character at the time.[11]

It is not easy now to assess exactly what changed through Lowe's involvement in the writing – but there are some traces, and one example that may indicate their character. Sam – a very flawed colonial character indeed in the initial concept – seems to have become more sympathetic, more a man caught up in his time and pulled against his moral judgement. His involvement in gun sales was always central to his plotline, but the warmongering profiteer who was resonant of colonial Auckland drops away in the revised script; in the story as it went to screen, viewers were invited to align their sympathies with the industrialist and trader Sam against the aristocratic Sir Geoffrey, now the primary origin of the drama's evils. In Nottingham-based Lowe's hands, colonial tensions seem to have been realigned around class tensions. Alongside this change, the script's tone seems to have tilted away from the self-consciously playful use of costume drama apparent in the initial concept, to become a vehicle for Sam's noble but doomed aspirations – losing the edge of his colonial unscrupulousness and some of the playful self-parody of the series in the same move.

Compounding the problems, there were tensions between the writers and the Māori advisors, too. Don Selwyn was cultural advisor and then associate producer, and Waihoroi Shortland was script consultant. McGee and Shortland had an ongoing conflict over a previous production, so there were existing tensions among the locals.[12] Shortland's view was that the script 'wasn't worthy of the history it was trying to portray':

> We came in after the BBC writer came in – their writer's hands were all over it. It'd been written like a BBC period drama reflecting the times, so not only do we have that, then we have Māoris speaking like that, so there were other areas where we were constantly having clashes, in our minds anyway.[13]

He was unhappy with a narrative that played so fast and loose with history when there had been so few opportunities to convey it with accuracy. Scholes, who had worked with Selwyn before, remembers:

> we had plenty of heated discussions about Greenstone, just as we had had previously about Once Were Warriors. I expected to be challenged. We did change the script on Don and Waihoroi's advice. The one thing I wouldn't compromise on was the inclusion of the Treaty. Don and I argued strongly about this. I thought a different series was needed to tell this story.[14]

The casting also generated some debate. Before *Greenstone* went to air, Selwyn voiced his concern over the casting of Simone Kessell in the lead role of Marama. Kessell had the beauty the genre demanded for the heroine, but she is obviously of mixed descent, with fair skin and features that look as much European as Māori. Selwyn had no complaint about her acting ability, but she did not speak Māori and was not visually convincing: 'No intermarriage had taken place [at the time the series was set], so, for me, you needed to have a visual look

Greenstone (1999): One battle echoes Te Ngutu o te Manu, although this is a topsy-turvy 'history' with events from the 1820s to the 1860s. TOP: Rongopai (Robin Kora, centre) sets a trap reminiscent of Tītokowaru's strategy; CENTRE: Te Manahau (George Hēnare) is broadly modelled on Hongi Hika; BOTTOM: unsuspecting troops approach.

that was going to give that character some credibility.'[15] Selwyn sent Kessell several pages of Māori dialogue for the audition.[16] He had wanted Nancy Brunning, an experienced actor and a fluent te reo speaker with a distinctively Māori beauty; Miriama Smith was also considered. Bailey, who was involved with the casting, recalled that the potential for international sales had been a deciding factor in the choice of actor: 'Don had talked about Nancy, the Māoriness, but there was an international dimension in there too, rightly or wrongly … I think at that stage it was the key issue.'[17] Kessell, who was 18, stepped up to the role and from that point the tensions ceased.

The title 'Greenstone' was the subject of objections by McGee and Parker on the one hand, and Shortland on the other. All had reservations about it. For McGee and Parker it smelt of Aussie arrogance:

> McGee: *Mike Lattin [said], what are you going to call it? And I had a number of titles, ideas for titles, and Mike said no no no we're going to call it Greenstone, cause, you know, and we all thought, well, that's it, face it, you give some ownership of the title, and away it went.*
>
> Parker: *And then Greg came back to me, and said it's going to be called Greenstone, and I said, but there's no greenstone … It was never greenstone, it was just Mike Lattin, an Aussie, deciding what he knew about Māori culture was they had this lovely greenstone, jade, so that's what we'd call it.*[18]

A shipment of greenstone was added in the opening scenes – perhaps to give some backing to the name – and this was what troubled Shortland:

> *you never see it, it's got no whakapapa to it at all, wasn't built into the story ... you don't know where it came from, from the Māori point of view you don't know what value they gave it ... We had this huge problem, from a Māori perspective, because greenstone has an intrinsic value, really.*[19]

These objections speak to a tension that has partly to do with genre, and partly to do with Selwyn and Shortland's sense of insufficient authority over the cultural values of the production. It may be that as the production moved away from the lightness and irony of costume drama and ceased to be a bodice-ripper with no pretensions otherwise, there was an increased uncertainty and concern about its relationship to the past. Shortland recalls another incident that highlights a desire for greater congruence with cultural practice:

> *at the end of the series, [Sam] ... gets shot – Māoris would never forgive him, he'd changed sides, he'd given their guns away or something ... and they wanted him to die a hero's death ... some redemption, well he doesn't get redemption, but what they wanted was in the very last scene, and this is where we had a real huge falling out, they said, oh, would the Māoris gather to pay Sam respect at his burial, and [we] said why? We're more likely to rip his heart out, eat it, and hang his head from the top of a tree. Now that could probably have more respect than anything else ...*[20]

For Chris Bailey, brought in as director when the BBC director did not work out, the project was an uncomfortable assignment. McGee's blunter view was that the involvement of the BBC, and specifically Lowe, resulted in the production becoming 'a sort of bastard child of the imperialists, it perfectly replicated what it was conveying [colonial exploitation]'.[21] When asked about the differences between the context of *The Governor* and of *Greenstone*, he responded that he thought the international investment in *Greenstone* had caused problems that were almost irresolvable:

> *my impression of* The Governor *was that, there was a show made with integrity, and you know, it may have been an eccentric approach, but it was a wholly New Zealand approach, whereas after ... the whole deregulation of the industry ... what we got with* Greenstone *was a kind of a real stepping back into almost imperialist dynamics where the foreign money started determining what we could do ... . And* The Governor *didn't have that, there was a purity about* The Governor *because it was locally funded. And dare I say it, that's probably the key of getting integrity into telling our own stories.*[22]

Scholes saw it otherwise: she commented that the New Zealand writers and Māori advisors had been employed to advise on and protect the story. She acknowledged the varying points of view but insisted that 'in the end, the finance came mainly from New Zealand sources and no one was controlled by international writers and/or producers'.[23]

Greenstone did retain a hefty proportion of its initial maverick approach to the documented past, even if it became more laboured about some of its debts to history. It swashed, buckled and haka'd, trading on stock figures from all sides of the colonial world: the Māori princess, several varieties of warrior chief, the alienated Irishmen finding common cause with Māori, the northern English arms manufacturer aghast at the impact of his industry, the aristocrat unscrupulous in land and sexual conquest, the idealistic cleric, and two varieties of Irishwoman – the fallen girl and the driven ex-nun.

There are loose appropriations of historical individuals

and events, including incidents brought in from the period of the wars of the 1860s: the compressed timeframe squeezes Musket Wars and Land Wars cheerfully together. Gun running is a thriving industry. Surveyors map out land, summoning resistance from the angry chief Wahana. British troops arrive en masse to deal with rebellious Māori. When tension builds between the angry young Wahana and the elder statesman Rongopai (a character with a debt to Tītokowaru), Rongopai at first maintains Christian and pacifist principles but then – when artillery is used on a peaceful village – turns uncompromisingly to war. A bloodthirsty attack on a redoubt echoes the attack on Turuturumōkai. In a battle echoing Tītokowaru's strategy at Te Ngutu o te Manu, imperial soldiers are lured into attacking a flimsy-looking pā only to find themselves trapped as warriors emerge on all sides to fire on them. Rongopai, dressed in the formal European style favoured by Tītokowaru, looks on. The Irish priest Father Michael/Mikaere, who adopts a partial moko to signal his Pākehā–Māori status, is the Kimble Bent in Rongopai's camp. He often sounds more like Joseph Conrad's Kurtz in the Congo than Kimble Bent in Taranaki: 'a horror has descended upon us,' he gasps when faced with the unfolding violence.

Eight episodes was fewer than the 13 originally planned – and fell far short of the briefly projected several seasons, taking the series into the twentieth century – but this still allowed *Greenstone* to follow its several plotlines in some detail and to entwine them as the series killed off its villain and sacrificed its martyr by the conclusion. It races across interracial love affairs, the European hunger for land, Māori political manoeuvring for claims on European technologies and resources, the remaking of class in the new world, unscrupulous colonial government and business and, of course, armed conflict. The creators, when they spoke about it, talked more about what might have been rather than celebrating what was. As some of them remarked, the late 1990s may not have been the easiest time to mount a multi-episode historical drama. Nor, perhaps, was the state of bicultural relations in the industry, or the country, yet ready for history as bodice-ripper, although that was not, in the end, exactly what *Greenstone* became.

While the series did not abandon many of the trappings of costume drama, elements of its plotting and characterisation shifted towards more serious colonial questions. It wavered between an ironically melodramatic tone – dastardly Sir Geoffrey is finished off after a night of passion – and more serious echoes, with the class tensions between the settler characters, and the voices of colonial resistance heard in characters such as Marama (even as she rode across a midnight landscape in billowing silk) and Rongopai. The culture-crossing Father Mikaere, too, became a more fraught and earnest figure.

Bailey observed in 2015 that 'now's the time when *Greenstone* would probably pull together really well'. Scholes made a similar comment in 2010:

> *In retrospect I think it became too pc … I think you could do it now, I think you could do a historical bodice-ripper, which is what I wanted it to be, now. You know, like hindsight's a wonderful thing, but at the time I felt I didn't have any other option, because I respected … Don Selwyn … who was a great mentor and educator for me, so, I wanted to respect what he had to say, and in the process I do believe that it became a bit more boring.*[24]

There were tensions running in many directions, and they are visible in the series. Trisha Dunleavy has observed that '*Greenstone* was the first historical drama serial to negotiate the export challenges of a bicultural colonial story', and that

Greenstone (1999): Soldiers Larry Snowden and Khai Scott tuck into lunch as they await action on the set. Newspix.co.nz

the production demonstrated 'the limitations of foreign co-production as an approach to New Zealand colonial drama'.[25] The first episode rated well, but audience numbers dropped off quickly to a chorus of poor reviews. Linda Herrick noted the odds stacked against it: 'Hyped to the heavens before its release expectations were too high in a country starved of ambitious local television drama and hypercritical of local product.' Nevertheless, she quoted commentators who had watched right through and liked it well enough. Selwyn defended it; as he pointed out: 'People had preconceived notions about it. Those who saw it for what it was got a lot more out of it.'[26] Scholes had noted that when Tainui Corporation came in as backers to replace the BBC, they 'had an opportunity to act as cultural advisors for the series, but preferred to keep the relationship on a totally financial level'; their main concern was that it would be shown on mainstream television. After the series went to air, Tainui spokesperson Nathan York commented on this: 'People took it too seriously – it wasn't a documentary. We are definitely proud of our involvement.'[27] Peter Hawes, in a review in the same issue of the *Sunday Star-Times*, complained that the series had worn its history both too heavily and too lightly:

> The English will remain a 'bloodthirsty tribe' and the tangata whenua will remain noble until we have the courage to de-homogenise our history and give it back to the individuals who lived, heartily and unselfconsciously, in the block of ex-time in question. Aunties have to stop being old and wise, kaumatua have to stop having four gonads, colonial secretaries have to stop circling victims with their hands behind their backs ...[28]

Diana Wichtel, who did see the series for what it was, or at least, for what it could have become – 'a slightly mad, melodramatic blast of fresh air' – was 'forced to consider the possibility that I liked it'. She appreciated its nod to the genre when Marama's bodice was indeed ripped off in an English ballroom. 'At its best,' she announced happily, 'this is the complex past as viewed through the eyes of the bewildered present … Local drama having a laugh at its own expense. This is surely a good sign.'[29]

*

At the start of the new millennium two more documentaries screened – *Von Tempsky's Ghost* (2002) and *Frontier of Dreams* (2005), a general historical survey in which the wars received their due share of airtime. They were very different treatments, but both made substantial use of footage from past screen productions. The older films had become historical artefacts in their own right, and these recent productions could now draw on 75 years of screen stories about the New Zealand Wars.

Von Tempsky's Ghost

Von Tempsky's Ghost, screened in 2003 in TV One's *Documentary New Zealand* series, reconsidered the reputation of the Prussian-born Major Gustavus von Tempsky, leader of one of the Forest Ranger units. He was an important but contentious figure in the Waikato War and later in Taranaki, and was killed at Te Ngutu o te Manu. The documentary featured a dashing historical individual, came with a shamelessly populist title, and was fronted by a comedian. With these popular elements, it could have been history lite. But what it became was something more interesting – and it offers an example of the ways filmmakers could creatively circumvent the straitened circumstances of documentary under deregulation. Officially, *Von Tempsky's Ghost* was granted a slim $140,862 by NZ On Air at the end of 2001 – close to the very tight $150,000 usual funding limit for a one-off documentary. It was not actually made within this

Von Tempsky's Ghost (2002): 'These are our stories, our people, and our children need to learn about them.' Narrator Mike King speaks from the memorial at Te Ngutu o te Manu, where Von Tempksy encountered Titokowaru and met his end.

All frame enlargements from *Von Tempsky's Ghost*, courtesy of John Milligan

grant. In order to bypass funding constraints that would have ruled it out of contention, producer John Milligan pitched two documentaries concurrently, and made an unwritten deal that he would deliver both for $300,000. The actual cost of making *Von Tempsky's Ghost* was $201,000.[30]

Milligan researched, wrote, directed and produced most of his work, and had specialised in documentaries on a variety of New Zealand cultural topics. Ken Burns' *Civil War* series had been influential for him, just as it had been for Colin McRae and Tainui Stephens. He had directed two series, *Epitaph* (1997–2002) and *Shipwreck* (2000), using a popular history series format of one-off stories, fronted by actor Paul Gittins.

OPPOSITE: *Von Tempsky's Ghost* (2002): Robin Kora reenacts Tītokowaru's oration over the body of von Tempsky: 'In the days of the past, you fought here and you fought there, and you boasted that you would always emerge safely from your battles, to the bright world of life. But when you encountered me, your eyes were closed in their last sleep. It could not be helped. You sought your death at my hands, and now you sleep forever.'

Von Tempsky's Ghost (2002): The documentary featured a number of historians, including Rose Young and Tom Roa.

Along the way he developed skills in creating reenactments 'on a shoestring'. New Zealand military history led him eventually to von Tempsky, who he thought 'had had a bum rap' largely as a result of his Prussian origins. Milligan was interested in von Tempsky's shifting reputation, and it struck him that the charges of atrocities levelled at him did not seem to come from Māori sources.[31]

Von Tempsky's Ghost, like *The New Zealand Wars*, aimed to provoke a reevaluation of the colonial past, and it was willing to take a freer approach to reach its audiences. With *The New Zealand Wars* it was plain from the outset that this would be an academic approach, and Belich would be the historian narrator, in charge of his own script. The narrator of *Von Tempsky's Ghost* was Māori comedian Mike King (Te Māhurehure) – on a suggestion from TVNZ's Irene Gardiner, who had heard that King had been doing a stand-up routine about von Tempsky. King was more than a comedian: he had consistently tackled race issues and engaged with a range of social and cultural topics, and had played an active role in brokering these to broader audiences. As presenter for *Von Tempsky's Ghost* he was the first Māori narrator of a primetime programme about the New Zealand Wars, and this was an important first. The narrator's voice and onscreen presence carry an implicit priority in relation to truth-telling, maintaining the thread of narrative between other perspectives but functioning as a programme's anchoring authority; now for the first time, that authority was Māori.

The documentary portrayed von Tempsky as a lively historical figure, a soldier of fortune who had ranged across the colonial world. His arrival in New Zealand had helped create a new style of colonial warfare: bush-fighting – an attempt by colonial soldiers to fight Māori on their own terms and in their own fashion. The film investigated the reputation that von Tempsky had skilfully fashioned for himself but that had later

attracted controversy – all of which made for engaging popular history. The documentary's path into colonial history through a distinctive individual opens up reflection on how we can assess the past from the present.

Several commentators are interviewed about his career in *Von Tempsky's Ghost* – among them his biographer Rose Young, and military historians Tim Ryan and Richard Stowers, who discuss his personal life and military career, including his development of close combat in bush warfare with the Forest Rangers, using the Bowie knife, which he introduced to New Zealand. Māori historians interviewed include Danny Keenan (Ngāti Te Whiti, Te Ātiawa), Tom Roa (Ngāti Maniapoto, Waikato) and Te Miringa Hohaia (Ngāti Kura); they consider von Tempsky's career, and the attitudes of Māori towards him historically and in the present. As with King, their appreciative stance towards a colonial soldier, and the reasons they articulate for it, take viewers into the complexity of colonial warfare. Another Māori commentator is actor Nicola Kawana, who played the kūpapa guide and von Tempsky's lover Lucy Takiora in the play *Hundred Birds – Manu Rau*, and who later discovered she was a descendant of Takiora.[32]

This Māori appreciation of von Tempsky – something that many viewers might not have expected – becomes a central theme of the documentary. It opens with the actor Robin Kora performing Tītokowaru's documented oration over von Tempsky's burning body, initially in English translation; it is repeated towards the end in Māori with English subtitles. In this way the narrative is framed by a custom in Māori warfare: respect for adversaries who have proved their worth. The narration then shifts to King's point of view. He takes viewers into the story through his own interest in this 'swashbuckling' historical figure. 'These are our stories, our people,' he says.

'Our children need to learn about them.' The documentary tracks von Tempsky's varied career as mercenary, artist and adventurer: a duel here, a revolution there, fighting Comanches in the United States, on to goldfields, journalism, and then to fighting again.

As the documentary moves into von Tempsky's New Zealand period, it uses two types of reenactment footage. The first is reenactment of battle scenes made for the documentary, drawing on Milligan's expertise in military costuming and props. This is lively footage and well filmed, with definite 'bloke appeal'; the battles pitch the past as cut and thrust, with historic firearms featuring prominently. Mike King strides across battle sites narrating vigorously as he interprets the action.

Second, the documentary used archived film that featured von Tempsky, including footage from Hayward's silent *Rewi's Last Stand* that portrays von Tempsky as a dashing athlete, and several sequences from *The Last Stand*, including some of the Ōrākau footage. The arrival of regiments is borrowed from *The Governor*, using its large-budget capacity to portray massed troops marching and attacking the retreating defenders. As the documentary charts von Tempsky's growing discontent with the colonial project, this archived footage includes *Governor* footage of the retreat from Ōrākau, with the cavalry mowing down the retreating defenders and a young girl falling to the ground wounded. As the Forest Rangers move on to Taranaki in the later 1860s, the attack on Turuturumōkai is portrayed through footage from *The Killing of Kane*. Sequences from Iain Rea's multimedia stage play about von Tempsky, *Hundred Birds – Manu Rau* (1999), are incorporated as he is shown becoming increasingly frustrated.

This use of archival material endorses the effort made in the documentary to maintain an open perspective on the past:

The faces of von Tempsky trace his shifting reputation: von Tempsky's own elegantly fashioned look in the photograph he commissioned; Hayward's von Tempsky in his 1925 *Rewi's Last Stand*; and actor Richard Thompson in a reenactment created for *Von Tempsky's Ghost*.

The original photo of von Tempsky is held in Alexander Turnbull Library, Wellington, 1/2-050850-F. *Rewi's Last Stand*, Ngā Taonga Sound and Vision

every generation revisits the past, we realise. King's concluding comments underline this openness: 'We as a people have still not lain to rest the ghosts of the wars our ancestors fought against each other. Little wonder that we can't decide whether those who fought in them were heroes or villains.' And Tom Roa concludes: 'Sometimes we have the view things are black and white. They aren't – [von Tempsky] could be termed an anti-hero, or anti-villain – he's got all these shades, he's a fascinating character …'

Von Tempsky's career opens up opportunities to explore some of the less examined aspects of the wars. The Māori historians in the documentary discuss the mentality of colonial soldiers and those who worked with them. Danny Keenan notes that it is 'hard to separate this generation of men from their strong belief that they were on a civilising mission, that Māori were ordained to die out'. Tom Roa makes a similar point: 'I think he was a product of his time, that there would be no doubt in his mind that it was right for him to come here and do certain things to further his cause.' Te Miringa Hohaia talks about Lucy Takiora: he is surprised that she survived, when others who played a similar role were killed.

One incident that was covered only briefly in *The New Zealand Wars* and that still seldom reached public consciousness outside of the Māori world was the attack on Rangiāowhia towards the end of the Waikato War, which was still highly contentious for Tainui. Von Tempsky's presence at this attack creates an opportunity for the Māori contributors to *Von Tempsky's Ghost* to talk about what happened there, including the firing on women, children and the elderly sheltering in the church, and the burning of the whare in which people died. Tom Roa comments on both incidents.

> *Mike King: Inside the Catholic church that day was the tupuna or ancestor of Tom Roa. Her eyewitness account has been passed down in her family's oral history.*
>
> *Tom Roa: [She remembered] hearing gunshots, hearing screams, a woman running down and telling them, run away, get out, Pākehās come, the soldiers are here.*

An old woman shoots at von Tempsky; he responds by ordering a soldier to take her prisoner, but he also gives instructions that she should be quietly released. Roa asks:

> *If he did that with that woman, what other things did he do … am I being romantic in expecting an honour of von Tempsky and his treatment of this woman? If that's so then maybe his respect for Māori, and Māori women, extended further than just that one incident.*

Some people, King informs us, have said the fire that burned down the whare with defenders inside was deliberately lit – by von Tempksy. The commentators, including King and Roa, doubt this story: they point to archived letters that describe his memory of the incident and his feelings later about what happened there. King points out that von Tempsky felt 'sickened' and haunted by the memory of Rangiāowhia, and wrote of his respect for the bravery and determination of the Māori who were there.

These are careful, nuanced assessments that contributed to what was the distinctive feature of this documentary: that it drew on Māori sources and commentators to question Pākehā stories and to reframe the reputation of the Prussian soldier.

Frontier of Dreams

In 2005 a major New Zealand history documentary series aired on TV One. It had been in process since 2001, when Vincent Burke of Top Shelf Productions and Jock Phillips won an initial seeding grant from NZ On Air. Phillips was chief historian at the Department of Internal Affairs, had done a stint as concept leader for history at Te Papa Tongarewa and had established the online encyclopedia *Te Ara*, all roles in which he had sought to take New Zealand history beyond the university – conscious as he was that much of New Zealand's historical scholarship did not reach a broad audience. Like *The New Zealand Wars*, *Frontier of Dreams* came in the wake of a similar series, this time in the UK – *A History of Britain* (2000), written and fronted by the historian Simon Schama. The three grants the series was eventually awarded amounted to around $4 million – a very substantial amount in NZ On Air terms but, once again, a tight budget for the end result: thirteen 50-minute episodes. By now it was assumed that a history series would include Māori personnel, and two Māori senior in the industry were among the directors appointed: Ray Waru (Ngāpuhi) and Michael Bennett (Te Arawa).

The series used a format and tone that were relatively conventional for a national history; but, unlike *The New Zealand Wars* and Schama's *History of Britain*, its narrative was not carried through the persona of a single historian narrator. Essays by prominent historians of each period were adapted for the

Frontier of Dreams (2005): Historical advisor Buddy Mikaere surveys the site at Rangiriri.

All frame enlargements from *Frontier of Dreams*, Top Shelf Productions. With the permission of Buddy Mikaere

scripts, and in each episode there were interviewees and a range of other specialists, or people whose ancestors were important in the episode. Other historians, including Buddy Mikaere (Ngāti Pūkenga, Ngāti Ranginui), co-scripted the narrative. The voiceover narration linking the episodes came in the well modulated, authoritative and (to contemporary audiences) familiar tones of Pākehā actor Peter Elliot. A mix of archival images, landscape shots and reenactments accompanied the script. The style signalled epic national history from the outset: the opening credits featured aerial coastal footage and sailing ship, with the series title in monumental graphics rising from the sea to the accompaniment of swelling orchestral sound. The series was pitched to inform and educate, and it presented audiences with a far more nuanced history than many would have been familiar with. But it did not set out to provoke or challenge, and where it did, it did so fairly discreetly.

The series used archival images and, like *Von Tempsky's Ghost*, footage from earlier dramatisations – *One Hundred Crowded Years*, *The Governor* and *Greenstone* – accessed through government and TVNZ archives. Where this history of representation had been used in *Von Tempsky's Ghost* to illustrate and elaborate on the shifting portrayals and reputation of von Tempsky, here the clips are used essentially to create a visual narrative, an analogue to the script rather than a narrative in its own right.

The wars were dealt with as they arose: the Northern War occupies a substantial portion of Episode 4, written by Claudia Orange, and the Waikato War is the main subject of Episode 5, written by Judith Binney. The series did not foreground the cut and thrust of historical debate to the same degree as *The New Zealand Wars*, but nor was it a history devoid of commitment. In Episode 5, 'The Explosive Frontier' especially, the affiliations and recognition of injustice that had driven much of the historical research into this period emerge. The episode begins with the prelude to war in the Waikato and settler dependence on Māori agriculture – the 'golden years' of Māori–Pākehā relations when the Māori economy was strong and trade was vigorous. It continues through the emergence of the Kīngitanga and the settler government's increasing pressure on land, to the outbreak of war first in Taranaki and then in the Waikato. To fit

the 50-minute episode format the filmmakers illustrate only a few battles – Rangiriri, Ōrākau – and the fallout for the defeated Māori; the confiscations; and then the source of most of the land loss – the Māori Land Court and the individualisation of title. The interviewees for this period are all well known: historians Judith Binney and Buddy Mikaere, a director of the Waitangi Tribunal, and Joe Williams, chief judge of the Māori Land Court. Consistent with the impact this period had on Māori, the tone in this episode is more impassioned than the previous ones. Mikaere explains that after the wars, it didn't matter what side you had been on, your land was taken anyway, 'so there's a whole truckload of grievance and injustice coming out of that whole thing'. Binney conveys the shock she felt when she began working on what Māori called 'the land-taking court'. She had not recognised until then the sheer scale of the loss, she says:

Frontier of Dreams (2005): The series also used reenactments and aminations: here, Wiremu Tāmihana reading his Bible; and the graphic of Rangiriri.

TELEVISION HISTORIES IN UNCERTAIN TIMES

Frontier of Dreams (2005): Footage from *The Governor* evokes the battle of Ōrākau; and Ramai Hayward's poster for *Rewi's Last Stand* – by now, a well-known image in its own right – is selected to represent the refusal to surrender.

'that's why [the Court] becomes the engine of destruction'. And Williams speaks with measured emphasis as he spells out the effects of the legislation:

> *Individualisation of title probably was the single most significant thing in the breakdown of tribal society. And, that was its purpose. There's no question but that the settler politicians believed that the destruction of tribal society was, one, necessary to achieve colonisation, and two, for the Maoris' own good.*

The invasion of Parihaka is the subject of the final segment of Episode 5. Te Miringa Hohaia – who had featured in *Von Tempsky's Ghost* – joins Binney and Mikaere for this part of the story. He had been active in researching the Taranaki claim and was involved with curating the major art exhibition, *Parihaka: The art of passive resistance* (2000–01) and organising the annual Parihaka Peace Festival, which began in 2005. Again Binney registers her sense of injustice, and a descendant is in tears as she recalls the lasting effects on women she knew who had been raped during the invasion of Parihaka.

The episode conclusion emphasises that the wars had been contentious, 'because they were civil wars, wars about who would rule this country'. The concluding narration, accompanied by news footage of the signing of the Waikato settlement in 1995, brings the subject of the episode into the present by underscoring how it relates to the contemporary settlement process: 'But in 1995, the New Zealand government accepted responsibility for the invasion of the Waikato and apologised in a deed of settlement with Waikato tribes.' Prime Minister Jim Bolger and the Māori Queen Dame Te Ātairangikaahu bend to sign the settlement together, and the narration continues: 'This was one of many actions that in our time are aimed at putting to rest the legacy of the past.' Prime minister and queen embrace in a gesture of reconciliation as the episode ends.

What *Frontier of Dreams* could do that shorter format documentary could not, of course, was to place the wars in the larger historical context. Especially in the case of Episode 5, it situated armed conflict within the longer history of colonisation and ongoing Māori dispossession as the wars were succeeded by the Māori Land Court. In this context, the story of 'what happened after' the wars, which Colin McRae had wanted to tell but for which he was unable to get funding, could be told in some detail.

Conclusion

Greenstone, Von Tempsky's Ghost and *Frontier of Dreams* – a cluster of television programmes that took up the subject of the wars in their separate genres – were all developed in the context of the first big push towards deregulation of broadcasting. All operated within the constraints of having to pitch to broadcasters whose executives were required to prioritise ratings. The ambitious *Greenstone*, a response to an explicit call from a broadcaster and which pioneered the co-production process, and *Von Tempksy's Ghost*, made possible only because of a behind-the-scenes arrangement to circumvent the financial cap, charted the new seas in different ways. *Frontier of Dreams* followed a little later and, sustained perhaps by the success of *The New Zealand Wars* and with the impetus of the millenium as a justification for a major historical survey, had fewer hoops to negotiate. All three, though, were trimming their sails to a very light wind.

AFTERMATH AND MEMORY
In Spring One Plants Alone and *Rain of the Children*

Thirty years ago I made a documentary, In Spring One Plants Alone. *Now I've gone back to make a feature film, a drama, interviewing a lot of people as well, to try and unravel the mystery and the extraordinary events of this woman's life that I didn't question at that time. And what I've found is this immensely dramatic tale.* —VINCENT WARD

In the first decade of the new millennium Vincent Ward made two feature films about colonial wars. Each was filmed in a place where the past of colonial conflict attached powerfully to a defining landscape and the memories of the mana whenua. The fiction feature *River Queen* (2005) was filmed on the Whanganui River and draws loosely on events there and in Taranaki in the 1860s and 70s. *Rain of the Children* (2008), a very personal documentary, deals with Rua Kēnana's community at Maungapōhatu, its invasion by police in 1916, and how the aftermath of the invasion shaped the life of a woman who was there, Te Puhi Tatu. Both films were indebted to *In Spring One Plants Alone* (1980), an early documentary Ward had made about Puhi, and his experiences during its filming. The production of *Rain*, which includes footage of Puhi from *In Spring*, had the curious result that this, the most recent feature about the New Zealand Wars, incorporates film of a woman who was present at the last of the conflicts: for the first time since Hayward's *Te Kooti Trail* in 1927, a survivor of the conflicts appeared on screen in a film about the wars.

The filming of *In Spring One Plants Alone* began in a pivotal moment for this book – the late 1970s, only a few years after Barry Barclay's *Tangata Whenua* series, as *The Governor* was going to air, and while Geoff Murphy was working over the drafts of *Utu*. Twenty-one years old and with art school just behind him, speaking no Māori, Ward headed into Te Urewera hoping to make a film about Māori people who still lived in the old ways. He was interested in the spiritual world:

> as I travelled amongst the Tuhoe Maori, roaming from place to place, I listened to their stories of dreams and visions and ancestors, tales of kaitiaki (spiritual guardians) and patupaiarehe (the little people of the forest). It was a world of mysteries that I was drawn to, perhaps because of my Catholic upbringing. I was trying to understand that world and, in searching for this film, I suppose I was also seeking to learn more about myself.[1]

It took him quite some time and several trips to Te Urewera and other parts of the country to find the person he was looking for. Crucially, during this time Tūhoe leaders John Rangihau and Sam Karetu decided to support him.[2]

> One old woman I knew, she knew a number of elderly women, … and she said why don't I meet them and I went and met them and then she said there's one woman I wouldn't want to meet, the burdened one, and I went … so I went and saw her and she seemed very much the real McCoy, you know, the way she sat was

Rain of the Children (2008): Vincent Ward when he filmed *In Spring One Plants Alone*. 'I was young, 21, naïve, inexperienced … This person, who I hardly recognise, looks kind of funny to me now.'

All frame enlargements from *Rain of the Children*, Forward Films. Where acknowledged, images are courtesy of the NZ Film Commission; others are created by the author.

very much the way the old people sat at that time, they didn't sit in chairs, they didn't like sitting in chairs, a lot of the women they sat on their haunches, they did karakias over everything.[3]

Ward had by now almost given up on the film, but he kept talking to John Rangihau and visiting the old lady. She was Puhi, and she lived with her son Niki in Matahī, the last home and burial place of Rua Kēnana. Puhi allowed Ward into their lives, and for 18 months from late 1978 he lived in a shack near Puhi's house and worked on what became a moving and beautiful documentary, observing their sparse, difficult existence and Puhi's care for her mentally ill 40-year-old son.

Although Ward at this stage did not have a great deal to do with local people other than Puhi and Niki, John Rangihau's backing smoothed his path, and it facilitated his relationships with Tūhoe people later, after both Puhi and Rangihau himself had died. Ward, though, 'learned on the job': he helped Puhi, learned how to take his time through the filming, and was willing to spend the time to become part of her life. In the end, *In Spring One Plants Alone*, which Ward had hoped to film in a matter of weeks, took over 18 months to complete – a sign of Ward's singular determination about his vision for the film and his commitment to Puhi.

Remarkably for someone at this stage in his career, Ward was able to enlist two of the country's most talented cinematographers, Alun Bollinger and Leon Narbey, for some of the filming. Most of the time, though, he worked by himself, documenting the daily round of Puhi's life with Niki who periodically became violent, destroying household items and threatening Puhi. The film tracks the day-to-day labour of the little, doubled-over kuia as she carries water, cooks, cleans, bathes Niki and gives him his pills, and takes him into town for a haircut. There is little commentary; Puhi's muttered prayers and the conversation between mother and son constitute most of the dialogue. From time to time Puhi speaks to Ward; once she explains to him that she cannot leave because Niki needs her but that her presence provokes his violent outbursts that threaten and frighten her. In the film their isolation is striking. The house and its inhabitants are framed in wide shots of the bush-covered hills, and other people are hardly seen near the house. Lynette Read discusses the aesthetics of the film in terms of a Romantic vision that echoes German art cinema.[4] Ward describes it as a 'fly-on-the-wall' documentary – but its aesthetic is highly crafted.

When Ward first headed into Te Urewera he was very young. So was the renewal of Pākehā interest and engagement with te ao Māori, and the terms of encounter were in the process of being reconfigured. A major shift in bicultural relations was taking place in the 1970s – politically, culturally and, for many, in terms of identity and emotion. To go 'into the Ureweras' for Pākehā then was to approach te ao Māori in an almost mythical way, going into the most remote of Māori communities. No other Pākehā lived at Matahī, where Ward found Puhi, and the legacy of Rua's separatist community there remained among people who continued to follow his religious practices.

Ward was not the first to see Te Urewera as a last place where traditional Māori life might still be found: nearly a century before the ethnographer Elsdon Best had made a similar journey. As Jeffrey Paparoa Holman has argued, Best went to Te Urewera in pursuit of a world unaltered by contact between Māori and Europeans; and this is what he thought he found in his collaborator Tūtakangahau. Yet, as Holman shows, Best was documenting a culture, and talking with a speaker, who were already greatly affected by colonial encounter and confronting the large questions of how Māori might deal with European influence and economies.[5] Ward made a similar discovery. He hoped to film a life being lived 'in the old ways' and shaped by traditional beliefs. His return nearly 30 years later to explore what lay behind Puhi's life in the late 1970s yielded a story not only about tradition, although that was part of it, but about the legacies of violent colonial encounter. Puhi and Niki's circumstances could be traced back to the beginning of the century and from there back to the 1860s, to colonial events that Ward began to learn about after Puhi died, as he talked to Tūhoe people and as historical work on Rua Kēnana was published – created through collaborations between Tūhoe people and Pākehā researchers.

The journey into Te Urewera was not the first of Ward's encounters with Māori communities and places that were resonant with a Māori past. He had grown up on a farm in Greytown, near Pāpāwai marae, one site of the Kotahitanga or Māori parliament in the late nineteenth century. This proximity to a place that had been prominent in nineteenth-century Māoridom gave him a sense of a once-vigorous Māori past that, even through his childhood in the 1960s, was slipping out of view in the Pākehā world:

you know, I always remember the carvings lying on the ground, covered in mud, these beautiful carvings that surrounded the fence and so I was always aware of that and I was aware that the numbers had diminished even from when I was a wee child, dramatically, when I'd seen Māori … sitting on the streets, I don't know what it was, when I was a kid and then by the time I was fourteen or fifteen most Māori had disappeared from the area. But we had close friends at the marae, my father did and I did.[6]

The son of an Irish New Zealand father and a German Jewish mother, Ward felt intuitively alert to questions of cultural difference, alienation and dispossession. He traces his interest in the colonial past to this complex background. When I asked him about the influence of written history on his work he made it plain that although he had drawn on historical work it was not what drove him to the subject of colonial encounter:

it has to do with being a New Zealander, living in a Māori community, being part of societies both on my father's and mother's side that are societies that have been preyed upon, so it's empathy, Irish and Jewish, so it's actually got nothing to do with Judith [Binney] or James [Belich], it's got to do with living in a Māori community, empathising with people, and coming from minorities that basically have been picked on, and saying that history is not just ... what's written down by the winners, it's actually, history is our history which is of the losers. It's much more basic and instinctive and, you know, it's actually got zero to do with those writers, it's just endlessly more powerful.[7]

Unusually for a Kiwi filmmaker, Ward continued to work mostly in art cinema: he made *Vigil* (1984) and *The Navigator* (1988), and then spent the next 20 years working in the international market, producing and writing as well as directing. His credits during this time include two films that concern cultural encounter: he directed *Map of the Human Heart* (1993), a crosscultural romantic drama about the fallout of colonialism in the Canadian Arctic, and he was involved in making *The Last Samurai* (2003), the story of an American soldier in nineteenth-century Japan.[8]

By the time he turned his attention again to films set in Aotearoa, even if he was not personally driven by changes in thinking about colonialism, the landscape of cultural memory had shifted. More of the film and television productions discussed in earlier chapters had appeared, and historical work on the wars and the history behind Treaty settlements had acquired some degree of recognition in the broader cultural imagination. By the time he adapted Tītokowaru's story as the implicit backdrop of *River Queen*, Belich's work had given it a narrative shape in the Pākehā world: no longer an obscure and ill-understood conflict, it had a presence as a striking narrative of indigenous resistance with a distinct dramatic form. Similarly, when Ward was filming Puhi in 1978–79, knowledge of what had happened in Te Urewera in the aftermath of the wars was almost entirely limited to Ngāi Tūhoe and those with close links to them, but even then researchers were beginning the work that would bring this past to a wider public awareness. Judith Binney and her colleagues, in collaboration with Tūhoe elders, were writing the story of Rua Kēnana for a national readership – as was anthropologist Peter Webster.

The national cultural and political sea changes of the 1970s and 80s played out in the hearts and minds of some Pākehā people in more personal ways. John Newton's study of the poet James K. Baxter and Jerusalem, the utopian community that Baxter founded in 1969 on the Whanganui River, looks at one group that experienced these changes intensely at the beginning of this period. Newton asks whether Baxter's young followers' love, gratitude and indebtedness to the Ngāti Hau kuia at Jerusalem are characteristic of a changing 'structure of feeling' among some Pākehā. He argues that Baxter's own apparently naïve openness about his emotions towards Māori allows an unusual insight into a broader – although still minority – pattern characterised by a search for love:

> *Again and again one hears in these accounts how disoriented young Pākehā made this discovery, and of the warmth and acceptance in which they felt enveloped in the company of these charismatic women. I have come to think of this as the emotional core of the Jerusalem commune narrative: the testimony of those who, taken under the wing of the Ngāti Hau kuia, remember feeling loved in a way they had never felt before ... What I believe we are looking at here ... is a characteristic attachment of the Pākehā imaginary.*[9]

Newton argues that such attachments and desires are as worthy of investigation as racial antagonism, which tends to attract more attention.[10] The arc of *In Spring* through to *Rain of the Children* by way of *Map of the Human Heart* and *River Queen* charts a path through this minority Pākehā reconsideration of its relation to Māori and the past. Ward is hardly typical of Pākehā, but his recuperation of his formative experience in

Matahī echoes this 'characteristic attachment of the Pākehā imaginary'.

River Queen, a romantic historical epic, features international stars and was largely funded from international sources. *Rain of the Children* is a harder film to categorise. It is technically a docudrama but that term is too stolid to encapsulate it. It mixes footage from *In Spring* with interviews, historical reenactment, direct-to-camera and voiceover narration, and historical photographs. The film investigates memory and its absences as it returns to Ward's encounter with Puhi in the 1970s in order to reexamine her life, the history that shaped it, and Ward's transformative relationship with her.

Although three years separate their release dates, the making of *River Queen* and *Rain* was contemporaneous and intertwined. Ward had been working on the story of *River Queen* for some years and was in the protracted process of raising funding for it as he began making *Rain of the Children*. *Rain*, funded by the Film Commission, NZ On Air, Te Māngai Pāho and Ward himself, was made in stages as he researched, interviewed elders and incorporated their stories into the film's larger story, then returned for more interviews. The filming had begun but was interrupted when the funding for *River Queen* came through and he turned to the larger film; when that was completed he went back to work on *Rain*.

Despite the very different genres, tone and scale of these two films, they are approaches to the same themes, and in some respects they move the colonial war film off its tracks in similar ways. In both films Ward deflected the primary narrative away from a heroic or anti-heroic leader as protagonist, and centred it on a woman's story. As a result they became stories of people whose lives are caught up and thrown around by colonial war. In their emphasis on those who never asked for it, the films render war less as action – although both include scenes of conflict – than as a trauma to be endured. Both films explore cultural encounter, and people 'who go into a different culture and are transformed by the process'. As we have seen, this is a persistent theme in the New Zealand Wars canon, but perhaps nowhere is it more explicit than in these later films of Ward's.

In both films Ward worked with Tainui Stephens. When Ward enlisted him, Stephens' role as director of the *New Zealand Wars* documentary series was only a few years behind him. He was experienced in negotiating between film crews and iwi, and conversant with issues surrounding the representation of Māori on screen. He was very familiar with Belich's rereading of the New Zealand Wars, and brought this expertise and perspective to his historical and cultural advice on Ward's films. Stephens first became involved in *River Queen* when he was asked to advise on the script; he was eventually appointed co-producer, and he was a producer on *Rain of the Children*.

Rain of the Children

In Spring One Plants Alone was a remarkable film in its own right. Ward gained Puhi and Niki's trust, and he brought a sympathetic visual aesthetic to his documenting of their lives. The film pulled off the feat of creating extremely beautiful images of lives of material poverty without diminishing the great difficulties Puhi and Niki confronted. Yet even by the time of its completion, Ward was well aware that much more lay behind Puhi and Niki's lives in the late 1970s. Their daily hardships and the ways they dealt with them were not simply remnants of the 'old ways' – a window into the Māori past – but the aftermath of a particular colonial history:

> *I started it before I did* River Queen. *I had been thinking about it for years and years and years and then many things about it that sort of niggled me, something about the woman in the film, the Tūhoe woman, plagued me, just plagued me, I couldn't get her out of my mind and these questions about her ... I'd formed certain conclusions about her when I made the first film, which were to some degree accurate, but there was also, there were also other readings that were also accurate and possibly even deeper and I couldn't go into those when I made the first film.*[11]

Ward was not a 'disoriented' youth like Baxter's followers at Jerusalem: he may have been youthfully naïve but he was also highly focused. But nor was he much like the filmmakers discussed in earlier chapters. His Romanticism and intensely visionary style set his work apart from the dominant modes of filmmaking in Aotearoa, and from the character of earlier filmmaking about the New Zealand Wars. While the emotional drama of interracial encounter is a characteristic of almost all the screen stories discussed here, it moves from subplot to main plot in Ward's films. There is something akin to the 'structure of feeling' that Newton ascribes to the emotions that bind Baxter and his followers to the kuia of Ngāti Hau. In *Rain*, Ward addresses Puhi directly and indirectly in the narration:

> *I didn't speak Māori, didn't know anyone and I definitely didn't have any idea what I was getting myself into. Perhaps that's why you took me in, because I was so vulnerable. I didn't know my grandmothers, but in Puhi I found a unique care. It was as if she'd taken me in, as if I was a mokopuna, a grandchild, and when I'd come back she'd say mokopuna mā, mokopuna mā, we're very mokemoke since you've been away, which means, we're very sad since you've been away.*

In a screentalk after *Rain* was released he reflects on the lifelong importance of this connection for him:

> *all through my life I've felt that if I would encounter hardship, somewhere she would be standing behind me, that she would kind of walk with me, even though she's dead, and that I could always in my mind turn towards her for inspiration, that she went through so much, and would always get up again no matter what hit her. And I think I'll always have that, I don't think having completed this story and conveying the fullness of the life that she will disappear, I always feel she will be with me, with a gift of knowledge and, you know, love, and – kindness.*[12]

This emotional connection resonates throughout *Rain of the Children*. It makes sense of Ward's desire to understand Puhi better, and it is also apparent in the film's preoccupation with the mother–son bond. Even more acutely than *In Spring*, *Rain* centres on Puhi's devotion to Niki, the last of her children; in the screentalk Ward described it as: 'that kind of love you know that goes beyond, that anybody with a son, that's challenged in some way, has ... to deal with'.[13] Ward feels that he, too, is the recipient of this kind of all-compassing devotion.

Encounters such as Ward's relationship to Puhi go back a long way: James Cowan greatly valued his relationships with Māori, even if they were not described in these terms. And the attachment took a practical form for both Ward and Puhi.

Back to the past

Ward describes *Rain of the Children* as the outcome of an effort to understand Puhi and, now, the past that had made her:

> Rain of the Children *and* In Spring *was really trying to understand who my neighbours are and understand where I come from ... in the second instance,* Rain, *it was about trying to understand someone I knew, who was something of a riddle to me, who I thought I knew pretty well but there were things about her that I didn't know and obviously her culture's very much, her history is very much part of who she is.*[14]

The way Ward's own reflections and the accumulation of material that came to light after the release of *In Spring* are integrated into *Rain of the Children* is central to the film's mode of contemplating the past.

It is helpful to trace how the various historical resources emerged. Ward insisted that the emergence of new historical work was not the impetus for his return to the material of *In Spring*. But when he did come to make *Rain of the Children* there was a great deal more information in the public domain than there had been in the late 1970s. Several central figures in this research contributed directly to the film. Judith Binney, Wharehuia Milroy and Pou Temara, all of whom had been involved with publications about the Tūhoe past or in work on Tūhoe's Treaty of Waitangi claim, advised on the history and appeared on camera.

Rain of the Children is simultaneously an exploration of Puhi's past, Ngāi Tūhoe's past, and Ward's past: a venture into cultural and personal histories and memories. This is plain in the title of Ward's book *The Past Awaits* and in the temporal layers of its cover image, which incorporates the three distinct time scales of *Rain of the Children*.[15] The first is from the film's narrative present: Ward photographed from behind, walking towards Puhi's now abandoned house, evoking his filming there in the 1970s; above this hovers a dramatised image from *Rain of the Children*, of Puhi as a child bride in her wedding dress and veil; and behind both, another image from *Rain*, recreated from a historical photograph of the round council house at Maungapōhatu.

Ward used the word 'haunted' or 'haunting' in talking about Puhi; he associated the haunting with his sense that there was another story to be told about her, beyond the story of *In Spring One Plants Alone*.[16] Memory – his own, and that of others – is

The cover of *The Past Awaits*, with its temporal layers, echoing the structure of *Rain of the Children*: it shows Ward in the early 2000s, returning to Puhi's house which he had known in the 1970s, and Puhi at Maungapōhatu at the beginning of the twentieth century.

Rain of the Children (2008): This frame from the title sequence signals a return to two pasts. In footage from *In Spring One Plants Alone*, Niki stands waiting in the dark as the lights of Vincent's van approach. The font design, echoing the playing-card symbolism Rua Kēnana used in the architecture of Maungapōhatu, takes us further back into Puhi and Niki's history.

his way in to this story. In this sense the film is, above all, Ward's personal return journey. He finds his way back to Puhi partly by way of allusions to the films he had made in the intervening years. The white horse that is such a powerful image in *The Navigator* (1988) reappears in a similarly surreal scene in *Rain*. Footage of constabulary approaching Maungapōhatu in one of the dramatised sections is borrowed from *River Queen*, converted to monochrome to align with *Rain*'s other dramatisations. Young Puhi in her wedding dress echoes a striking shot of Sarah O'Brien in *River Queen*, or Toss in her tutu from his first feature, *Vigil* (1984). These visual allusions integrate the assembling of Puhi's story into the assembling of Ward's own.

The film engages with the past more explicitly through two closely linked sets of historical evidence. The first is the body of published historical work about Rua Kēnana and Ngāi Tūhoe, which had only just begun in the late 1970s; and the second is Ward's filmed interviews, undertaken over several years, with people who had known Puhi.

Rua Kēnana was an enigmatic figure to the Pākehā world in his lifetime: as well as being a charismatic leader, he was a superb photographic subject. The colonial government initially found him an ally in the opening up of Te Urewera, but it grew suspicious of the increasing autonomy of his settlement and, finally, suspected him of revolutionary activity. Many, including Cowan, regarded his utopianism with some skepticism.

In the late 1970s, Maungapōhatu attracted attention again as interest in alternative, utopian communities spread from the hippy counterculture to the more mainstream left. Anthropologist Peter Webster, in his doctoral thesis and subsequent book on the community, took an ethnographic approach that Ward found valuable – especially Webster's emphasis on the coexistence of multiple interpretations of the past.[17] Webster's book had less public impact, though, than the work of another group of researchers, whose interest was initially sparked by a collection of photographs of Rua and his followers (the Iharaira or Israelites) taken at the beginning of the twentieth century. These photographs reemerged at a perfect cultural moment in the 1970s, with its romantic utopianism and experiments in communal living. Rua's support of polygamy, too, appeared at first glance to fit perfectly with the era of free love, even if the historical realities of child marriage, which was Puhi's situation as a young girl, were at odds with these liberationist impulses.

In 1908 the *Auckland Weekly News* photographer George Bourne went to Maungapōhatu and, with Rua's collaboration, photographed the settlement with its striking buildings prominently on display and its healthy, well-dressed inhabitants making preparations for Christmas Day. Bourne's collection was eventually deposited at the Auckland Museum, where the photographer Gil Hanly saw them, and she told anthropology student Craig Wallace about them.

Wallace saw immediately that the photographs were important, and began research on the community. He was living in the house of the pianist Ivan Wirepa at the time, and he still recalls an incident that confirmed that he was working with something unusually important. 'I was just writing away, and [Ivan] wasn't Tūhoe so I hadn't shared anything … Ivan always dreamt, he had a Māori grandmother who he'd been raised by, and so he and her both had spiritual guides in their dreams.' But one morning Wirepa described to Wallace a dream that referred to details in the Bourne photographs. Wallace was electrified:

So I grabbed the photos, I took them out, those photos of the Iharaira with their intense eyes and everything, that jump out at you, and he looked at them and he said, 'You be really careful with this material mate,' he said 'you be really careful because look how strong that tapu is. You can still see the mana from them.' So, that made me really, I have to say that made me wary of what I did with the material.[18]

With a new sense of the power of the images, Wallace worked on a chronology of Rua's life and the community. Early on he asked Binney if she knew anything about Rua, but at that time she did not; then, he found that Webster was also writing about Rua, and stopped his own work. Some years later Binney made contact with him again – she was interested in a project of her own. With the photographer Gillian Chaplin, she went to Te Urewera to interview elders.

As it turned out, Binney and Chaplin were interviewing and photographing elders in Ruatāhuna, Waimana and Matahī at the same time as Ward was living in the Matahī valley and filming Puhi and Niki. They took the historical photographs back to the people whose tīpuna were represented in them, and the images, which were welcomed with great emotion, came to be central to the relationships they formed there. They interviewed older people at length about Rua, the Maungapōhatu community and the 1916 police invasion – including Te Puhi Tatu, who was one of the kuia still living who had been present in 1916. Webster had also interviewed Puhi. For Binney, these interviews began the work of the rest of her life, and her development of a closely collaborative mode of research involving long-lasting relationships with Tūhoe kuia and kaumātua. These interviews later provided some of the material for Puhi's story in *Rain of the Children*.

Binney, Chaplin and Wallace's *Mihaia: The prophet Rua Kenana and his community at Maungapohatu*, about the story of the community at Maungapōhatu, and the police invasion and its aftermath, was published in 1979.[19] *Mihaia* was structured around the photographs – those that Wallace had found in the Dominion Museum and others provided by the elders – with an accompanying text informed by the point of view of the Tūhoe informants. With Webster's book published in the same year, Tūhoe perspectives on these events began to claim the attention of a wider audience, mediated through Pākehā researchers.

Mihaia was followed by Binney and Chaplin's *Ngā Mōrehu: The life histories of eight Maori women* (1986), a series of oral histories of women associated with Te Kooti, Rua and the Ringatū church.[20] Although Puhi was not one of the eight women who feature in the book, she is acknowledged there. *Ngā Mōrehu* ('The Survivors') offers other connections between Ward's work and Binney and Chaplin's, too. Both deal not so much with the events of the wars themselves as with the long aftermath of conflict; and not so much with the chiefs or prophets, who are usually seen as the central figures, as with those who bore the longer-term burdens – the women, and the descendants.

Binney and Chaplin, when they were talking over historical photographs with Tūhoe elders, did not encounter Ward filming in Matahī – although they heard he was 'up the valley'.[21] He knew little of their work. Puhi was an informant for Binney and Chaplin as well as for Ward, but for whatever reason she saw no need to connect their enquiries. Binney and Chaplin were talking about the past. Ward was filming Puhi's day-to-day life. At that time, Ward was hesitant about enquiring too closely into her past, because she seemed reluctant to dwell on it. In *Edge of the Earth* (1990) he records a conversation that suggests the way she steered discussion away from the traumas of the past, even while she seems to be reflecting on them. She asks Ward if he was born before the flu epidemic of 1918. He reminds her of how young he is, then asks her what she was doing during World War One. She replies: 'Staying in Maungapohatu. Staying with Rua's son. One of Rua's sons, ne?' Ward goes on:

> I know of Rua Kenana, the charismatic Maori prophet who created a town called Maungapohatu deep in the hills for his disciples and followers, as Puhi has mentioned him before. But I can sense she wants to talk some more, so I ask where she was when the police launched their brutal raid on the community in 1916. Typically, she doesn't respond to me directly, but begins to talk about how she had lived with Whatu, one of Rua's sons. 'And then after four years he left me and married another wahine, woman ...'²²

The conversation touches on her children at that time, and then it ends.

In the production notes for *Rain of the Children*, Ward describes how the film came about. As he began to research it, he realised that Binney had information that could help piece together Puhi's past life:

> I was also in touch with the historian Judith Binney, who uncovered a whole range of things about Puhi from school records and births and deaths records. There was also an affidavit from a police case about a manslaughter, which was Puhi's testimony into the accidental death of her third husband, Clarkie. I realised I had in print things that Puhi had said and also Judith gave me access to the interview that she'd done in which Puhi talked about the 1916 police raid on Maungapōhatu. So, I had these key pieces of research that would allow me to dramatise her life. I saw that I could make something of Judith's photos and I could interview Puhi's descendants and Tūhoe historians to hear the stories about Puhi first or secondhand and I could dramatise those stories.

Binney is interviewed in the film, and her position as historical advisor facilitated a flow of information – specific and conceptual – that she had accumulated over a life's work:

> Judith was invaluable ... she gave me a couple of real keys ... the exact names and dates and deaths of the children. That was her. She had dug up that information and it was absolutely precise. The whole thing was great and also some insights into belief systems and the fear of ... trying to understand why they were all dying ... feeling that their god wasn't powerful enough and they had to adopt the Pākehā god in order to not all die ... she knew a lot about Rua and his sons and so on ... and she allowed me to use, borrow from interviews she'd done as well so ... Judith was just really a saint, she was just wonderful. She was very kind to me.²³

Binney's value for the film is evident in a cameo of Temuera Morrison filmed during one of the shoots and now included in the NZ On Screen material about *Rain of the Children*. Morrison, who played the role of Rua in some of the dramatisations, is chatting while he sits waiting to be made up. He begins by talking about his own connections – his father had been a teacher near Ruatāhuna, so he has a personal sense of what it means to be there. He echoes Ward's early sense of Tūhoe people as 'the last place really in New Zealand where they still, you can still get a glimmer into the old world'. But as he talks, Morrison is leafing through a copy of *Mihaia*: he reads up on what it has to say as he prepares to take on the role of Rua.²⁴

Rain of the Children traces the course of Puhi's life, how it was shaped by the colonial history of Tūhoe and Rua Kēnana's leadership, and the aftermath of the police raid on Maungapōhatu in 1916. The story is framed by Ward's return to Matahī, and is structured as a journey of investigation into the past. It begins in conventional documentary style as Ward

Temuera Morrison (Te Arawa) waits to be made up for the role of Rua Kēnana. He talks about the time he spent in a Tūhoe community as a child, as he looks through a heavily stickered copy of *Mihaia*, one of the historical sources for the film.

Rain of the Children DVD interviews

returns, looking to find out more about Puhi and Niki. He describes meeting Puhi and making *In Spring*, and talks about his desire to know more about what made her who she was. From Ward speaking to camera from a shiny new car on the way to Matahī, the film cuts to Puhi praying in the back of his old van in the 1970s.

To bring together Tūhoe's colonial past with Puhi's and Ward's past, the film uses historical photographs, dramatisation and interviews to tell the story of the bush-scouring military invasion of Te Urewera in the 1860s and 70s and the starvation and disease that followed; the rise of Rua as a prophet and the migration to form a religious community at Maungapōhatu, where Rua planned economic development and implemented health regimes to protect the people from the European diseases devastating communities without immunity. Puhi was the daughter of one of Rua's apostles, and we witness the growth of the settlement through her eyes (the younger Puhi is played by girls and young women from the Waimana area). At 12 years old she is married to Rua's son Whatu because the community needs children, and she lives with Whatu and his brother Toko. Then comes the police invasion of 1916, a catastrophic event in which Toko is killed. Heavily pregnant when the police invade, Puhi retreats into the forest and returns days later with her baby. Rua and Whatu are imprisoned, and the prosperity of the community begins to diminish.

The film now turns to the aftermath of the invasion, as the community seeks explanations for the disasters. Puhi's marriage collapses after Whatu returns from prison. Things go badly in her subsequent relationships, and her behaviour attracts criticism. She has many more children but they sicken. The film increasingly centres on the sickness and deaths of her children, a long catalogue of loss and damage as the children who do survive are taken from her. Standing outside her old house, Ward turns to the camera and reels off the sad list of deaths and illnesses; he wonders how she could keep going. The last segment of the film turns to the story of Niki, her last child and the only one who grows up with her, and the causes and course of his mental illness both before and after Puhi's death.

Composition

Rain of the Children is composed from several types of footage, constituting a narrative that reaches back and forth between timeframes and across multiple points of view. These include

Rain of the Children (2008): Archival photographs and reenactments were combined to recreate historical sequences.
LEFT AND BELOW: the police approach Maungapōhatu;
OPPOSITE, TOP LEFT: Rua (played here by Temuera Morrison) turns as someone fires a shot.

The original photograph of police crossing the river was taken by Arthur Breckon and is held in the Alexander Turnbull Library, 1/2-028071-F

OPPOSITE, TOP RIGHT AND BOTTOM: Young Puhi (Mikaira Tawhara) during and after the police attack, in reenactment: as the bullets fly around her; in the bush after the attack, with her newborn baby.

the original footage for *In Spring One Plants Alone* (1977–78); historical photographs of Maungapōhatu; film of the interviews Ward conducted in the 2000s with Tūhoe elders; and dramatised sequences in which the events of Puhi, Rua and Niki's lives are reenacted – some by professional actors, but also by actors drawn from among Tūhoe people from the Waimana area. The dramatisations stage events ranging from the 1870s to the 1980s. They touch briefly on the end of Te Kooti's War, concentrate in most detail on Puhi's childhood and young womanhood, the community at Maungapōhatu and the police invasion, then move forward to events in Niki's childhood, his life with Puhi as an adult, and episodes late in his life after her death.[25]

There are several narrative points of view. The primary one is Ward's own as the film tracks back into his search for Puhi.

He talks about making *In Spring* and his relationship with Puhi and Niki, narrates sections of the larger historical story, and frames his interpretation of Puhi within that larger story. Rena Owen, who plays Puhi as an older woman in the film, narrates from Puhi's point of view, describing her early childhood, the creation of Maungapōhatu, and her family. Other points of view come from the kuia and kaumātua interviewed, who tell some of the longer history of Maungapōhatu and also speak about Puhi and Niki. These speakers explain across cultures, translating Puhi's beliefs and Tūhoe understandings in terms that will be explicable to the contemporary world and to Pākehā people. But the film also marks the limits of translation and of access to knowledge. There are moments when the elders pause, deciding how – or whether – to respond to Ward's questions. At times they are obviously reluctant to discuss a subject. Some things do not readily translate: at one point one of the kuia says 'there is a word for it, but I don't know how to say it [in English]'.

The early footage

The footage from *In Spring* was restored and digitised for *Rain of the Children*. As a result, this film now acquired a clarity that even its first audiences never experienced. Co-producer Catherine Fitzgerald recalled how entrancing it was to see the images emerge from the digitisation process.[26] The beautiful camerawork includes many closeups of Puhi and Niki that bring us into their world through an intimate lens. Some may see this closeness as invasive – the camera tracks Puhi persistently as she carries water, chops wood, bathes Niki or phones the butcher – but this concentration on Puhi's daily life is a considered attentiveness that values her labours and accords her recognition. One scene shows the kuia giving Niki an ice

Rain of the Children (2008): Puhi unwraps an icecream for Niki. 'For me, it's the best moment of the whole film' says Ward.
BOTTOM LEFT: Puhi. BOTTOM RIGHT: Vincent Ward and Puhi, late 1970s, off for a trip in Vincent's van.

cream. He can't unwrap it, so she gently takes it out of his hands, unwraps it for him and puts it back in his hands. The camera is patient and intimate. Of this scene, which is included in *Rain*, Ward says, 'For me, it's the best moment of the whole film.'[27]

Such images are countered by scenes of disorder when Niki periodically becomes violent, making Puhi afraid for her safety and leaving the house a chaos of broken and dirty things – which she then sets about cleaning up. During one of these episodes she speaks to Vincent outside the house, waiting for Niki's violence to be over. She is afraid, she says, and if Vincent wasn't there she would run away while Niki was angry, as he might kill her. Sounds of banging come from the house that squats, isolated, under the dark hills behind.

Puhi did not always appreciate the filming, and she placed limits on how long she was willing to be filmed for: this was the main reason why it took far longer to make than Ward had originally planned. Alun Bollinger recalls one occasion when she got tired of the filming and said, 'You've taken enough' – and, he said, she *meant* 'taken'. Sometimes she put her foot down. One day the crew filmed her as she arrived home with heavy bags of shopping: when she spotted the sturdy young men lurking behind the house with the camera she put down the shopping and told them off for not helping her.[28] But Bollinger also recalled that 'the relationship between Vincent and Puhi, it was of mutual benefit, you know. Vincent wanted to record her story, her way of being, her way of life with Niki. And, Vincent had a van. So that was quite convenient.'[29]

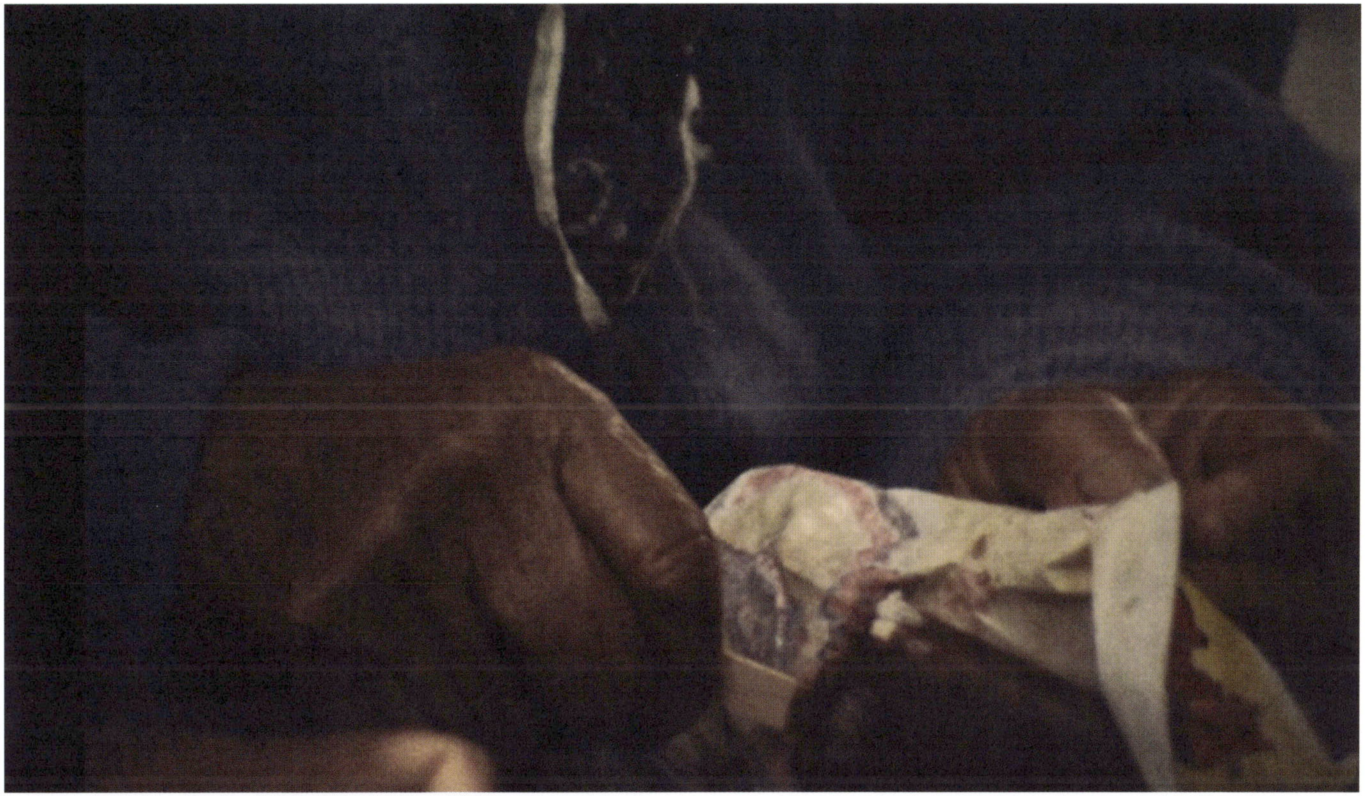

Rain of the Children (2008): Rua Kēnana's visual imagination was evident in the symbolic architecture of Maungapōhatu and in the care he gave to personal appearance, both his own and his followers'. Photographers recognised him as a superb subject, and Ward incorporated many of their images in *Rain of the Children*.

ABOVE: Rua Kēnana, Christmas 1908. The playing-card symbolism used on many buildings at Maungapōhatu can be seen on the gateway. The original photograph was taken by George Bourne, and is held in the Auckland War Memorial Museum Tāmaki Paenga Hira, PH-1976-6-16

LEFT: Rua Kēnana, in a portrait by the ethnographer and filmmaker James McDonald. The original image is held in the Alexander Turnbull Library, Wellington, 1/2-019618-F

Photographs

The historical photographs from a variety of sources chart Tūhoe history from the late nineteenth century. A smaller group of images of Puhi herself traces the more intimate story within it. This rich photographic archive interpreted by voiceover narrative provides a thread of documentation through much of the film. The camera pans across grainy images from the late nineteenth century illustrating the poverty, starvation and makeshift housing. The images of the police invasion in 1916 show the police and the people, and reveal evidence such as the fact that the women and children were held under armed guard.

The archive of news photographer Bourne, who went to Maungapōhatu in 1908, provides many of the images showing the creation of the 'City of God', of Rua and the Iharaira when Rua had taken on the mantle of a prophet, and of community celebrations, especially his photographs of the Christmas Day celebrations. Many of these early images reveal how Rua fashioned the representation of his religious community – in the stylised buildings with their decoration based on playing-card symbols, the attention to dress and hair, and the way the people are presented for the photographs. Well-known portraits of Rua and his followers by the ethnographic photographer James McDonald and others also appear. The Maungapōhatu images are strikingly staged and Rua's visual imagination, so attractive to Bourne and McDonald, obviously also appeals strongly to a filmmaker like Ward. Many of these images find their way into *Rain of the Children* and Rua's symbolism is carried through in the design of the film, including in the credits. Where text appears onscreen, Rua's playing-card imagery is reproduced in the font design.

Interviews

The production notes record that about 50 hours of interviews were shot, with 30–40 people. With the exception of Judith Binney, the interviewees are Tūhoe people, most from the Waimana area. To set up the interviews, Ward worked with Kēro Nancy Tait as iwi co-producer. Leon Narbey commented on what she brought to the production: 'she was brought up by her grandmother ... so that was her beauty, she knew all the old stuff from her grandmother'. Tainui Stephens described how this came about:

> Vince is unafraid to approach anyone. Through various circumstances he ended up with Nancy ... Vinnie already had a relationship with kaumātua down there, anyway. And subsequently – cause he did the hard yards, he went back ... those old people [who gave iwi commitment to the film] were old people that Nancy respected and they saw that she was assuming an assisting role and advising role and liaising role, and she respected the fact that they wanted the story to be told. So if she was grumpy at Vinnie, she could never ever doubt the wish of her old people that the story be told. So she was very committed not just for her own interest ...
>
> [AC: Were the old people happy with him telling the story?]
>
> Yes. Yes. Because they knew Vince. Not necessarily the filmmaker. Some of them didn't like the filmmaker (laughs), but they liked Vince.[30]

Nancy Tait was interviewed when she came to the Wairarapa for the launch of Ward's *The Past Awaits* in 2010. Asked what it was like to work with him, she responded 'challenging', because he was a perfectionist, but she went on to comment appreciatively on the way he had worked with Tūhoe people: he was '"very willing and very giving" in living and working with Tuhoe for more than two years, respecting and fitting in with the community. "He did that really well; he had the utmost respect for my elders; if he was able to do anything it was because of that."³¹

Tūhoe historian Pou Temara, whose whānau came from Maungapōhatu and who regularly stayed there through his childhood, decided to contribute to *Rain of the Children* after watching *In Spring One Plants Alone*:

> *Vincent Ward brought that along and showed me and I was impressed by that, in fact I was struck by it, in a very Māori way, and a very Tūhoe way, because what was there was the past greeting me, and I knew the main character in* In Spring One Plants Alone, *I knew her … so this was the past greeting me.*³²

Reflecting on the making of the film, he saw Ward's arrival as an opportunity for Ngāi Tūhoe:

> *The stories contained in* Rain of the Children *are stories that are well known [to us] … it's a story that had to be told, I mean it's probably lain dormant within the conscience of the people, but when Ward turned up, it was almost a god-given release, to tell those stories, so people would have viewed Vincent Ward as someone who could launch the stories about Maungapōhatu and its beginnings, into the twenty-first century.*³³

When asked about the film's preoccupation less with Rua, the leader, and more with the life of Puhi – someone who was caught up in the larger history – he said he saw the film as acknowledging the part of people like Puhi in the story of Maungapōhatu, and recording these more intimate stories for descendants:

> *it's those stories that are also very important to the people of Maungapōhatu, the people of Waimana, and then on to the people of Tūhoe. They are real stories, of characters that have descendants and they're still around today.*

Most of the interviewees were descendants or whānau of people whose lives were traced in the film. He said that, in general, they were happy to be interviewed:

> *Generally they were, yes, generally they were. I can't recall anyone who was outwardly concerned about being interviewed, or concerned about those who were being interviewed. In fact I think they were more concerned about not being interviewed. So, if there were dissenters we didn't see or get to hear of them.*

The camerawork for the interviews, like that of *In Spring One Plants Alone*, is mostly interior, in familiar spaces – either homes or marae spaces. Some are filmed at Maungapōhatu, on the historical site. One distinctive quality of these interviews does depart from *In Spring*, where Puhi and Niki are often filmed alone; indeed, the early film emphasises their isolation, and not only in its title. In the interviews in *Rain* almost every speaker is filmed together with others, who might witness or acknowledge what they say and sometimes contribute or add to the kōrero. In this way the filming follows the practice of speaking from and within a community. Leon Narbey, who shot these interviews, has spoken of the logistics of bringing these groups of people into shot – Ward was very insistent that he wanted the frames to include family.³⁴ At first there was little control over where the crew could film, so that, as Narbey explained, they might have to film people around a table against 'white walls, and fluorescent lights, and four very dark-skinned Māori people, and you can hardly see their features … in echo-y, reverberant rooms' – a lighting cameraman's nightmare. The system they evolved was to use the form seating on the marae they visited, so that they could group people side-by-side, 'and usually, we were more often cutting the light back, and then amplifying one direction or

Rain of the Children (2008): Interviewees are seldom alone as they speak; they are usually grouped with their whānau. LEFT: Te Uru McGarvey with her daughter Turuhira Julie Hare. With the permission of Turuhira Julie Hare; RIGHT: Sebastian Black and Judith Binney.

two directions only, so there was a nice, softer wrap-around of the features, and usually an eyelight … so this would give a stronger modelling of their features'.[35] The result of this skilful, careful camerawork is a series of unusually beautiful interview scenes.

Nancy Tait and Ward usually worked together in the interviewing, which was often done in te reo, as Narbey recalled, 'usually in a line-up, where [Nancy] would be just in front of me, by the camera, then behind her would be Vincent, over her shoulder, then I would be behind them': in this way the collaborative process in the interviewing could be integrated and the eyeline of the speakers could be kept aligned. The accumulation of speakers conveys the sense that this story is being told by Tūhoe, from the people's perspective. They tell a multifaceted story: they decide how they will respond and exactly what they are willing to talk about.

Ward is interested, for example, in the idea that Puhi may have believed she was cursed and that that was why her children kept dying. He asks whether that might be why she prayed all the time. Some of the interviewees assent to this view; others are not so willing to discuss it. There is some uneasiness for the viewer, in this part of the film: is Ward pushing this point too hard, overstating it, pressing for agreement with this interpretation? The voiceover narration gives it force as an explanation. But then an interview with a kuia suggests some reluctance about the explanation, opening up the space for conflicting interpretations, and keeping the film's historical perspectives open.

At times the interviews and dramatisations work in counterpoint. One example is a witty sequence in which a mother and daughter, the Tūhoe kuia Te Uru McGarvey and Turuhira Julie Hare, are filmed together. Te Uru McGarvey talks about her aunt, who was one of Rua's wives. She points her out in a photograph, and then Ward prompts her for some information he obviously already knows:

> Ward: So how did he actually choose his women …
>
> [Both women's expressions change slightly; the same thought has crossed both their minds, and they are amused, but they are not about to accede readily. The kuia gives a little laugh.]
>
> Ward: … or did they fall for him?
>
> Te Uru McGarvey: [deflecting] Well I don't know, must have been just a look, I suppose.
>
> Ward: [prompting] There's a story about his dog, that his dog chose some of the women.
>
> Te Uru McGarvey: [deciding she will address this] So somebody has talked about the dog. I didn't want to say it, but now I will say it.
>
> [Cut to monochrome dramatisation, with soundtrack of female vocals. A beautiful young woman sits among others on a porch. Rua arrives, smiles, and his dog runs up to her; there are glances between Rua and the young woman. The scene is romantic, innocent.]
>
> Te Uru McGarvey: Rua's got this dog with him, and the dog went up to my aunty, and it went to the other ones … [she pauses, then continues, both amused and forthright] In my own views, blowed if I let a dog come and choose me …
>
> [As she speaks, her daughter anticipates that she is about to speak her mind, and is already smiling at what she knows is coming.]

The scene is engaging and cleverly edited, with its contrast between the kuia and her daughter – strong and appealing women – on the one hand, and on the other, the 'choosing' by the dog, which the dramatisation subordinates to the exchange of glances between Rua and the young woman. The kuia's final statement then cuts across any idea that this was a romantic way for a marriage to begin. What the scene also tells us is that there were many decisions going on, among those interviewed, about what was appropriate to tell the filmmaker. Another example concerns a kuia who is pressed to respond to the idea that Puhi felt herself to be under a curse. She is reluctant to talk about it; she thinks carefully before she decides to do so, and then she speaks slowly and with deliberation.

This production process was episodic, evolving through the process of the interviews and emerging out of the stories that were told. The dramatisations were developed in a modular process over 4–5 years. Ward describes this process in the production notes:

> I didn't know what was going to be revealed, what new path I would find myself going down … It was a film that evolved because I didn't know quite what stories I would get from the elders and so we would start editing those stories to see how they shaped up and then we would go off and shoot a drama for a week or so and then come back and edit some more and then shoot another drama. In all, we did about 13 shoots with various-sized crews. It took a long time, but we kept it small, which gave me tremendous freedom to allow this film to grow into the best shape that I felt it could be.[36]

When Leon Narbey, who shot the interviews, spoke about filming them he recalled being struck by Ward's intuition. One day began with filming Judith Binney in Auckland:

> by the time we'd worked out where to film her, typical Vincent, it was so interesting, we just had to get her right against the window, and it was a bit of fiddle to get the light right in their small house … it seemed like she was only talking for a very short time and Vincent said right, that's enough, we've got to go to this other interview. I felt really pissed off. I thought, but she knows all this stuff, and we had to shoot out to … a very old lady, and

it was all dealing with the curse … and she couldn't give us very much, but her expression was amazing … and when I saw the final film I thought, yeah, right, OK. Yeah, that was the right decision, Vincent.

Dramatisations

Although most of the roles in the dramatisations, including Puhi as a child and young woman, were played by people from the Waimana area, some professional actors were also cast, and Nancy Tait was not always happy with this. The negotiations between iwi priorities and filmmaking priorities are apparent in Ward's description of what was at stake and how it was handled:

> Rain of the Children *involved a wide range of elders and had people act in it and so that inevitably means a grass roots participation in the film and a sense of ownership of it, a sense of participatory ownership … We weren't allowed, my kaitiaki, my guardian Nancy Tait, she and Marewa Hillman her daughter … they wouldn't let me have actors that weren't from that immediate area. I managed to get Tem [Morrison, who is from Te Arawa] involved, you know, yeah … well, Tem was easy … Rena [Owen], they didn't like Rena being involved, because her accent was totally different from theirs, and … to the end they weren't happy with that choice. But I needed an experienced actress …*
>
> [AC: her accent was the key issue?]
>
> *Yup. And I think probably more than that … she was a northerner.*[37]

Several people said later that they had not liked the voicing of Puhi in the dramatised narrations. Pou Temara had a specific reservation about it: ' If I compare the reality of Puhi's English language and the actor that played Puhi, then I think Puhi's language was much more melodic.'[38]

Waihoroi Shortland played the part of Niki in one of the film's most striking dramatised scenes. He accepted the part because several of his closest mates were from Tūhoe and they had known the people involved, including Puhi. For him, the fact that the film included Puhi 'who was there on the day' in 1916 gave it a particular magic. The scene where he played Niki shows him beaten up and stripped naked, lying in the main street of Waimana at night. A white horse approaches slowly all the way up the street, and stops when it reaches him:

> *[Vincent] said to me, you know, we can play this half clothed … we can throw a thing over you. I said 'All I need to know is, did it happen to Niki?' He said 'Yeah, it happened to Niki, they would drink his benefit money … and they beat him up and then they just threw him out into the street without his clothing' … 'I said, well, we'll play it the way Niki went through it,' and you know, it's one of the marvellous scenes I've played because that horse came right up the street, from the bottom of the street, from about 100 metres away, they pulled it into the scene on a fishing line, and at any time the horse could have just shook its head and gone off … although they played it in stop-start shots, the horse walked all the way up.*[39]

Pou Temara commented that the dramatised sequences made Puhi's life seem more complicated than it was: 'If there was criticism … it would have been about the overstatement of what actually happened, I think it was much simpler than that, but if you're making a film to capture the minds and attention of people, you probably needed to overdramatise it.'[40]

This points to something else that was going on in the dramatisations. The horses, the monochrome images of people in the snow, the powerful but harsh landscapes, the entwining of curse and disease, prophecy and salvation, the deaths of children, the permeable boundary between life and death, the transformative impact of cultural encounter, spirituality and the inexplicable – all were motifs that appeared in Ward's body of work between *In Spring* and *Rain*. This is an oblique thread that operates like a personal code within the film, through which Ward connects his own creative career to Puhi's story and also links European-inflected art cinema to Tūhoe symbolism, integrating a crosscultural exchange into the film that is both affective and visual. In tracing the paths of memory back to Puhi through his own subsequent career, shadowing his other films, he intimates that Puhi and Matahī shaped the later films.

All three, Puhi, Niki and Ward, are 'haunted': Puhi by the Tūhoe past and by her dead children; Niki by catastrophic events, a hard history and a more diffuse body of kehua or ghosts; Ward by Puhi herself and everything he had not understood about her when she was alive, as well as by his own Irish and Jewish family histories. His endeavour to explain her is an archaeology of his own memory and of Pākehā memory, an unearthing of things that Pākehā have not known and understood. But it aims for more than this: it seeks to bring Tūhoe interpretations of the colonial past to the information Ward uncovers.

Reception

Rain of the Children was screened for Tūhoe in Rotorua early in 2008, and had a world premiere in Sydney in June 2008 and a New Zealand premiere at the New Zealand International Film Festival in July 2008. Between the completion of the filming and the film's release, something happened that brought past and present uncannily together: for some people, it shaped the way they viewed the film. In 2007, 91 years after 1916, police raided Tūhoe again. The 'terror raids', as they came to be called, followed ongoing police surveillance of 'training camps' held in Te Urewera that involved, among others, the Tūhoe activist Tame Iti, one of the interviewees in *Rain of the Children*. Armed police cordoned off roads around Tūhoe communities, entered houses and made arrests in the middle of the night. In one incident a bus full of children on the way to school was stopped and boarded by armed police in combat uniform and balaclavas. Many of the cases were dismissed but four people were eventually tried, including Tame Iti.[41] The case attracted national attention.

This very recent event must have been present in the minds of some of the Tūhoe people who were first to view the film. But Pou Temara felt that 'Tūhoe appreciated the film'. Merata Mita, after a film hui in Waitakere, recounted one response to Tainui Stephens:

> *And she said a young Tūhoe guy got up, and talked about* Rain of the Children *as being* my *film [putting his hand to his chest], and I thought that was fabulous, that he took ownership of the story. Because it was challenging, I mean, it wasn't easy and some of the family are still embarrassed that we exposed some of what people may think of as lack of care of the old lady or whatever ... That's being emotionally transparent, honest about this tragedy. So for that young Tūhoe guy ... and I've found that from everyone, really, there were a couple who didn't like it ... it's the kind of film that provokes ... that's cool. But yeah, the on-the-ground people, they really get it, they're proud of it, which is fantastic.*[42]

One Tūhoe commentator expressed strong objections to the film. In a long critical column, Taiarahia Black argued that the film did not situate Puhi and Niki's story in Tūhoe history and

---

Rain of the Children (2008): Niki (played by Waihoroi Shortland) lying in the street as the horse approaches. Courtesy of NZ Film Commission.

did not convey enough of the history; that it told an outsider's story; and that it blamed Puhi herself for the curse.[43] Some of these criticisms misrepresent the film. Other viewers, including the present author, have had doubts about the pursuit of the idea that Puhi was the object of a curse – yet, as Ward has pointed out, this information had come to him from older people who knew Puhi.[44] But Black's main objection – and that of Puhi's granddaughter, whom he quotes in his column – was a concern that her story was being told by an outsider.

It is hard to know how widespread this objection was. Black is not from the Waimana area where Puhi lived and where the film was made. Tūhoe leadership had supported the film: this meant Ward could draw on substantial support and a sense of ownership from within the iwi as the film was made, and many Tūhoe people were involved at all levels of the production. Tūhoe names outnumber all others in the credits. Several hundred Tūhoe people travelled to Auckland for the New Zealand premiere at the film festival in Auckland in July 2008. Yet many Māori do have concerns about Pākehā telling Māori stories, and these concerns have been expressed in relation to *Rain of the Children*.

The film appears to have contributed to public historical knowledge of Tūhoe. When the centenary of the police invasion of Maungapōhatu was marked with a reenactment in April 2016, *Newshub* reported: 'The raid by 70 armed police affected Tūhoe for decades, as told in the movie *Rain of the Children*.'[45] The news coverage included reenactment footage from the film.

In a review of an exhibition of Ward's paintings, *Breath*, in New Plymouth in 2012, Anthony Byrt situated Ward's practice within a certain type of crosscultural relationship – and his comments apply equally to Ward's films.

> [Ward's] connection with the central North Island, from Tūhoe country in the east through to the Taranaki and Whanganui regions in the west [is] one of the major forces in his career, as are his relationships with various iwi. Kaumatua from across the North Island travelled to New Plymouth for the exhibition's opening-day blessing, with Tūhoe particularly strongly represented.
>
> Tūhoe's fusion of Christianity and self-determination has long been a subject of fascination – and often frustration to the point of violence – for Pakeha. Alongside Colin McCahon and Judith Binney, Ward is one of the few Pakeha figures who have managed to harness Tūhoe history and highlight its immense cultural significance for New Zealand/Aotearoa as a whole. Tūhoe's presence at the gallery confirmed that the respect is mutual, and close …
>
> Just like McCahon and Binney, Ward has never shied away from the truth: he digs and digs until he gets somewhere other filmmakers and artists don't often visit: a psychic space where violence, memory, myth, sex and religion mingle in a landscape scarred by its history.[46]

ENCOUNTER, ROMANCE AND CONFLICT
River Queen

I was interested in trying to tell something of a founding story, a foundation story ... the moment where we became, as a people to some degree, even though it was a bloody becoming. —VINCENT WARD

Between trips to Te Urewera to shoot the initial interviews for *Rain of the Children*, Ward was raising funds for a larger film, the fiction feature *River Queen*. More than 20 years had passed since *Utu*, and now another New Zealand Wars epic was on the horizon. Much had changed in those years. The industry had grown and professionalised, but it had become far harder to raise funds for a film on this scale. The sources of local funding – primarily the Film Commission – offered part-funding, but the amounts fell well short of the budget of a substantial historical drama. The newly elected Labour government had sought to address the gap confronting mid-sized productions with a Film Fund in 2000, but still the level of funding came nowhere near the scale of the budgets necessary.

River Queen was made in a bicultural climate that had altered since *Utu*: cultural advice and iwi permissions to film in an area such as the Whanganui River were now formal processes that were part and parcel of film production. When the Whanganui iwi was approached to participate in the production, it came backed by a substantial iwi organisation that had a good sense of the cultural values behind its involvement, and expected tangible benefits for its people in return for their commitment. The days of the 'shy conversation' that Gaylene Preston had observed in the making of *Utu* were past.

For Ward, this film was primarily a woman's film set against a background of colonial war. It was also a film about cultural transition that hinged on affinities between Māori and Irish as colonised peoples. The protagonist Sarah O'Brien's Irishness predisposes her to an alignment with Māori rather than the English, who are represented most forcefully by Major Baine – a ruthless Englishman like *Utu's* Colonel Elliot. The film combines its New Zealand-derived stories, Māori performers and cultural elements with the look and feel of Irish historical romance, drawing on a Celtic-inflected score and mystical dream sequences.

Ward worked on the script over several years, with Toa Fraser as co-writer. In 2001 he asked Tainui Stephens to look at it. Stephens liked the script and was impressed with the historical research (the work of Ward's sister Ingrid Ward). Some time later Ward and Don Reynolds asked him to be co-producer: 'They wanted my cultural input, Vinnie wanted to work with me with regard to that, and Don wanted my involvement with regard to setting up iwi things and be responsible for the Māori elements of the film. I didn't realise how big it was going to be.' Stephens was doing preliminary work with Ward on *Rain of the Children* at the same time. Having directed the *New Zealand Wars* documentary series only a few years earlier, he brought a considerable depth of knowledge about Tītokowaru's War to a film that drew on that history.[1]

In Whanganui

As with Tūhoe, Whanganui was a highly distinctive iwi with a deep and present sense of its past. Its identity centred on the Whanganui River, the defining landscape of the film. Whanganui people had fought on both sides during the wars. In the 1840s they fought against the British; but from 1864 the lower Whanganui people, who lived closer to the settlers, tended to ally with the Crown, while the upper tribe further inland, which adopted the Pai Mārire faith, remained resistant. In 1864 a battle that took place on Moutoa Island in the river brought upper and lower tribes into direct conflict.[2] The protests that took place in 1995, when Whanganui people occupied Pākaitore/Moutoa Gardens to challenge the presence there of colonial statues and memorials that celebrated the kūpapa victory and its defence of the town in this battle, were a recent reminder of contentious events.

Stephens and Ward approached the Whanganui River Trust Board and, specifically, the kaumātua Rangitihi Tahuparae to request iwi support and involvement in the film. Discussions with Whanganui iwi began upriver at Pipiriki in early 2002, and the Whanganui Awa Film Working Party was formed to manage iwi involvement with the film. Rangitihi Tahuparae and Julie Ranginui became the film's kaumātua, and an agreement was drawn up that covered employment, creative contributions, cultural security and the protection of the river and sensitive landscapes during filming. When Tahuparae became ill several weeks into the filming he asked Gerrard Albert to step in for him; Albert, who happened to be on the set on the first day, had already become a de facto cultural advisor and continued in this role throughout the filming.[3] The film credits include a substantial list of marae – and the Pātea Maori Club, 30 years after it was credited in *The Killing of Kane*. Ward recalls that although some people in the industry had told him he would have difficulty because of Whanganui's history of protest, the relationship was very good:

> So this became an us situation, our film and us situation. And you know everybody had said at that time … everybody said are you crazy, wanting to do a film with Whanganui iwi, what are you, it'll just mean you'll have lots of problems … And we never had any, we just had … it was a dream. We … found the iwi just fantastic and very collaborative and very can-do and … I formed some very close friends with some of the people there and they really participated, they were fantastic. Really … they really went into the film heart and soul.[4]

Alun Bollinger also emphasised the commitment that Whanganui put into the production:

> there's commitments at so many levels from so many people. You know we've got Māori extras turning up in the dark to get moko put on and then they're standing around all day half dressed ready to do whatever the bidding is, you know that sort of level of commitment from people, you can't just treat that as – sure it's Vincent's film – but actually now there's a lot of heart and soul in this.[5]

River Queen (2005): The Whanganui River, star of the screen.
All frame enlargements are from *River Queen*, Silverscreen Films

River Queen (2005): Charles Mareikura trained the Whanganui performers in haka, and in movement.

Albert recalls that his advice was frequently sought on cultural matters, and he was sometimes asked to resolve debates. He advised on the way that a waka should be carried, for example; and he was asked to resolve an argument over how the body of the sick chief should be touched. He and Tahuparae thought a few of the onscreen results were 'a bit off', but they acknowledged the film was fiction. Albert appreciated Ward's open, amenable approach to taking cultural advice.[6]

Stephens described how young Māori gained expertise through their work on the film. Whanganui people were cast in the film; iwi artists and craftspeople contributed to the design; and locals participated through cultural performance, ranging from waka paddling to haka and military manoeuvres.[7] Charles Mareikura, the trainer for much of this performance, brought a high level of martial arts and kapa haka expertise to the film: 'the way that the warriors walked, in that stylised way as they approached the village, the kūpapa, you know how they walked … that … came from those guys, their kapa haka'.[8] Tahuparae and Albert worked with language coach Wiha Te Raki Hawea-Stephens to advise Māori actors from other areas, including Cliff Curtis and Temuera Morrison, on the distinctive Whanganui dialect.

The Whanganui River itself was the star of the superb cinematography – the deep greens of the bush and of the river under the high cliffs, and the scenes shot in low light deepened and enriched the film's palette. The wintry conditions created enormous problems for the production, but they also helped to produce magnificent images: the colours deepen in the moisture, and the cold is palpable.

Production dilemmas

The film made headlines during production for a series of problems that centred on two issues. The first was money. *River Queen* was caught squarely in the ever-growing dilemma of funding historical film in Aotearoa. The costs of historical drama had risen far more rapidly than the available local funding. This meant an ever-widening shortfall that had to be met by obtaining international funding – a difficult task. *River Queen* had a substantial price tag by New Zealand standards, with its historical sets and costuming, large cast and remote locations on a wintry river. Alun Bollinger, who had also worked on *The Piano*, recalled that the two productions had a roughly similar budget – around $13 million – but that *The Piano* had been made over a decade earlier and was a much smaller-scale production.

In 2003 Margot Butcher profiled Ward for *North and South* as he was trying to raise the funding for *River Queen*. Butcher pointed out that the limited budget allotted to the Film Fund effectively defeated its very purpose – to fund mid-size films that were beyond the scope of the Film Commission. She criticised the government's inability to recognise the yawning gulf between the available funds and the actual costs of such films, and she pointed out that no other country's film investors were likely to step into such a breach.[9] When the production did get under way, with funding from New Zealand (the New Zealand Film Production Fund, the New Zealand Film Commission), Britain (the Film Consortium, the UK Film Council, Invicta) and the United States (Endgame), it was still several million short of the forecast budget.[10]

There was another catch, too. International funding for the film came with two conditions: its contracts with international stars, and a requirement to use the funding within that tax year. When the film's English lead Samantha Morton accepted a role in another film, thereby delaying production for several months, these two conditions threatened to become incompatible. The only solution was to shoot through the winter months – and this, besides making it a more arduous shoot for everyone involved, added to the cost of making the film; the production proceeded on a wing and a prayer rather than an adequate budget. This meant that when problems arose and the filming ceased for six weeks (for reasons discussed below) the film's production guarantor was the person in charge of the schedule when filming resumed. Scenes were cut and compromises were made: some story threads were closed off.

The second, and related, problem centred on Morton herself. Ward had been very keen to cast her in the role of Sarah, to harness the 'raw' quality of her acting. Morton found herself on the Whanganui River among a New Zealand cast and crew, and, unlike her character, was not transformed by the experience. She obviously found this environment unfamiliar, physically hard, and uncomfortable. The international funding was contingent on the recognition of its bankable stars – Morton, Canadian Kiefer Sutherland and Irish actor Stephen Rea. Morton's decision to accept another role not only delayed the shoot and forced up the costs, it had implications for a film that was set on a cold river between high cliffs and in dense bush. It shortened the daylight hours for filming each day, and the cold affected everyone – perhaps none more so than Wī Kuki Kaa, veteran of *The Governor* and *Utu*, who had been so keen to work with Ward that he kept his diagnosis of terminal cancer secret. He was afraid the waka in which several of his scenes took place would capsize and tip him into the freezing river, and that he might not survive it.[11]

When Samantha Morton came down with the flu she returned to England for six weeks, and the filming came to a halt. Tension already surrounded her; she had reportedly been unwilling to work with some cast members, and there were varying degrees of hostility and tolerance towards her among cast and crew. Then her relationship with Ward deteriorated. At this point as Temuera Morrison saw it, 'She was not just unsupportive, she was actively opposing Vincent'.[12] Ward is known as a director who places high demands on cast and crew, but it seems that Morton was unprepared for the antipodean all-pitch-in culture of filmmaking. Finally she refused to work with Ward. But because she was now essential to the film's completion – many scenes involving her had already been shot – it was Ward who was fired. Many wondered if this would spell the end of the film but, as Morrison recalled, there was a strong sense of loyalty to Ward which meant 'we wanted to finish the movie for Vincent'.[13] Bollinger, who as director of photography had worked closely with Ward throughout, stepped in as director for the final period of the shoot. Ward returned for post production, and to film some sequences to compensate for scenes that could not be shot and pull the film together.[14]

The 'media spotlight' didn't help, either. As soon as word of trouble was out there was a high level of media interest. Stephens recalls how a newspaper report of a curse placed on the production gave him 'one of the darkest days of my life':

> *going on to the set about five in the morning when we didn't know whether we were carrying on because of Samantha's condition … and then we see in the fuckin headlines a curse being put on the [film] and that struck to the core of what I was meant to be responsible for … As it turns out, the so-called said curse was a bullshit thing and just some inter-hapū rivalry things happening. And our people, John Tahuparae and kaumātua got onto it and, you know, put a stop to it pretty much, but the headline was out and the media hounds were baying.*[15]

The story

At the opening of *River Queen*, Sarah O'Brien lives with her Irish colonial surgeon father and her sister in a remote outpost on a river, Te Awa Nui (the Great River – the Whanganui). Sarah falls in love with a boy from the local Māori community, son of the tohunga Rangi; they become lovers, but he later dies. Sarah gives birth to a son, Boy (Rāwiri Pene), but while he is still small, her father (Stephen Rea) violates tapu by clearing bush from a burial ground. In retaliation Boy is seized by his grandfather Rangi (Wī Kuki Kaa), and taken away up the river. Sarah searches for him for years without success. Then, as the colonial army launches an unprovoked attack on a Māori settlement, Sarah finds Rangi – but as she asks him about Boy the English commander Major Baine (Anton Lesser) shoots Rangi; he dies predicting a 'river of blood'. Rangi's other son Wiremu (Cliff Curtis), a scout fighting with the colonial troops, takes part in the attack on the settlement; but when war breaks out between the colonial forces and the Māori, led by the chief Te Kai Pō (Temuera Morrison) – a character modelled primarily on Tītokowaru – Wiremu switches allegiance back to the resistant side. He asks Sarah to come up the river to treat Te Kai Pō, who is suffering from 'the coughing sickness'; there, he tells her, she will find her son. Sarah is taken up the river blindfolded: she cures Te Kai Pō's illness, is reunited with Boy, and falls in love with Wiremu. Boy refuses to return downriver with her and declares his affiliation with the iwi. Meanwhile the colonial army advances up the river, falls into Te Kai Pō's carefully laid trap and suffers heavy losses; the Irish soldier Doyle (Kiefer Sutherland) who loves Sarah is wounded and dies. At the outset of this battle Wiremu's small, crippled son is killed by a kūpapa warrior. Sarah returns to Whanganui, where Baine suspects her loyalty but commandeers her surgical skills for the army. Again the troops advance up the river; in the lead-up to the final battle Boy is captured by the colonial troops and Wiremu crosses again to the enemy side, to negotiate his release. Boy, Wiremu and Sarah then run from the colonial troops. The resistant Māori campaign falls apart when Te Kai Pō is discovered with the wife of one of his allies; his forces disperse and retreat inland. Sarah elects to make her home with Wiremu and Boy and the film's coda, years later, sees them incorporated into the daily life of the Māori community.

The background

The research for *River Queen*, in contrast to that for *Rain of the Children*, was mostly archival and was oriented to a specific idea. Ward asked his sister Ingrid to search for historical evidence of European women who had gone into te ao Māori in the nineteenth century. Two stories in particular derived from the Whanganui and Taranaki areas: those of Anne Evans and Caroline ('Queenie') Perrett (later Queenie Ngoungou).[16] There was a third woman who was the subject, not of a story but of an enigmatic photograph taken at Pāpāwai around 1900 – 'of I think it's about six women and one of them's Pākehā but she has a moko, in the middle of the group'.[17] Boy's story as well as Sarah's derives from Queenie Perrett's story.

The other main historical antecedent for *River Queen* was Tītokowaru's War, which had acquired some public prominence by this time. It was the basis for several characters and the overall trajectory of the war forms the background story.

Once again, Ward's own imperative for telling this historical story can be traced back to his experience as a young Pākehā growing up in Te Urewera, and his ongoing interest in stories of cultural encounter that emerged from it. He had more recently become interested in telling a woman's story set against a background of conflict – as a result of his development work on the film *The Last Samurai*. The studio he was working for had wanted that film to centre on the male lead, but Ward liked the character of a female translator in the story. The studio was unwilling to risk a female lead, so Ward withdrew from directing it; he found a replacement director and stayed on as executive producer instead. But the idea of a woman character operating between cultures in a nineteenth-century war had stuck, and he began thinking towards setting it in New Zealand. For him, the war story in *River Queen* was definitely secondary to the story of cultural encounter:

The story I was doing … had a Tītokowaru character in it but it was not the inspiration. The inspiration was Annie the Doctor

River Queen (2005): Rangi (Wī Kuki Kaa) looks back as the waka carries Boy away from his mother.

and Caroline Ngoungou … those two women were the inspiration and, you know, I liked the Tītokowaru story but mine is such an angle into it … Probably the biggest inspiration [was] work I did on The Last Samurai.[18]

Ward's desire to tell a woman's story of cultural encounter introduced a new thread into the long tradition of telling the story of Tītokowaru's War from the sympathetic insider perspective first established by Kimble Bent. Bent told his story to Cowan and it featured in *The Killing of Kane*, Belich's *I Shall Not Die* and Shadbolt's *Monday's Warriors*. Sarah's perspective continues the story's history of entanglement with a Pākehā–Māori viewpoint – in her case Irish. Bent was less important, though, than Perrett and Evans in the shaping of Sarah's and Boy's stories. To make the point-of-view character a woman also made her more vulnerable, less culturally dominant, especially in the nineteenth-century context.

Shifting history

The cultural narrative of colonial conflict in the historiography of the New Zealand Wars had been reconfigured by the 2000s – even if, as Belich observed, it was a shift largely among 'the cognoscenti'.[19] The realignment is evident in *River Queen*'s background story, especially in the renewed prominence of Tītokowaru in the pantheon of resistance leaders alongside others such as Hōne Heke, Rewi Maniapoto and Te Kooti. Whereas in *Utu* resistance was reactive, as Te Wheke was impelled into violence by the codes of warfare – a trajectory dictated by the prevailing interpretation of Te Kooti's War – in the wake of Belich's work the narrative of resistance now centred on the figure of the proactive intelligent strategist.

A second dimension of the changing historiography, if not necessarily of popular wisdom, was the idea that the wars were integral and founding events rather than marginal affairs in New Zealand's past. This view had been put forward by earlier historians such as Keith Sinclair, but the *New Zealand Wars* series gave it a greater reach – for a while at least.

Third, and somewhat at odds with Belich's emphasis on masculine stories of 'great men', there was more of a focus on women and on apparently marginal figures. Binney's work, especially *Ngā Mōrehu/The Survivors* in collaboration with Gillian Chaplin, was the best-known example in this context. *Utu* moved away from the powerful man as protagonist to the quiet Wiremu, but despite its forthright women characters it was still a very masculine narrative. Women's stories gain greater prominence in Ward's films – in *Rain*, with its attention to the long aftermath of conflict and as a film about Puhi more than Rua Kēnana; and in *River Queen*.

River Queen makes extensive use of historical referents, although it also (with one exception) marks out its fictional status. Tainui Stephens commented on the way the film sits at a carefully judged distance from its historical sources. The place of historical fiction might be a delicate matter in contexts where events are still contested, or where historical events or figures might be tapu. His experience with the *New Zealand Wars* series involved him in dealing with many iwi about their history, including in Whanganui.

> *Because what is on documentary is considered to be truth, or purporting to tell the truth, you have more cause for tribal versions and dissent about what story should be told. If you make it a fiction there's less cause for dissent, no matter how thinly disguised some of the incidents [are] … I mean* River Queen *was a mixture of some of Te Kooti's story, some of the Tītokowaru story, and others, and it's a smart melding, I thought. And it was certainly an easier sell for Whanganui iwi, and Taranaki iwi, to be telling the* essence *of their story but not the* tapu.[20]

The makers of *Utu* were working with similar concerns and adopted a similar strategy: a recognisable connection with the history, but overt fictionalisation. Stephens' comment suggests something more, too: that while there was concern that the story did not stray into tapu areas, there was nevertheless enthusiasm for having some version of a local story told on the big screen. Even though Tītokowaru's is a Ngā Ruahine (Taranaki) story, and Caroline Perrett's story began with events that happened in Taranaki, the iwi that was involved in the film was Whanganui – since they were mana whenua for the filming on the Whanganui River. Stephens had met with representatives of Ngā Ruahine and had maintained contact with kaumātua Tom Ngātai, whom he had come to know well through *The New Zealand Wars*.[21]

Ward has another take on *River Queen*'s relation to history:

> *There was another aspect for* River Queen *... I was interested in trying to tell something of a founding story, a foundation story ... the moment where we became, as a people to some degree, even though it was a bloody becoming ... [I] was trying to tell that story through this woman and her experiences, and her son and relationships.*[22]

The film's epic foundational claim figures in its spectacular setting, and in its large-scale battle scenes that situate the story of the character who crosses the cultural divide as a mythic story, an origin story that, in the shifting bicultural context of the early twenty-first century, has become a story of Pākehā assimilation. 'Could I have found a home here?' asks Sarah, and the answer by the end of film is 'āe'.

Sarah's assimilation into the Māori world has some origin in the story of Anne Evans, or 'Anne the Doctor', who was living in Whanganui in the early 1870s. A group of Māori asked her to go with them to treat a sick man, and she agreed. She was blindfolded for the last part of the journey to the patient, who turned out to be Tītokowaru: he had spent two years living in hiding inland after his campaign collapsed in early 1869. Evans nursed him through pneumonia. This event from after the war is brought into the period of conflict in the film, providing the plot device for taking Sarah into the Māori community. In a spectacular sequence, Sarah is blindfolded (as Evans was) and taken up the river to a secret location to nurse the chief who is afflicted with 'the coughing sickness'.

The more important historical figure behind Sarah's character was Caroline Perrett, the subject of one of Aotearoa's few narratives of captivity. In 1874 when she was eight, Perrett was seized after her father, disregarding warnings from local iwi that he was violating the tapu, cleared the ground of an urupā in Taranaki where the dead of the Battle of Sentry Hill were buried. Her family searched for her for years, but the people who took her moved frequently around the North Island. Caroline grew up knowing that she was European but thinking of herself as Māori. She married twice, both times to Māori men. In Whakatāne, more than 50 years after her capture, her niece saw her and recognised the family resemblance. Caroline was reunited with her surviving family, but she preferred to stay living in the Māori world. Her story was published in 1929 in several newspapers as a story of childhood capture that resulted in her eventual happy integration into Māori society.[23]

Caroline (Queenie) Perrett was interesting to Ward in much the way that Kimble Bent was interesting to James Cowan. Like Cowan, Ward regarded go-betweens as pivotal figures in the cultural formation of New Zealand. In discussing *River Queen* he explicitly traces his interest in such figures to the experience of making *In Spring One Plants Alone*:

> *I always wondered if I could transfer my experience into a feature film, the experience of someone who goes into a community thinking they will learn about the community but in fact learning as much about themselves.*
>
> *My story doesn't tell Queenie's story or Doctor Annie's story directly but they were the lodestones for a story about a woman who went into another community and is changed by the experience. That's a real New Zealand story because New Zealand has been formed not by Māori and Pākehā so much as by the people in between Māori and Pākehā trying to find a way of co-existing.*[24]

These themes are familiar from films already discussed in this book. But *River Queen* stands out from the other screen stories – with the exception of *The Killing of Kane* – in its interest in Pākehā assimilation. Perrett appealed strongly to Ward, and he described her willingness to be absorbed into

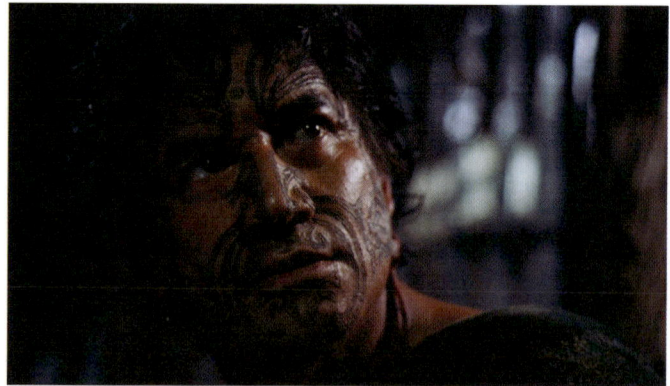

River Queen (2005): Te Kai Pō (Temuera Morrison). Anticipating the movements of the advancing colonial and kūpapa troops, he explains the trap he is setting for them, in a strategy modelled on that of Tītokowaru at Te Ngutu o te Manu.

another culture as 'humility'.[25] Here there is another echo of the characterisation of Bent in *The Killing of Kane*, in which the two Pākehā – Kane and Bent – are distinguished from each other on just this axis: Kane is arrogant, whereas Bent is willing to adapt.

River Queen's reworking divides the historical person of Queenie Perrett between the characters of Sarah and Boy. It is Boy who is seized and grows up to affiliate with the iwi, and Sarah who searches for him over many years, as the Perrett family searched for Caroline. But then it is Sarah who 'crosses over' and eventually, like Caroline, marries and becomes absorbed into the iwi. The crucial difference here is that the film accords Sarah an active choice that Queenie did not have: rather than growing up within the iwi, Sarah makes the decision to transfer her allegiance to it. It is a choice motivated by her desire to be with her son and her lover, and to become part of te ao Māori rather than remain in the European world – which we only ever see, in the film, as an abrasive military world.

In the background story, the character of Te Kai Pō draws from the figure of Tītokowaru, especially as Belich had reinterpreted him – in the charismatic strategic leader using his knowledge of the Europeans to craft carefully provocative military strategies; his one blind eye; his illness that brings a nurse to care for him; and in the sexual indiscretion that was said to be the cause of his retreat. The character of Major Baine in the film melds the sartorial flair of Gustavus von Tempsky and the ruthlessness of Thomas McDonnell. Wiremu, the film's male lead and its third culture-crossing figure, derives from the scout Wiremu Kātene Tūwhakaruru, whom Cowan called 'that hero of many fights'.[26] Wiremu's shifting allegiance between resistant and colonial forces is like Kātene's, and both are renowned marksmen. Wiremu reiterates Kātene's injunction to 'never trust a Maori. Some day I may remember that I have lost my land, and that the power and influence of my tribe has departed, and that you are the cause …'.[27] In *River Queen*, Wiremu tells Baine, 'Never trust a Maori eh? Because sooner or later, he's going to want his land back.' In earlier drafts of the film the names Tītokowaru and Kātene were used; by the final draft they have been replaced, although Kātene's first name, Wiremu, is retained.

The course of the war approximates Tītokowaru's War. The first battle, for example, uses a decoy like the battle of Te Ngutu o te Manu, but instead of a deceptively weak palisade, a group of bare-breasted women playing at skipping rope trick the troops into thinking their approach has not been detected. In the aftermath of this battle, though, there is no funeral pyre of constabulary bodies and no consumption of human flesh. Cowan records Kātene partaking of the flesh of the attacking enemy after the battle, in revenge for the death of his son;[28] but Wiremu grieves in a far milder fashion when his young son is killed. *River Queen* does hint at Tītokowaru's final great fortification, Tauranga Ika; and the story of his alliances collapsing there when he is caught with the wife of another chief is suggested in the scene that shows Te Kai Pō in a sexual encounter in the middle of an earlier battle and again on the eve of the next battle, which never takes place as a result – as supposedly occurred at Tauranga Ika.

Alun Bollinger, who was in the director's seat at the time, was not aiming to replicate that almost-battle with any precision – apart from anything else, he was cutting costs as hard as he could, and battle scenes are expensive. Instead he foregrounds the exchanges back and forth across the lines, beginning as provocative verbal exchanges (as occurred at Tauranga Ika) but turning suddenly serious when Boy is captured and nearly executed – finally forcing Sarah to choose sides.

The film does not engage with the larger politics of the war, either, although it shows events that lead up to it. The skirmishes we see are sometimes explained, but the war's overall trajectory and the details of its implications for either side inform the film's background rather than constituting its main plot. The enmity is apparent, and the strategies, and the compelling detail that gives the flavour of the past, but the reasons for it are less apparent: as Ward emphasises, this is not a war film but a story of lives caught up in a war.

One historical detail suggests how Tītokowaru's capacity for a compelling gesture proved irresistible to storytellers – and here is the point where the film uses a historical document, one of Tītokowaru's letters to settlers, almost word for word. Dibble's script for *The Killing of Kane* quoted the same letter, as did Belich in *I Shall Not Die*, where it rounded off a chapter with a dramatic flourish. In *River Queen* Sarah is its shocked first audience:

> *A word for you. Cease travelling on the roads. Stop forever the going on the roads, lest you be left there as food for the birds of the air and the beasts of the field, or for me, because I have eaten the European as beef. He was cooked in a pot. The women and children partook of the food. I have begun to eat human flesh. Kua haumama toku koro koro ki te kai i te tangata. My throat is constantly open for the flesh of man. I shall not die. I shall not die. When death itself is dead, I shall be alive.*[29]

But Te Kai Pō then adds colloquially, 'That should raise their temperature a bit, don't you think?' – casting the threat as strategic provocation. Bollinger and Gerrard Albert both expressed reservations about this direct quotation which, they thought, brought the film too close to the Tītokowaru story. For Albert this was part of an underlying concern about 'what our Taranaki relatives thought' about the film's use of Tītokowaru's War.[30] Temuera Morrison on the other hand, from the perspective of a professional actor, loved the opportunity to deliver Tītokowaru's provocative phrases – indeed, he relished the part, which he describes as 'one of the best characters I've ever had the chance to play'. He read up on the history as he prepared for the role, 'and learnt a lot about my people and my country'.³¹

The use of history in *River Queen*, then, is no casual borrowing: with the exception of this letter, the film tracks the historical record but also maintains a distance from it. Names, events and locations are alluded to – Anne Evans, Caroline Perrett and Tītokowaru are acknowledged in the closing credits – even though they are altered.³² We are invited to recognise at least some of the history while understanding that what we are watching is a fiction – in the names Wiremu and Queenie, and in the fact that Wiremu's son, like Kātene's, is killed by a kūpapa warrior approaching a battle. Bruce Babington describes the film as 'fabulous history', suggesting its shift into a slightly surreal register with its grand narrative sweep, its characters caught up in semi-mythical and sometimes supernatural events, and the epic scale of its spectacular landscapes;³³ but its allusion to real people and events underlines its claim to be telling an origin story: while it may have surreal elements we are to understand the film's fiction as a truth.

River Queen's allusions to other colonial fictions illustrates its claim to tell a distinctly New Zealand colonial story. It is not the first narrative about the New Zealand Wars to allude to Joseph Conrad's *Heart of Darkness* – a novel that became a touchstone for postcolonial critique of colonialism and violence. Errol Braithwaite's novel *The Evil Day* and the television series *Greenstone*, both of which draw on Tītokowaru's War, also invoked *Heart of Darkness* with its rendition of a 'horror' emanating from violent colonial encounter and attaching to a white man gone native. Each echoed the 'savage' Congolese interior that Conrad's character Kurtz has discovered and which is mirrored in what he becomes. But *River Queen* summons the spectre of *Heart of Darkness* in order to reverse its stance and its outcome. Ward's colonial traveller Sarah, like Kurtz, journeys upriver 'into the interior' (the Conrad reference is explicit in the use of this word, which sits oddly in the New Zealand context) and into the unknown – but in the end what she finds is a home. The film's images of the Māori settlement repeatedly situate it in this way: the rich colours, the earthy exteriors and interiors in the temporary settlement, the dim light of an early-morning wharenui, the daily work of gathering, growing, cooking and eating food and caring for children and elders. Unlike Conrad's Marlow, Sarah stays to reconstitute her family and make a life in a place that is already a home in the landscape, and in the way that has already been established there. Having called up the *Heart of Darkness* trope – as well as other Conrad-referencing colonial river journeys like those in *The Mission* (1986; set in Argentina) and *Black Robe* (1991; set in Canada) – *River Queen*'s detailed visualisation of domestic life in the Māori community explicitly refuses 'horror' – raising but disrupting the trope of 'native savagery'. Taking us into life in a Māori community in the midst of the wars, the luminous cinematography and the deep, saturated palette of the film's design and costuming portray a tranquil visual harmony between the Māori settlements and their spectacular settings. There was impressive expertise behind the look of the film, in the cinematography of Bollinger and his team, Rick Kofoed's design and Barbara Darragh's costume design.

River Queen also references John Ford's ambivalent western *The Searchers* (1956), based on the capture of Anglo-American Cynthia Ann Parker by a Comanche war party in 1836 and her family's protracted search for her. One scene echoes the well-known episode from *The Searchers* in which Cynthia Ann's uncle and brother seize her and run from the Comanche: in a spectacular escape they slide down a long dune and elude their

River Queen (2005): Sarah (Samantha Morton), Wiremu (Cliff Curtis) and Boy (Rāwiri Pene) escape down a sandy bank, in a reversal of a similar scene in John Ford's *The Searchers*.

pursuers. In a direct reversal of this, in *River Queen*, Sarah and Wiremu rescue Boy and make their escape by sliding down a long, sandy cliff face – only they are running away from the colonial forces.

Despite its thematic importance, Sarah's cultural transition happens largely off-camera: the film jumps forward several years to show her now absorbed into the 'upriver' community and her family there. Her assimilation is figured on her skin and in her costume. Through much of the film her pale Celtic complexion and her vivid clothing mark her out against the browns and greens of the landscapes and settlements, the dark uniforms of the soldiers, and the brown skin of the Māori. In the night as she lies blindfolded in the bottom of a boat and talks with the young man who turns out to be her son, her white skin is stark against the darkness. In the midst of the battle she is jarringly pale. In a later scene where she finds a white wedding dress in an abandoned house and puts it on, she stands out bright white against the dark background. She is routinely framed alone and apart from the Māori women, her skin and bright clothes insistently setting her apart from their darker, softer clothing and skin. In a discussion of the parallels between *River Queen* and *The Piano*, Olivia Macassey comments on this whiteness of the female lead against a dark background, and notes the 'imperial imagery of a "civilised" European picturesquely seated in an open boat'. She points to a distinction between them, however: *The Piano*, which is set in the period of the wars, never refers to them; while 'the process of colonisation is underscored, and made explicit through detailed conflict in *River Queen*'.[34]

When Sarah asks Boy to give her a moko – which, as she has earlier warned him, will make a return downriver impossible – the marks on her skin define the transition she is undertaking.

The flashforward to the end of the film tells a longer story. As the scene begins the camera pans across a beach and a Māori settlement. A wagon runs along the sand, a child scampers, and a group of women working in a garden come into view. Only when one of them turns do we recognise her as Sarah. She works among the other women and, brown-skinned from the sun and wearing a deep green, she is visually incorporated with the group. This transition towards her assimilation is plainly designed to be central to the film's narrative arc – although viewers may not notice it, as this 'brown, assimilated' Sarah makes only a brief appearance whereas the 'white' Sarah who stands apart and prominent dominates almost the entire film.[35]

The historical plausibility of Sarah's character is pushed close to its limits. It is unlikely that a woman could have travelled safely alone on the river searching for her son, as she does; or that if, like Anne Evans, she had been escorted upriver to heal the chief, she would have been free to circulate within the Māori settlement. (Kimble Bent was constrained in his movements and was often anxious for his safety.) Similarly, instances of European women marrying Māori were rare, and the women were commonly regarded as having been degraded by such a marriage.[36] Sarah's father and Major Baine in *River Queen* both condemn her choices of lover, echoing the attitudes of nineteenth-century Pākehā communities: she is a whore, says her father; she will be prey to madness, says Baine. But *River Queen* situates Sarah's love affairs within the frame of romance, and in its terms Sarah's choices define her as one of the people 'in between' who were making a new society.

Nevertheless, these uncommon freedoms and romantic choices place the film, again, as 'fabulous history', and they suggest a kind of imagining back into an origin story that is less prejudicial than was actually the case. Sarah's Irishness

River Queen (2005): Sarah's bright clothing and white skin distinguish her visually from the people around her and the settings for most of the film. She is transported up the river like a 'river queen' (top). But in the final scene her skin has browned, she has a moko, and she is at first indistinguishable among the group of women gardening.

predisposes her toward alliance with the Māori against the English, following an existing tradition of rendering Irish as already-colonised immigrants – no doubt familiar to Ward from his own Irish descent. The Celtic quality of the score enhances this disposition to link Irish and Māori, against the 'bad Englishman' Baine in particular. Still, the question that confronts us is how far Sarah's freedoms and choices might be analogous to the 'dishonesty' of which Sandra Coney accused *Pictures*, in that film's projection of a 1980s sensibility back onto the nineteenth-century Burton Brothers. To what extent is Sarah's lack of nineteenth-century racism equivalent to the fictionalised Burtons' anachronistic disquiet about colonialism?[37] Does her willingness to cross over ('that border did not exist for me,' she says at the beginning, explaining her choice of 'a Māori boy') offer Pākehā a more attractive foundation story than they are entitled to?[38]

It becomes harder to answer this question when the complexities of the creation and performance of the character of Sarah are taken into account. A more productive way of looking at the character, rather than labouring over its plausibility, might be to see it as a difficulty within the film that is symptomatic of the risks to identity as Pākehā venture into te ao Māori. Ward, looking back at the film more than 10 years later, spoke frankly about the complexities of the character of Sarah: he had not achieved what he wanted with it, not just because Morton

LEFT: 'There was a photo taken at Pāpāwai ... of I think it's about six women and one of them's Pākehā but she has a moko, in the middle of the group, and she's looking very staunch ...'

1/1-007842-G, Alexander Turnbull Library, Wellington.

RIGHT: Caroline Perrett in a photograph taken for *The Sun* in 1929.

FAR RIGHT: *River Queen* (2005): Samantha Morton, staunch as Sarah O'Brien.

was unwilling to produce what he was looking for but, as he intimated, because the character itself was difficult. While the story of Anne Evans being taken to Tītokowaru had provided a plot element, it was Caroline Perrett he was more interested in as a character because of her capacity for transformation through encounter. In talking about this he also referred to the Pāpāwai photograph. He explained the layers of complexity within the character that were entangled with the performance and in the various qualities he was drawing together through the character:

> I felt that the story of Caroline had a more interesting inner transformation that I don't think the film captured, and I actually think that was to do with the arrogance of the actress, you know. You know Caroline had a sort of humility, incredible humility to her and Samantha didn't ... There was a photo taken at Pāpāwai ... of I think it's about six women and one of them's Pākehā but she has a moko, in the middle of the group, and she's looking very staunch ...

> ... in some respects in terms of the transformation of the central character, I didn't feel totally that I got what I wanted, that it didn't move me in the way I would have liked to have been moved, and as I say, that was to do with the humility, but there were ... things in my mind to do with where that story went and one of them, which is slightly contradictory to the Caroline Perrett story, is that image from Pāpāwai which had the slightly haughty look in the woman, who is so cocksure of herself and she's got this moko ... and that was a destination for the story and I think Samantha captured that destination, but I didn't feel that the story ultimately had the feeling of someone who'd really suffered, and yet found a way to grow, suffered but found their own truth and managed to grow with it ...[39]

Ward's emphasis on humility *and* self-assurance – the idea that to be willing to be transformed you might need both – is reminiscent of other culture-crossing characters discussed in this book. His comments are a reminder that he himself had such an encounter at a formative point in his life.

Morton's performance cannot be entirely separated from

ENCOUNTER, ROMANCE AND CONFLICT

the dynamics of the production – a matter on which everyone involved, apparently, had a view. In his study of Ward's films, Dan Fleming argues that Morton's intense practice of acting had mixed success in the role of Sarah: like Ward, he sees her as reluctant to deliver the role that Ward was asking for. His discussion helps explain how the difficulties in production contributed to the story of encounter as it finally appeared on screen: Morton, he says, was recognised for a style of performance that refused easy emotional expression and delivered an intensely inward depth of character. Fleming points out the risk of Morton's practice: that it might end up 'failing to connect with much else that is going on in the film … [and] closing out the other actors'.

Over the film as a whole, Fleming argues, Morton hoped that the charge of emotion might be stored up:

for a symbolic release at a key chosen point in the narrative … but this method got progressively out of step with the kind of film it was – an expansive, multi-layered narrative with a complex time structure and very little by way of a centripetal organisation of narrative material around only one role.[40]

Other reports on the production also suggested that Morton, through her performance, insisted on a specific approach to her role – including that the film circulated more around the character of Sarah. This didn't meant that her performance was not respected: Wī Kuki Kaa admired it, and Ward praised it in interviews after the film's release. Tainui Stephens voices his respect for Morton's performance:

I learned a lot about working with actors, and learned a lot about how brave you have to be as an actor to really put yourself out there but also that … there are different ways for different actors to get into the emotional zone that they need to get into, I mean if you're going to have anger on the set at 2.30, for a very difficult scene, it might actually turn up at 5.30 at makeup and fuck you up for the rest of the day.[41]

The film does circulate around Sarah, and of course Ward intended her to be the centre of its narrative arc. Yet, as Ward said, the 'cocksure' quality of the Pāpāwai woman comes through in Morton's performance at the expense of Perrett's 'humility'.

The very context of the production – the cultural nuances of it, as well as the role itself – may have contributed to the mutual incomprehension and unwillingness to work together which seems to have created such problems: apart from Anton Lesser (who played Baine), Morton was probably the only actor on the set who had no experience of a settler colonial society and, therefore, no concept of the ongoing cultural politics of such a society. As a result she came cold into a long cultural conversation that everyone else in the production had been having for decades, often without realising it, and which had

River Queen (2005): Boy's anger at Sarah smoulders through much of the film: seized as a child, he now has no wish to return to the white world. But standing across the river from Sarah he sings a Māori-language rendition of 'Danny Boy' – he's Māori *and* Irish.

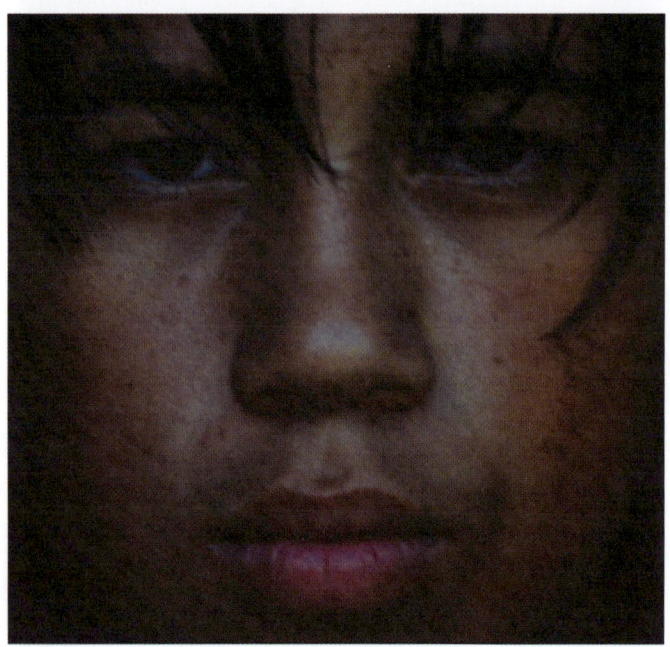

shaped the role which she was being asked to play. Rather than acquiring cultural literacy over time, she had to make all her cultural mistakes at once and in an already fraught setting. And then, she had to play a character at the cultural interface. Given that intercultural relationships, in Aotearoa at least, hinge so often on embodied nuances such as when to speak and when to listen, what to touch, and when *not* to make yourself the centre of attention – and there is a gendered element here – this may have been difficult and perhaps incomprehensible territory for her to negotiate. These complexities were overlaid with the discrepancy between the respect paid to stars in the global film industry and the all-in culture of the antipodean industry.

Unlike *Rain of the Children*, *River Queen* was never conceived as 'a Māori story', but it does depend on extensive involvement of Māori – historical, fictional and contemporary – in the Pākehā transformation story. What does it make of these stories and characters – Wiremu, Boy and Te Kai Pō – that sit around the edge of Sarah's narrative? Whether it was a result of the way the production played out, or whether it was already in the screenplay, they remain relatively underdeveloped. For example, by contrast with Wī Kuki Kaa's Wiremu in *Utu*, whose move to the centre of the narrative is integral to that film's plot, Cliff Curtis's Wiremu in *River Queen* is developed largely through the actor's strength of performance rather than through the film's plotting. Historian Danny Keenan finds 'the general ambivalence of Wiremu's position ... disappointing; Maori audiences wanted to see him more strongly defined'. He notes, of Wiremu's supporting role:

> *If* River Queen *is Sarah's story, Wiremu's problem in this movie is obvious; he only appears as a counterpoint to Sarah – Maori as counterpoint to Pakeha in a film located in Maori country. This is how screenplays like* River Queen *often develop. It is far easier on an audience if complex historical stories and locations (if not cultural processes) are shaped around one central character, with others attached in support or as back stories.*[42]

In *River Queen* Sarah, the colonial character, does dominate to the exclusion of the indigenous go-betweens – not only Wiremu but Boy, characters whose antecedents were also 'the people in between Māori and Pākehā trying to find a way of co-existing'. Like Kaa in *Utu*, Curtis is an actor from a historically Crown-allied iwi (Te Arawa) playing a kūpapa warrior, and he conveys the dilemmas of this situation with depth and economy – but is not given much opportunity to develop them. His character does push the development of 'the warrior' into areas that go well beyond stereotype. The brief, wordless scene where

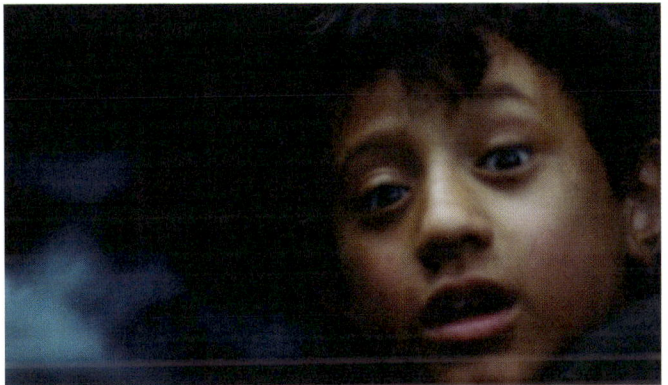

River Queen (2005): Wiremu's young son Timoti (Brandon Lakshman) turns to the kūpapa warrior about to kill him; after the battle, he is found by his father.

he finds and holds the body of his dead son is one of the most powerful in the film.

Te Kai Pō (Morrison) is developed in a direction that is both interesting and troubling. On the one hand he is the far-seeing strategist of Belich's reinterpretation, whose thinking is difficult for Sarah to fathom, but who – the film suggests – is ahead of everyone else in his plan to deflect the final battle and salvage what he can for his people from the war. On the other hand, his authority in the film expands on the story of Tītokowaru's infidelities to define his military power through sexual dominance. A disturbing series of cuts during the battle, between a sexual act and the scene of the fighting, suggests a link between sex and killing – connecting his prophetic and military power to his sexual power. In a similarly disquieting scene the armed constabulary, tricked by a glimpse of semi-naked women into thinking their approach is undetected, are mown down in a barrage of rifle fire.

Reception

River Queen did moderately well at the box office, and to mixed reviews. There was general agreement on the spectacular chemistry between two of its stars: the Whanganui River and Alun Bollinger's camera. The use of voiceover narration – which, as several critics surmised, does appear to have been a strategy for pulling together a story that was missing crucial scenes – was unpopular. The dialogue and the score attracted criticism, too, and the narrative was described as confusing.[43] Peter Calder disliked the film and was unimpressed with Morton's performance; he commented that 'she displays about as much emotional turmoil as a Central Otago farmer at the saleyards', and Kate Stables described her performance as 'sullen underplaying'.[44] Others, though, thought Morton was one of the film's strengths. Graeme Tuckett was surprised by what had been achieved under such adversity: 'And yet, and this really is a bloody miracle, *River Queen*, mis-shapen and ill-starred bastard child that it may be, actually works as a film, as an entertainment, and as easily the most accurate authentic portrayal of land wars era New Zealand ever filmed.'[45]

Among Whanganui people and other Māori interested in film, not everyone was happy about the production or the film. In an online debate after the film's release, some people who had been sceptical about the filmmakers' engagement with local iwi and opposed to iwi involvement from the outset gave their views. Cheryl Smith, for example, said:

> *Some of the highs were those of us who secured roles, work in the picture; our old people visiting the film set and being treated extremely well by the cast, crew and support staff. The lows included late payment of wages especially for those who counted on this income; the four weeks hold up of filming while the main actress recovered from illness and other hiccups due to misunderstandings. All in all, however, it is important to note that some positive things came out of the filming on our beautiful Awa Tupua. The faces of our people and the roles they played in the film will be everlasting. The experience and skills gained by some in several areas, set, art, props, transport, filming and recruitment provide a favorable base for employment consideration in future undertakings.*[46]

Smith reported that the benefits were not as great as she had hoped; and she found it 'surreal' to see a Te Arawa man playing a character based on Tītokowaru and speaking a Whanganui dialect. Others were more outspoken in their objections. Some had not seen the film and didn't want to: they were frustrated at the lack of 'ability to tell our own stories and to represent ourselves to ourselves and the wider Indigenous and global world,' as film scholar Leonie Pihama put it. 'The control of filmic representation of our people remains in the hands of the few dominant Pakeha film companies who are in turn supported by a Film Commission that does little to promote the fact that we as tangata whenua have a right to access the resources and technical support to tell our own stories.' This discussion expressed a larger, ongoing objection to outsiders telling Māori stories, and suspicion of filmmakers' motives and strategies in involving Māori in filmmaking.[47] In a different context, another Whanganui person said bluntly, 'They used us.'[48] But another industry veteran added the comment, 'Filmmakers use people all the time. It's what they do. Otherwise films would never be made.'[49] These remarks about *River Queen* could apply just as well to other productions. They reflect the conflicting priorities of people involved in filmmaking for differing purposes and with differing expectations and concerns.

Gerrard Albert was a senior Whanganui iwi member who was often on the set, and because he had stepped in when Rangitihi Tahuparae became sick he ended up being more closely involved than he had anticipated. His reflections on the production and the film give insight into the many implications and considerations involved for iwi in their relationships with filmmakers. He had similar concerns to the participants in the online debate, but came to a different conclusion: he saw the advantages of being there to protect cultural values and landscapes, and to look out for possible economic and training benefits for iwi members.[50]

Albert thought the story was overly complex, but this was not his main concern. He was pleased that 'some of our people were captured on film', and that a lot of effort had gone into training outside performers in Whanganui dialect, although he wished there had been time to tidy up some of the problems with its delivery – in the difficult post-production process it did not get the remedial attention he had expected, so some of the reo was poorly delivered and 'we got a bit of stick for that'. He felt some disquiet, too, about the way the Tītokowaru story seemed to have been adapted, although he was cautious about stating this as he was unsure of what exactly had happened in consultation with Ngā Ruahine. On the set itself he found Ward very alert to cultural concerns, ready to respond to local cultural traditions, and keen to incorporate local practices into the action of the film.

On more pragmatic matters, Albert was involved in advocating for some of the local extras on the set when they were the last to be fed and had to wait outside in the cold; the issue was resolved when he spoke up about it. He realised that it was a matter of coming to terms with some of the routine unglamorous realities of film work. Some of the people contracted found themselves waiting around until they were needed, and had passed up other work while they waited for the production. This problem came to a head for many during the unplanned six-week break in production: they had not anticipated this, and tradespeople had no other work lined up. Albert had hoped that the film might bring more contracts for local people, but while some did get work, they found out through the process of the film that some types of contracts, such as catering, always went to specialist companies. The Awa Films Working Party formed for the production went on to be involved in other films, however, and took the knowledge gained on *River Queen* into later negotiations. Albert commented that, while he recognised that the production had had troubles and had not resulted in the film that was hoped for, he would have liked Whanganui's commitment to have been reciprocated through a stronger film: 'If you're going to come, do a quality job, don't leave it.' This was not a personal criticism of the director. He had appreciated Ward's integrity, his willingness to invite and take cultural advice, and that his relationship with Whanganui had continued well beyond the film.

Conclusion

The 30-year path from *In Spring One Plants Alone* to *Rain of the Children* via *River Queen* charts a path of personal encounter, set against the larger context of two fields of cultural memory – iwi memory and the broader national memory – but also within the context of historical work that was closing the gaps between those fields of memory. *River Queen*'s story of a woman negotiating cultural identity sits within a background story that recognisably portrays Tītokowaru's War. *Rain*'s story of putting together fragments of knowledge is a personal drama embodying changes that were happening in the broader cultural memories and identities of Pākehā. Ward looks back at *In Spring*, at what he thought he was seeing, and realises that there is much more to see, in the film and beyond it, than he had thought at the time. *Rain* reflects on that earlier state of limited knowledge, and charts the search for the information that will provide what was missing; *River Queen*'s difficult engagement with the emotions of encounter echo the complexities of cultural change in process.

MĀORI CREATIVE CONTROL AND NEW SCREENS

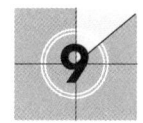

'... at some stage we've got to have this conversation and we've got to find a place where we can talk about our own wars.' —Mihingārangi Forbes

'We've got a lot more people on the ground than we did twenty years ago.' —Cliff Curtis

Māori were actively involved, one way or another, in the making of films about the New Zealand Wars right from the beginning. The conjunction of the subject of colonial war and screen media, with their combined requirements for personnel and collaboration, meant that these films stood or fell on the willingness of Māori to participate. The Pākehā whose passions for history or storytelling drew them into this territory found themselves involved in crosscultural collaborations and dialogue of various kinds with Māori actors, advisors and mana whenua about a shared past. Māori actors found leading roles, Māori advisors were in demand, and several productions facilitated the expansion of Māori expertise into a greater range of filmmaking occupations.

Nevertheless, by the beginning of the twenty-first century only two Māori had claimed director's or producer's credits in high-profile productions: Lee Tamahori for first assistant director on *Utu*, and Tainui Stephens for directing *The New Zealand Wars* and for his production roles on *River Queen* and *Rain of the Children*. Māori cast, crew and advisors still negotiated the terms of their involvement in productions that had been conceived and largely managed by Pākehā. Tama Poata wrote that '*Once Were Warriors* and *Utu* ... have a lot of Māori content and many people think they are Māori films, but they are not, because the tino rangatiratanga, the absolute authority has belonged to someone other than Māori.'[1] As Cliff Curtis observed in 2016 of New Zealand film in general:

> we were allowed to be employed as advisors, cultural advisors is big on the list of crew for Māori, but not in a lot of other departments. You know, we could be writing consultants, we could be employed in front of the camera, they don't mind hiring us in essence, but we still have to compete a lot with others who see the value in our stories, and see the commercial value, and the artistic and cultural value of our stories.[2]

There had been calls for greater authority for a very long time. Merata Mita's influential 'The Soul and the Image' pointed out that Māori had immediately gravitated to the camera: 'the reproduced likeness had mana, and the introduction of those first frozen portraits added a new dimension to our remembrances'. In an essay that both criticised and acknowledged Pākehā-made films featuring Māori, and that described how film contributed to carrying on oral histories, Mita discussed the competing demands on Māori filmmakers: they had to meet the expectations of 'the cinema, the demands of their own people, the criteria of a white male-dominated value and funding structure, and somehow be accountable to all'. She pointed to the absence of 'Maori technicians, directors, producers and production houses that would concern themselves with Maori projects and aspiring Maori film makers'.[3] Mita herself played a part in bringing about change. Stephens' role in direction and production from the late 1990s signals the changes that were taking effect, and as Curtis noted in 2016, 'We've got a lot more people on the ground than we did twenty years ago.'

Some of the productions discussed earlier had fostered Māori careers. Ramai Hayward became the first Māori director: if her marriage to Rudall was the determining factor, she was already a professional photographer and was ready to extend her skills. *The Governor* gave Don Selwyn an opportunity to cast many Māori in leading roles, but also to contribute to the shape and the ethos of the series and to expand Māori expertise behind the camera, as he remarked at the time.[4] Geoff Murphy's strategic decision on *Utu* to promote Lee Tamahori helped facilitate Tamahori's progression to director on other films. Slow as it was to change, the industry eventually expanded beyond Māori inclusion to productions where Māori had creative control. Ramai Hayward, Barry Barclay, Selwyn, Mita and Stephens all helped to broaden expertise, shifting the terms of Māori involvement and laying the foundations of a Māori-centred screen industry. Barclay's influential theory of 'fourth cinema' – indigenous filmmaking on indigenous terms – provided a manifesto for Māori cultural authority.[5]

Since its establishment in 2004 the Māori Television Service, through its own news and current affairs production and in creating a demand for Māori content, has extended the opportunities available through TVNZ's Māori Programming Department, made a major contribution to the filmmaking skill base among Māori and facilitated the growth of Māori-led production houses. Opportunities on the big screen have grown, too, with a rising interest in feature-length documentary made for theatrical release, and a greater representation of documentary in film festivals internationally and in Aotearoa. The New Zealand International Film Festival, the Māoriland Film Festival and the Wairoa Māori Film Festival have all supported the new era of Māori documentaries. Bodies such as the Māori screen production organisation Ngā Aho Whakaari with its publication *The Brown Book* – a guide for working with Māori in screen production – have created a better-informed environment for crosscultural and Māori filmmaking.[6] Cheaper screen technologies have given emerging filmmakers an entry into production. As a result, Māori filmmakers and Māori-owned production companies now feature more strongly in the twenty-first century climate.[7] The success of Lee Tamahori and Taika Waititi in Aotearoa and internationally, and the justly acclaimed *Waru* (2017) directed by Māori women, are recent examples. Libby Hakaraia and Tainui Stephens celebrated with their documentary *Hautoa Ma! The rise of Māori cinema* in 2016.

To date, there has been no dramatic feature film from a Māori filmmaker that is primarily about the New Zealand Wars.[8] The high cost of historical drama is still a major hurdle. The budget for creating content that screens on Māori Television is reportedly, on average, 40 per cent lower than for content on mainstream television, and funding is still highly competitive.[9] In the years before his death, Tama Poata still hoped to 'make the world's best film, a period film called *Tattooed Generals*', about Tītokowaru;[10] Lee Tamahori did some work with the script, but it never made it to production. Tamahori has spoken about an idea for a Te Kooti film but, perhaps taking a pragmatic approach to cost, he envisages a modern-day adaptation.[11] Waititi's *Hunt for the Wilderpeople* (2016) gives a sideways glance to the Te Kooti story: as the young hero Ricky (Julian Dennison) lines up his sights along a rifle he tells Bella (Rima Te Wiata), 'I'm a Māori warrior, and that bottle over there is a British soldier. And I'm defending all my wives.' 'All right Te Kooti,' Bella responds, and that seems to be that – except that the film becomes a chase through Te Urewera as Ricky and his uncle Hec (Sam Neill) evade pursuit by latter-day kūpapa – a welfare officer and a member of the constabulary (Oscar Kightley), whose allegiance to the state is reluctant and, in the end, ambiguous.[12]

Another possible reason for the absence of Māori-led drama on the wars is that Māori are more likely to be conscious of the sensitivities and the competing local stories relating to historical events and so may encounter greater impediments than Pākehā, who are not answerable in the same immediate way to relatives and kaumātua. And young Māori filmmakers are perhaps more interested in the present than in the past, and may see young people as their strongest market. It is no surprise that Tearepa Kahi's *Mt Zion* and *Poi E! The story of our song*, both films about popular music, gained far more attention than his documentary on a nineteenth-century printing press (see below). There are fewer constraints in contemporary subjects and, although there are still burdens of responsibility to tīpuna and to iwi, they are usually less complex than in contentious historical subjects.

Māori-led stories of the wars are appearing in documentary though, and they are discussed below. A few of these are explicitly about the wars and are mostly commemorative. Where earlier productions mined the past for its stories and, in the process, performed a duty of remembrance, in these works the duty to remember comes first. Others deal with the wars in the context of other topics. None of these documentaries initiates a major shift in the story of 'what actually happened', but their orientation, focus and address to their audiences show some marked changes from earlier productions. Tainui Stephens' work on *The New Zealand Wars* anticipated some of these new directions.

In these Māori-led documentaries the past is conveyed primarily through people in the present who speak and bear witness. Some are kaumātua who speak directly to camera about stories that have come down to them; others, such as the children from Parihaka, learn as they go and the viewer is invited to learn along with them. Where Pākehā-led productions made varying use of interviews, here there is greater priority given to elders as the source of knowledge and to face-to-face relationships as the medium through which knowledge is conveyed. Mihingārangi Forbes and Mahanga Pihama, for example, both spoke with great feeling about the kōrero of kaumātua in the documentaries they made.

The orientation to the past in the present – the uses and purposes of remembering – sometimes takes a different course from that of earlier productions, too. Shared pasts are often consolidated through the films' selection of speakers, making explicit links between the nineteenth and the twenty-first centuries. Iwi speakers ask viewers to remember the past, but also to remember its meaning in and for the present.

These films pay far less attention to Pākehā or imperials as individuals – whether as 'good Pākehā' confronting moral dilemmas, as go-betweens, or as villains: Pākehā are more often an outside threat than protagonist. The absence of historical drama is a factor in this, but in general the theme of interracial affections and alliance disappears – none of the Māori filmmakers seems remotely interested in it. Crown-allied Māori are no longer central either, in part perhaps because most of these productions to date, which are made largely by people with Tainui or Taranaki affiliations, have centred on the Waikato, Taranaki or Northern Wars, and on the early phases of the 1860s or Parihaka in 1881 – which means they are concerned with events either before or after the main period of Māori alliance with the Crown. These emerging Māori narratives are about tribal strategies, leadership, survival, land and commemoration.

Another difference has to do with the period of the action, although here there is a less marked distinction. These films tend to deal in longer timeframes: they are as likely interested in subjects such as the rise of the Kīngitanga, the longer aftermath of Māori Land Court processes and changing economies, or the effects of imprisonment after Parihaka, for example, as in the period of open conflict. This pattern is not entirely absent from earlier films such as *The Governor* and *Rain of the Children*, but it is more dominant here.

These productions take a range of stances on the balance between Māori and Pākehā contributions. Vincent O'Malley, who wrote his major history of the Waikato War over this period, is interviewed in and gave advice for several productions over this period. There is a balancing agenda at work in general: a sense that it is now time for Māori to tell these stories their way. Sometimes this takes the form of inclusion of Pākehā in a Māori-controlled bicultural story. In others, the decision has apparently been made to prioritise Māori voices, on screen at least: *The Prophets* includes Māori speakers only, although Leon Narbey, a Pākehā, held the camera.

Changing memory, changing screens

A somewhat reluctant shift in public attention to the wars as nationally important events gathered momentum with the sesquicentenaries of the wars of the 1860s. The highly publicised centenary of World War One prompted a series of commentators to object to the lack of attention to the 150th anniversaries of New Zealand Wars events by comparison; to calculate the discrepancy between the minimal government funding accorded to these iwi-managed events and the millions sustaining the World War One events; and to ask once again why the wars that took place at home carry so much less weight in national memory than those that took place overseas.[13]

The commemorations of the Taranaki Wars in 2010–11 were mainly local events and hardly reported beyond the region, with the exception of the major exhibition *Te Ahi Kā Roa, Te Ahi Kātoro Taranaki War 1860–2010*, which opened at Puke Ariki in 2010.[14] The exhibition toured to other centres and may have contributed to the growing scale of commemorations of the Waikato Wars that followed. There was very little attention paid to the commemorative events on mainstream television news bulletins. Māori Television and TVNZ's *Te Karere* did report more fully on commemorations, as did TVNZ's *Waka Huia* series, indicating that the commemorations were perceived to be events largely of concern to Māori. One important exception to the general media disinclination to cover the anniversaries was Mihingārangi Forbes' groundbreaking Radio New Zealand report on Anzac Day 2016.

A strong call for a national day of commemoration was made at the 150th anniversary of the Battle of Ōrākau in 2014, followed by a petition led by two Ōtorohanga school pupils, Leah Bell and Waimārama Anderson in 2015. With some reluctance and delay, government agreed and an announcement was made in August 2016. In order to avoid nominating the anniversary of a specific battle and skewing commemorations towards a single theatre of conflict, a hui was held to determine a date: 28 October was decided on – the anniversary of the Declaration of Independence signed in 1835. The day is to be hosted by a different region each year. The date was not a unanimous decision, and when the first Rā Maumahara National Day of Commemoration was to be held in the North, the major commemorations were in fact held over until March 2018, the anniversary of the battle of Kororāreka.

Although the cost of producing historical drama has continued to rise, new technologies have reduced the cost of creating screen stories in other genres. High-quality digital cameras have dispensed with the prohibitive cost of film stock, and almost all New Zealand films are now shot digitally. Drones have replaced helicopters. Editing has been digitised. While expected production values have risen in mainstream cinema to keep up with changes in international cinema, the proliferation of other media platforms has made it more possible to create local media and make it accessible. RNZ (formerly Radio New Zealand) has begun developing its online offerings with forays into visual programming, including a flagship work – an interactive production on the New Zealand Wars. The takeup of personal devices such as tablets and smartphones has radically altered the relationship between users (who are no longer simply 'viewers') and screens, shifting the spaces and contexts of screen use and making it more individualised and interactive: the full implications of this transition are yet to play out. And there is now a large Māori audience online – just as Māori adopted print with alacrity and enthusiasm in the nineteenth century, they have been rapid adopters in the online space.

Productions that relate to the wars are taking up the storytelling opportunities provided by these cheaper and more diverse technologies and types of screens. The New Zealand Wars are not the major focus of most of these productions, but a wider survey of screen histories reveals the wars' far-reaching impact on many aspects of Māori history, shaping its course through the nineteenth century and beyond.

The Flight of Te Hookioi (2009)

Tearepa Kahi's documentary *The Flight of Te Hookioi* (2009) follows the journey of two men from Tainui, Hemara Te Rerehau and Wiremu Toetoe, to Vienna, where they meet the Emperor Franz Josef, learn the trade of printing and, on their departure in 1860, are gifted a printing press. With this technology the newly formed Kīngitanga could establish its first newspaper, *Te Hokioi*, to promote the king's views. The story of the press and of the rival press established in Te Awamutu by the governor's agent John Gorst is told against the larger background of the Waikato War as it unfolds. The film declares its Tainui perspective: 'there are stories and then there are our stories,' the filmmaker–narrator tells us in one of the direct-to-camera pieces. Tearepa Kahi makes the film a personal journey that restores the connection between Tainui and Vienna, and a journey that links past and present. As he arrives at the archive in Vienna he greets his hosts formally in te reo Māori; he greets the portrait of Franz Josef with Hemara's words; and when he arrives home he tells the descendants of the travellers about the documents that he is bringing back from Austria. The film traces a history and simultaneously reforms connections for the present.[15] It screened on Māori Television and at the Wairoa Film Festival in 2013.

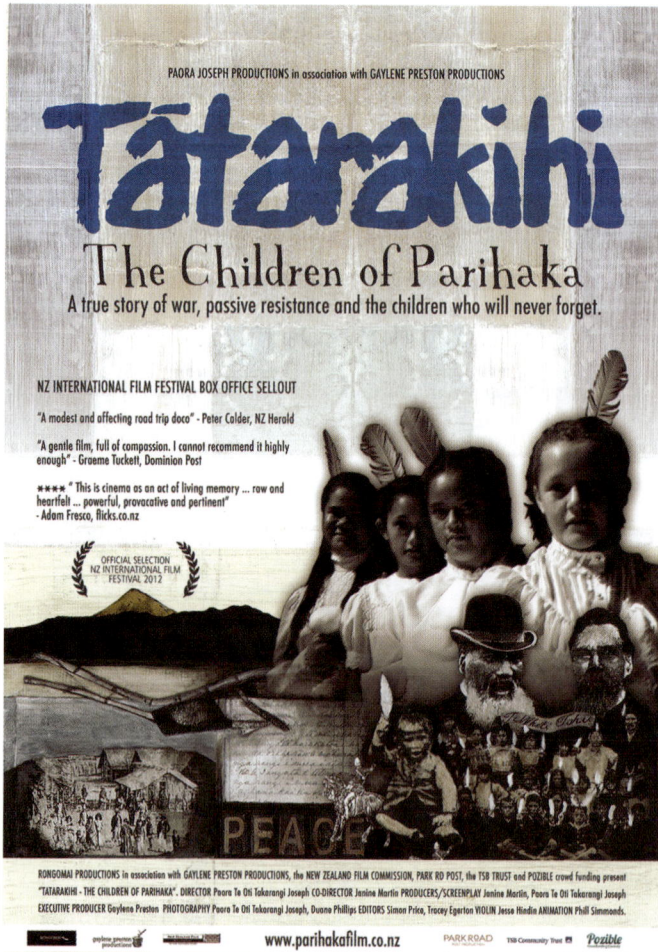

The poster for *Tātarakihi*. With the permission of Maata Wharehoka

Tātarakihi (2012)

Tātarakihi: The children of Parihaka (dir. Paora Joseph, 2012) also follows a journey, this one taken by the people of one of the Parihaka marae, Te Niho o Te Ātiawa. The journey – and the film – commemorate the arrest and exile of the ploughmen of Parihaka from the 1870s to the 1890s and the invasion of Parihaka by government troops on 5 November 1881. Filmmaker Paora Te Oti Takarangi Joseph is from Whanganui but his connection to Parihaka goes back to his great-grandfather Huru Hohepa, who had lived there. Joseph's own commitment to the cause of peace led him to think, initially, of creating a drama about the history; 'However, when Maata [Wharehoka] and Te Niho and Te Kura o Tamarongo generously made available the opportunity to film the hīkoi, it became apparent to me that this would be the right way to go about making a film as it was coming from the people of Parihaka themselves.'[16]

Maata Wharehoka (Ngāti Kuia) has lived at Parihaka and been caretaker of Te Niho o Te Atiawa for over 30 years. She and Joseph saw the need for Māori to tell a history that had been well traversed by Pākehā writers but not publicly told by Māori, and they both realised that film would make the story readily accessible.[17]

The original narrative structure of a bus trip in which people from the marae visit the sites where the Parihaka ploughmen were exiled was developed further in collaboration with Gaylene Preston. Maata Wharehoka, who organised the trip, thought Joseph's idea of shaping the film around the children's point of view was 'brilliant'; 29 children of the kura wrote stories and poems for the narration and created artwork, and they also helped with sound and camerawork.[18] The directness of the children's perspective, drawn from their words, invites viewers to share the experience and emotion of this commemorative journey. It has a symbolic purpose too, echoing the role played by the children during the invasion of Parihaka in 1881, when troops marched into the village and were welcomed by children and women singing and offering them bread.

Tātarakihi opens with the children beginning their journey early in the morning, and a farewell shot of Mt Taranaki as they leave. They travel to the site of Mt Cook Prison – now the National War Memorial – in Wellington, to Nelson, to the Christchurch Cathedral where Sir Paul Reeves preaches about the effects of nineteenth-century legislation, to Addington Prison and to Fort Jervois on Rīpapa Island where the boys haka against a grey Christchurch day, and on to Dunedin. There are tears as they visit the sites of imprisonment and respond to the unfolding history. They travel to places where the prisoners laboured, and find that they built many roads and public works in Dunedin and other South Island centres. The children pay their respects at memorials to the ploughmen in Dunedin and Hokitika, observe the street names ('Hau Hau Rd' occurs more than once), and visit marae where they meet the descendants of people who welcomed their tūpuna in the late nineteenth century. At the Ōtākou marae on Otago Peninsula, from where Rāniera Ellison led the support for the ploughmen in Dunedin, the happiness of reforging ties across generations balances the mamae (hurt) of visits to other sites.

The apparent ordinariness of the children – like any bunch of kids on a school trip, except that they are talented performers – points up the extraordinariness of what they are learning and how they come to accommodate their history. The graphics used to trace the film's journey on a map suggest a children's storybook, and the raukura, the three-feather symbol of Te Whiti's association with nonviolent resistance, marks each stop on the way – enhancing the contrast between the ordinary present and the extraordinary past.

Intercut with the journey, segments that use archival images develop the historical background. The invasion of Parihaka, where journalists and photographers followed the troops as they advanced on the settlement, was the first intensively photographed incident in the New Zealand Wars. Co-director Janine Martin integrated these historical photographs into 'scenes' (like those of the *New Zealand Wars* documentary) to dramatise the encounter between the approaching troops and the children and women who walked out to greet and welcome them. Elsewhere, the sad photographs of the men at Parihaka and at the various sites of exile accompany the ploughmen's story; and sound – of marching feet during the invasion, elegiac violin for the scenes of exile, and the children narrating their stories and poems – contributes to summoning the past.

In another strategy similar to that of *The New Zealand Wars* series, the road trip in *Tātarakihi* operates as a way of marking the unknown past of familiar places, reminding viewers of what lies behind everyday landmarks. Katie Kenny, in her response to the film in Otago University student newspaper *Critic*, confessed her ignorance of the past of the city she thought she knew. In a commentary that must have pleased the filmmakers, she wrote of the prisoners' work on the built environment of Dunedin and gave an account of Parihaka and the legacies of Te Whiti o Rongomai and Tohu Kākahi.[19]

Tātarakihi featured in the 2012 New Zealand International Film Festival and drew sell-out crowds as it toured with Paora Joseph and Maata Wharehoka. It also screened at international festivals. At completion, Joseph 'gave the Mauri of the film back to the people of Parihaka' and Wharehoka took on the role of kaitiaki.[20] According to the wishes of the children in the film, it is screened with an accompanying presenter, usually Wharehoka herself.

Paora Joseph concluded his communication about the film by marking its personal and historical significance for him:

> My middle name Te Oti Takarangi was given to me by my Kuia from Whanganui. Te Oti Takarangi was a chief from Whanganui who lived at the time of Te Whiti and Tohu, who led many warriors to Parihaka in support of Taranaki when the crown was encroaching upon Parihaka. He left with his warriors when Te Whiti and Tohu asked them to, so bloodshed could be avoided. When I completed the film I turned to Huirangi Waikerepuru and said that the film is a gift from my namesake as a whakautu because we could not be there when the soldiers invaded.[21]

The Prophets (2013)

In 2013 Māori Television screened a series that included episodes about Te Ua Haumēne, Te Kooti Arikirangi, Te Whiti o Rongomai and Tohu Kākahi.[22] *The Prophets* dealt with these men not so much as resistance leaders, but as the leaders of a faith. Megan Douglas (Te Arawa), head of Scottie Productions, had developed the concept with Māori Television. The style adopted by directors Tainui Stephens and Libby Hakaraia echoed Stephens' earlier work on *The New Zealand Wars* series, combining interviews, archival material, location filming and evocative soundscape, and using a specialist narrator. The narrator was Anglican priest and historian Hirini Kaa (Ngāti Porou, Ngāti Kahungunu, Ngāti Rongomaiwahine), who researched and wrote the script with Michael Bennett, a broadcasting veteran who had also worked on *Frontier of Dreams*, as well as Stephens.

In *The Prophets* the interviews with people from the faith communities took centre stage. The decision to prioritise these speakers rather than academics, said Kaa, 'was about whose voice was going to be privileged, and obviously it had to be the voice of the people themselves'.[23] The production team centred the series on 'faith to faith' kōrero. In *The Prophets*, everyone onscreen is Māori: beneath the apparent similarities, this was quite another kind of documentary to *The New Zealand Wars*.

In an interview for *Te Ahi Kaa* on RNZ, Kaa pointed out that Judith Binney's writing discussed prophets such as Te Kooti as resistance leaders. He did not reject this perspective but said that, for Māori, their relevance was 'broader than the politics of their situation': the prophets were – and still are – primarily religious leaders. The wars, he added, could be thought of as 'religious conflicts', 'Mihināre vs Pai Mārire … underpinned by religion'. He came to look at these movements first as a historian, but was compelled by their work of faith: 'they're huge movements, they're quiet, humble, they don't grab power, they go about their work'.[24]

Rather than the story of brilliantly executed escape from Wharekauri (Chatham Islands) as told in *The New Zealand Wars*, for example, Kaa's narration tells a story of deliverance for a prophet sustained by visions:

> Here at Whareongaonga, in this wāhi tapu, in this sacred space, Te Kooti had arrived. God had delivered him and his people, had removed the obstacles from their pathway, and they had escaped the seemingly inescapable. Soon the first part of [Tohiroa's] prophecy would be fulfilled, and Te Kooti would lead his people in giving thanks for their biblical deliveries. But soon, as they leave this space, the second part would come to fruition. The sword would appear and Te Kooti's prophecies and visions would be tested in the fiery crucible of war.[25]

The score by Warren Maxwell of Trinity Roots enhances the difference: instead of the energetic combative percussion backing Belich's narrative, *The Prophets* accompanies its story with joyous ecclesiastical music.

Kaa has discussed the shifting historical perspectives on the Māori prophets, and the fact that they had now become 'the good guys' of the story of colonisation, heroes who spoke truth to power.[26] The research and script development involved a concerted endeavour to move beyond what are now routine oppositions – 'oppressor/oppressed, resistance/collaborator, you know, those easy dichotomies, when actually it's normally a lot more complicated'.[27] Parts of the series that cover the war period explore the strategies iwi adopted as they sought to deal with the impact of colonisation. The speakers, in their kōrero about these leaders, put forward perspectives that had not often been aired in other productions. The Tūhoe and Te Aitanga a Māhaki leader Haare Williams explains the raid on Matawhero – often seen as the most notorious of Te Kooti's expeditions – by pointing out its cultural logic as utu. In the episode on Te Whiti o Rongomai and Tohu Kākahi, women from Parihaka talk about the sadness still felt about the rape of the women and the resulting pregnancies that interrupted whakapapa.

Although the prophets' work had been precipitated by war, the series took their stories beyond wartime. Episode 3 on Te Kooti continues on to his religious teachings after the war had ended, and his gifting of meeting houses and prophesies to many communities. At Te Whāiti in Te Urewera the memories of Ngāti Whare people are not of warfare but of Te Kooti living there; Robert Taylor relates with gratitude that 'we held a special place in his heart. Because we're only a small people, we're a humble people, and even though we were trodden on, we're beaten and battered, by many bigger tribes, Te Kooti came,

The Prophets (2013): Haare Williams (Tūhoe, Te Aitanga a Māhaki) speaks about Te Kooti's arrival at Whareongaonga, after the escape from Wharekauri.

Frame enlargements from *The Prophets*, Scottie Productions. With permission of Haare Williams

The Prophets (2013): Robert Taylor talks about how Te Kooti came and looked after the Ngāti Whare people at Te Whāiti. Beside him are (at left) Jack Ohlson, and (right) Kohiti Kohiti and mokopuna Ria.

With the permission of Lydia Taylor, Raukura Ohlson and Kohiti Kohiti and stayed with us and looked after us.' The camera lingers on the exquisite painting of the house Eripitana, and that of other painted houses. Later in the episode art historian Ngārino Ellis talks about the carvings in these meeting houses.

Aired on Māori Television, this series could assume an audience that was knowledgeable about te ao Māori and highly receptive to interviews conducted in te reo Māori, as many of these were. The membership of the Māori churches is mostly Māori and their leadership entirely Māori, 'and they all have te reo at their heart', said Kaa.[28] In Episode 4, which deals with Parihaka, the distinctive reo of Taranaki is prominent among the speakers, and in the episodes set in Te Urewera, Tūhoe reo is noticeable.

Both Kaa and director of photography Leon Narbey found the location-oriented dimension of the series a powerful experience as they visited places such as Maungapōhatu, Parihaka and Whareongaonga.[29] Narbey's camerawork produces evocative images of the whenua, and here there is a further continuity with *The New Zealand Wars* and Stephens' emphasis on images of whenua in that series. Narbey's landscape images are sometimes intimate, as when a fence trembles in the wind; at other times spectacular, such as in a glimpse of Taranaki from Parihaka. In the filming of iwi speakers, some of the techniques he had developed during *Rain of the Children* are evident: speakers sit in whānau groups, often in a row, their faces carefully lit. These are beautiful sequences in which, as in *Rain*, the camerawork pays tribute to the speakers.

Kaa's stories about *The Prophets* remind us, though, that if Pākehā making films with Māori communities could find themselves in complex negotiations, so could Māori. His descent from major Crown-allied iwi and his Anglicanism did not always smooth the way:

The Prophets (2013): Taranaki, viewed from Parihaka.

the production crew turned up to meet Rua Kenana's people, in the Urewera village of Matahi. A really staunch powhiri met them on arrival, with pointed reminders of Hirini's own Ngati Porou forbears coming through and killing people there. In initial negotiations with the Ratana Church, difficult histories were raised again: 'Well, there are only two groups of people we don't get along with,' said one kaumatua, 'And those are ... Ngati Porou and Anglicans.'[30]

Nevertheless, in shifting the emphasis of these stories to their ongoing meaning for the followers of the prophets' faiths, and hence to their relevance in te ao Māori today, *The Prophets* satisfied the faith communities that had contributed to the production. Reactions to the series were very positive, and Kaa found he was often recognised by schoolchildren: 'it's a real go-to for schools ... as a resource in history in schools'.[31] The series streams on Māori Television on demand, and recently sold to the Australian SBS channel. Kaa, although he is pleased with the series, had one telling reservation about it: he pointed out that most Māori engagement with Judaeo–Christian traditions had been through 'mainstream' churches such as Anglican or Catholic, and he observed that it was much harder to make a case for programming about this history. The drama of the wartime origins had, ironically, helped make the case for a series about faiths born of conflict.[32]

Waka Huia (2014)

Through May 2014 TVNZ's long-running *Waka Huia* documentary series ran a series of four episodes on the 150th anniversaries of the Waikato War. Each covered events staged by iwi to commemorate battles or attacks: Rangiriri, Rangiāowhia, Ōrākau and, finally, Pukehinahina (Gate Pā) and Te Ranga.[33] Following *Waka Huia*'s usual style of interviewing speakers in depth and usually in te reo, the episodes were shaped by interview material with kaumātua from the iwi involved, cutting to footage of the commemorations and brief soundbites from participants and people attending the commemorations. Almost all the interviews were in Māori, subtitled in English. The programmes, which ran close to the time of the actual commemorations – and between the two final commemorations at Pukehinahina and Te Ranga – took the experience of these big iwi events out to a larger audience.

Commentators were kaumātua with connections to the events. The attack on Rangiāowhia is told largely by Tom Roa (Ngāti Apakura, Ngāti Maniapoto), who had already discussed this event in other contexts, including for *Von Tempsky's Ghost*, and who is a direct descendant of people who were present at Rangiāowhia during the attack. In the episode on Ōrākau, however, the first speakers are Tūhoe elders Pou Temara and Wharehuia Milroy, who recount the decision of a group of Tūhoe men and women to go to Waikato and their determination to fight there; it then moves to Tainui kaumātua Paraone Gloyne and Tom Roa. This balance of speakers echoes the emphasis in the episode on the connections between Ngāi Tūhoe, Ngāti Apakura and Ngāti Maniapoto and other iwi – on the fact that these affiliations went back well before the war; that the Battle of Ōrākau consolidated them; and that the commemoration in 2014 remembered and acknowledged this relationship. This episode is a good example of the performative orientation of the *Waka Huia* programmes: their function is not only to document but to reaffirm the iwi-to-iwi affiliations that have been created through that history. A similar process occurs when Awanuiārangi Black (Ngāti Pūkenga) speaks early in the Rangiriri episode to recount the presence of people from Tauranga Moana who came to fight in support of Waikato; and in the fourth episode, Waikato's support of Tauranga Moana at Pukehinahina. Here *Waka Huia*'s kaupapa Māori approach to filmmaking is evident.

Except for the episode on Rangiāowhia, which is characterised by a tone of lament, footage from the massed haka and peruperu created and rehearsed for these occasions is the central visual element in showcasing the events of the day. The Rangiriri, Ōrākau and Gate Pā episodes all begin with short clips of these haka, and later in the episode each is shown more fully, displaying the results of many months of preparation. Each episode also includes clips of the major speeches. The priority given to these performances reflects the commitment of iwi in mobilising around the events. These are community-building events, and the programmes themselves, which ensure a wider audience than those who could be there on the day and also ensure an ongoing record so that the events can be watched later, are part of that community-building effort.

The Battle of Gate Pā Told with Sand (2014): These images from Marcus Winter's story of Pukehinahina shows Hēni Te Kiri Karamū bringing water to the wounded after the battle, and a lament for the dead. With the permission of Marcus Winter

The programmes tell the historical narratives entirely from iwi points of view. Mention is made of sovereignty and Grey's objection to the degree of independence that the Kīngitanga posed, but speaker after speaker emphasises greed for land as the driver of the Pākehā invasion. Some stories told have seldom been heard in the national domain. Tom Roa talks about the people who were at Rangiriri and who do not appear in published sources. Tamati Tāta tells a story about a woman who helps wounded soldiers after Pukehinahina, but it is not the well-known story of Hēni Te Kiri Karamū; rather it is about Harata Te Auetū who, concerned for her father and uncles, rode to the battlefield, but when she found only the wounded government soldiers still there, helped them to safety.

The Battle of Gate Pā Told with Sand (2014)

One event that was staged during the 2013–14 commemorations was a dinner, held on the eve of the anniversary of Pukehinahina (Gate Pā). On 21 April 1864 the officers who would lead the attack on the pā next day had dined together at the Elms in Tauranga, the home of the archdeacon: in the catastrophic defeat suffered by the British the following day, only one of them survived. The dinner marked 150 years since the officers sat down for their last meal, but also commemorated some of the other stories of Pukehinahina, a battle which as well as being a remarkable Māori victory, is also remembered for the code of conduct ('rules of engagement') drawn up by the defending chief Hēnare Taratoa, and the act of mercy shown by Hēni Te Kiri Karamū, the woman soldier who took water to the dying British soldiers during the night after the battle.

The 2014 dinner was a large event, with good-humoured guests entertained by a number of performances. The last of these captured the legendary elements of Gate Pā well. It was an ephemeral screen story created by Marcus Winter (Ngāpuhi) using sand on a lightbox projection. His narrative employed all the well-known motifs as it followed the arrival of troops, the 'rules of engagement', the battle that surprised and devastated the British, and the woman taking water to the dying officer. An accompanying score using both European and Māori instrumentation as well as songs in te reo moves from threat to martial drama to pathos, and concludes with the popular hymn 'Whakaaria Mai'. A year later, when Winter reproduced a version of the sand-on-lightbox narrative for uploading to YouTube, the story moved beyond its immediate audience and transitory form.[34]

The Kiingitanga (2016)

In 2016 Māori Television screened a three-part documentary called *The Kiingitanga: Behind the throne* – a portrait of the Kīngitanga that profiles King Tūheitea, his family and the contemporary Kīngitanga.[35] The series incorporated historical sequences, including the creation of the movement in the 1850s and the events of the wars that followed. Its director, Mahanga Pihama (Waikato, Taranaki), belongs to the rising generation of Māori screen professionals whose bread and butter lies in creating content for Māori Television, and his previous work had been in contemporary, youth-oriented Māori-language television. He had been turning over the idea of a series on the Kīngitanga for several years, and had gone through a long process of discussion with senior Kīngitanga kaumātua Rahui Papa, Tukoroirangi Morgan and King Tūheitea himself. With co-producer Viv Wigby-Ngatai, he put a proposal to Māori Television and then applied to NZ On Air for funding.[36]

Brad Haami, the researcher and writer on the series, recalled that the brief resulting from the negotiations with Māori Television emphasised the contemporary Kīngitanga: the network wanted a 'forward looking' approach to ensure that it addressed its younger demographic.[37] Neither Pihama nor Haami, though, thought it possible to separate the contemporary Kīngitanga from its history. To express the historical dimension, rather than telling a chronological story they shaped the documentary's three episodes into three broad topics. Each episode weaves between past and present, explaining the present-day movement with reference to its origins. There are two distinctly Māori dimensions to this: the Māori perspective on the past as 'ahead of' (ngā rā o mua) rather than 'behind' (ngā rā o muri) the present; and that the programme, in drawing on the past, advocates for the Kīngitanga in the present, supporting its ongoing relevance as a voice for iwi 'across the motu'. There is an urgency to this message. King Tūheitea's opening voiceover speaks of 'a monarchy at a crossroad, fighting for survival'. He is referring to the general problem of the disengagement of younger Tainui people, and this message is also articulated by his daughter Ngāwai Paki – but at the time the programme was made the Kīngitanga was also dealing with the fallout of the arrest of the king's younger son, Korotangi Paki.[38] This event and its aftermath is openly discussed in the series.

Many senior figures within Tainui are interviewed, such as Rāhui Papa, Tukoroirangi Morgan, the king's sister Heeni Katipa, MP Nanaia Mahuta and Tom Roa, as well as kaumātua from other iwi closely connected to the Kīngitanga, including Sir Wira Gardiner (Te Whānau a Apanui) and Pou Temara (Ngāi Tūhoe). The series narrator Chris Winitana – a careful choice – signals the way the series worked to maintain intertribal relationships with deep roots, connecting past and present. Winitana is an experienced broadcaster, but more importantly he is from Ngāti Tūwharetoa, so his role as narrator acknowledges a specific history: the definitive part played by that iwi in the establishment of the Kīngitanga, when Iwikau

The Kiingitanga (2016): King Tāwhiao, juxtaposed against an archival image of a haka with raised tūpara.

All frame enlargements from *The Kiingitanga*, Enter the Dragon Productions

Te Heuheu hosted the decisive hui at Pūkawa in 1856. Young people, especially the king's children, have their say, too. The only Pākehā speaker is the historian Vincent O'Malley, who was completing his history of the Waikato War as the series was made.

Like previous documentary series, this one draws on archived materials: historical maps, drawings, paintings and photographs. It also uses a series of short, symbolic reenactments, dramatising events such as the coronation of King Pōtatau; or politically charged encounters such as Wiremu Tāmihana making peace with Ngāti Apakura by handing over his daughter in marriage, King Tāwhiao making peace by laying down his guns, and his efforts to regain land through the courts.

The first episode sets out the reason for the Kīngitanga's existence: the threat posed to Māori land by settlers and government. The speakers explain how the arrival of the world's then dominant power and the desire for land by government and settlers forced Māori to unite against a common enemy. Those who had visited England and seen the authority of Queen Victoria recognised the value of monarchy as a uniting force. The episode traces the emergence of the movement in the journey of Mātene Te Whiwhi and Tāmihana Te Rauparaha around the iwi of the central North Island, meeting one iwi after another in a sequence of hui to debate the question of a king; then the process by which one chief after another was offered, and refused, the kingship. Cuts between past and present draw explicit parallels between Pōtatau Te Wherowhero's reluctant acceptance of the title, and King Tūheitia's reluctant acceptance of the role in 2006; and between the case for the Kīngitanga at its beginnings and today. A visual link is made when the

The Kiingitanga (2016): Taking the petition for a day of commemoration for the New Zealand Land Wars to parliament, 10 September 2015. Waimārama Anderson and Leah Bell, who led the petition, third and fourth from left.

kingmaker Wiremu Tāmihana's bible is used both to crown Pōtatau king in 1858, in a reenactment, and to make Tūheitia king in the television footage from 2006.

It is in the second episode that the historical background covers the period of the Waikato War. Here the link between past and present connects the war and its aftermath with the long process of working for and achieving compensation through the Waitangi Tribunal. King Tāwhiao had gained some attention in previous films, mainly in the *New Zealand Wars* series, but this was the first time that the leader so revered among Tainui had become definitively central to a film or television production. The episode opens in the present and with a contentious event: the signing of Tainui's settlement by Dame Te Ātairangikaahu and Prime Minister Jim Bolger in 1995. As it shows, one school of thought considered that Tainui's negotiator, Robert Mahuta, had settled for too little and there was intense division within the iwi surrounding this agreement. In tracing the history behind the settlement and then the changes that have resulted from it, the episode makes the case that the settlement allowed Tainui to move on and to benefit its people. A second contemporary event is introduced later in the episode: the 1915 petition for a national Land Wars Day.

The historical sections in this episode begin with the standoff between the prewar government desire for land and Māori reluctance to sell. Vincent O'Malley argues that Waikato's natural pasture made it a prime target. Tom Roa sets out the situation by the early 1860s: 'It was very clear. They invaded for the land. They had aspirations for the land that Māori didn't share and the only way they could get it was by breaking the back of this major land league we called the Kīngitanga.'

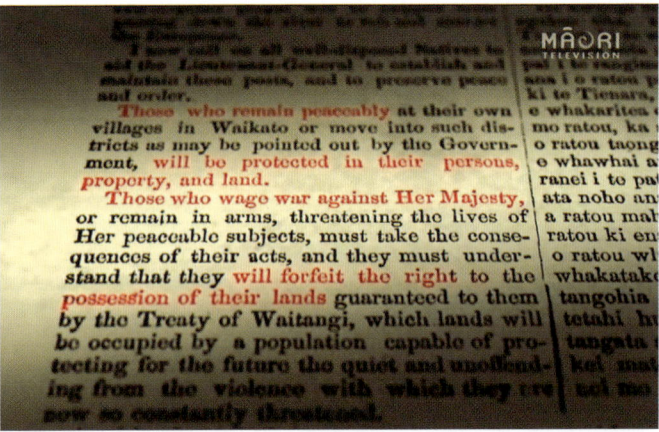

The Kiingitanga: Documents from the archives: Governor George Grey's proclamation warning that those who fought against the Crown would forfeit their lands.

The major figures are introduced: King Tāwhiao and Wiremu Tāmihana, who argue for peace for as long as they can; and Rewi Maniapoto – 'we call him Manga … a person who is more than human'. Tāwhiao sets up a pou just north of the Mangatāwhiri Stream, marking the border; Governor Grey demands that all Māori living north of this point swear allegiance to the government, but many go south instead. Then there is a second proclamation, but O'Malley points to the deceptiveness behind this: he notes that it was still being drafted after the invasion had commenced. Speakers rebut Grey's notorious claim (made to support his request for troops) that Waikato Māori were planning to invade Auckland.

This was not the first time the history of the Waikato War had been told from a Māori point of view – *The Governor* and *The New Zealand Wars* had both offered strong representations of Tainui perspectives. But what was new here was the consistency with which the point of view now came from south of the Mangatāwhiri – the 1863 border. Huirama Matatahi explains how Waikato's world changed: 'for us in Waikato, 1863, 1863 was the turning point between a normal that we once knew, 1863 happened, the crossing of the Mangatāwhiri River, all of a sudden everything became abnormal'.

Another example of this point of view is how Tainui oral sources are prioritised. Tom Roa's explanation of Tainui strategy, for example, came down through his family. He describes:

a very significant but not widely known way of waging war in Tainui. You have your skirmishes and then you have a bit of a pitched battle. But that's not where the war is going to be. You have another second line, and then most often it's at the third line where the major battle is to be.

O'Malley and Roa both comment on the attack on Rangiāowhia. O'Malley explains that Rangiāowhia still causes huge anger and bitterness among Waikato Māori 'because people are torched in their whare there, burnt to death'. Roa continues with a story told to him by his grandmother:

it was Sunday morning, prayers had started in one of the churches, and then this attack took place. The soldiers set light to the whare. These people, a child about ten years old, running out of the whare, and then being shot, and falling flat on her face. And then there are stories of about twenty people in the building actually being burned and killed.

Mahanga Pihama was keen to give prominence to these voices, to 'personalise it to that particular rohe, that iwi – for me anyway, listening to Tom Roa give those interviews was quite special. It highlights the darkness around the Waikato War at that time.'[39]

The episode turns to the aftermath of the war and to the confiscations in the Waikato. Many followed King Tāwhiao into exile in Te Rohe Pōtae (King Country), where they lived in difficult and impoverished conditions – in striking contrast to the thriving prewar economy in the Waikato. Tukoroirangi Morgan explains the loss of prosperity, from the era of rich trade to the dramatic loss of land and wealth after the raupatu or confiscation. King Tāwhiao's leadership through this period now becomes the subject: his efforts to create peace, and to regain the land by negotiation and by making a journey to England in an attempt to meet Queen Victoria – an attempt that is frustrated by the colonial government. One of his methods of strengthening Tainui from within is the tradition of the poukai, the king's annual sequence of visits to Kīngitanga marae: here the episode turns to footage of contemporary poukai.

With the historical context now established, the episode returns to the late twentieth-century negotiations through the Waitangi Tribunal. It addresses the intense arguments within Tainui over whether the settlement should have been accepted, and the accusation of a sellout levelled at Robert Mahuta and others in the leadership of the claim. The episode shows how the signing of the apology to the iwi by Queen Elizabeth herself is a partial resolution of Tāwhiao's frustrated effort to meet Queen Victoria in 1884. In 2016 the leadership looks back at the economic gains made by the iwi since the settlement and the growth of the Tainui asset base resulting from it. The case gains implicit endorsement from a debate that would have been resonant among many viewers in 2016: the arguments that came up frequently in the news about another large iwi, Ngāpuhi, who had not yet been able to negotiate their claim.

In its arguments, *The Kiingitanga* was not such a radical departure from the historical account that Belich and others had set out in historical discussions since the 1970s and 80s. These written histories, and the television histories that followed them, drew from and fed back into iwi knowledge. The *Kiingitanga* series differed in making its tribal authorities *the* authoritative voices, moving beyond inclusion. O'Malley as the sole Pākehā speaker is just one speaker among others, his claim grounded in his historical research. Where *The Kiingitanga* – and other Māori-led productions – stand out most distinctly from earlier productions is in the audience they assume. Pihama and Haami were accustomed to creating programming for Māori viewers, using te reo. This series uses both te reo and English, but it is primarily addressed to Māori and people interested in te ao Māori. *The New Zealand Wars*, commissioned by TV One, had to speak to a national audience and had to work to 'bring in' viewers who might be sceptical of its message. *The Kiingitanga*, on the other hand, was made for Māori Television and this gave it the opportunity to prioritise the perspectives of its Māori audience.

Music video

Stories that have been told on marae, narrated in carving and performed in haka or waiata have also been making their way into popular music and music video. Here they reach audiences who are not so interested in documentary – and the young. Live performances of reggae artist David Grace's *Rua Kēnana*, a song that featured on the soundtrack of the film *Once Were Warriors* in 1992, now appear on YouTube. In early 2017 the young metal band Alien Weaponry's *Raupatu* went online: the story of Treaty breaches and confiscations is shouted out in te reo against thumping percussion and thrash metal.[40] Later in the year the song won the APRA Maioha Award at the Silver Scrolls

Raupatu: Contrasting styles. TOP: Alien Weaponry perform their song *Raupatu* in the official music video. CENTRE AND BOTTOM: At the Silver Scrolls in 2017, Ariana Tikao, Alistair Fraser (both shown here), James Webster and Horomona Horo performed the song on taonga pūoro, with a backdrop of historical images and flags.

With the permission of Ariana Tikao and Alistair Fraser

music awards. The Scrolls ceremony allocates winning songs to a different artist or artists to perform on the night, and the contrast here could hardly have been more marked, or more effective. The Alien Weaponry music video features pounding sound accompanied by heavy-metal images of performers' hair flying in limelight, crashing waves and a succession of intense faces directed at the camera, as the names of places where iwi made a stand against the colonial government are chanted. In an inspired choice, the Scrolls gave *Raupatu* to Ariana Tikao, James Webster, Alistair Fraser and Horomona Horo to perform: in a mix of Māori and nineteenth-century European costume, against tino rangatiratanga and United Tribes flags and slides showing historical photographs of the invasion of Parihaka, they performed the song using traditional Māori instruments.[41]

Then in October 2017, timed for the eve of the first Te Rā Maumahara, Ria Hall released her concept album *Rules of Engagement*, named in reference to Hēnare Taratoa's 'rules of engagement' for battle, drafted and sent to the British on the eve of Gate Pā. Hall (Tauranga Moana) tells the story of the war in Tauranga through several tracks on this album, written and performed in collaboration with others, including Tiki Taane (Ngāti Maniapoto). In an interview with Kirsten Johnstone (RNZ) on the album release, Hall talked about its origins in the kapa haka she was involved in at high school when 'she'd tell the stories of Tauranga iwi through waiata and haka', after researching the history.[42] A music video for *They Come Marching* makes explicit the song's tribute to Rāwiri Puhirake, the tactician whose strategy defeated the British at Gate Pā in 1864. The video opens with a young Māori girl in martial – apparently colonial – uniform, drumming; it then frames the singer ('If it's war/you wanna press on me/I'll be ready, I'll be ready …/Don't underestimate/what you don't know') with warriors laying down a wero with taiaha and patu; and it closes on the Gate Pā flag and the words 'Ko Te Manawarerekia U'/ Rawiri Puhirake/ Pukehinahina 1864'.[43] In the RNZ interview Hall walks through the Gate Pā and Te Ranga sites, articulating Taratoa's stance towards the British as an insistence on compassion despite the arrival of war; the defenders' strategies that resulted in the great Māori victory; and the finality of the defeat of the Tauranga iwi at Te Ranga. Interviewed on TV3's *The Cafe*, Hall explained that she had found archived audio of her great-uncle Turirangi Te Kani speaking about Gate Pā and Te Ranga. She uses this audio in her music.[44] Structured around the war in Tauranga, this is a history of the wars from a young Māori artist that is likely to attain a broad reach, especially among young Māori.

Digital histories, mapping landscapes

Digital histories started appearing online. Some did the work of print histories with added features made possible by the online format. The most notable example was the section on the New Zealand Wars by historian Danny Keenan (Ngāti Te Whiti Ahi Kā, Te Ātiawa) in the online Te Ara – the Encyclopedia of New Zealand, which charts the wars from 1843 to 1916 with more detailed sections on major theatres of conflict.[45] Keenan had previously developed and maintained a website on the New Zealand Wars over some years. This site, pitched at a broad audience and with pages catering to secondary school students, covers battlesites, landscapes, events and claims, and provides maps, a bibliography and an accessible illustrated overview.[46]

Online productions, because of their portability on smartphone or tablet, create the opportunity for their users to

Rules of Engagement. Images from Ria Hall's music video for *They Come Marching* include this drummer at the site of Pukehinahina; intense stripped warriors; and Hall – 'If it's war / You wanna press on me / I'll be ready …'

With the permission of Ria Hall

make sense of historical sites as they make their way around them. Some of the landscapes of the New Zealand Wars are marked by monuments, and some are defined by the roads that were used for military invasion, such as the Great South Road which took troops from Auckland to the Waikato, or the road from the Bay of Plenty into Te Urewera. But unless you come from iwi who tell the stories of conflict and confiscation, or research the history beforehand, you can travel around Aotearoa with little or no idea of the movements of troops and equipment, the fortifications that were built or the battles that raged over what are now farms, towns or, occasionally, still bush-clad hills. Precisely because of the dispossession resulting from the wars and their aftermath, the historic sites around the country are held in disparate ownership – by farmers, churches, the Department of Conservation or Heritage New Zealand – and information on each location from a variety of sources expresses the past of the landscape in a variety of ways (or not at all), with no interconnection. Guidebooks, in the past, provided some access to the landscapes of the wars and helped to restore connections between them. David Green's *Battlefields of the New Zealand Wars: A visitor's guide* concentrates on tours of war sites.[47] Nigel Prickett's *Landscapes of Conflict: A field guide to the New Zealand Wars* is an archaeological study with aerial photography and detailed descriptions of sites.[48] Each new edition of Jeremy Pope and Diana Pope's excellent guides to the North and South islands included more detail on the wars, before publication of these guides ceased.[49]

Site information has increasingly moved online: one example is Ruapekapeka, one of the best-preserved historic sites, which benefited from a collaboration between the Department of Conservation and iwi and, later, the Ruapekapeka Trust through the late 1980s and the 1990s. The Ruapekapeka website provides histories of the Northern War and the battle of Ruapekapeka, as well as a detailed study of the site itself.[50]

The phone or tablet app is now replacing the guidebook as an aid to travellers who want to engage with the past of landscapes. The first of these digital guides was the Waikato War Driving Tour app, a history of the war created by the Māori Heritage team of Heritage New Zealand in 2013; others include the 1846 War in Wellington app developed by the Ministry for Culture and Heritage, and the Taranaki Wars app developed by Heritage Taranaki. They connect sites that appear separate in the landscapes, allowing a traveller to follow the paths of the wars while listening to the words of people who fought at each waypoint.[51]

As some of the sites are developed as memorials their presence in the landscape becomes more apparent to travellers; now, if you stop at any point on the route shown in the Waikato app, for example at Rangiriri, to look at what is happening there as the site is recreated to show how the pā was laid out, the panels at the site may prompt you to access the app and listen to the words of people who were present at the battle. The app will also inform visitors that Rangiriri is just one point in the long Waikato campaign; that the road they are travelling on was created to invade the Waikato; and that a series of battles and negotiations occurred there over the months of the war.

Heritage 'trails' pamphlets tracing the routes of the wars have been produced in Taranaki for many years, and Heritage Taranaki drew on these when it created the Taranaki Wars app. A road tour of sites of the First Taranaki War is online, and four more tours are planned.[52]

NZ Wars: Stories of Ruapekapeka (2017)

The first annual Day of Commemoration of the New Zealand Wars, Te Rā Maumahara, was set down for 28 October 2017, although in the event, as noted above, the larger commemoration was held in March 2018. Mihingārangi Forbes was one person very happy to see the day established: it gave her the opportunity to initiate an online series about the wars for RNZ. RNZ was in the process of expanding from radio to a greater online presence, and in the process looking to increase the diversity of its content and audiences. The appointment of Carol Hirschfeld (Ngāti Porou) as head of content in 2014, and of Forbes to the role of Māori issues correspondent in 2015, signalled RNZ's seriousness about reaching a more diverse demographic. Both had migrated from positions at Māori Television.[53]

A collaboration between Hirschfeld and Forbes resulted in a full hour of coverage of the New Zealand Wars on Anzac Day 2016: the first time a national broadcaster had acknowledged the New Zealand Wars on Anzac Day. Prior to 2017 it had not been easy to find the right occasion for New Zealand Wars coverage but Forbes, who is known for tackling contentious issues, was characteristically persistent:

> I think if we had thought about [the Anzac Day feature] for too much longer it may not have happened because as the day came closer people were saying 'oh, do you think the Anzacs will be annoyed that you're talking about other wars', and I said 'yes, possibly, yes, and the RSA [Returned Services' Association] might be too and I can understand where they're coming from but at some stage we've got to have this conversation and we've got to find a place where we can talk about our own wars'.[54]

In this audio coverage Forbes interviewed four iwi experts: Peeni Hēnare (Ngāti Hine), Awanuiārangi Black (Ngāti Pūkenga), Paraone Gloyne (Ngāti Raukawa) and Te Kahautu Maxwell (Whakatōhea). The programme was aired in the prime 7am hour and and began with a karakia, 'Homai te rā' (bring us the day) – endorsing the petition for the national day.[55] There was 'lots of very good feedback' that demonstrated that Pākehā were as interested as Māori.[56]

In 2017, the scheduling of 28 October meant there was a date that called for programming – Forbes could apply to NZ On Air in collaboration with production company Great Southern Television. *NZ Wars: Stories of Ruapekapeka* is planned as the first in a series of online interactive features, telling the stories of one iwi after another as they take their turn in hosting Te Rā Maumahara. A series will depend on repeated funding applications, as NZ On Air's grants operate on a year-by-year basis.

This was the first attempt at a substantial documentary series since *The New Zealand Wars* aired in 1998. It is planned to roll out with one documentary a year, rather than one a week – so comparisons between the two are premature. The online format appealed to Forbes because 'Māori audiences are all online.' The core content is a 30-minute documentary – usually regarded as an appropriate limit for online content of this kind – but users can click into its separate elements such as animations or interviews. She envisages the series as an ongoing resource.

The balance of authoritative voices, as in *The Prophets*, reveals that a shift had taken place since the making of *The New Zealand Wars*: RNZ, at least, was receptive to a programme where Māori speakers were predominant. But the difference also has to do with how each documentary was initiated: the 1998 series was sparked by a history PhD and, although Stephens' direction shaped it with Māori elements and iwi speakers, it was inevitably defined by the overarching argument of its Pākehā historian narrator James Belich. *Stories of Ruapekapeka* arose from another source. Forbes recalls the long periods she spent around the country as a reporter, and her recognition that the mainstream news routinely ignored events that were important to Māori:

> *I've spent so much time up in the north, with Waitangi, at Te Tī marae, sitting around those hui, with the Crown not coming, all that kind of stuff, reporting them, and I've heard so many of these rich great stories, from these descendants like Hirini Hēnare, who's Kawiti's descendant, and Peeni's relations, and Kīngi Taurua, and all these people that you normally see in the Waitangi One News stories that are trying to negotiate with the government about the pōwhiri, and those kind of meaningless stories. But I'd heard, I knew all the rich stories behind them, I'd heard them, and I just thought – you don't really hear those in the official documentaries …*[57]

Stories of Ruapekapeka's bicultural production team included Forbes, directors Simon Bennett and Cameron Bennett, and executive producers Carmen Leonard (Te Arawa), Annabelle Lee-Harris (Ngāi Tahu) and Philip Smith. Two veterans of the earlier *New Zealand Wars* joined the team: Ian Taylor (Ngāti Kahungunu) and Animation Research created the animations; and Colin McRae returned as one of producers, along with Samoan–Swiss Adrian Stevanon. The tikanga for the production was directed toward developing the story out of interviews with kaumātua in collaboration with Vincent O'Malley, the historian who had also appeared in *The Kiingitanga*.

> *I thought … if we're going to do something let's do it truly bicultural, let's make sure that Māori can have their stories told, or woven in … We went to the authority in Northland, which was the Ruapekapeka Trust, and they handed us a number of names of kaumātua who were storytellers, storyholders for them. And so we then decided we'd get a Ngāpuhi researcher [Tamati Rakena], not one of ours, and we'd send him out, and he went around and he recorded their stories. And then he brought them back and we went through them all and we selected the ones we thought we'd like to include in the documentary. And then we had to run those by Vincent – his job as a historian was to see if he could find links … he had to be comfortable that they would be part of a documentary where he would be the key historian.*[58]

The interviews relate the intimate detail of the war. Three kaumātua are interviewed on screen, partly in te reo and partly in English. Peeni Hēnare is one of the guardians of the Ruapekapeka site. Forbes notes that he whakapapas to both Māori and British sides of the conflict; and she also notes her own link with the surname on one of the English soldiers' graves in the Russell cemetery. The carver and tohunga Te Warahi Hetaraka (Ngāti Wai) talks about mental and spiritual preparation for battle as he and Forbes sit in his workshop among his carvings. Arapeta Hamilton (Ngāpuhi) reflects on the longer-term aftermath for northern Māori and, especially, the deprivation in the region. O'Malley sketches out the broader picture: he locates the origins of the Northern War in the discrepancies between what the Treaty meant for British and for Māori.

The bilingual and bicultural emphasis carries through from the research practice of the production process to the onscreen shifts between te reo Māori and English, and the transitions between the broad history sketched out by O'Malley and the finer details such as Hēnare's explanation of the landscape of Ruapekapeka. It extends to the onscreen performance of tikanga – such as when Forbes washes her hands and flicks the water around her head to lift the tapu on leaving the cemetery at Ōhaeawai – and to the haka and mōteatea that introduce the documentary and thread through it.

Stories of Ruapekapeka (2017): TOP: The aerial view of Ruapekapeka shows the design of its defences, 170 years later.
CENTRE: The animation shows the detail of the firing positions.
BOTTOM: Mihingārangi Forbes leaps into a trench at Ruapekapeka.

Stories of Ruapekapeka, RNZ

As in the earlier series, whenua is a dominant element in film footage of the site and in animation. The programme opens with drone shots sweeping across islands, seashore and bush-covered hills, and aerial views of Ruapekapeka pā. Because the pā is so well preserved its design is clearly defined from above, and a higher view shows us the British positions too. Through the documentary Forbes takes us to one site then another, with animations and dramatisations shuttling between timescales and taking us back to the landscape as it was in the 1840s.

The animations are briefer than those created for *The New Zealand Wars*. They continue the style of Animation Research's work for the earlier series, but this is a generation of animation that allows for more fluency and detail, in the way the past is reconnected to the present landscape, for example. Forbes opens with a piece to camera as she introduces herself, then the drone camera pulls back, the screen shifts into animation, palisades and the pā's internal structures spring up on the site, and the animated occupants of the pā appear around her as she continues the narration. She presents from the landscape as Belich did, but adopts a more energetic, physical style, placing herself in the position of both sides. She runs up the long, once-lethal approach to Ōhaeawai like the doomed redcoats of 1845, and leaps into the trenches at Ruapekapeka like the defending Ngāpuhi. The plan was to create an intimate connection with the landscape for the audience through Forbes' onscreen engagement:

Stories of Ruapekapeka (2017): Girls load the muskets in a dramatisation.

[Carmen Leonard] said this has to be different, we have to engage with our audience, we're already going to have this amazing virtual reality, we're going to have these beautiful animations, and then we're going to have you, and we have to have something different for you, [not just] I'm Mihingārangi Forbes the reporter. We just have to be right there [...] touching, and allowing people to be with us in the land and the trenches and all over the place. So I think that was the idea about it ... we're retelling the story but we're also walking in the steps.[59]

O'Malley and the Ngāpuhi speakers' historical analysis of the Northern War is consistent with Belich's revisioning of the historiography. This was a war over sovereignty and the threat to the Māori economy; the British confronted an enemy they had expected to overcome with ease but Māori developed innovative military and strategic means to defeat them in several encounters. The war in the North resulted not in Māori defeat but a standoff: the British returned to Auckland, and there was no immediate land loss for Māori and no loss of freedom or mana for Heke or Kawiti. The felled flagstaff was re-erected permanently only a dozen years later – by Kawiti's son. In these respects at least, the documentary supports the view that Belich's broader revisioning of the wars had become the prevailing orthodoxy of historians and of iwi.

Stories of Ruapekapeka is nevertheless a narrative for a new cultural moment – as is apparent onscreen and in the shifting emphases of the production process. The particularity and the prioritising of the iwi information, for a general audience, is one important change. The attention paid to people other than warriors is another. Forbes asks about wāhine and tamariki, and Hēnare explains that the fighting involved whole communities: kuia for their healing capacities; younger women for helping to build the pā and for their role in battle of following the warriors and finishing off the wounded. There are stories such as that of the young girl whose task was to run out and collect mortars and defuse them before they exploded, and bring them back so the gunpowder could be reused. Te Warahi talks about children reloading the muskets, and there is a reenactment of this dangerous work. The inclusion and prominence of women is signalled from the outset: the opening mōteatea begins with women's voices and faces.

Another distinctive subject of this documentary, as for the *Kiingitanga* series, is the long economic aftermath. Although the Northern War did not result in defeat for Māori, it was followed by longterm economic decline and the loss of land and resources. The reasons for these are not elaborated in the documentary, with its emphasis on the war, but the speakers comment on the effects of poverty and the lack, to date, of a Ngāpuhi settlement. At the beginning and end of the documentary the physical manifestations of poverty – houses with peeling paint, a caravan that looks like someone's home – unfold as Forbes drives through the landscape.

It is too early to assess the reception of this documentary. But after it went live Forbes had an immediate call from a West Auckland school that had been studying the Northern War and had gone up north for the October commemoration:

> *they had planned their studies around that commemoration date. So [the teacher] rang me and she said 'Oh, we've just been to Ruapekapeka this week, we had no idea your documentary was coming out and we have just woken up in Waitangi and the school watched it all together.' And she said, 'There was not a peep or a squeak in the room, the kids just were fixed, and thoroughly enjoyed it.'*[60]

*

Māori creative control has grown through the increasing presence of Māori in the screen industries, the diminishing costs of digital media, and the rise of Māori-led or supportive production houses, in part as a response to the establishment of the Māori Television Service in 2004. The Māori-led productions discussed here do not inevitably tell a greater historical truth than any of those discussed in earlier chapters, but in giving voice to a range of points of view and in according greater priority to Māori audiences, they illustrate just how much was missing from the broader landscape of public discussion of the wars, despite the appearance of productions led by Pākehā who were deeply committed to putting the wars back into the national memory. These were perspectives heard on marae and in other iwi contexts, and on Māori airwaves, but rarely on nationally broadcast media. The establishment of Te Rā Maumahara and its consolidation in coming years will provide a demand for new content. Historical programming continues to struggle for airtime, nevertheless, and there is little sign that the more expensive dramatic genres will be any easier to fund in this changing economic and cultural climate.

CONCLUSION

In charting the productions about the New Zealand Wars this book has sought to 'set them deep', situating each of them in the cultural politics of their time; in the structures, cultures and economies of the screen industries; in the particular milieux – the personalities, relationships and networks – that produced them; in the histories they drew from; in the places, the whenua, where they were made; and in their relation to mana whenua. We have seen that each production is a snapshot of a complex cultural moment, and moving from one to the next enables us to follow the path of cultural change as successive generations reimagined the colonial past and its aftermath. Filmmakers were driven by storytelling and historical passions: whatever the balance between these imperatives in each case, they knew they were dealing with the legacies of a difficult past. Each film reflects its own moment of production – the time of its making, but also the more immediate context in which ideas about the past crystallise through encounters among people who converge, usually if not invariably on an uneven field, to create a story that embodies those ideas. As filmmakers spent time in historical locations and consulted and worked with mana whenua, familiarity often bred complexity, nuance and respect.

Over almost a century of screen productions about the wars, understandings of Māori and Pākehā pasts were repeatedly revisited and reshaped in written and oral histories, in iwi and family memories, in politics, in legal claims – and in screen stories. Cultural identities and cultural politics have undergone huge transformations. The history of these screen productions shows us how the wars have altered in cultural memory, as attention has shifted from one conflict or historical figure to another and the meanings derived from them have changed. But it also shows us how the ways we negotiate the past have altered. The productions themselves – their filmmaking practices, conversations and negotiations – provide evidence of a shifting cultural–political landscape, an ambiguous and incomplete decolonising process, and an underlying continuity of desires and dilemmas as Māori and Pākehā have dealt with each other about the past.

How might film shape a national past? On what terms can film tell history? Can film claim to inform the present with a rich and nuanced understanding of the past? If one dilemma of written history is its limited reach and the difficulty of representing complexity while still engaging readers, does film overcome these impediments, and what might it lose in the process? Many of these films have drawn audiences much larger than the readership of books and, to greater or lesser degrees, they catch us up in their narratives in ways that written histories usually struggle to do. Film freights the past with emotions: it hooks viewers into engagement with historical protagonists, whether fictional archetypes or based on actual individuals; it makes claims on the viewer's identity and shapes their sense of cultural belonging. It has an appetite for national pasts, and in return it invests them with emotional resonance. The old critiques of film histories – that they focus too narrowly, or that they provide such a plausible appearance of the past that they persuade us to suspend our critical judgement too easily – are not to be lightly dismissed. Nevertheless, film's capacity to engage us in the past cannot be disregarded either.

*

Historical films about the New Zealand Wars are artefacts of the layered cultural and industrial processes that produced them, and these complex origins have implications that have played out through the films. Each film, consistent with the workings of cultural memory that it contributes to, speaks to the present even while it recreates a past, and it does so out of specific social contexts. Each generation and each community's preoccupations, anxieties and unconscious omissions mark their films, from the cluster of peoples freighted with diverse colonial experiences who converged on Tāneatua to make *The Te Kooti Trail* in the wake of World War One, to the pressing concerns of an economically thriving yet politically beleaguered Kīngitanga contending with issues of leadership in 2016.

By recreating the past, film intervenes in the present: it changes those who make it and those who watch it. Belich's revelation as he dug the trenches of Ruapekapeka in the summer of 1976–77 is one of the more striking exemplars of film's interventions here, but the medium's collaborative character brought people and ideas together in all sorts of ways as it demanded their knowledge and then remade it, thrust them into relationships of trust or disagreement with each other, opened their eyes to other points of view, and forged working relationships. Pākehā filmmakers ventured into unknown places, and found themselves surprised. For viewers, too, these productions could have a lasting impact. *Rewi's Last Stand* helped to ensure that generations of schoolchildren remembered Ōrākau. '*Utu* was the one,' said Cliff Curtis as he recalled the way his horizon expanded when he watched that film for the first time in Rotorua; and many years on, Zac Wallace's performance is still widely remembered and beloved. Many young Māori drew pride and confidence from *The New Zealand Wars* – including Tainui Stephens, who went on to make other productions about the wars and to foster Māori filmmaking.

As a subject for film in a settler colonial society, the 'colonial past' could hardly be more contentious for the very reason that the colonial is *not* past, but structures the everyday circumstances that underpinned the making of these films: the differential access to funding, to occupations within the film world, to the cultural authority that allows a voice to be heard about historical legacies. Even as the subject appeals on many levels and for many reasons – for the intensity of its drama, for a sense of a wild and adventurous national past, for its provision of searching and troubling origin stories, for its capacity to unsettle the present – it is also a subject that has demanded confrontation with the privileges and disadvantages that unfolded and persisted over generations. This aftermath clung to filmmakers, performers and mana whenua as they negotiated their way through the manifold dealings of film production.

While these films were shaped by the local context, the film and television of a small nation continued their unequal competition with more powerful global industries. Hollywood's scale of production and its budgets vastly exceeded local capacity. Film on such an apparently local subject was, for better and for worse, informed and sometimes driven by genres, aesthetics and styles of narrating colonial pasts that came from Hollywood but also from other national cinemas and television industries – Japan, Ireland or Britain. Film has never even looked like being a 'pure' New Zealand product. The terms on which it has engaged aesthetically, financially and ideologically with transnational film and television have shifted dramatically over the 90 plus years. Here lies the ongoing dilemma of the screen as the vehicle for stories of local origin: its capacity to tell 'our stories' may be energised by its borrowings from other cinemas, or unravelled by its demands for the exotic or the globally legible.

*

The films' themes and motifs have shifted and mutated over the 90 years, and the character of some themes has altered radically. Hayward's silent films of the 1920s betray little doubt that the march of empire and colonial paternalism, personified in Governor Grey and the archetypal native-born Pākehā Gilbert Mair, brought benefits to coloniser and colonised alike. No such confidence is apparent in any of the later productions; even Hayward's second *Rewi* portrays a more complicated and troubled colonial past, and every film since has addressed colonialism as a disturbing ongoing question – some more forcefully than others. In dramatic fictions imperial commanders either feel moral disquiet over their role (Cameron in *The Governor*) or are outright villains increasingly at odds with colonials as well as Māori (Elliot in *Utu*, Baine in *River Queen*). The colonial's dilemma – what are the terms of belonging? – is a pressing question for settlers or native-born Pākehā, whose endeavour to be a 'good colonial' preoccupies protagonists in most dramatic fictions. To a greater or lesser degree, though rarely explicitly, what has come to be discussed as 'whiteness' is at the centre of these dilemmas.[1] Not surprisingly this is one respect in which fiction tends to diverge from the documentary and from the written histories. The motif, common in dramatic productions, of colonial soldiers who were more perceptive and less ruthless than imperial soldiers, offered a comforting separation to audiences who were descended from settlers, but was hardly consistent with the plentiful evidence that settler demand for land pushed governments towards wars in Taranaki and the Waikato. A related subtheme derives from the history of internal colonisation within Britain. Irish and Māori and, at times, Scots and Māori find common interest in a shared distrust of the English: *River Queen*'s Irish, Sarah and Doyle, express more affinity with the Māori 'enemy' than with the English. This cushioning distinction between the good colonial and the bad imperial is questioned more often in documentary: in *The Governor*, the *New Zealand Wars* documentary series and the recent documentaries created under Māori direction.

The cultural go-between – an archetype of a national identity in formation – persists across the history of these productions and occurs in several forms. The colonial soldier travels from Hayward's egalitarian, chivalrous, knockabout irregulars, to *The Killing of Kane*'s cautious Pākehā and the soldiers of *The Governor* wondering what they are fighting for, to *Utu*'s Lieutenant Scott and Ward's Doyle. In drama the colonial soldier inevitably invites comparison with the hero of the western, a form that all of the dramatic features produced in New Zealand echo in some way. Yet it is striking that none of these films has what could be described as a stock western hero – the loner who carries the weight of justice on his shoulders, and/or who furthers anything like the great imperative of Western expansion. If there is a consistent mission for this masculinity-in-formation, it centres on the creation of interracial bonds and even, as Kenneth Marc Harris argued in relation to *Utu*, the deliberate dismantling of the white-hat hero, his cultural dominance and his civilising mission.[2]

White women's place in the story varies more. Cecily, the love-interest who bookends the real drama in Hayward's first *Rewi*, is replaced in *The Te Kooti Trail* by the more adventurous though still peripheral Alice; but by the 1940 *Rewi* she has gone, and the Māori woman is the centre of the film's romance. *Utu*'s doomed Emily Williamson is a good shot and brave enough to get killed trying to defend her husband, but this film is still largely about masculinity. The *Greenstone* series – colonial saga more than war film and therefore stocked with a more varied cast – makes more space for immigrant women. Not until *River Queen*'s Sarah, though, do we find a female Pākehā–Māori, the first European female lead, and the first European woman to take up with a Māori man: it is no coincidence that this was less a western than a woman's film.

The portrayal of Māori, historical or fictional, can be mapped out against shifting historical perspectives. Several historical figures prove irresistible over the generations, but they alter over time. Te Kooti, whose reputation guaranteed audiences in the 1920s, appears in *The Te Kooti Trail* and, later, as a source for Te Wheke in *Utu*, as well as in several documentaries. Despite Belich's assertion that Riwha Tītokowaru had been forgotten as settler terror sought to erase him from memory, he was in fact the subject of the first colour television drama. Belich's attention to him in written history and documentary series influenced the character of Te Kai Pō in *River Queen*. Both leaders, magnetically attractive to storytellers, have been the subject of other scripts that have not made it to the screen. Rewi Maniapoto, well known and admired in Māori and Pākehā worlds, is the title character if not the lead in Hayward's two versions of *Rewi's Last Stand*. Rua Kēnana's story is traced through *Rain of the Children*, but this documentary turns aside from masculine leadership to the fallout and aftermath of historical events on little-known people like its subject, Te Puhi Tatu.

If *The Killing of Kane* played an underacknowledged role in its foray into the historical portrayal of Māori on television, it was *The Governor* that really made an impact, through the scale and the seriousness of its commitment to this task. The creators were deliberate in their intentions, but *The Governor*'s intervention in the representation of Māori on the small screen was driven by Don Selwyn, whose networks in Māori theatre facilitated the casting and performance of many historical figures in that production.[3] The series also included scenes set entirely in the Māori world, though it was not the only production to do so. If *The Governor* did rely on an overdrawn opposition between 'peaceable' Tamihana and 'fiery' Rewi, it was in tune with mid-century historians' emphasis on the political decisionmaking of Māori leaders as they grappled with the ever-growing implications of colonisation. In Tainui Stephens' direction of *The New Zealand Wars* documentary

In Spring One Plants Alone/Rain of the Children: Te Puhi Tatu, survivor.

CONCLUSION

series, Māori descendants and wider hapū members speak about what they know of major historical figures, a pattern that continued through *Rain of the Children* and was a persistent characteristic of Māori-directed documentaries.

The warrior recurs constantly as a figure of Māori masculinity. Hayward's Māori men are well and mostly sympathetically realised, aided by his recruiting performers who were familiar with these historical figures; *Utu*'s fearsome warrior characters arguably evade the spectre of the 'savage' through the film's narrative of injustice, its complexity, but also its anarchic comedy. The warrior chief Te Kai Pō in *River Queen* echoes Belich's recasting of Māori military leaders, and Cliff Curtis's go-between Wīremu extends the conception of warrior masculinity into the realms of fatherhood and tragedy. Both characters may be informed by the *New Zealand Wars* documentary series, which made an explicit case for revisiting the warrior: it argued that the Māori defenders were neither victims nor savage fighters but successful military innovators. This documentary series, like *The Governor*, attends to Māori leadership – a theme that becomes central in the Māori-led documentaries. Here new figures come to prominence, or familiar figures are considered for different reasons – in *The Kiingitanga*'s emphasis on King Tāwhiao, for example, and in *The Prophets*' concern with religious leadership.

Māori allied with the Crown are another generic figure of the cultural go-between, prevalent in the fiction especially. From 'friendlies' defined by admirable loyalty to the government side in the 1920s, in later fictions, as historical sympathies swung in the other direction, kūpapa become troubled figures who are dealing with conflicting loyalties – a correlative to the colonial soldier in the process of becoming native and questioning his own loyalty. Māori allied with the Crown are fully developed central characters in some films – such as the tragic figures of Te Wheke and Wiremu in *Utu* – but less so in others. In drama, crosscultural friendships and love affairs connect kūpapa and colonials, and test their commitments and perspectives: the relationships between them serve as emblems of the nation-in-the-making. In documentary or drama-documentary, these cultural go-betweens on both sides are important and symbolic figures in the imaginary of national race relations: Kimble Bent, George Grey's Māori aides, Gustavus von Tempsky, Lucy Takiora.

The high death rate of Māori women in the dramatic productions invites comparison with the treatment of Native American women in film who, as M. Elise Marubbio argues, are routinely assigned passive, self-sacrificial roles.[4] Yet despite their short lives, Māori women and girls have plenty to say for themselves and are active in these films' narrative arcs: Monika in *The Te Kooti Trail*, Kura in *Utu* and Marama in *Greenstone* are all forceful characters (and Marama survives). Oddly, the character who looks most conventional now is Ariana in the second *Rewi*, whose performance has dated as a result of the film's adherence to the codes of melodrama. But another recurring and most often female figure is the wounded child or woman, the victim of colonial attack and often a symbol of atrocities – and many of the heroines come to occupy this role. Te Puhi Tatu, whose life Vincent Ward traces, is also a figure of suffering and Ward unravels her story as one of lasting colonial damage as well as of determined endurance. And it is only in *Rain of the Children* and the Māori-led documentaries that Māori women gain full authority as speakers.

Romance is often more than just love interest. Main plots that veer dangerously towards racial antagonism are interrupted and mitigated time and again with subplots of interracial romance, military alliance, mutual protection, friendship and familial bonds. In a settler society where intermarriage occurred early, and where there was some settler ambivalence about the wars, this is not historically anomalous, although it is an open question whether Māori filmmakers will maintain this tradition if and when they turn to fictional treatments of the wars.[5] In the fiction features and television dramas it is women, and men of ambiguous alliance, who stand between warring or mutually incomprehending sides and create the spaces of affectionate or passionate encounter. These stories of interracial affections, beginning with Takiri and Ken (1925) and continuing to Te Puhi and Vincent (2008), alter in nature substantially over time, and the changes they undergo constitute a little history of crosscultural relations in themselves. This pattern in the Pākehā fiction films seldom featured strongly in documentary, except in *Rain of the Children*.

Another theme concerns the question of *which* wars came to prominence for each generation of filmmakers: which historical figures and events caught their imagination or seemed to speak to their contemporary moments? The decision to focus on one historical conflict raises other questions; and as historiographic interpretations shift over time, the same conflict can raise different questions altogether. From the Waikato War – the largest theatre of the wars that encompasses the widely disparate events at Rangiriri, Rangiāowhia and Ōrākau – filmmakers derived themes ranging from Māori heroism and 'mutual interracial respect' to imperial invasion and atrocities. But, beginning with *The Governor* and emerging again with the recent Māori documentaries, the significance of the Waikato War centres more and more on one issue: land. Taranaki's complex role in the beginning of the wars of the 1860s is charted in *The New Zealand Wars*, but fictional treatments are associated mostly with Tītokowaru, whose intuitive understanding of effective public theatre has served filmmakers well. To venture into the later phases of the wars in Taranaki, or in Te Urewera and the surrounding region, is to deal with the period after the imperials had departed: the drama shifts away from a struggle between Māori and empire and/or colonial government towards murkier, more troubling conflicts between resistant Māori and combined forces of colonial and Crown-allied Māori troops. Here lie complex stories with long colonial legacies. They have been attractive to filmmakers for a variety of reasons: if Hayward's *Te Kooti Trail* praised the attachments between colonial and Māori allies, *Utu* took up these events as troubling and tragic. Vincent Ward's *Rain of the Children* and Paora Joseph's *Tātarakihi: The children of Parihaka* are both concerned with the long shadow of colonial impact from the invasions of Maungapōhatu and Parihaka respectively.

The way the films handle physical violence echoes to some degree the growing tolerance for onscreen violence in cinema as a whole, although no film here is distinguished by extreme onscreen violence and, indeed, most step back from it. Where, precisely, acts of violence occur, and between whom, is invariably telling. In dramatic film this plays out through the plotting. Hayward's use of violence is highly judicious: in *The Te Kooti Trail*, he avoids the most extreme historical incidents of violence on both sides. By the time the sound version of *Rewi's Last Stand* is made, the most violent acts are the work of imperial soldiers, and this is also the case in *The Governor*. *The Killing of Kane* shows frightening violence perpetrated by Māori towards a renegade soldier, in a confrontational assault on viewer sentimentality; but it also shows the unsavoury path that led to this rough justice. Several films portray the notorious imperial assault on Rangiāowahia. Both *Utu* and

River Queen portray bloodshed on both sides, but they situate the imperatives differently. The increasingly lethal Te Wheke and *River Queen*'s cool strategist Te Kai Pō are both countered by cruel and vindictive English commanders. Across these divides, the central characters in each film struggle to come to terms with the bloodshed they are caught up in. Documentary-makers also had decisions to make about how they handled violence: they had to weigh up the excitement to be derived from the war story and, increasingly, potential audience delight in stories of triumphant Māori underdogs, against the pathos and tragedy of the historical reality.

Land is inevitably a major theme and its presence is enhanced by the processes of filmmaking. In fiction and in documentary, the filmmakers' gravitation towards the landscapes where history happened had several implications. Documentary can use location to mark continuities, as when a kaumātua speaks from the ridges and hollows that still mark the earthworks of Ruapekapeka pā; or disjunctures, as when traffic whizzes along behind a historian as he explains what once happened in a place now called Manners Street or Greenlane. Dramatic productions gain a dimension of authenticity through location, too. *Utu's* opening shots summon the great sweep of Te Urewera and its associations with the wars of the late 1860s and early 1870s; its grand epic footage of the volcanic plateau draws resonance from the historical pursuit of Te Kooti across this region, and the bush camp in the final scenes – the dense, damp vegetation and the river – seems fitting for a story that references Te Kooti's War. Hayward rebuilt the mill at Tāneatua where the historical events of *The Te Kooti Trail* had occurred, and was able to use some relatively unchanged historical locations. With Tainui Stephens' involvement in a series of productions we find a deeper attention to land as whenua, first in *The New Zealand Wars* with its signature footage of whenua in each episode. Stephens, with the designers and directors of photography associated with the films he worked on, defines landscape as whenua in each of them.

*

To some extent it is possible to investigate what filmmakers sought to achieve, to what extent they were able to realise it, and how other people participated in and contributed to the productions. The story the sequence of films reveals is, for the most part, a story of engagement – of Pākehā filmmakers whose interest in the wars was genuine and who recognised that substantial injustice had occurred; and of Māori who contributed their expertise or knowledge to the creation of the films. Most of the filmmakers aimed to make injustice apparent to their audiences, and their stories often unsettled assumptions of 'natural' settler dominance in Aotearoa. Māori – usually hapū or iwi with a connection to the historical events – were involved in almost all productions, and often in formative ways. Filmmakers have sought advice and been keen to take it as they worked out how to represent the past, and in quite a few productions Māori contributions went well beyond advice. Things did not always go smoothly: there was often turbulence at the cultural shorelines.

Nevertheless, in placing the stories of these films in sequence, one overall pattern becomes obvious: only very recently has the control of the story or the camera passed out of the hands of Pākehā men to any degree. Cultural authority and narrative authority were long the preserve of the white male, in neat alignment with seniority in the screen industries and access to funding. Although some of the filmmakers discussed here have been aware of this and have sought to mitigate what they recognised as a problem, Māori creative control has been a long time coming. By the end of the twentieth century Tainui Stephens, hired for *The New Zealand Wars* and then on Vincent Ward's productions, was involved in developing Māori capacity behind the camera. His work on the productions discussed here was important, but it was only part of his contribution to a much longer game – involving the efforts of many people including Don Selwyn, Merata Mita and Barry Barclay: the development of a Māori screen industry. The final chapter was an exciting one to write, with new productions emerging, encouraged by the creation of a national day of commemoration, and with digital platforms providing opportunities for Māori creative attention to the wars. Each time I thought I had finished, someone would tell me about something new.

In this phase – which is very likely only beginning – more varied points of view and approaches are emerging as Māori acquire greater authority behind the camera. The preoccupations and concerns of Māori reimagining the difficult past will not be the same as those of Pākehā, even those who invited Māori involvement. These are not only 'Māori stories', as Geoff Murphy said; they are Pākehā stories too – but it is past time that Māori had equivalent opportunities to tell them as they see them. The films discussed in chapter 9 are the first indications of how such stories might look in the future – provided, as ever, that there is funding.

Here, then, is a colonial story that is also distinctly a story of Aotearoa New Zealand: a story of a very uneven field, but also a story of negotiation, argument, inquiry and conflicting points of view aired and in varying degrees accommodated; of change and fluctuation and shifting understandings; and also of some remarkable examples of indigenous agency, as far back as the earliest films. Although the taiaha, guns and bayonets were now only props, the filmmakers, actors, cultural advisors, crews and the mana whenua all lived and worked in the world that colonial violence had made. In turning to the past, in looking to make sense of it in these successive presents, and trying to undo as well as record its legacies, they played out its complexities over again in their encounters: like their historical antecedents, they were go-betweens, lovers, innovators, strategists and fighters. In the process, they created a body of screen stories that charts the slow, inconsistent and incomplete decolonising of a nation.

NOTES

Abbreviations

ATL   Alexander Turnbull Library
DNZB   *Dictionary of New Zealand Biography*
NZJH   *New Zealand Journal of History*
NZW   Cowan, *The New Zealand Wars: A history of the Maori campaigns and the pioneering period* (2 vols)

Introduction

1. Kynan Gentry, *History, Heritage and Colonialism: Historical consciousness, Britishness and cultural identity in New Zealand, 1870–1940* (Manchester: Manchester University Press, 2015), 93–124.
2. There is argument about the dates: the Wairau Affray of 1843 was an isolated incident rather than properly a war; and the police invasion of Maungapōhatu in 1916 was a sorry incident in colonial history but not, in its scale, a war. Its aftermath, however, was serious and long-lasting for those involved.
3. O'Malley, *The Great War for New Zealand*, 220.
4. In this brief introductory summary I have relied on James Cowan, James Belich and Vincent O'Malley for a general overview: Cowan, *The New Zealand Wars: A history of the Maori campaigns and the pioneering period* (Wellington: Government Printer, 1922–23); Belich, *The New Zealand Wars and the Victorian Interpretation of Racial Conflict* (Auckland: Auckland University Press, 1986) and *Making Peoples: A history of the New Zealanders from Polynesian settlement to the end of the nineteenth century* (Auckland: Allen Lane/Penguin, 1996); O'Malley, *The Great War for New Zealand: Waikato 1800–2000* (Wellington: Bridget Williams Books, 2016).
5. Patrick Wolfe sets out this distinguishing element of settler colonial societies, that 'the colonizers come to stay – invasion is a structure not an event', in the Introduction to Patrick Wolfe, *Settler Colonialism and the Transformation of Anthropology: The politics and poetics of an ethnographic event* (London: Cassell, 1999), 2.
6. For a detailed discussion, see Michael Belgrave, *Historical Frictions: Maori claims and reinvented histories* (Auckland: Auckland University Press, 2005).
7. James Edward FitzGerald, 'Ake! Ake! Ake!', *Press*, 16 April 1864.
8. John Bryce sued Rusden over the claim that Bryce had attacked women and children; Bryce won his case in the High Court in London. Hazel Riseborough, 'John Bryce', *Dictionary of New Zealand Biography*, vol. 2, 1993.
9. James E. Alexander, *Incidents of the Maori War, New Zealand, in 1860–61* (London: Bentley, 1863); George S. Whitmore, *The Last Maori War in New Zealand under the Self-Reliant Policy* (London: Sampson Low, Marston & Co., 1902); John Featon, *The Waikato War, 1863–4* (Auckland: Free Lance, 1879, 2nd edn 1923); Frederick Edward Maning, 'Heke's War in the North', in *Old New Zealand* (Auckland: Whitcombe & Tombs, 1906); George W. Rusden, *History of New Zealand*, 3 vols (London: Chapman & Hall, 1883) and *Aureretanga: Groans of the Maoris* (London: W. Ridgeway, 1888). For the libel action, see Ann Blainey & Mary Lazarus, 'Rusden, George William (1819–1903)', *Australian Dictionary of Biography*, vol. 6 (Melbourne: Melbourne University Press, 1976); William Pember Reeves, *The Long White Cloud: Ao Tea Roa* (London: Horace Marshall & Son, 1898); T. Lindsay Buick, *New Zealand's First War, or The rebellion of Hone Heke* (Wellington: Government Printer, 1926).
10. Cowan's friend and later informant Colonel Porter approached Joseph Ward, then prime minister, to argue that Cowan should be commissioned to write the official history of the New Zealand Wars. There appears to have been some question about the appointment, as Ward's successor Massey wanted someone else, but T.W. Leys, editor on the *Auckland Star* and Cowan's former employer, lobbied successfully in his favour. Alan Mulgan, 'Cowan's history of the Maori Wars', in *Great Days in New Zealand Writing* (Wellington: A.H. & A.W. Reed, 1962), 76.
11. James Cowan, *The Maoris of New Zealand* (Christchurch: Whitcombe & Tombs, 1910) and *The Adventures of Kimble Bent: A story of wild life in the New Zealand bush* (London: Whitcombe & Tombs, 1911).

12. James Cowan, *The New Zealand Wars: A history of the Maori campaigns and the pioneering period*, 2 vols (Wellington: Government Printer, 1922–23). For more on Cowan, see Chris Hilliard, 'James Cowan and the frontiers of New Zealand history', *New Zealand Journal of History*, vol. 31, no. 2, 1997, 219–33; the special issue 'James Cowan and the legacies of late colonial culture in Aotearoa New Zealand', *Journal of New Zealand Studies*, eds Annabel Cooper & Ariana Tikao, vol. NS19, 2015; Greg Wood, 'Revisiting James Cowan: A reassessment of *The New Zealand Wars* (1922–23)' MPhil thesis, Massey University, 2010.
13. In his documentation of Cowan's sources, Greg Wood shows that the interviews covered all sides of the wars, but he suggests Cowan's personal networks enabled him to find more resistant Māori sources for some conflicts (such as Ōrākau) than for others (such as Te Kooti's War). Wood, 'Revisiting James Cowan'.
14. cf. Hilliard, 'James Cowan and the frontiers'.
15. Henty, *Maori and Settler: A story of the New Zealand War* (London: Blackie, 1890); Boldrewood, *War to the Knife: or, Tangata Whenua* (London: Macmillan, 1899); Hamilton-Browne, *With the Lost Legion in New Zealand* (London: T. Werner Laurie, 1911); *Camp Fire Yarns of the Lost Legion* (London: T. Werner Laurie, 1913); Satchell, *The Greenstone Door* (London: Sidgwick & Jackson, 1914); Tracey, *Rifle and Tomahawk: A stirring tale of the Te Kooti rebellion* (London: Harrap, 1927); Bruno, *Black Noon at Ngutu* (London: R. Hale, 1960); Braithwaite, *The Flying Fish* (London: Collins, 1964); *The Needle's Eye* (London: Collins, 1965); *The Evil Day* (London: Collins, 1967).
16. Dick Scott, *The Parihaka Story* (Auckland: Southern Cross Books, 1954); *Ask That Mountain: The story of Parihaka* (Auckland: Heinemann/Southern Cross, 1975); Keith Sinclair, *The Origins of the Maori Wars* (Wellington: New Zealand University Press, 1957); Keith Sinclair, *A History of New Zealand* (London: Oxford University Press, 1959); Ian Wards, *The Shadow of the Land: A study of British policy and racial conflict in New Zealand 1832–1852* (Wellington: Historical Branch, Internal Affairs, 1968); Alan Ward, *A Show of Justice: Racial 'amalgamation' in nineteenth-century New Zealand* (Auckland: Auckland University Press, 1973). Also, Harold Miller's *Race Conflict in New Zealand 1814–1865* (Auckland: Blackwood & Janet Paul, 1966) and B.J. Dalton, *War and Politics in New Zealand 1855–1870* (Sydney: Sydney University Press, 1967).
17. Tony Simpson, *Te Riri Pakeha: The white man's anger* (Martinborough: Alister Taylor, 1979); Tim Ryan & Bill Parham, *The Colonial New Zealand Wars* (Wellington: Grantham House, 1986).
18. Judith Binney, Gillian Chaplin & Craig Wallace, *Mihaia: The prophet Rua Kenana and his community at Maungapohatu* (Auckland: Oxford University Press, 1979); Judith Binney & Gillian Chaplin, *Ngā Mōrehu/The Survivors: The life histories of eight Māori women* (Auckland: Oxford University Press, 1986); Judith Binney, *Redemption Songs: A life of Te Kooti Arikirangi Te Turuki* (Auckland/ Wellington: Auckland University Press/ Bridget Williams Books, 1995); Judith Binney, *Encircled Lands: Te Urewera, 1820–1921* (Wellington: Bridget Williams Books, 2009).
19. Belich, *The New Zealand Wars and the Victorian Interpretation of Racial Conflict* (1986) and *I Shall Not Die: Titokowaru's War, New Zealand 1868–1869* (Wellington: Allen & Unwin/Port Nicholson Press, 1989); *The New Zealand Wars* (dir. Tainui Stephens, Landmark Productions, 1998). For critique see for example Chris Pugsley, 'Maori did not invent trench warfare', *New Zealand Defence Quarterly* (1998), 33–34.
20. Ranginui Walker, *Ka Whawhai Tonu Matou: Struggle Without End* (Auckland: Penguin, 1990).
21. Danny Keenan, *Wars Without End: The Land Wars in nineteenth-century New Zealand* (Auckland: Penguin, 2009); Danny Keenan, *Te Whiti o Rongomai and the Resistance of Parihaka* (Wellington: Huia Books, 2015). I have covered only a few of the published histories here – there are many more, involving many debates that there is not scope to address here.
22. Maurice Shadbolt, *Season of the Jew* (London: Hodder & Stoughton, 1986); *Monday's Warriors* (Hodder & Stoughton, 1990); *The House of Strife* (London/Auckland: Bloomsbury/Hodder & Stoughton, 1993); Witi Ihimaera, *The Matriarch* (Auckland: Heinemann, 1986); *The Trowenna Sea* (Auckland: Raupo, 2009); *The Parihaka Woman* (Auckland: Random House, 2011); Witi Ihimaera with Hēmi Kelly, *Sleeps Standing Moetū* (Auckland: Vintage, 2017); Hamish Clayton, *Wulf* (Auckland: Penguin, 2011).
23. Binney, *Encircled Lands*; O'Malley, *The Great War for New Zealand*; Belgrave, *Dancing with the King: The rise and fall of the King Country, 1864–1885* (Auckland: Auckland University Press, 2017).
24. The debate began with M.P.K. Sorrenson, 'Towards a radical reinterpretation of New Zealand history: The role of the Waitangi Tribunal', *NZJH*, vol. 21, no. 1, 1987, 173–88, and intensified with W.H. Oliver, 'The future behind us: The Waitangi Tribunal's retrospective Utopia', in Andrew Sharp & Paul McHugh (eds), *Histories, Power and Loss: Uses of the past – A New Zealand commentary* (Wellington: Bridget Williams Books, 2001), and Giselle Byrnes, *The Waitangi Tribunal and New Zealand History* (Auckland: Oxford University Press, 2004). Belgrave, *Historical Frictions* traced the course of evidence in a series of claims.

25. Keenan, *Wars Without End*, 29–43, gives a good account of the arguments over naming.
26. The national implications of such films are suggested by the fact that *Battleship Potemkin* was discussed in New Zealand papers but was banned because of its heroic portrayal of revolution in Russia.
27. Robert Burgoyne argues that in the US, fiction features are the most important source of national history but also contest understandings of nation. In New Zealand the films are fewer and further between, but they have nevertheless played a similar role. Robert Burgoyne, *Film Nation: Hollywood looks at U.S. history* (Minneapolis: University of Minnesota Press, 1997).
28. Robert A. Rosenstone, *History on Film/Film on History* (Harlow: Pearson Longman, 2006), 118.
29. Hayden White, 'The fictions of factual representation', in *Tropics of Discourse: Essays in cultural criticism* (Baltimore: Johns Hopkins, 1978), 121–34.
30. Geoff Murphy, interview with author, Wellington, 11 November 2015.
31. Wolfe, *Settler Colonialism*, 2.
32. Jacquelyn Kilpatrick, *Celluloid Indians: Native Americans and film* (Lincoln: University of Nebraska Press, 1999); Angela Aleiss, *Making the White Man's Indian: Native Americans and Hollywood movies* (Westport: Praeger, 2005).
33. Giacomo Lichtner, 'The Age of Innocence? Child narratives and Italian Holocaust film', *Modern Italy*, vol. 17, no. 2, 2012, 198.
34. Maurice Halbwachs, *On Collective Memory*, trans. Lewis A. Coser (Chicago: University of Chicago Press, 1992).
35. Thanks to Michael Belgrave for this comment.
36. www.nzonscreen.com
37. In this and other points, the films discussed here have parallels elsewhere: see Brad Evans & Aaron Glass (eds), *Return to the Land of the Headhunters: Edward S. Curtis, the Kwakwaka'wakw, and the Making of Modern Cinema* (Seattle: University of Washington Press, 2013).
38. Peter Limbrick, *Making Settler Cinemas: Film and colonial encounters in the United States, Australia, and New Zealand* (NY: Palgrave Macmillan, 2010), 131–32.
39. 'It will be taking the historical narrative and updating it and then changing it radically – the story of a wronged man imprisoned, who comes out and wreaks vengeance on those who did him wrong.' Lee Tamahori, interviewed by Kim Hill, *Saturday Morning*, Radio New Zealand National, 27 February 2016.
40. Merata Mita, 'The soul and the image', in Jonathan Dennis & Jan Bieringa (eds), *Film in Aotearoa New Zealand* (Wellington: Victoria University Press, 1992), 43.
41. Limbrick, *Making Settler Cinemas*, 11–15.
42. Geoff Murphy, interview with author, Wellington, 11 November 2015.
43. Paul Willemen, 'The national revisited', in Valentina Vitali & Paul Willemen (eds), *Theorising National Cinema* (London: British Film Institute, 2006), 36.
44. Duncan Petrie, 'New Zealand', in Mette Hjort & Duncan Petrie (eds), *The Cinema of Small Nations* (Edinburgh: Edinburgh University Press, 2007), 160–76. New Zealand cinema's contentious engagement with the state had launched itself with Roger Donaldson's *Sleeping Dogs* (1977).
45. Bruce Babington, *A History of the New Zealand Fiction Feature Film* (Manchester: Manchester University Press, 2007), 68.
46. Petrie, 'New Zealand', 165.
47. Diane Pivac, Frank Stark & Lawrence McDonald (eds), *New Zealand Film: An illustrated history* (Wellington: Te Papa Press, 2011).
48. Trisha Dunleavy & Hester Joyce, *New Zealand Film and Television: Institution, industry and cultural change* (Bristol: Intellect Books, 2011), 31–68.
49. Roger Horrocks, 'Introduction', in *Re-inventing New Zealand: Essays on the arts and the media* (Pokeno: Atuanui Press, 2016); Lawrence McDonald, 'Waking from fretful sleep: New Zealand film in the 1970s', in Pivac et al., *New Zealand Film*; Susy Pointon, 'Risky Business: The creation of a New Zealand film industry', PhD thesis, University of Auckland, 2006.
50. Dunleavy & Joyce, *New Zealand Film and Television*, 82–84.
51. Other funding comes from Te Māngai Paho (for Māori language productions), Creative New Zealand, and – for a period – the Film Fund created in 2000 in order to facilitate the funding of mid-budget films and attract successful New Zealand filmmakers working overseas back to make films in New Zealand. By the late 1980s the departure of filmmakers who had made their first films locally and then found they were unable to finance larger-scale films in New Zealand's small market had become a regular pattern. Petrie, 'New Zealand', 167.
52. Ibid., 166–67.
53. Dunleavy & Joyce, *New Zealand Film and Television*; Petrie, 'New Zealand'; Margot Butcher, 'What films may come', *North and South*, May 2003, 80–88.
54. Jo Smith, *Māori Television: The first ten years* (Auckland: Auckland University Press, 2016), 18–19.
55. Blythe, *Naming the Other: Images of the Maori in New Zealand film and television* (Metuchen, NJ: Scarecrow Press, 1994); Jonathan Dennis & Jan Bieringa, *Film in Aotearoa New Zealand* (Wellington: Victoria University Press, 1992); Babington, *History of the New Zealand Fiction Feature Film*; Pivac et al., *New Zealand Film*; Trisha Dunleavy, *Ourselves in Primetime: A history of New Zealand television drama* (Auckland: Auckland University Press, 2005), Dunleavy & Joyce, *New Zealand Film and Television*; Smith, *Māori Television*; Mary Debrett, 'Branding

documentary: New Zealand's minimalist solution to cultural subsidy', *Media, Culture and Society*, vol. 26, no. 1, 2004, 5–23; and Mary Debrett, 'Representing cultural diversity or serving local industry? An exploration of the future prospects of subsidised documentary', *International Journal of Diversity in Organisations, Communities and Nations*, vol. 5, no. 3, 2006, 94–101; Horrocks, *Re-inventing New Zealand*; James E. Bennett & Rebecca Beirne (eds), *Making Film and Television Histories: Australia and New Zealand* (London: I.B. Tauris, 2012); Alistair Fox, Barry Keith Grant & Hilary Radner (eds), *New Zealand Cinema: Interpreting the past* (Bristol: Intellect Books, 2011); Limbrick, *Making Settler Cinemas*.

56. Pivac, 'Filming the pages of New Zealand history', BA Hons dissertation, VUW, 2002; Cross, 'The forgotten soundtrack of Maoriland: Imagining the nation through Alfred Hill's songs for *Rewi's Last Stand*', MMusicology, Te Kōkī, New Zealand School of Music, 2015; Wood, 'Revisiting James Cowan'; Perrott, '*The New Zealand Wars* documentary series: Discursive struggle and cultural memory', PhD thesis, University of Waikato, 2007; Read, 'Vincent Ward: The emergence of an aesthetic', PhD thesis, University of Auckland, 2004; Lacey, 'To settle the settler: Pathologies of colonialism in New Zealand history films 1925–2005', PhD thesis, University of Auckland, 2010.

1: Hayward in the Bay of Plenty

1. Rudall Hayward, interview with Ray Hayes & Walter Harris, 1962, A0644, Audio Collection, Ngā Taonga Sound and Vision. My thanks to Diane Pivac for alerting me to this interview and to other sources relating to Rudall Hayward; and for sharing her extensive knowledge about Hayward and *The Te Kooti Trail*.
2. Chris Pugsley, 'The magic of moving pictures: Film making 1895–1918', in Diane Pivac, Frank Stark & Lawrence McDonald (eds), *New Zealand Film: An illustrated history* (Wellington: Te Papa Press, 2011), 40.
3. Rudall Hayward, interview with Ray Hayes & Walter Harris, 1962; 'West End sensation', *New Zealand Herald*, 28 October 1921, 12.
4. Chris Pugsley, 'The magic of moving pictures: Film making 1895–1918'; Diane Pivac, 'The rise of fiction: Between the wars', in Pivac et al. (eds), *New Zealand Film*, 29–52, 53–78.
5. Ibid.
6. Jacquelyn Kilpatrick, *Celluloid Indians: Native Americans and film* (Lincoln: University of Nebraska Press, 1999), 16–35.
7. 'Entertainments', *NZ Herald*, 29 December 1910.
8. Minette Hillyer, '"Greetings to our distant kinsmen!": "Paramount's Red Indians" come to Aotearoa', paper presented at *Film in the Colony* symposium, Ngā Taonga Sound and Vision, 12 July 2017; 'Paramount Week', *Auckland Star*, 27 August 1926; 'Entertainments: "The Vanishing Race"', *NZ Herald*, 20 January 1927, 15. Grey, who met with Cowan on his visits to New Zealand, was an 'outspoken critic of the [US] government's treatment of American Indians' (Kilpatrick, *Celluloid Indians*, 29–33).
9. Rudall C. Hayward, 'Was Layla Raki necessary?', MA2244, 5146/10, Ngā Taonga Sound and Vision; Rudall C. Hayward, Papers: *Rewi's Last Stand* (1940 version), MA2244, 5146/10, Ngā Taonga Sound and Vision.
10. Bruce Babington, *A History of the New Zealand Fiction Feature Film* (Manchester: Manchester University Press, 2007), 68.
11. The film 'concerned an episode in the Maori Wars, which resulted in a beautiful girl being brought up by an elderly Maori on an island out from the coast of New Zealand': Hayward, interview with Ray Hayes and Walter Harris. The serial, *My Lady of the Cave* by H.T. Gibson, was published in the *New Zealand Herald* between September 1921 and March 1922. It continued a dominant theme in treatments of the wars: interracial relationships (in this case the young woman being raised as a daughter by an elderly Māori man).
12. Rudall Hayward to James Cowan, 13 December 1924, MS-Papers-11310-120, ATL.
13. Kynan Gentry discusses the circumstances in which the New Zealand Wars attracted attention in the years following World War One in *History, Heritage and Colonialism: Historical consciousness, Britishness and cultural identity in New Zealand, 1870–1940* (Manchester: Manchester University Press, 2015), 93–124.
14. James Cowan, *The New Zealand Wars: A history of the Maori campaigns and the pioneering period* (*NZW*), vol. II (Wellington: Government Printer, 1923), 502. On the anniversary of Ōrākau in 1914, newspaper articles linked the two wars in ways that overrode the ongoing consequences that Māori were still trying to resolve: 'W.F.G' praised the heroic defence and the bravery of the defenders, and quoted a speech given at the presentation of its new colours to the 16th Waikato Regiment, 'in which our sons and your sons are serving side by side'; the regiment's new motto echoed Rewi Maniapoto's words 'Ka whawhai tonu matou, ake, ake, ake': 'Fifty years ago', *Hawera and Normanby Star*, 12 March 1914.
15. Rudall Hayward to James Cowan, 13 December 1924, MS-Papers-11310-120, ATL.
16. Hayward, interview with Hayes & Harris.
17. Prospectus of Maori War Films Limited, MS-Papers-11310-120, ATL.
18. Ibid.
19. Rudall Hayward to James Cowan, 31 December 1924, MS-Papers-11310-120, ATL.
20. Rudall Hayward to James Cowan, 25 March 1925, MS-Papers-11310-120, ATL.

21. Virginia Callanan, 'Gaston Méliès', in Pivac et al. (eds), *New Zealand Film*, 45.
22. Vincent O'Malley, *The Great War for New Zealand: Waikato 1800–2000* (Wellington: Bridget Williams Books, 2016), 320.
23. Hayward, interview with Hayes & Harris.
24. Michael King, *Te Puea: A biography* (Auckland: Hodder & Stoughton, 1977).
25. Rudall Hayward, interviewed by Ray Hayes and Walter Harris. Although Hayward added that she would never allow him inside Turangawaewae, Te Puea did however purchase a few shares in Frontier Films, the company that funded the second *Rewi's Last Stand* (Frontier Films List of Shareholders at 27 July 1939, ARC3003.8, Te Awamutu Museum Archives); and she supplied canoes, extras and the use of the Turangawaewae marae for sequences in that film. 'Rewi's Last Stand'. Pamphlet produced for 50th Anniversary, n.d. 1987/88, ARC3630.2, Te Awamutu Museum Archive.
26. 'Arawa veterans', *Evening Star*, 8 September 1925, 2.
27. Hayward, interviewed by Hayes and Harris.
28. Ibid.
29. Diane Pivac, 'The rise of fiction', 63–72; Hayward, interview with Hayes & Harris.
30. Thomas McDonnell was 'brave and physically powerful ... skilled in bushcraft and the use of weapons. He flaunted his ability, often carrying two revolvers and indulging in mock duels using a taiaha against his comrades' swords: "Von Tempsky was the only man whom I had tried that I could not touch."' James Belich, 'McDonnell, Thomas', *Dictionary of New Zealand Biography* (*DNZB*): www.teara.govt.nz/en/biographies/1m33/mcdonnell-thomas
31. Cowan's account is in Cowan, *NZW*, vol. I (Wellington: Government Printer, 1922), 270–71. McDonnell was later awarded the New Zealand Cross for his part in the expedition; by this time von Tempsky was dead.
32. 'The story', press kit for *Rewi's Last Stand*, Maori War Films, 1925, Ngā Taonga Sound and Vision.
33. James Edward FitzGerald, 'Ake! Ake! Ake!', *Press*, 16 April 1864.
34. *NZ Herald* and *Auckland Star* clippings, n.d., 'Album (Press and Publicity) Rudall Hayward', MA2767, D5146, Box 11, Hayward Collection, Ngā Taonga Sound and Vision.
35. Hayward, interview with Hayes & Harris.
36. Ibid.
37. One newspaper report of the filming in Whakatāne mentions Hilda working together with Rudall at the back of a canoe as the shots are set up of the romantic couple at the other end of the canoe. Hilda's contributions have been obscured, however, in part because of Hayward's instinctive self-promotion and also, very likely, because by the time he gave the interviews about his work that are the primary source of our knowledge about it, he had divorced her and was much more willing to speak about his collaboration with his second wife, Ramai. See Diane Pivac, 'New Zealand film pioneer: Hilda Maud Hayward (1898–1970), *Screening the Past*, no. 40, 2015: www.screeningthepast.com/2015/08/new-zealand-film-pioneer-hilda-maud-hayward-1898–1970/; and Deborah Shepard, *Reframing Women: A history of New Zealand film* (Auckland: Harper Collins, 2000).
38. The account given here is Cowan's, *NZW*, II, 305–16.
39. 'Taking a film. Life of Te Kooti. Interest at Whakatane', *Auckland Star*, 24 August 1927.
40. Cowan, *NZW*, II, 387.
41. Ibid. More recent historians have taken a different view of Te Kooti's intentions regarding Te Arawa, but Cowan's was a common view at the time.
42. George Hamilton-Browne, *With the Lost Legion in New Zealand* (London: T. Werner Laurie, 1911); see also Bryan D. Gilling, 'George Hamilton-Browne', *DNZB*: www.teara.govt.nz/en/biographies/2h10/hamilton-browne-george
43. Hamilton-Browne, *With the Lost Legion*, 1.
44. Ibid.
45. In the *Otago Witness*, serialisation began on 9 August 1927; in the *New Zealand Herald*, 24 September 1927. The *Auckland Weekly News* also ran it.
46. Ernest Renan, 'What is a nation?' (1882), trans. in H.K. Bbabha (ed.), *Nation and Narration* (New York: Routledge, 1990), 8–21.
47. Hayward met Mair on a fishing trip in the early 1920s while Hayward was scouting locations for *My Lady of the Cave* (1922): '[I] learnt more about the Maori Wars and was given first hand information on some of the material which I was to use later in films like *Rewi's Last Stand*.' Rudall Hayward, interview with Hayes & Harris.
48. The nature of Mair's relationship with Te Arawa people was always more ambiguous than the film suggests, and it became more controversial over time. While he led Te Arawa troops during the later period of the wars, and arguably prevented the attack by Te Kooti on Rotorua in 1870, after the wars he was instrumental in a series of land sales (some of which he appears later to have regretted); his relationship with at least one Māori woman resulted in his ownership of some valuable land; and he was adept at exploiting his position in the iwi to ensure he was 'gifted' many taonga. See Paul Tapsell (ed.), *Ko Tawa: Maori treasures of New Zealand* (Auckland: David Bateman, 2006).
49. Review of *The Te Kooti Trail*, *Auckland Star*, 26 November 1927, 14.
50. 'No stone, no memorial of any kind, marks the spot defended by "John the Frenchman" with such heroic valour. In a few years, but for this record, the memory of Jean Guerren's gallant stand would have perished. New Zealand should mark as one of its national monuments the ground made sacred by the

51. Gilbert Mair, 'When Mount Edgecumbe trembled', in Gilbert Mair, *Reminiscences and Maori Stories* (Auckland: Brett Printing and Publishing Co., 1923), 80.
52. Intertitle, *The Te Kooti Trail*.
53. Rudall Hayward to Ray Hayes, 3 October 1962, AAOJ W5077 7811 Box 23, 50/1/1, Archives New Zealand (ANZ).
54. He considered making a comedy in this mode based on some of Pat Lawlor's 'Hori' comedy in 1928, but backed off. 'Maori Comedy Films', 86–105–042, ATL.
55. Rudall C. Hayward, 'Was Layla Raki necessary?', MA2244, 5146/10, NTSAV; Rudall C. Hayward, Papers: Rewi's Last Stand (1940 version), MA2244, 5146/10, Ngā Taonga Sound and Vision.
56. My thanks to Paerau Warbrick for his advice on this subject.
57. *NZ Herald*, 2 August 1927, 1.
58. Interviews with Pauline Butt, Hamilton, 22 November 2012 and Jim Davies, Whakatāne, 11 December 2012.
59. Interviews with Pauline Butt and Jim Davies.
60. Documentation Collection, Series 2: Correspondence – Letters to Hilda Hayward (nee Moren) from Rudall Hayward Ref. no. MA2884, Ngā Taonga Sound & Vision. Courtesy of Hayward-Book Collection.
61. 'Too realistic: The Te Kooti film', *Northern Advocate*, 7 September 1927; 'Outdoing Tom Mix: Young Maori film actor', *Auckland Star*, 26 August 1927.
62. This is, of course, another form of institutionalised racism. See Angela Wanhalla, *Matters of the Heart: A history of interracial marriage in New Zealand* (Auckland: Auckland University Press, 2013), and Damon Salesa, *Racial Crossings: Race, intermarriage, and the Victorian British Empire* (Oxford: Oxford University Press, 2011).
63. The debate began with Martin Blythe who suggested that, despite an emergent tradition of crosscultural romance in New Zealand film, *The Te Kooti Trail* appears to echo Griffith's *Birth of a Nation* in a condemnation of miscegenation (Martin Blythe, *Naming the Other: Images of the Maori in New Zealand film and television* (Metuchen, NJ: Scarecrow Press, 1994), 38–39. Alistair Fox adopts a similar stance in a more recent analysis ('Rudall Hayward and the cinema of Maoriland: Genre-mixing and counter-discourses in *Rewi's Last Stand* (1925), *The Te Kooti Trail* (1927) and *Rewi's Last Stand/The Last Stand* (1940)', in Alistair Fox, Barry Keith Grant & Hilary Radner (eds), *New Zealand Cinema: Interpreting the past* (Bristol: Intellect Books, 2011), 45–64. Blythe qualified his view by noting that if the 'half-caste' was demonised in the figure of Peka, the interracial marriage of Erihapeti and Jean was lauded; perhaps, he suggests, Peka represented 'the unacceptable face of union between Maori and Pakeha – unacceptable when the half-caste identifies with Maori nationalism'.
64. 'The big half-caste Peka Makarini, who fell to Mair's carbine, was a man with an atrocious record. It was estimated that he had been guilty of over thirty murders': Cowan, *NZW*, II, 395.
65. See Cowan, *NZW*, I, 396.
66. Pivac, 'The rise of fiction', 69; Babington, *A History of the New Zealand Fiction Feature Film*, 73.
67. Judith Binney, *Redemption Songs: A life of Te Kooti Arikirangi Te Turuki* (Auckland: Auckland University Press/Bridget Williams Books), 308–11.
68. It was the Te Arawa soldier Te Warihi who killed Peka, but Mair had already shot and disabled him after hours of running pursuit. Cowan, *NZW*, II, 393.
69. Paerau Warbrick, email communication, 19 September 2012.
70. Cowan, *NZW*, II, 393.
71. It is possible that Hayward met Te Pairi while he was making a film about New Zealand's primary industries – a commission he took on reluctantly to earn some income at the same time as he was raising funds and forming the company that would make *The Te Kooti Trail*. In early 1927 he wrote to Hilda: 'Have to go out to the Waimana gorge to a cheese factory a sheep station and film a railway bridge and a few stacks of hay besides climbing the young mountains hereabouts to get a panorama of the country surrounding.' Here we have a sense of Hayward working on the bread-and-butter income while scouting for actors and locations for his next feature. (Rudall to Hilda Hayward, March 1927, Hayward files, Ngā Taonga Sound and Vision).
72. Pou Temara, 'Te Pairi Tūterangi', Te Ara – The Encyclopedia of New Zealand: www.teara.govt.nz/en/biographies/3t16/te-pairi-tuterangi
73. 'Chief laments cultural loss. "Polluted by Pakeha influences"', c. 1957. Clipping file, Whakatāne Museum, 65B, Bay of Plenty History.
74. I would like to thank Pou Temara for his sage advice on this matter.
75. 'Rangatira on the film', *Auckland Star*, 2 September 1927. This report identifies him as 'Te Pairi Oterangi', a misidentification that has turned up repeatedly in later critical literature.
76. Binney, *Redemption Songs*, 554.
77. 'Chief as film actor', unsourced clipping, MA2767, D5146, Box 11, Hayward Collection, Ngā Taonga Sound and Vision.
78. '"Te Kooti Trail" re-screening makes district history', *Bay of Plenty Beacon*, 2 November 1964.
79. Ted Coubray, transcript of an interview by Jonathan Dennis, 10 January 1995, MA1683, 1009.054.01, 80–81. Ngā Taonga Sound and Vision.
80. 'In Rua's country: Villagers act for film', *Auckland Star*, 15 September 1927.
81. The journey resulted in another short film being made – now known as *Rua 1927* –

and another group being included in the opening scene: Rua Kenana's community at Maungapōhatu. Some footage was shot specifically for the film, but Hayward seems to have taken the opportunity to film this community that many people were curious about, as the government invasion of Maungapōhatu had taken place only 11 years before in 1916. It was also one of the most remote and isolated Maori communities in the country. For some Tūhoe people now this short film has a greater memorial significance than *The Te Kooti Trail*.
82. Pou Temara, 'Te Pairi Tūterangi'.
83. Pou Temara noted that the killing of Monika was entirely within the protocols of Māori warfare – in the terms of customary practice and belief, it was dangerous for her to be left alive; and this act would not necessarily have been seen as needlessly cruel by contemporary Māori. Interview with author.
84. Paerau Warbrick, interview with author.
85. *Sun*; undated clipping, Hayward Collection, Ngā Taonga Sound and Vision.
86. 'Taking a Film. Life of Te Kooti. Interest at Whakatane', *Auckland Star*, 24 August 1927.
87. Cowan, *NZW*, II, 217–18.
88. Refusal of Censor to approve Film, signed W. Tanner (censor), 12 November 1927, MA1663, Miscellaneous Papers: 'The Te Kooti Trail', MANS 0013.01, Ngā Taonga Sound and Vision. Furious at having to delay his premiere, Hayward flung back his suggested replacement titles – shown here with the censor's underlining and editing:

> '(1) Te Kooti in a looted uniform, aped the British officer, and with quotations from a mission Bible, incited his followers to kill all white men.
> (2) The half-cast, Baker-McLean (Peka Makarini) Te Kooti's notorious lieutenant, <u>plays a practical joke</u>. *No*'

The censor refused the last phrase 'because the following scene (which I assume to be the scene of the illuminated crosses) is eliminated, so that there is no practical joke to follow'. The replacements, and the fact that they were accepted with this minor amendment, suggest that there was no objection to portraying Te Kooti as harbouring lethal animosity towards whites. The correspondence between Pōmare and Ngata, whose constituency in the Bay of Plenty included a sizeable number of Ringatū adherents, sought to ensure 'that the film is satisfactory from the point of view of the Maori people' (Letter from Māui Pōmare to Āpirana Ngata, 13 September 1927. IA 12/135. Cited in Pivac, 'Filming the pages of New Zealand history', 45).
89. Censor to R.C. Hayward, 15 November 1927, IA 83 Box 7, Dept of Internal Affairs, ANZ.
90. I have discussed this disjuncture between mise-en-scène and intertitles elsewhere: A. Cooper, 'Imagined community, performed: *The Te Kooti Trail*', Film in the Colony symposium, Wellington, 12 July 2017.
91. 'J.C. [James Cowan], 'Te Kooti the Atua', *Auckland Star*, 18 November 1927.
92. 'Maori war film: Retention by censor', *New Zealand Herald*, 10 November 1927.
93. 'Imagined grievances', *Sun*, 11 November 1927.
94. Hayward did in fact create a later cut and took out some of this material.
95. '"The Te Kooti Trail", N.Z. history at the Strand', *Sun*, undated clipping, Album (Press and Publicity) Rudall Hayward, MA2767, D5146, Box 11, Hayward Collection, Ngā Taonga Sound and Vision.
96. Interviews with Pauline Butt and Jim Davies, 2012.
97. Email, Jonathan Mane-Wheoki to Annabel Cooper, 14 February 2013.
98. Phone interview with Brad Haami, 21 November 2012.
99. Ibid.
100. Ibid.

2: Hayward in the Waipā

1. Chris Hilliard, 'James Cowan and the frontiers of New Zealand History', *New Zealand Journal of History*, vol. 31, no. 2, 1997, 219–33.
2. *One Hundred Crowded Years* (New Zealand Government Film Studios), 1941. The National Film Unit had been established to promote the government war effort, so it is not surprising that it took a conservative line.
3. Rudall Hayward to President of the Te Awamutu Historical Society, 10 February 1937. Te Awamutu Historical Society archive, Te Awamutu Museum. (The letter is dated February 1936 but this is likely an error, given the dates of other documents.)
4. 'Rewi's Last Stand', *Te Awamutu Courier*, 1 October 1937, 5.
5. Ibid.
6. Lindsay S. Rogers to Rudall Hayward, 18 February ?1937. Te Awamutu Historical Society, Te Awamutu Museum.
7. 'The Battle of Orakau. Reconstruction for motion pictures?' *Te Awamutu Courier*, 31 May 1937, 4; '"Rewi's Last Stand": Project to reproduce picture in sound', *Te Awamutu Courier*, 8 June 1937, 4.
8. Prospectus of Frontier Films Ltd, 30 August 1937, Te Awamutu Museum.
9. Ibid.
10. Te Huia's father Raureti Paiaka, according to Cowan, was the chief intermediary during the famous negotiation with the government interpreter William Mair (*NZW*, I, 391–92).
11. Rovina Maniapoto-Anderson, interviewed by the author, Te Awamutu, 30 October 2012; Richard Swarbrick, interview with author, 6 October 2013.
12. Minute Books of the Te Awamutu Historical Society, 1937–40, Te Awamutu Museum ARC2057.
13. Frontier Films, Prospectus, filed 30 August 1937, ARC3003.9, Te Awamutu Museum Archives. The *Te Awamutu Courier*

reported on 1 October 1937: 'A strong and representative committee of Maoris, with Mr. J. Rust, headmaster of the Parawera Native School as chairman, has been set up to attend to a lot of detail work in which the Maori race will be prominent, to ensure accuracy and assist in the selection of suitable types for the personnel of the defending forces,' 5.

14. Hitiri Te Paerata, 'Description of the Battle of Orakau as given by the native chief Hitiri Te Paerata of the Ngatiraukawa tribe' (Wellington: Government Printer, 1888).
15. Ibid, 10.
16. Years later, Te Rongonui Paerata's wife and daughter recalled that he had been so outraged at receiving only 'a pittance' for his part in the film that he had asked for footage including him to be removed. Thia Priestly to Jennifer Evans, 30 March 1993, ARC3630.1, Te Awamutu Museum Archive. Hēnare Toka replaced him in this role.
17. R. Amohanga to Hon. W.E. Parry, 8 February 1938, IA1W2578 113, Archives New Zealand.
18. 'Rewi's Last Stand', *Te Awamutu Courier*, 2 February 1938; 4 February 1938.
19. 'Filming Waikato Maori Wars: Wild Urewera as background', *Auckland Star*, 11 December 1937.
20. Hayward, '"Rewi's Last Stand": An epic of the battling Sixties. A scenario by R. Hayward copyright 1937', D5146, MZ2301, Folder 52, Hayward, Collection Ngā Taonga Sound and Vision.
21. 'Frontier Films Ltd. Producing Rewi's Last Stand. General Meeting Elects Directors', Report of ordinary general meeting of Frontier Films, *Te Awamutu Courier*, 7 September 1938.
22. A.W. Reed, based on the film scenario by Rudall C. Hayward, *Rewi's Last Stand* (Wellington: A.H. & A.W. Reed, 1939).
23. 'Maori war film', *Auckland Star*, 12 August 1939, supplement; Critique from 'The Dominion', Wellington, 1940. Rudall Hayward Papers, Ngā Taonga Sound and Vision; '"Rewi's Last Stand": Private screening held', *Auckland Star*, 26 February 1940.
24. '"Rewi's Last Stand". N.Z. picture at Strand', *Auckland Star*, 11 April 1940.
25. Keith Sinclair, *A Destiny Apart: New Zealand's search for national identity* (Wellington: Unwin Paperbacks/Port Nicholson Press, 1986), 239.
26. Hill's score is the subject of a detailed study by Melissa Cross, who shows how precisely it shapes the 'Maoriland' themes of the film; and that because the score survives in full, it is the best remaining evidence about what was cut from the film for the 1949 release. Melissa Cross, 'The forgotten soundtrack', Master's thesis, Te Kōkī New Zealand School of Music, Victoria University of Wellington, 2015.
27. Rudall C. Hayward, 'Was Layla Raki necessary?', MA2244, 5146/10, NTSAV: 'Papers: Rewi's Last Stand' (1940 version).
28. Rudall Hayward, interview with Ray Hayes & Walter Harris.
29. Jennifer Evans, 'Making of Orakau Battle film was major event in district', *Footprints of History*, vol. 12, 1994, 20–23.
30. 'News of the films. Plays and players: *Rewi's Last Stand*', *Evening Post*, 20 June 1940, 18.
31. Hayward, interview with Hayes & Harris.
32. Belich, *The New Zealand Wars*; O'Malley, *The Great War for New Zealand*. For the Kīngitanga see also Michael Belgrave, *Dancing with the King: The rise and fall of the King Country, 1864–1885* (Auckland: Auckland University Press, 2017).
33. As Bruce Babington also notes: Babington, *A History of the New Zealand Fiction Feature Film*.
34. Damon Salesa, 'A tender way in race war', *Racial Crossings: Race, intermarriage, and the Victorian British Empire* (Oxford: Oxford University Press, 2011); Vincent O'Malley, *The Great War for New Zealand* (Wellington: Bridget Williams Books, 2016).
35. Salesa, 'A tender way'; Vincent O'Malley, *The Great War*, 35–60.
36. Ibid; Tom Roa, interview with author, Waipā Valley, 25 January 2011.
37. See Salesa, 'A tender way in race war', on the 'cold war', and the complex 'racial crossings' in the Waipā area.
38. James Cowan, *The Old Frontier: Te Awamutu. The story of the Waipa Valley* (Te Awamutu: The Waipa Post, 1922), 81–83.
39. For example, 'A maori maiden and her admirers', *Evening Post*, 22 February 1865, 3; here cited from Cowan, *The Old Frontier*, 81–83.
40. Hayward, interview with Hayes & Harris.
41. Babington, *A History of the New Zealand Fiction Feature Film*, 78.
42. Here Hayward follows Cowan's account.
43. Martin Blythe, *Naming the Other: Images of the Maori in New Zealand film and television* (Metuchen: Scarecrow Press, 1994), 44–46; Babington, *History of the New Zealand Fiction Feature Film*, 76–77.
44. Jennifer Evans, 'Making of Orakau battle film was major event in district', *Footprints of History*, 20.
45. 'A new look at Rewi', *NZ Listener*, 3 April 1970, 9.
46. Evans, 'Making of Orakau battle film was major event in district', 21.
47. The film was perceived locally as having 'accuracy'. Jennifer Evans recalls that when she worked at Te Awamutu Museum in the 1990s she took film stills with her when she spoke to school groups on fieldtrips run by the museum: local amateur historians thought the film gave a good representation of the battle. Jennifer Evans, personal communication, September 2013.
48. Hītiri te Paerata, quoted in *NZW*, I, 386.
49. It is difficult to determine exactly what happened here. Even in the 1937 script, the two parts are confused and conflated: when Hītiri creeps out across the lines for water,

49. Bob sees him and recognises him as Tama, even though the script identifies him as Hītiri.
50. Hītiri Te Paerata, translation by Gilbert Mair, quoted in Cowan, *NZW*, I, 401.
51. Cowan, *NZW*, I, 400–01.
52. This scene marks another departure from the script. The script includes a fight between Bob and a ranger in which Bob, armed with a taiaha, proves his worth – and his crosscultural credentials – by defeating the sceptical ranger who is confident that his sword is the superior weapon. The film, at least as we have it, replaces this scene with the contest between Bob and Tama over Ariana, fought entirely with taiaha – a scene that does not appear in the plot in the script. Hayward may have been keen to capitalise on Toka's expertise with the taiaha. It is possible that both fight scenes were in the original script and the 1940 film but that only one survived in the *Last Stand* cut.
53. Ramai's songs unfortunately did not survive the 1949 cut.
54. Ramai Hayward, interviewed by Lawrence Wharerau in 'Nga Pikitia, Koha, 1987': www.nzonscreen.com/title/koha-nga-pikitia-maori-1987
55. Diane Pivac, 'New Zealand film pioneer: Hilda Maud Hayward (1898–1970), *Screening the Past*, no. 40, 2015: www.screeningthepast.com/2015/08/new-zealand-film-pioneer-hilda-maud-hayward-1898-1970; and Deborah Shepard, *Reframing Women: A history of New Zealand film* (Auckland: HarperCollins, 2000).
56. This is shown in A. Cooper, 'Nō Ōrākau: Past and people in James Cowan's places', *Journal of New Zealand Studies*, no. 19, 2015, 63–78.
57. Cowan, *NZW*, I, 391. For a broader discussion of the history of mythologising about Ōrākau, see Kynan Gentry, *History, Heritage and Colonialism: Historical consciousness, Britishness and cultural identity in New Zealand, 1870–1940* (Manchester: Manchester University Press, 2015), 93–124.
58. 'Rewi's Last Stand' script, 1937. April 1864 sequence, 30.
59. Curiously, the volume of Cowan used here and at the beginning of the film to anchor the film to 'real history' is volume II of *The New Zealand Wars*; Cowan's account of the Waikato War comes in volume I.
60. 'Rewi's Last Stand' script, 1937. April 1864 sequence, 23. Here Hayward follows Cowan, *NZW*, I, 382.
61. Cross, 'The forgotten soundtrack', 43.
62. Cowan, *NZW*, I, 379.
63. A point of clarification: Major William Mair was Gilbert Mair's older brother.
64. Cowan, *NZW*, I, 382.
65. Reed with Hayward, *Rewi's Last Stand*, 134.
66. Lost footage showed this in more detail, as Melissa Cross demonstrates in her analysis of the cues in Hill's score. Cross's discussion of how Hill frames viewers' perceptions of Māori through the score is comprehensive: Cross, 'The forgotten soundtrack'.
67. Reed with Hayward, *Rewi's Last Stand*, 147–48.
68. Ibid., 145.
69. See Angela Wanhalla, *Matters of the Heart: A history of interracial marriage in New Zealand* (Auckland: Auckland University Press, 2013).
70. Rudall Hayward, interview with Ray Hayes & Walter Harris.
71. Mair, Ben and Bob find Tama's body in *The Last Stand*. Because it is obvious that Tama dies in the 1949 cut, it must have been included in the 1940 film.
72. 'Rewi's Last Stand', *Auckland Star*, 13 April 1940.
73. Michael King, *Te Puea: A biography* (Auckland: Hodder & Stoughton, 1977).
74. James Cowan, *Settlers and Pioneers* (Wellington: Government Printer, 1940).
75. James Cowan, 'Settlement of the Waikato', paginated typescript, 1939, Cowan Papers, 39/54D, ATL. Cited and discussed in Chris Hilliard, 'James Cowan and the frontiers of New Zealand history', *NZJH*, no. 31, 1997, 219–33. As Hilliard observes, the strength of these views came late in Cowan's career, and he himself had valorised pioneering in the Waikato in his other writing.
76. 'Film subjects', *Auckland Star*, 13 March 1940.
77. 'Critique from the "Dominion", Wellington'. Undated ms, Ngā Taonga Sound and Vision.
78. 'Rewi's Last Stand', *Auckland Star*, 13 April 1940.
79. 'Enters second week: "Rewi's Last Stand"', *Auckland Star*, 20 April 1940.
80. '"Rewi's Last Stand": Notable N.Z. production', *Evening Post*, 27 July 1940.
81. 'J.C.', '"Stand Fast": Brave words. In battles against odds: Maoris at Orakau', *Auckland Star*, 25 May 1940.
82. Hayward wrote an account of his frustrations with this process to the directors of Frontier Films on 30 January 1947. Frontier Films, Te Awamutu Museum.
83. Cross, 'The forgotten soundtrack'.
84. See Ramai Hayward, quoted in Russell Campbell, 'In order that they may become civilized: Pakeha ideology in *Rewi's Last Stand*, *Broken Barrier* and *Utu*', *Illusions*, no. 1, 1986, 5.
85. 'A new look at Rewi', *NZ Listener*, 3 April 1970, 9. Rorke's Drift, a battle in the Anglo-Zulu War, was notable for the successful defence by a tiny British and colonial garrison against several thousand Zulu warriors. It was often referred to as an emblem of British heroism.
86. Rudall C. Hayward & John Batten, radio talk, 'Papers: Rewi's Last Stand' (1940 version), MA2244, 5146/10, Ngā Taonga Sound and Vision.
87. Swarbrick, interview.
88. Correspondence between Walter Harris and Rudall Hayward, 17 June 1958, 4 September 1958; letter to D. Garratt, 3 July 1963, 'Rewi's Last Stand', AAOJ W5077 7811 Box 23, Archives New Zealand; Vincent O'Malley, '"Recording the incident with a monument":

The Waikato War in historical memory', *Journal of New Zealand Studies*, no. 19, 2015, 89.
89. Diane Pivac, 'The rise of fiction: Between the wars', in Pivac et al. (eds), *New Zealand Film: An illustrated history* (Wellington: Te Papa Press, 2011).
90. Robert Sklar, 'Rudall Hayward, New Zealand film-maker', *Landfall*, vol. 98, 1971, 148.
91. John O'Shea, *Don't Let It Get You: Memories, documents* (Wellington: Victoria University Press, 1999), 62.
92. Merata Mita, 'The soul and the image', in Jonathan Dennis & Jan Bieringa (eds), *Film in Aotearoa New Zealand* (Wellington: Victoria University Press, 1992), 43.
93. 'Rewi's Last Stand', *Te Iwi o Aotearoa*, February 1990, 19.
94. Personal communications with author, 2012.
95. Cited in Murray Horton, 'Of Flicker-Drammers and Maori Oscars', *Rolling Stone*, 12 April 1973, 43.
96. Ramai Hayward, interviewed by Lawrence Te Wharerau, *Koha* Special Episode on Ramai Hayward, 1989: www.nzonscreen.com/title/koha-ramai-hayward-1989

3: Wars in the living room

1. Kelvin Day, 'Introduction', in Kelvin Day (ed.), *Contested Ground/Te Whenua i Tohea: The Taranaki Wars 1860–1881* (Wellington: Huia, 2010), xi–xxvii; Vincent O'Malley, *The Great War for New Zealand* (Wellington: Bridget Williams Books, 2016), 29; and Vincent O'Malley, '"Recording the incident with a monument": The Waikato War in historical memory', *Journal of New Zealand Studies*, no. 19, 2015, 79–97.
2. Keith Aberdein, interview by author, Sydney, 30 November 2010.
3. Donna Awatere, *Maori Sovereignty* (Auckland: Broadsheet, 1984). The book was based on articles first published in *Broadsheet* magazine in October 1982; Aroha Harris, *Hīkoi: Forty years of Māori protest* (Wellington: Huia, 2004); James Belich, *Paradise Reforged: A history of the New Zealanders from the 1880s to the year 2000* (Auckland: Allen Lane/Penguin 2001); Ranginui Walker, *Ka Whawhai Tonu Mātou – Struggle without end* (Auckland: Penguin, 2000).
4. Michael Noonan, interview by the author, Auckland, 14 July 2010; Trisha Dunleavy & Hester Joyce, *New Zealand Film and Television: Institution, industry and cultural change* (Bristol: Intellect Books, 2011), 56.
5. Over this period King was beginning to make his name with books about Māori that had a broad reach; he had already published *Moko: Maori tattooing in the 20th century* (1972).
6. *Uenuku* (dir. Geoff Murphy, Peach Wemyss Astor, 1974) was an early production of the community at Waimārama in Hawke's Bay, many of whom went on to be involved in Murphy's *Utu*.
7. Trisha Dunleavy, *Ourselves in Primetime: A history of New Zealand television drama* (Auckland: Auckland University Press, 2005), 66–71.
8. Dunleavy & Joyce, *New Zealand Film and Television*, 40.
9. Michael Scott-Smith, interviewed by Catherine Fitzgerald, n.d., Blueskin Films.
10. Dunleavy, *Ourselves in Primetime*, 15–16.
11. Dick Scott, *Ask That Mountain: The story of Parihaka* (Auckland: Heinemann/Southern Cross, 1975).
12. Errol Braithwaite, *The Flying Fish* (London: Collins, 1964); *The Needle's Eye* (London: Collins, 1965); *The Evil Day* (London: Collins, 1967).
13. Warren Dibble, interview with the author, Sydney, 30 November 2010.
14. Ibid.
15. Ibid.
16. Ibid.
17. Ibid.
18. Riwha Tītokowaru Collection, Alexander Turnbull Library, MS-Papers-3006-02.
19. Quoting an earlier letter written by Tītokowaru on 25 June 1868: Riwha Tītokowaru Collection, Alexander Turnbull Library, MS-Papers-3006-02.
20. Taketake's account to Tahupōtiki Haddon, written probably in the late 1920s. Reproduced from Tony Sole, *Ngāti Ruanui: A history* (Wellington: Huia, 2005), 321–22.
21. Warren Dibble, annotation on newspaper clipping, n.d. Copy supplied by Warren Dibble.
22. Alexander Fry, 'Death to the Pakeha', *NZ Listener*, 3 May 1971, 4–6.
23. Napi Waaka, telephone interview with author, 14 November 2012.
24. Fry, 'Death to the Pakeha'.
25. Waaka, telephone interview.
26. Peter Vere Jones, telephone interview, 3 April 2013.
27. Te Rau Oriwa Davis, telephone interview with author, 21 February 2018.
28. Ibid., and email communications to author, 13 March 2018.
29. Fry, 'Death to the Pakeha'.
30. Dermot McNeilage, email to author, 27 April 2018.
31. Michael Noonan, interview with the author; Dunleavy, *Ourselves in Primetime*, 57–60, 96. 'TV One takes Grey areas out of its $1m splash', *Dominion*, 3 September 1977; 'Grey series faces cost probe', *Dominion*, 6 September 1977.
32. William Pember Reeves, *The Long White Cloud: Ao Tea Roa* (London: Horace Marshall & Son, 1898), 229–30.
33. Keith Sinclair, *The Origins of the Maori Wars* (Wellington: New Zealand University Press, 1957; 2nd edn 1961), 33. In a similar vein, see also Ian Wards, *The Shadow of the Land: A study of British policy and racial conflict in New Zealand 1932–1852* (Wellington: Historical Branch, Internal Affairs, 1968).
34. Noonan, interview.

35. Grey, too, had acquired some critical views on English colonialism during his service in Ireland.
36. Selwyn's work in the development of Māori performance in theatre and film is charted in *Don Selwyn: Power in our hands* (Catherine Fitzgerald, Blueskin Films/Māori Television, 2017).
37. George Hēnare, interview with the author, Dunedin, 29 April 2016.
38. Keith Aberdein, interview with the author, Sydney, 30 November 2010.
39. Noonan, interview.
40. Ibid.
41. Ibid.
42. George Hēnare, *ScreenTalk* interview: www.nzonscreen.com/interviews/george-henare-acting-on-screen-and-stage
43. The line of descent is through Kawiti's eldest son, who had remained behind in the Bay of Plenty after Ngāpuhi raids in the area in the 1820s. Napi Waaka, telephone interview.
44. Noonan, interview.
45. Aberdein, interview.
46. Don Selwyn, interview with Selwyn Muru, *Te Puna Wai Kōrero*, Radio New Zealand, 11 June 1977. Audio Collection, 45346. Ngā Taonga Sound and Vision.
47. Keri Kaa, interview with Nancy Brunning, 2007. © Blueskin Films.
48. Noonan, interview.
49. Kaa, interview with Brunning.
50. Noonan, interview.
51. Kaa, interview with Brunning.
52. Waihoroi Shortland, interview with the author, Auckland, 29 January 2015; Kaa, interview with Brunning.
53. Richard Campion, 'They wouldn't have stood for it on the small screen', *NZ Listener*, 5 November 1977, 82.
54. Dunleavy & Joyce, *New Zealand Film and Television*, 57.
55. The exact circumstances of the fall, or abandonment, of Ruapekapeka are still debated. The series opts here for one of the more widely held interpretations.
56. James Belich, *The New Zealand Wars and the Victorian Interpretation of Racial Conflict* (Auckland: Auckland University Press, 1986).
57. Warwick Roger, 'Governor good – not great', *Dominion*, 8 October 1977, 8.
58. '"The Governor" goes to top of the polls', *Dominion*, 1 November 1977, 9.
59. Vincent O'Malley, 'A tale of two rangatira: Rewi Maniapoto, Wiremu Tamihana and the Waikato War', *Journal of the Polynesian Society*, vol. 125, no. 4, 2016, 341–57.
60. Keith Sinclair, *The Origins of the Maori Wars* (Wellington: New Zealand University Press, 1957).
61. The specific events of the hui are invented, but the enmity and the need to overcome it was real, dating from an unavenged killing of Te Wherowhero's aunt by Ngāti Hauā decades earlier. O'Malley, *The Great War*, 79–80.
62. J.C. Beaglehole was professor of history at Victoria University. Noonan, interview.
63. Ibid.
64. Ibid.
65. Ibid.
66. Aberdein, interview with the author.
67. Hugh Nevill, 'Good Governor Grey', *NZ Listener*, 1 October 1977, 38–41.
68. D.A. Hamer, 'The Governor', *NZ Listener*, 29 October 1977, 11; Keith Sinclair, '"Terrible and fateful" Grey', *NZ Listener*, 5 November 1977, 18–19. Aberdein's novel was *The Governor* (Wellington: Hamlet Books, 1977).
69. Richard Campion, 'Television review', *NZ Listener*, 5 November 1977, 82.
70. Graeme Douglas, 'Epic better for pace', *NZ Herald*, 24 November 1977, 15.
71. '"Governor" rekindles fighting spirit', *Star Weekender*, 5 November 1977, 1.
72. Barry Shaw, 'And for the next epic?' *Auckland Star*, 7 November 1977, 6.
73. www.nzonscreen.com/title/the-governor-1977-13c/series. Episode 1 was uploaded on 14 April 2009, Episode 4 on 1 June 2010, and Episode 5 on 1 February 2011. *The Killing of Kane* was uploaded on 7 October 2010. Thanks to Natasha Harris at NZ On Screen for this information.
74. Russell Campbell, 'The New Zealand Wars', in *Observations: Studies in New Zealand documentary* (Wellington: Victoria University Press, 2011), 102.
75. With the economy that had already become customary in the film world, they also hired out to *The Governor* the costumes their partners had made for their Māori-language drama *Uenuku* (1974).
76. George Hēnare, interview with the author.
77. James Belich, interview by the author.
78. Sandra Coney, '*Pictures*', *Broadsheet*, July/August 1983, 45.
79. Cherie Lacey, 'Unsettled historiography: Postcolonial anxiety and the burden of the past in *Pictures*', in Alistair Fox, Barry Keith Grant & Hilary Radner (eds), *New Zealand Cinema: Interpreting the past*, (Bristol: Intellect, 2011), 99–118.
80. Peter Vere Jones, interview with author.
81. In Kristen Warner, 'This movie is not *Utu*', *Auckland Star*, 28 May 1983, cited in Lacey, 'Unsettled historiography'.

4: The pūhā western

1. Gaylene Preston, interview with author, Wellington, 29 October 2013.
2. Cliff Curtis, in *Hautoa Ma!*, directors Libby Hakaraia and Tainui Stephens, 2016.
3. Diane Pivac, personal communication, August 2013.
4. Gilbert Mair recorded the events surrounding the death of Monika in a letter to Cowan of February 1923, which Cowan included in *The New Zealand Wars*, vol. II, 319; and Mair told Cowan the story of the capture and 'bush court martial' of Wī Heretaunga, which Cowan wrote up as 'A bush court martial' for

The Auckland Star in 1926 and then revised for *Tales of the Maori Bush* (Dunedin: Reed, 1934): it became the basis of the final scene of *Utu*.

5. For a detailed discussion see Susy Pointon, 'Risky business: The creation of a New Zealand film industry', PhD thesis, University of Auckland, 2006.
6. Geoff Murphy, interview with the author, Wellington, 11 November 2015.
7. Geoff Murphy, *Geoff Murphy: A life on film* (Auckland: HarperCollins, 2015), 170. The tax shelter began in 1979 and lasted five years, during which local film blossomed, but so did predatory international investment. See also Trisha Dunleavy & Hester Joyce, *New Zealand Film and Television: Institution, industry and cultural change* (Bristol: Intellect Books, 2011), 82–83.
8. Interview with Geoff Murphy & Graeme Cowley, *Saturday Morning*, National Radio, 20 July 2013.
9. Merata Mita, 'The soul and the image', in Jonathan Dennis & Jan Bieringa (eds), *Film in Aotearoa New Zealand* (Wellington: Victoria University Press, 1992), 46.
10. Leon Narbey, email communication, 13 July 2016.
11. Gerd Pohlmann, email communication, 18 May 2015.
12. Geoff Murphy, interview.
13. Aroha Harris, *Hīkoi: Forty years of Maori protest* (Wellington: Huia, 2004); Ranginui Walker, *Ka Whawhai Tonu Mātou: Struggle without end* (Auckland: Penguin, 1990).
14. *Patu!* was not edited and released until after *Utu* was completed.
15. Poata's long relationship with radical politics and with film, which often converged, is documented in his memoir *Poata: Seeing beyond the horizon: A memoir* (Wellington: Steele Roberts, 2012).
16. Keith Aberdein, interview with the author, Sydney, 30 November 2010.
17. At one point in *Patu!* the documentary actually borrows from *Utu*, as protestors stream down a hillside accompanied by a snatch of orchestration from *Utu*'s score. Mita and Pohlmann did some of the editing in Napier while Mita was working on *Utu*. Gerd Pohlmann recalls showing *The Bridge* to some cast and crew of *Utu*: 'I wanted the others to learn about [Zac Wallace], to show that there was much more to him than his physicality and violent reputation, that he had been through some tough working class battles and politics and had shown some remarkable leadership qualities.' Gerd Pohlmann, email communication, 26 July 2016.
18. Pohlmann, email communication, 26 July 2016.
19. Gaylene Preston, interview with the author, Wellington, 29 October 2013.
20. Murphy, *Geoff Murphy*, 222.
21. Ibid., 220.
22. Murphy, interview.
23. Ibid.
24. Murphy, *Geoff Murphy*, 225.
25. Murphy, interview.
26. Murphy had given responsibility for speeches in Māori to Māori actors before, in the short film *Uenuku*, and had become convinced that this produced far better results than attempting to retain directorial control. Murphy, interview.
27. Ibid.
28. Sylvia Kaa, phone interview with the author, 9 November 2016.
29. This Waimārama–Wellington network was a kind of Petrie dish for developing talent; it included Alun Bollinger, Martyn Sanderson, Bruno Lawrence and John Charles (who wrote the score for *Utu*), not to mention women such as Pat Murphy, Helen Bollinger, Veronica Lawrence and Liz Sanderson, who raised a generation of film professionals and, at the same time, supplied expertise and support for film productions.
30. Preston, interview.
31. Jane Clifton, 'Maoris rally round set', *New Zealand Times*, 20 June 1982.
32. Preston, interview.
33. Murphy, interview.
34. Clifton, 'Maoris rally round set'.
35. In fact, Belich sets them aside in his book, *The New Zealand Wars*, noting only that they were of such complexity that they warranted separate treatment.
36. Cowan, *NZW*, II, ch. 40.
37. Ibid., 440.
38. 'J.C.', 'Bush Court Martial: A story of the Urewera', *Auckland Star*, 18 December 1926, 25; James Cowan, 'A Bush Court Martial', *Tales of the Maori Bush* (Dunedin: Reed, 1934), 83–91.
39. Cowan, 'A Bush Court Martial', 85.
40. Ibid, 89–90.
41. Ibid, 90–91.
42. Interview with Geoff Murphy and Graeme Cowley, Kim Hill, *Saturday Morning*, National Radio, 20 July 2013.
43. Geoff Murphy, 'Puha western', 30 pp, Ngā Taonga Sound and Vision; Geoff Murphy & Keith Aberdein, 'Utu', 4th draft, Utu Archive. Ngā Taonga Sound and Vision. Tony Noble, Utu Productions press release, 18 December 1981. Aberdein, interview with the author.
44. Aberdein & Murphy, interviews with the author.
45. Murphy, interview.
46. Bridget Orr discusses this transition at greater length: 'Birth of a nation? From *Utu* to *The Piano*', in Felicity Coombs & Suzanne Gemmell (eds), *Piano Lessons* (London: John Libbey, 1999), 148–60.
47. Direction from 'Utu' script, 4th draft. Utu Archive, Ngā Taonga Sound and Vision.
48. Unlike Monika, Kura was not based on a specific historical individual, but her death, which focuses Matu's anger on Te Wheke, may derive in part from the detail in 'A Bush Court Martial' when the captured women

gave evidence of Wī Heretaunga's murder of his wife.
49. M. Elise Marubbio, *Killing the Indian Maiden: Images of Native American women in film* (Lexington: University Press of Kentucky, 2006).
50. Kenneth Marc Harris, 'American film genres and non-American films: A case study of *Utu*', *Cinema Journal* 29, no. 2, 1990, 36–59.
51. 'Zac Wallace finds rebirth in "Utu"', *Christchurch Star*, 8 February 1983; 'They're making a film about revenge', *Star*, 29 May 1982, 5.
52. *Daily Post*, 23 December 1981; *Star Weekender*, 29 May 1982, 5; *Media Times*, February 1982, cited in *Daily Post*, 23 December 1981.
53. Bruce Ansley, 'Kept his eyes out to be tasteful', *Christchurch Star*, 26 May 1982.
54. Harold Coop, 'Utu film may spark bitterness', *Auckland Star*, 19 July 1982; Irene Gardiner, 'Tauroa says Utu cultural', *Dominion*, 17 September 1982.
55. David Manning, '"Utu" – working hard but failing to inspire', *Nelson Evening Mail*, 12 February 1983; Nicholas Reid, '"Utu"– entertaining, yet rotten at the core', *Auckland Star*, 12 February 1983; Marc Knowles, 'Blood for blood', *Evening Post*, 14 February 1983; David Lawrence, 'Pretentious but hectic', *NZ Herald*, 12 February 1983.
56. Bob Williams, 'Utu another Kiwi triumph', *Evening Standard*, 12 February 1983; Erica Short, 'Ersatz cowboys Utu's drawback', *New Zealand Times*, 13 February 1983; Rob White, '"Utu" captures the past and the present', *Christchurch Star*, 15 February 1983; Aline Sandilands, 'Rebels with a cause', *Otago Daily Times*, 12 February 1983.
57. Bill Gosden, 'Sport and politics', clipping, source untraced. Utu archive, Ngā Taonga Sound and Vision.
58. '"Utu" actor Kaa says NZ films can still improve', *Evening Post*, 9 February 1983; Kirsten Warner, 'Time for Kaa to come home', *Auckland Star*, 14 April 1983.
59. Sylvia Kaa, phone interview with the author, 9 November 2016.
60. Evans, 'Utu', *Broadsheet*, May 1983; 'Premiere of "Utu" fuels many talking points', *Christchurch Star*, 1 February 1983; Aberdein, interview.
61. Witi Ihimaera, '*Utu* mirrors contemporary agony of Waitangi', *Dominion*, 28 February 1983.
62. Stephen (Tipene) O'Regan, 'Utu', *PPTA Journal*, Term 2, 1983, 66.
63. 'French critic accords "Utu" high praise', *Evening Post*, 16 February 1983; Brigitte Cornand & R.P. O'Malley, 'Maoris, Magie et Sales …' *Actuel*, n.d., *Utu* files, Ngā Taonga Sound and Vision.
64. Pauline Kael, 'The current cinema', *New Yorker*, 15 October 1984.
65. Preston says of Murphy that 'he's a born teacher', but the concentration of expertise on the production went beyond the director. Reviewing *Utu Redux* in 2013, Tainui Stephens commented: 'When you look at the credits at the end of *Utu*, you can't help but be struck by the many names in the cast and crew who kickstarted, inspired and trained many of the current generation of Maori filmmakers.' Tainui Stephens: 'Maori are passionate filmmakers', *New Zealand Herald*, 2 December 2013.
66. Preston, interview.
67. Dunleavy & Joyce, *New Zealand Film and Television*, 82–84, gives an account of the tax shelter and its demise.

5: Documentary adventures

1. Diana Wichtel, 'Great guns!', *NZ Listener*, 11 July 1998, 71; Neville Peacocke, cited in Mark Revington, 'War of words', *NZ Listener*, 18 July 1998, 24.
2. James Belich, interview with the author, Wellington, 23 April 2009.
3. Ibid.
4. Colin McRae, interview with the author, Devonport, 24 March 2017.
5. Trisha Dunleavy & Hester Joyce, *New Zealand Film and Television: Institution, industry and cultural change* (Bristol: Intellect, 2011) 113, 115.
6. Roger Horrocks, 'Documentaries on New Zealand television', in *Re-inventing New Zealand: Essays on the arts and the media* (Pokeno: Atuanui Press, 2016), 262.
7. Dunleavy & Joyce, *New Zealand Film and Television*, 122.
8. Ibid.
9. McRae, interview.
10. Horrocks, 'Documentaries on New Zealand television'; Mary Debrett, 'Representing cultural diversity or serving local industry? An exploration of the future prospects of subsidised documentary', *International Journal of Diversity in Organisations, Communities and Nations*, vol. 5, no. 3, 2006, 94–101.
11. Horrocks, 'Documentaries on New Zealand television', 268.
12. Mary Debrett, 'Branding documentary: New Zealand's minimalist solution to cultural subsidy', *Media, Culture and Society*, vol. 26, no. 1, 2004, 5–23.
13. Debrett, 'Representing cultural diversity'.
14. Gary Edgerton, 'Ken Burns's rebirth of a nation: Television, narrative and popular history', *Film and History*, vol. 22, no. 4, 1992, 118–33.
15. McRae, interview; Six months earlier in December 1993, Communicado had received $900,000 for its six-episode series *New Zealand at War* – also the largest grant of that year. Belich noted that the NZ On Air board happened to have 'the right people' on it, and mentioned its chair, Ruth Harley, as one who strongly supported the programme.

16. *Pounamu* seems to have straddled the old and new systems. Made by staff from the old TVNZ (produced by Morehu McDonald), it was nevertheless funded by the new Broadcasting Commission. Descendants of Te Kooti performed in reenactments, making a case for revisiting the reputation of their tipuna. The influence of Belich's written history *The New Zealand Wars*, published four years earlier, is evident in the inclusion of Kawiti among the historical figures profiled. Don Selwyn was the narrator, and he took care to use the reo of each region. *Pounamu* made use of *The Governor* with a fairly free hand – footage of Selwyn as Wiremu Tāmihana, ploughing his fields, becomes a representation of the Parihaka ploughmen, and *The Governor*'s attack on Gate Pā serves to illustrate war in Taranaki. The series was evidently made on a small budget and does not appear to have screened beyond the Sunday morning slot. Kept to 'niche' Māori programming, it was hardly mentioned in publicity and reviews, and its separate episodes remained uncatalogued. This Māori-led production, pitched largely to Māori, effectively dropped out of sight until recently, when Ngā Taonga Sound and Vision began cataloguing the TVNZ archive.
17. Also relevant is the *New Zealand Maori Council v. Attourney-General* (1987) decision of the Court of Appeal, which gave the Treaty weight in the New Zealand legal system for the first time. (Thank you to Vincent O'Malley for this information.)
18. Claudia Orange, *The Treaty of Waitangi* (Wellington: Allen & Unwin/Port Nicholson Press, 1987); Hugh Kawharu, *Waitangi: Maori and Pakeha perspectives of the Treaty of Waitangi* (Auckland: Oxford University Press, 1989).
19. The Maori Language Act 1987 followed tribunal recommendations on the Te Reo Māori claim.
20. John Newton, 'Becoming Pākehā', *Landfall*, vol. 218, 2009, 38–48.
21. Belich, interview.
22. Military historians objected to several claims that Belich made. The most contentious was his claim that Māori had 'invented trench warfare'. Chris Pugsley responded in 'Maori did not invent trench warfare', *New Zealand Defence Quarterly* (1998), 33–34; and John Gates wrote a counter-argument in 'James Belich and the modern Maori pa: Revisionist history revised', *War & Society*, vol. 19, no. 2, 2001, 47–68. Both Pugsley and Gates pointed out that defensive features that Belich had argued were novel in the development of pā already existed in European fortifications. Belich has since noted that his claim was, rather, that Māori had independently invented these features. This compelling 'invention of trench warfare' point has nevertheless proved long-lasting; it was reiterated in the most recent productions about the wars in 2016 and 2017 (see chapter 9).
23. Tainui Stephens, interview with the author, Ngāruawāhia, 3 July 2009.
24. This was the claim that drew most flak: see note 22 above.
25. Belich's television persona, and its appeal to audiences, is discussed at greater length in A. Cooper, 'Televisual memory and *The New Zealand Wars*: Bicultural identities, masculinity and landscape', *European Journal of Cultural Studies*, vol. 14, no. 4, 2011, 446–65.
26. Belich, interview.
27. Ibid.
28. In 2009 Belich reflected that 'given infinite time' he would have attempted to seek out Pākehā descendants also, but at the time the team had felt that since he was Pākehā, it was Māori perspectives that most needed representing. Belich, interview with the author.
29. Ibid.
30. Ibid.
31. Ibid.
32. Stephens, interview.
33. Belich, interview.
34. Stephens, interview.
35. Ibid.
36. Hayden White, 'Historiography and historiophoty', *American Historical Review*, vol. 93, no. 5, 1988, 1193–99.
37. Stephens, interview.
38. One might add Colin McRae here, given his contribution to the images; and Stephen Ellis, for the distinctive design.
39. Lisa Perrott, '*The New Zealand Wars* documentary series: Discursive struggle and cultural memory' (PhD thesis, University of Waikato, 2007), 331.
40. Stephens, interview.
41. Ibid.
42. Ibid.
43. Belich, interview.
44. Stephens, interview.
45. Perrott, '*The New Zealand Wars* documentary series', 311, 332.
46. Stephens, quoted in Mark Revington, 'War of words', *NZ Listener*, 18 July 1998, 24.
47. See note 22; and 'Author defends his claim on Maori trench warfare', *New Zealand Herald*, 23 June 1998, A13.
48. Paul Diamond, 'Potshots fired over Belich's wars', *Evening Post*, 8 July 1998, 5.
49. Belich, interview.
50. Figure supplied by Television New Zealand, 11 July 2009.
51. Criticism as documented by Diamond, 'Potshots', 5; Revington, 'War of words', 24; Perrott, 'Rethinking the documentary audience', 67–79. Praise as documented by Diamond, 'Potshots'. Belich, interview; Stephens, interview.
52. Margot White, 'Titokowaru, unsung hero', *NZ Listener*, 27 June 1998, 70.
53. McRae, interview.
54. Wichtel, 'Great guns!', 71.

55. Ibid.
56. Debrett, 'Branding documentary', 16.
57. I discuss this further in Annabel Cooper, 'Televisual memory and the New Zealand Wars'.
58. http://maorilandfilm.co.nz/facebook-event/ra-maumahara/
59. Stephens, interview.

6: Television histories in uncertain times

1. John Milligan, interview with the author, 13 March 2013; Greg McGee, in McGee, Parker & Bailey, interview with the author, Auckland, 29 January 2015. McGee was speaking about the environment of the late 1990s as well as the situation in 2015.
2. Robin Scholes, email communication, 26 May 2017.
3. Robin Scholes, email communication, 24 May 2017.
4. McGee, in McGee, Parker & Bailey, interview.
5. Scholes, email communication, 24 May 2017.
6. Ibid; and McGee, Parker & Bailey, interview.
7. 'Rhodes to nowhere: BBC's epic tale flops', *Independent*, 25 September 1996.
8. Greenstone, 'Outline of opening episodes'. Thanks to Dean Parker for providing a copy.
9. David Lawrence, 'Brits polish Greenstone', *NZ Herald*, 21 September 1996, B8.
10. Scholes noted that the other international investor Beyond International would have pulled out if Stephen Lowe had been removed.
11. Bailey, in McGee, Parker & Bailey, interview.
12. McGee, in McGee, Parker & Bailey, interview.
13. Waihoroi Shortland, interview with author, Auckland, 29 January 2015.
14. Scholes, email communication, 24 May 2017.
15. Selwyn, cited in Margo White, 'Soapstone', *NZ Listener*, 29 May 1999, 18–20.
16. Ibid., 20.
17. Bailey, in McGee, Parker & Bailey, interview.
18. McGee & Parker, interview.
19. Shortland, interview.
20. Ibid.
21. McGee, in McGee, Parker & Bailey, interview.
22. Ibid. McGee went on, more optimistically, to note that he thought this had been achieved with Gaylene Preston's *Hope and Wire*, which was being made at the time of the interview.
23. Scholes, email communication, 26 May 2017.
24. Chris Bailey, in McGee, Parker & Bailey, interview; Robin Scholes, 'ScreenTalk', *NZ on Screen*, 2010.
25. Trisha Dunleavy, *Ourselves in Primetime: A history of New Zealand television drama* (Auckland: Auckland University Press, 2005), 270.
26. Herrick, 'Why Greenstone couldn't win: Viewers abandon overhyped epic', *Sunday Star-Times*, 18 July 1999, A3.
27. Leanne Moore, 'TV drama draws on bicultural heritage', *NZ Herald*, 4 June 1998, A20; Herrick, 'Why Greenstone couldn't win'.
28. Peter Hawes, 'Series smothered by cloak of "approved" history', *Sunday Star-Times*, 18 July 1999, A3.
29. Diana Wichtel, 'Past caring', *NZ Listener*, 26 June 1999, 70.
30. Milligan, interview.
31. Ibid.
32. Iain Rea, *Hundred Birds – Manu Rau*. Multimedia performance, Fuel 2000 Festival, Hamilton, June 2000.

7: Aftermath and memory

1. Vincent Ward, in Vincent Ward, Alison Carter, Geoff Chapple & Louis Nowra, *The Edge of the Earth: Stories and images from the antipodes* (Auckland: Heinemann Reed, 1990), 6.
2. Lynette Read, 'Vincent Ward: The emergence of an aesthetic', PhD thesis, University of Auckland, 2004, 139; and Clare O'Leary (interviewer), 'Vincent Ward: A very original filmmaker …', ScreenTalk, *NZ On Screen*: www.nzonscreen.com/interviews/interview-with-vincent-ward
3. Vincent Ward, interview with O'Leary.
4. Read, 'Vincent Ward'; ch. 4 on *In Spring One Plants Alone* is an illuminating discussion of the film.
5. Jeffrey Paparoa Holman, *Best of Both Worlds: The story of Elsdon Best and Tutakangahau* (Auckland: Penguin, 2010).
6. Vincent Ward, phone interview with author, 9 March 2016. See also Ward, Carter, Chapple & Nowra, *The Edge of the Earth*, 5–6.
7. Ward, interview.
8. *Map of the Human Heart* (dir. Ward); *The Last Samurai* (co-wrote, and production credit).
9. John Newton, 'Becoming Pākehā', *Landfall*, 218 (2009), 42. The term 'structure of feeling' comes from the cultural critic Raymond Williams.
10. Newton, 'Becoming Pākehā', 43.
11. Vincent Ward, interview with O'Leary.
12. '*Rain of the Children*: Interview with writer and director Vincent Ward', *NZ on Screen*: www.nzonscreen.com/title/rain-of-the-children-2008/awards
13. Ibid.
14. Ward, interview.
15. Vincent Ward with Lani-rain Feltham & Louis Nowra, *The Past Awaits: People, images, film* (Nelson: Craig Potton, 2010).
16. Vincent Ward, *NZ On Screen* interviews; Olivia Macassey takes up this term in her discussion of the film as 'postcolonial haunting': 'The edge of tears: Vincent Ward's *Rain of the Children*', *Illusions*, no. 41, 2009, 3–7.
17. Peter Webster, *Rua and the Maori Millenium* (Wellington: Victoria University Press, 1979).
18. Craig Wallace, phone interview, 22 February 2016.

19. Judith Binney, Gillian Chaplin & Craig Wallace, *Mihaia: The prophet Rua Kenana and his community at Maungapohatu* (Auckland: Oxford University Press, 1979).
20. Judith Binney & Gillian Chaplin, *Ngā Mōrehu/The Survivors: The life histories of eight Māori women* (Auckland: Oxford University Press, 1986).
21. Judith Binney, personal communication, June 2009.
22. Ward, *The Past Awaits*, 16.
23. Ward, interview.
24. 'Rain of the Children, Interview with Temuera Morrison', NZ On Screen: www.nzonscreen.com/title/rain-of-the-children-2008
25. Kevin Fisher and Brendan Hokowhitu discuss the complex relationships between the different types of footage and still images, and the shifting time scales, in 'Viewing against the grain: Postcolonial remediation in *Rain of the Children*', in Brendan Hokowhitu & Vijay Devadas (eds), *The Fourth Eye: Māori media in Aotearoa New Zealand* (Minneapolis: University of Minnesota Press, 2013), 60–75. The filming and editing of the police invasion is discussed in Dan Fleming, *Making the Transformational Moment in Film* (Los Angeles: Michael Wiese Productions, 2011).
26. Catherine Fitzgerald, personal communication, 2008.
27. Vincent Ward, interview with O'Leary.
28. Alun Bollinger, phone interview, 8 April 2016.
29. Ibid.
30. Tainui Stephens, interview with the author, Ngāruawāhia, 3 July 2009.
31. Gerald Ford, 'River Queen at Ward launch', *Wairarapa Times Age*, 19 November 2010.
32. Pou Temara, phone interview, 30 September 2016.
33. Ibid.
34. Andrew Whiteside (interviewer), 'Leon Narbey: Illustrious cinematographer …', *ScreenTalk*, NZ On Screen: www.nzonscreen.com/interviews/leon-narbey-illustrious-cinematographer
35. Leon Narbey, phone interview with author, 22 February 2018.
36. *Rain of the Children* Production Notes.
37. Ward, interview.
38. Temara, interview, 2016.
39. Waihoroi Shortland, interview with the author, Auckland, 29 January 2015.
40. Temara, interview, 2016.
41. Danny Keenan (ed.), *Terror in our Midst? Searching for terror in Aotearoa New Zealand* (Wellington: Huia, 2008).
42. Stephens, interview.
43. Taiarahia Black, 'That's my Nan!', *Pūkāea*, June 2016, 19–22.
44. He explained that he was told by a number of people that 'a curse existed and that Puhi suffered from its effects' (email communication, 3 June 2017). He makes clear in the film that he is less interested in whether or not a curse might be 'real', and more interested in how belief in a curse might affect the sufferer.
45. 'Pain felt 100 years on from Tuhoe arrest', *Newshub*, TV3, 3 April 2016.
46. Anthony Byrt, 'Vincent Ward: Breath – The Fleeting Intensity of Life review', *NZ Listener*, 7 January 2012: www.listener.co.nz/culture/arts/vincent-ward-breath-the-fleeting-intensity-of-life-review

8: Encounter, romance and conflict

1. Tainui Stephens, interview with the author, Ngāruawāhia, 3 July 2009.
2. James Belich, *The New Zealand Wars and the Victorian interpretation of racial conflict* (Auckland: Auckland University Press, 1986), 203–07.
3. Gerrard Albert, interview with the author, 9 May 2017.
4. Vincent Ward, interview, 9 March 2017.
5. Alun Bollinger, interview, 8 April 2016.
6. Albert, interview.
7. Tainui Stephens, 'A murky past and a full-blown civil war', *Tu Mai*, February 2006, 26–33.
8. Ward, interview.
9. Margot Butcher, 'What films may come', *North and South*, May 2003, 80–88.
10. NZ On Screen.
11. Sylvia Kaa, interview, 9 November 2016.
12. Paul Little, *Temuera Morrison: From haka to Hollywood* (Auckland: Penguin, 2009), 208.
13. Bollinger, interview; Little, *Temuera Morrison*, 208.
14. When some outside the production suggested to Bollinger that he could hold on to the direction and take a director's credit, he pointed out that it was Ward's film. This loyalty seems to have been characteristic of most people involved with the production.
15. Stephens, interview.
16. Ward, interview.
17. Ibid.
18. Ibid.
19. James Belich, interview with the author, Wellington, 23 April 2009.
20. Stephens, interview.
21. Tainui Stephens, email communication, 12 June 2017.
22. Ward, interview.
23. The most substantial report was J.R. Sheehan, 'My life among the Maoris', *Sun*, 27 July 1929. James Cowan wrote about her in the *Auckland Star*, wondering if she was the same white girl he often saw as a child in Kihikihi. She was 'living with the Maoris near the King Country border, the Puniu River. We used to see her in the township of Kihikihi when she came riding in with her native friends to shop at the stores.' She was 'barefooted, dressed like the native women in loose gown and blouse'. He guessed that she was Caroline Perrett because her age seemed right but also because 'the Maoris were not given to kidnapping white children': 'The Mountain Maid', *Auckland Star*, 19 July 1929, 6.
24. 'Vincent's obsession', *Weekend Herald*, 21 January 2006, 3.
25. Ward, interview.

26. Cowan, *NZW*, II, 173, 243.
27. James Belich, *I Shall Not Die: Titokowaru's War, New Zealand 1868–1869* (Wellington: Allen & Unwin/Port Nicholson Press, 1989), 45.
28. Cowan, *NZW*, II, 210.
29. Te Kai Pō, Vincent Ward, *River Queen* (New Zealand: Silverscreen Films, 2005). The Māori text is translated in the following sentence. Tītokowaru's letter of 25 June 1868 is held in the Riwha Tītokowaru Collection, MS-Papers–3006–01 and MS-Papers–3006–02, Alexander Turnbull Library, Wellington.
30. Albert, interview.
31. Little, *Temuera Morrison*, 206–07.
32. The credits situate *River Queen*'s relation to historical sources by naming three figures (Tītokowaru, Caroline Perrett and Anne Evans) 'without whose stories this one would not have happened'. Earlier drafts of the script used the names of historical figures, although the names had been changed by the final version so that the historical referencing was less direct: Russell Campbell, seminar for Department of Film and Media, University of Otago, 2008.
33. Bruce Babington, 'What streams may come: Navigating Vincent Ward's River Queen', *Illusions*, no. 39, 2007, 8–13.
34. Olivia Macassey, 'Cross-currents: River Queen's national and trans-national heritages', in Alistair Fox, Barry Keith Grant & Hilary Radner (eds), *New Zealand Cinema: Interpreting the past* (Bristol: Intellect, 2011), 119–34.
35. This was a criticism made of *The Piano* too, but it is also a motif that has attracted wider critical debate: see Bell Hooks, *Black Looks: Race and representation* (Boston: South End Press, 1992); and Richard Dyer, *White* (London: Routledge, 1997).
36. See Angela Wanhalla, *Matters of the Heart: A history of interracial marriage in New Zealand* (Auckland: Auckland University Press, 2013), 109–19.
37. See the discussion in chapter 4.
38. Roger Nicholson's argument that the film's organisation around the genre of romance comes at the expense of the colonisation story is also pertinent in this respect. Nicholson, 'Romancing the past: History, love, and genre in Vincent Ward's River Queen', *Journal of Popular Romance Studies*, vol. 2, no. 1, 2011.
39. Ward, interview. In fact, the woman at Pāpāwai in the photograph that Ward was interested in was probably of mixed descent (Angela Wanhalla, personal communication, 2016). This doesn't, of course, change the more important point that Ward saw her as Pākehā.
40. Dan Fleming, *Making the Transformational Moment in Film: Unleashing the power of the image* (Los Angeles: Michael Wiese Productions, 2011), 206.
41. Stephens, interview.
42. Danny Keenan, 'Finding Wiremu: Centre and substance in *River Queen*': www.newzealandwars.co.nz
43. For example, in Philip Matthews, 'Watery grave', *NZ Listener*, 28 January 2006; Sean Damer, 'Drama queen? The trouble and strife of Vincent Ward's River Queen', *Metro* 149 (2006), 48–51.
44. Peter Calder, 'Upriver without a paddle', *Weekend Herald*, 21 January 2006; Kate Stables, 'River Queen', *Sight and Sound*, no. 17, 2008, 75–76.
45. Graeme Tuckett, 'Apocalyse then', *Capital Times*, 25–31 January 2006, 9.
46. *River Queen*, eHui Discussion Forum on kaupapamaori.com, August to September 2006: www.rangahau.co.nz/assets/ehui/river_queen.pdf
47. Ibid.
48. Personal communication, 2016.
49. Ibid.
50. Albert, interview. Quotations in the next paragraphs are also taken from this interview.

9: Māori creative control and new screens

1. Tama Te Kapua Poata, *Poata: Seeing beyond the horizon, a memoir* (Wellington: Steele Roberts, 2012), 203.
2. *Hautoa ma! The rise of Māori cinema* (dir. Libby Hakaraia & Tainui Stephens, Blue Bach Productions, 2016).
3. Merata Mita, 'The soul and the image', in *Film in Aotearoa New Zealand*, 1992, 36, 49.
4. In *The Making of The Governor* (dir. Bob Barton, 1977): www.nzonscreen.com/title/the-making-of-the-governor-1978
5. Barry Barclay, *Our Own Image* (Auckland: Longman Paul, 1990).
6. Ella Henry & Melissa Wikaire, *The Brown Book: Māori in screen production* (Ngā Aho Whakaari/Association of Māori in Screen Production, Te Ara Poutama, 2013).
7. Jo Smith, *Māori Television: The first ten years* (Auckland: Auckland University Press, 2016).
8. The Māori-language action movie *The Dead Lands* (2014) deserves a mention here. Dealing not with the colonial period but with war in the precolonial era, this film was directed by Toa Fraser, a playwright and filmmaker of English and Fijian descent who arrived in New Zealand in his teens. While the cast were Māori, and Tainui Stephens co-produced it, Māori were not especially strongly represented among the crew.
9. John Bishara, cited in Smith, *Māori Television*, 58.
10. Poata, *Poata*, 251.
11. Lee Tamahori, interview with Kim Hill, *Saturday Morning*, Radio New Zealand. There is at least one other Te Kooti script: Curtis Bristowe's screenplay written as part of an MA. Joseph Curtis Bristowe, 'Indigenising the screen: Screenplay and critical analysis for *The Prophet*', MA thesis, Waikato University, 2009.
12. *Hunt for the Wilderpeople* (dir. Taika Waititi, 2016).

13. 'Danny Keenan: Time to shake Land Wars taboo', *Wanganui Chronicle*, 1 September 2016; Alison McCulloch, 'Lest we remember', *Werewolf*, 23 April 2014, http://werewolf.co.nz/2014/04/lest-we-remember/; 'Vincent O'Malley: Land Wars neglected orphan of New Zealand's history', *NZ Herald*, 11 November 2016.
14. *Te Ahi Kā Roa, Te Ahi Kātoro Taranaki War 1860–2010* (Puke Ariki, 17 March–1 August 2010).
15. *The Flight of Te Hookioi: From the Waikato to Vienna in 1859* (dir. Tearepa Kahi, 2009).
16. Paora Joseph, email communication, 4 December 2017.
17. Initial Lotteries Grant funding of $35,000 was supplemented by a small amount raised through crowdfunding, and post-production company Park Road Post and Gaylene Preston Productions donated their services. Preston, who had a longstanding association with Parihaka, mentored Joseph over the period of the film and took on the role of executive producer, and she made her house available to Joseph and to co-director Janine Martin and editor Simon Price as a postproduction studio where they took the film to edit for six months. This film was the result of a deeply felt commitment to Parihaka on the part of all these people, Māori and Pākehā. Maata Wharehoka, interview with author, Dunedin 24 November 2017; Paora Joseph, email communication.
18. Wharehoka, interview.
19. Katie Kenny, 'The children of Parihaka': www.critic.co.nz/features/article/2316/the-children-of-parihaka
20. Paora Joseph, email communication.
21. Ibid.
22. As noted in Chapter 5 note 16, the series *Pounamu* (1990) had covered some of this ground before.
23. Hirini Kaa, interview with author, Dunedin, 23 April 2018.
24. Hirini Kaa interviewed by Maraea Rakuraku in 'Hirini Kaa: Host of Maori TV show *The Prophets*', *Te Ahi Kaa*, RNZ, 26 May 2013: radionz.co.nz/national/programmes/teahikaa/audio/2556270/hirini-kaa-host-of-maori-tv-show-the-prophets; Kaa, interview in *Te Ahi Kaa*; email communication with author, 4 April 2018.
25. *The Prophets*, Episode 3.
26. Kaa, interview in *Te Ahi Kaa*.
27. Kaa, interview with author.
28. Ibid.
29. Hirini Kaa and Leon Narbey, interviews with author.
30. Julianne Clarke-Morris, 'The Prophets: A journey of faith', *Anglican Taonga*, 22 July 2013: anglicantaonga.org.nz/news/tikanga_maori/the_prophets_a_journey_of_faith
31. Kaa, interview.
32. Ibid.
33. Now uploaded to YouTube by *Waka Huia*, the programmes are: 'The 150th anniversary of the Land Wars – The battle of Rangiriri' (dir. Potaka Maipi, 3 May 2014, *Waka Huia*, TVNZ); '150th anniversary of the Land Wars – Battle of Rangiaowhia (dir. Meihana Te Huia, 10 May 2014, *Waka Huia*, TVNZ); '150th anniversary of the Land Wars in Waikato at Ōrākau' (17 May 2014, *Waka Huia*, TVNZ); 'Gate Pā – 150th anniversary of Waikato Land Wars' (dir. Piata Gardiner-Hoskins, 28 May 2014, *Waka Huia*, TVNZ). The final episode that included commentary on the final conflict at Te Ranga went to air a few days before the commemoration of that battle: www.youtube.com/playlist?list=PLOvRS8AyGe49QZCpuBW_rULwTdC-u5gq7
34. Marcus Winter, 'The Battle of Gate Pā told with sand': www.youtube.com/watch?v=V_ceI8RF2sM]
35. *The Kiingitanga* (dir. Mahanga Pihama), Māori Television, 2016.
36. Mahanga Pihama, phone interview, 21 June 2017.
37. Brad Haami, phone interview, 13 June 2017.
38. See, for example, Phil Taylor, 'The bad boy who would be king', *NZ Herald*, 16 August 2014.
39. Pihama, interview.
40. www.youtube.com/watch?v=CrGHGwH2wlg
41. www.youtube.com/watch?v=Y7eTKvyTxDU
42. Kirsten Johnstone, 'Ria Hall: Rules of engagement', RNZ Music, 26 October 2017: www.radionz.co.nz/national/programmes/nat-music/audio/2018619319/ria-hall-rules-of-engagement
43. 'Ko te manawarerekia u', Rāwiri Puhirake's instructions to the warriors awaiting the attack on Pukehinahina, is translated by Matiu Dickson as 'Be patient, hold your fire': 'Ngāiterangi Treaty negotiations: A personal perspective' in *Te Tai Haruru: Journal of Māori and indigenous issues*, vol. 5 (2017), 105.
44. www.youtube.com/watch?v=27hDGOkwnvg
45. https://teara.govt.nz/en/new-zealand-wars
46. http://newzealandwars.co.nz/
47. David Green, *Battlefields of the New Zealand Wars: A visitor's guide* (Auckland: Penguin, 2010).
48. Nigel Prickett, *Landscapes of Conflict: A field guide to the New Zealand Wars* (Auckland: Random House NZ, 2002).
49. Diana Pope & Jeremy Pope, *North Island: Penguin New Zealand travel guide* (Auckland: Penguin, 2009); Diana Pope & Jeremy Pope, *Mobil South Island Travel Guide* (Auckland: Penguin, 1995).
50. www.ruapekapeka.co.nz/
51. www.heritage.org.nz/apps/the-waikato-war; https://mch.govt.nz/news-events/news/1846-war-wellington-app; https://play.google.com/store/apps/details?id=com.mytoursapp.android.app1256
52. Deena Coster, 'New app launched to help get to grips with Taranaki land war history', *Stuff*, 22 August 2017: www.stuff.co.nz/technology/apps/96014326/new-app-launched-to-help-get-to-grips-with-taranaki-land-war-history
53. Smith, *Māori Television*, 71.

54. Mihingārangi Forbes, phone interview with author, 3 November 2017.
55. Mihingārangi Forbes, 'Māori and the New Zealand Wars', Radio New Zealand, 25 April 2016: www.radionz.co.nz/national/programmes/anzacday/audio/201798271/maori-and-the-new-zealand-wars. On Anzac Day 2017, RNZ followed this up with a much more controversial item, although many listeners would not have recognised its inflammatory potential. Australian historian Peter Stanley presented 'The first wars of Australia', setting out the case for recognising colonial conflict in Australia as warfare. In Australia this is still very contentious, and the focus of what have been called 'The history wars': Peter Stanley, 'The first wars of Australia', RNZ, 25 April 2017: www.radionz.co.nz/national/programmes/anzacday/audio/201841454/peter-stanley-the-first-wars-of-australia
56. Forbes, interview.
57. Ibid.
58. Ibid.
59. Ibid.
60. Ibid.

Conclusion

1. Robert Young's exposition set out the theory: *White Mythologies: Writing history and the West* (London: Routledge, 1990).
2. Kenneth Marc Harris, 'American film genres and non-American films: A case study of Utu', *Cinema Journal*, vol. 29, no. 2 (1990), 40–46. This impulse is of course quite consistent with that of the revisionist western, although it takes local forms.
3. See Catherine Fitzgerald, dir., *Don Selwyn: Power in our hands* (Māori Television, 2017).
4. As discussed, for example, by M. Elise Marubbio, *Killing the Indian Maiden: Images of Native American women in film* (Lexington, KY: University Press of Kentucky, 2006).
5. Some might, perhaps: Ranginui Walker, in response to the infamous Orewa speech of 2004, said: 'The lizards of our colonial past are being laid to rest in the bedrooms of the nation.' ('State of the nation', *NZ Listener*, 21 February 2004).

BIBLIOGRAPHY

PRIMARY SOURCES
Unpublished
R. Amohanga to Hon W.E. Parry, 8 February 1938, IA1W2578 113, Archives New Zealand, Wellington

Censor to R.C. Hayward, 15 November 1927, IA 83 Box 7, Dept of Internal Affairs, Archives New Zealand, Wellington

Correspondence from Rudall Charles Hayward, MS-Papers–11310-120, Alexander Turnbull Library, Wellington

Ted Coubray, transcript of an interview by Jonathan Dennis, 10 January 1995, MA1683, 1009.054.01, 80–81, Documentation Collection, Ngā Taonga Sound and Vision

Jonathan Dennis Library Vertical Files, 'Utu' Press Clippings/Articles, Ngā Taonga Sound and Vision

Warren Dibble, annotation on newspaper clipping, n.d. Copy supplied by Warren Dibble

Frontier Films List of Shareholders at 27 July 1939, ARC3003.8, Te Awamutu Museum Archives, Te Awamutu

Rudall C. Hayward, Files, MA2244, 5146/10; MA2767, D5146, Box 11; MA2884; MZ2301, D5146, Folder 52; Documentation Collection, Ngā Taonga Sound and Vision Archive, Wellington. Courtesy of Hayward-Boak Collection

Rudall Hayward correspondence, AAOJ W5077 7811 Box 23, 50/1/1, Archives New Zealand, Wellington

'Maori comedy films', 86-105-042, Alexander Turnbull Library, Wellington

Minute Books of the Te Awamutu Historical Society 1937–40, Te Awamutu Museum Archives, Te Awamutu, ARC2057

Miscellaneous papers: 'The Te Kooti Trail', MA1663, MANS 0013.01, Ngā Taonga Sound and Vision, Wellington

Geoff Murphy, 'Puha Western', Script I. Early draft, 30pp; Ref. no. MA1036 [SC0001.01], Box. no. 0962.025; Documentation Collection, Ngā Taonga Sound and Vision. Courtesy of Don Blakeney Collection

Geoff Murphy & Keith Aberdein, 'Utu', Script I, 4th draft; SC0001.04, Box. no. 0247.08.03 [Box L8]; Documentation Collection, Ngā Taonga Sound and Vision. Courtesy of New Zealand Film Commission Collection

Tony Noble, Utu Productions press release, 18 December 1981. Jonathan Dennis Library Vertical Files, 'Utu' press kits/press releases, Ngā Taonga Sound and Vision

Thia Priestly to Jennifer Evans, 30 March 1993, ARC3630.1, Te Awamutu Museum Archives, Te Awamutu

Prospectus of Frontier Films Ltd, 30 August 1937, ARC3003.9, Te Awamutu Museum Archives, Te Awamutu

Prospectus of Maori War Films Limited, MS-Papers–11310-120, Alexander Turnbull Library, Wellington

'Rewi's Last Stand', Pamphlet produced for 50th Anniversary, n.d., 1987/88, ARC3630.2, Te Awamutu Museum Archives

Rewi's Last Stand. Press & Publicity, Vertical Files, New Zealand Title, Documentation Collection, Ngā Taonga Sound & Vision.

Riwha Tītokowaru, 25 June 1868, Riwha Tītokowaru Collection, MS-Papers-3006-01 and MS-Papers-3006-02, Alexander Turnbull Library, Wellington

Published sources
Books and pamphlets
Alexander, James E., *Incidents of the Maori War, New Zealand, in 1860–61* (London: Bentley, 1863)

Boldrewood, Rolf, *War to the Knife: Or, tangata whenua* (London: Macmillan, 1899)

Buick, T. Lindsay, *New Zealand's First War, or The rebellion of Hone Heke* (Wellington: Government Printer, 1926)

Cowan, James, *Settlers and Pioneers* (Wellington: Government Printer, 1940)

——, *Tales of the Maori Bush* (Dunedin: Reed, 1934)

——, *The Adventures of Kimble Bent: A story of wild life in the New Zealand bush* (London: Whitcombe & Tombs, 1911)

——, *The Maoris of New Zealand* (Christchurch: Whitcombe & Tombs, 1910)

——, *The New Zealand Wars: A history of the Maori campaigns and the pioneering period*, 2 vols (Wellington: Government Printer, 1922–23)

——, *The Old Frontier: Te Awamutu. The story of the Waipa Valley* (Te Awamutu: The Waipa Post, 1922)

Featon, John, *The Waikato War, 1863–4* (Auckland: Free Lance, 1879; 2nd edn, 1923)

Hamilton-Browne, George, *With the Lost Legion in New Zealand* (London: T. Werner Laurie, 1911)

Henry, Ella & Melissa Wikaire, *The Brown Book: Māori in screen production* (Ngā Aho Whakaari/Association of Māori in Screen Production, Te Ara Poutama, 2013)

Henty, G.A., *Maori and Settler: A story of the New Zealand War* (London: Blackie, 1890)

Mair, Gilbert, *Reminiscences and Maori Stories* (Auckland: Brett Printing & Publishing Co., 1923)

——, *Description of the Battle of Orakau as given by the native chief Hitiri Te Paerata of the Ngatiraukawa tribe* (Wellington: G. Didsbury, Government Printer, 1888)

Maning, Frederick Edward, 'Heke's War in the North', in *Old New Zealand: A tale of the good old times* (Auckland: Whitcombe & Tombs, 1906)

Reed, A.W., *Rewi's Last Stand* (Wellington: A.H. & A.W. Reed, 1939)

Reeves, William Pember, *The Long White Cloud: Ao Tea Roa* (London: Horace Marshall & Son, 1898)

Rusden, George W., *History of New Zealand* (London: Chapman & Hall, 1883)

——, *Aureretanga: Groans of the Maoris* (London: W. Ridgeway, 1888)

Satchell, William Arthur, *The Greenstone Door* (London: Sidgwick & Jackson, 1914)

Tracy, Mona, *Rifle and Tomahawk: A stirring tale of the Te Kooti Rebellion* (London: Harrap, 1927)

Whitmore, George S., *The Last Maori War in New Zealand under the Self-Reliant Policy* (London: Sampson Low, Marston & Co., 1902)

Interviews and personal communication

Aberdein, Keith, interview with author, 30 November 2010

Albert, Gerrard, interview with author, 9 May 2017

Belich, James, interview with author, 23 April 2009

Binney, Judith, personal communication, June 2009

Bollinger, Alun, phone interview with author, 8 April 2016

Butt, Pauline, interview with author, 22 November 2012

Davies, Jim, interview with author, 12 December 2012

Davis, Te Rau Oriwa, telephone interview with author, 21 February 2018

Dibble, Warren, interview with author, 30 November 2010

Evans, Jennifer, personal communication with author, September 2013

Fitzgerald, Catherine, personal communication with author, 2008 and 2017

Forbes, Mihingārangi, phone interview with author, 3 November 2017

Haami, Brad, interview with author, November 2012

Hayward, Ramai, interviewed by Lawrence Te Wharerau in 'Nga Pikitia, Koha, 1987': www.nzonscreen.com/title/koha-nga-pikitia-maori-1987

Hayward, Rudall, interviewed by Ray Hayes & Walter Harris, 1962, A0644, Audio Collection, Ngā Taonga Sound and Vision Archive, Wellington

Hēnare, George, interview with author, 29 April 2016

Hēnare, George. *ScreenTalk* interview: www.nzonscreen.com/interviews/george-henare-acting-on-screen-and-stage

Joseph, Paora, email communication with author, 4 December 2017

Kaa, Hirini, interviewed by Maraea Rakuraku, *Te Ahi Kaa*, RNZ, 26 May 2013

Kaa, Hirini, interview with author, Dunedin, 23 March 2018; email communication with author, 4 April 2018

Kaa, Keri, interview with Nancy Brunning, Blueskin Films, 2007

Kaa, Sylvia, phone interview with author, 9 November 2016

Mane-Wheoki, Jonathan, email communication with author, 14 February 2013

Maniapoto-Anderson, Rovina, interview with author, 30 November 2012

McGee, Greg, Dean Parker & Chris Bailey, interview with author, 29 January 2015

McRae, Colin, interview with author, 24 March 2017

Milligan, John, phone interview with author, 13 March 2017

Morrison, Temuera, interview, NZ On Screen, 2008: www.nzonscreen.com/title/rain-of-the-children-2008

Murphy, Geoff & Graeme Cowley, interview, *Saturday Morning*, National Radio, 20 July 2013

Murphy, Geoff, interview with author, 11 November 2015

Narbey, Leon, email communication with author, 13 July 2016

Narbey, Leon, interview with Andrew Whiteside, 'Leon Narbey: Illustrious cinematographer …', *ScreenTalk*, NZ On Screen, 2011: www.nzonscreen.com/interviews/leon-narbey-illustrious-cinematographer

Narbey, Leon, phone interview with author, 22 February 2018

Noonan, Michael, interview with author, 14 July 2010

Pihama, Mahanga, phone interview with author, 21 June 2017

Pivac, Diane, personal communication with author, 2013–2018

Pohlmann, Gerd, email communication with author, 18 May 2015, 26 July 2016

Preston, Gaylene, interview with author, 29 October 2013

Roa, Tom, interview with author, 25 January 2011

Scholes, Robin, email communication with author, 26 May 2017

Scholes, Robin, interviewed by James Coleman, 'Robin Scholes: Producing the goods', *ScreenTalk*, NZ on Screen, 2010: www.nzonscreen.com/interviews/robin-scholes-producing-the-goods

Scott-Smith, Michael, interview with Catherine Fitzgerald, Blueskin Films

Selwyn, Don, interviewed by Selwyn Muru, Te Puna Wai Kōrero, Radio New Zealand, 11 June 1977. Audio Collection, ID45346 Ngā Taonga Sound & Vision, Wellington

Shortland, Waihoroi, interview with author, 29 January 2015

Stephens, Tainui, interview with author, 3 July 2009

Swarbrick, Richard, phone interview with author, 6 October 2013

Temara, Pou, interviews with author, 26 October 2012; 30 September 2016 (phone)

Vere Jones, Peter, phone interview with author, 3 April 2013

Waaka, Napi, phone interview with author, 14 November 2012

Wallace, Craig, phone interview with author, 22 February 2016

Wanhalla, Angela, personal communication with author, 2016.

Warbrick, Paerau, personal communication with author, 2012 & 2018

Ward, Vincent, interviewed by Clare O'Leary, 'Vincent Ward: A very original filmmaker', *ScreenTalk*, NZ On Screen, 2008: www.nzonscreen.com/interviews/interview-with-vincent-ward

Ward, Vincent, phone interview with author, March 2016

Wharehoka, Maata, interview with author, 24 November 2017

Periodicals and newspapers

Auckland Star, 24 August 1927, 26 August 1927, 2 September 1927, 15 September 1927, 18 November 1927, 26 November 1927, 18 November 1927, 19 July 1929, 11 December 1937, 12 August 1939, 26 February 1940, 13 March 1940, 11 April 1940, 13 April 1940, 20 April 1940, 25 May 1940, 7 November 1977, 19 July 1982, 12 February 1983, 14 April 1983, 28 May 1983

Auckland Weekly News, 1927 (serialisation of *The Te Kooti Trail*)

Bay of Plenty Beacon, 2 November 1964

Broadsheet May 1983, July/August 1983

Capital Times, 25–31 January 2006

Christchurch Star, 26 May 1982, 1 February 1983, 8 February 1983, 15 February 1983

Colonist, 27 March 1911

Daily Post, 23 December 1981

Dominion, 3 September 1977, 6 September 1977, 8 October 1977, 1 November 1977, 17 September 1982, 28 February 1983

Evening Post, 22 February 1865, 29 April 1939, 20 June 1940, 27 July 1940, 9 February 1983, 14 February 1983, 16 February 1983, 8 July 1998

Evening Standard, 12 February 1983

Evening Star, 8 September 1925

Independent, 25 September 1996

Media Times, February 1982

Metro, no. 149, 2006

Nelson Evening Mail, 12 February 1983

New Yorker, 15 October 1984

New Zealand Herald, September 1921–March 1922 (serialisation of 'My Lady of the Cave' by H.T. Gibson), 28 October 1921, 2 August 1927, 24 September 1927 (serialisation of *The Te Kooti Trail*), 10 November 1927, 24 November 1977, 12 February 1983, 21 September 1996, 4 June 1998, 23 June 1998, 2 December 2013, 16 August 2014, 11 November 2016

New Zealand Listener, 3 April 1970, 1 October 1977, 5 November 1977, 27 June 1998, 11 July 1998, 18 July 1998, 29 May 1999, 26 June 1999, 28 January 2006, 7 January 2012

New Zealand Times, 20 June 1982, 13 February 1983

North and South, May 2003

Northern Advocate, 7 September 1927

Otago Daily Times, 12 February 1983

Otago Witness, 9 August 1927– (serialisation of 'The Te Kooti Trail')

PPTA Journal, Term 2, 1983

Press, 16 April 1864, 25 July 1910

Pūkāea, June 2016

Rolling Stone, 12 April 1973

Sight and Sound, no. 17, 2008

Star, 8 October–6 November 1906 ('The white slave'), 29 May 1982

Star Weekender, 5 November 1977, 29 May 1982

Sun, 11 July 1929, 27 November 1927

Sunday Star-Times, 18 July 1999

Te Awamutu Courier, 31 May 1937, 8 June 1937, 1 October 1937, 2 February 1938, 4 February 1938, 7 September 1938.

Te Iwi o Aotearoa, February 1990

Tu Mai, February 2006

Wairarapa Times Age, 19 November 2010

Wanganui Chronicle, 1 September 2016

Weekend Herald, 21 January 2006

Films and television

The 150th Anniversary of the Land Wars, Waka Huia TV series, TVNZ, 2014

An Angel at My Table, dir. Jane Campion, Hibiscus Films, 1990

Don Selwyn: Power in our hands, dir. Catherine Fitzgerald, Blueskin Films/Māori Television, 2017

The Flight of Te Hookioi, dir. Tearapa Kahi, Monsoon Pictures, 2009

Frontier of Dreams, TV series, Whakapapa Productions, 2005

The Governor, TV series, dir. Tony Isaac, TV One, 1977

Greenstone, TV series, dir. Chris Bailey, Communicado, 1999

Hautoa ma! The rise of Māori cinema, dir. Libby Hakaraia & Tainui Stephens, Blue Bach Productions, 2016

Hunt for the Wilderpeople, dir. Taika Waititi, Piki Films, 2016

In Spring One Plants Alone, dir. Vincent Ward, Vincent Ward Films, 1980

Map of the Human Heart, dir. Vincent Ward, Australian Film Finance Corporation, 1993

My Lady of the Cave, dir. & prod. Rudall Hayward, 1922
One Hundred Crowded Years, New Zealand Film Unit, 1941
Pictures, dir. Michael Black, Pacific Films, 1981
Rain of the Children, dir. Vincent Ward, Wayward Films, 2008
Rewi's Last Stand, dir. Rudall Hayward, Maori War Films, 1925
Rewi's Last Stand, dir. Rudall Hayward, Frontier Films, 1940
River Queen, dir. Vincent Ward, Silverscreen Films, 2005
Tātarakihi: The children of Parihaka, dir. Paora Joseph, Gaylene Preston Productions, 2012
The Kiingitanga, dir. Mahanga Pihama, Enter the Dragon, 2017
The Killing of Kane, TV play, dir. Chris Thomson, NZBC, 1971
The Last Samurai, dir. Edward Zwick, Radar Pictures, 2003
The Last Stand, dir. Rudall Hayward, Frontier Films, 1949
The Making of The Governor, dir. Bob Barton, TVOne, 1977: www.nzonscreen.com/title/the-making-of-the-governor–1978
The New Zealand Wars, TV series, dir. Tainui Stephens, Landmark Productions, 1998
The Prophets, dir. Libby Hakaria & Tainui Stephens, Scottie Productions, 2013
The Te Kooti Trail, dir. Rudall Hayward, Whakatane Films, 1927
Uenuku, dir. Geoff Murphy, Peach Wemyss Astor, 1974
Utu, dir. Geoff Murphy, Utu Productions, 1983
Utu: Redux, dir. Geoff Murphy, Utu Productions, 2013
Von Tempsky's Ghost, dir. John Milligan, Bright Spark Television, 2002

Websites and apps

The 1846 War in Wellington, app, Ministry for Culture & Heritage: mch.govt.nz/news-events/news/1846-war-wellington-app
The Battle of Gate Pā Told with Sand, Marcus Winter: www.youtube.com/watch?v=V_ceI8RF2sM
Māoriland Film Festival, Facebook page: http://maorilandfilm.co.nz/facebook-event/ra-maumahara
'New Zealand Wars', Te Ara – the Encyclopedia of New Zealand: teara.govt.nz/en/new-zealand-wars
NZ Wars: The stories of Ruapekapeka. RNZ and Great Southern Television: www.radionz.co.nz/programmes/nz-wars/story/2018619186/nz-wars-the-stories-of-ruapekapeka
Ruapekapeka: www.ruapekapeka.co.nz
The Taranaki Wars, app, Heritage Taranaki: https://play.google.com/store/apps/details?id=com.mytoursapp.android.app1256&hl=en
The Waikato War Driving Tour, app, Heritage New Zealand Pouhere Taonga
They Come Marching, Ria Hall, music video: www.youtube.com/watch?v=tY_IRSkhQgs

SECONDARY SOURCES

Online

Clarke-Morris, Julianne, 'The prophets: A journey of faith', *Anglican Taonga*, 22 July 2013: http://anglicantaonga.org.nz/news/tikanga_maori/the_prophets_a_journey_of_faith
Coster, Deena, 'New app launched to help get to grips with Taranaki land war history': www.stuff.co.nz/technology/apps/96014326/new-app-launched-to-help-get-to-grips-with-taranaki-land-war-history
Forbes, Mihingārangi, 'Māori and the New Zealand Wars', Radio New Zealand, 25 April 2016: www.radionz.co.nz/national/programmes/anzacday/audio/201798271/maori-and-the-new-zealand-wars
Kenny, Katie, 'The children of Parihaka': www.critic.co.nz/features/article/2316/the-children-of-parihaka
McCulloch, Alison, 'Lest we remember', Werewolf, 23 April 2014: http://werewolf.co.nz/2014/04/lest-we-remember
Renan, Ernest, 'What is a nation', trans. Ethan Rundell, ucparis.fr/files/9313/6549/9943/What_is_a_Nation.pdf
'River Queen', eHui Discussion Forum on kaupapamaori.com, August to September 2006: www.rangahau.co.nz/assets/ehui/river_queen.pdf
Stanley, Peter, 'The first wars of Australia', RNZ, 25 April 2017: www.radionz.co.nz/national/programmes/anzacday/audio/201841454/peter-stanley-the-first-wars-of-australia

Theses and oral presentations

Campbell, Russell, Seminar for Department of Film and Media, University of Otago, 2008
Cross, Melissa, 'The forgotten soundtrack of Maoriland: Imagining the nation through Alfred Hill's songs for *Rewi's Last Stand*', MA thesis, Te Kōkī, New Zealand School of Music, 2015
Curtis Bristowe, Joseph, 'Indigenising the screen: Screenplay and critical analysis for *The Prophet*', MA thesis, Waikato University, 2009
Hillyer, Minette, '"Greetings to our distant kinsmen!" "Paramount's Red Indians" come to Aotearoa', paper presented at Film in the Colony symposium, 12 July 2017
Lacey, Cherie, 'To settle the settler: Pathologies of colonialism in New Zealand history films 1925–2005', PhD thesis, University of Auckland, 2010
Perrott, Lisa, '*The New Zealand Wars* documentary series: Discursive struggle and cultural memory', PhD thesis, University of Waikato, 2007
Pivac, Diane, 'Filming the pages of New Zealand history', BA (Hons) dissertation, Victoria University of Wellington, 2002
Pointon, Susy, 'Risky Business: The creation of a New Zealand film industry', PhD thesis, University of Auckland, 2006.

Read, Lynette, 'Vincent Ward: The emergence of an aesthetic', PhD thesis, University of Auckland, 2004

Gregory Wood, 'Revisiting James Cowan: A reassessment of the New Zealand Wars (1922–23)', MPhil thesis, Massey University, 2010

Articles

Belgrave, Michael, 'Looking foward: Historians and the Waitangi Tribunal', *New Zealand Journal of History*, vol. 40, no. 2, 2006, 230–50

Bruce Babington, 'What streams may come: Navigating Vincent Ward's *River Queen*', *Illusions*, no. 39, 2007, 8–13

Byrnes, Giselle, 'By which standards? History and the Waitangi Tribunal: A reply', *New Zealand Journal of History*, vol. 40, no. 2, 2006, 214–29

Campbell, Russell, 'In order that they may become civilized: Pakeha ideology in *Rewi's Last Stand*, *Broken Barrier* and *Utu*', *Illusions*, no. 1, 1986, 5

Cooper, Annabel, 'Nō Ōrākau: Past and people in James Cowan's places', *Journal of New Zealand Studies*, no. 19, 2015, 63–78

———, 'Televisual memory and the New Zealand Wars: Bicultural identities, masculinity and landscape', *European Journal of Cultural Studies*, vol. 14, no. 4, 2011, 446–65

Cooper, Annabel & Ariana Tikao (eds), 'James Cowan and the legacies of late colonial culture in Aotearoa New Zealand', *Journal of New Zealand Studies*, no. 19, 2015

Day, Kelvin, 'Introduction', in Kelvin Day (ed.), *Contested Ground/Te Whenua i Tohea: The Taranaki Wars 1860–1881* (Wellington: Huia, 2010), xi–xxvii

Debrett, Mary, 'Representing cultural diversity or serving local industry? An exploration of the future prospects of subsidised documentary', *International Journal of Diversity in Organisations, Communities and Nations*, vol. 5, no. 3, 2006, 94–101

Debrett, Mary, 'Branding documentary: New Zealand's minimalist solution to cultural subsidy', *Media, Culture and Society*, vol. 26, no. 1, 2004, 5–23

Dennis, Jonathan & Jan Bieringa (eds), *Film in Aotearoa New Zealand* (Wellington: Victoria University Press, 1992)

Edgerton, Gary, 'Ken Burns's rebirth of a nation: Television, narrative and popular history', *Film and History*, vol. 22, no. 4, 1992, 118–33

Evans, Jennifer, 'Making of Orakau Battle film was major event in district', *Footprints of History*, vol. 12, 1994, 20–23

Fox, Alistair, 'Rudall Hayward and the cinema of Maoriland: Genre-mixing and counter-discourses in *Rewi's Last Stand* (1925), *The Te Kooti Trail* (1927) and *Rewi's Last Stand/The Last Stand* (1940)', in Alistair Fox, Barry Keith Grant & Hilary Radner (eds), *New Zealand Cinema: Interpreting the past* (Bristol: Intellect, 2011), 45–64

Harris, Kenneth Marc, 'American film genres and non-American films: A case study of *Utu*', *Cinema Journal*, vol. 29, no. 2, 1990, 36–59

Hilliard, Chris, 'James Cowan and the frontiers of New Zealand history', *New Zealand Journal of History*, vol. 31, no. 2, 1997, 219–33

Lacey, Cherie, 'Unsettled historiography: Postcolonial anxiety and the burden of the past in *Pictures*', in Alistair Fox, Barry Keith Grant & Hilary Radner (eds), *New Zealand Cinema: Interpreting the past* (Bristol: Intellect, 2011), 99–118

Macassey, Olivia, 'Cross-currents: *River Queen*'s national and trans-national heritages', in Alistair Fox, Barry Keith Grant & Hilary Radner (eds), *New Zealand Cinema: Interpreting the past* (Bristol: Intellect, 2011), 119–34

———, 'The edge of tears: Vincent Ward's *Rain of the Children*', *Illusions*, no. 41, 2009, 3–7

McAloon, Jim, 'By which standards? History and the Waitangi Tribunal', *New Zealand Journal of History*, vol. 40, no. 2, 2006, 194–213

Mita, Merata, 'The soul and the image', in Dennis & Bieringa (eds), *Film in Aotearoa New Zealand* (Wellington: Victoria University Press, 1992)

Newton, John, 'Becoming Pākehā', *Landfall*, no. 218, 2009, 38–48

Nicholson, Roger, 'Romancing the past: History, love, and genre in Vincent Ward's *River Queen*', *Journal of Popular Romance Studies*, vol. 2, no. 1, 2011

O'Malley, Vincent, 'A tale of two rangatira: Rewi Maniapoto, Wiremu Tamihana and the Waikato War', *Journal of the Polynesian Society*, vol. 125, no. 4, 2016, 341–57

———, '"Recording the incident with a monument": The Waikato War in historical memory', *Journal of New Zealand Studies*, no. 19, 2015, 89

Oliver, W.H, 'The future behind us: The Waitangi Tribunal's retrospective Utopia', in Andrew Sharp & Paul McHugh (eds), *Histories, Power and Loss: Uses of the past: A New Zealand commentary* (Wellington: Bridget Williams Books, 2001), 1–26

Orr, Bridget, 'Birth of a nation? From *Utu* to *The Piano*', in Felicity Coombs & Suzanne Gemmell (eds), *Piano Lessons: Approaches to* The Piano (Sydney: John Libbey, 1999), 148–60

Perrott, Lisa, 'Rethinking the documentary audience: Reimagining the New Zealand Wars', *Media International Australia*, no. 104, 2002, 67–79

Pivac, Diane, 'New Zealand film pioneer: Hilda Maud Hayward (1898–1970)', *Screening the Past*, no. 40, 2015: www.screeningthepast.com/2015/08/new-zealand-film-pioneer-hilda-maud-hayward–1898–1970

Pötzch, Holger, 'Difficult pasts: Two documentary dramas on Bloody Sunday, Derry 1972', *Memory Studies*, vol. 5, 2011, 206–22

Pugsley, Chris, 'Maori did not invent trench warfare', *New Zealand Defence Quarterly*, 1998, 33–34

Sklar, Robert, 'Rudall Hayward, New Zealand film-maker', *Landfall*, vol. 98, 1971, 147–52

Walker, Ranginui, 'State of the nation', *NZ Listener*, 21 February 2004)

White, Hayden, 'Historiography and historiophoty', *American Historical Review*, vol. 93, no. 5, 1988, 119–99

Books

Aleiss, Angela, *Making the White Man's Indian: Native Americans and Hollywood movies* (Westport: Praeger, 2005)

Babington, Bruce, *A History of the New Zealand Fiction Feature Film* (Manchester: Manchester University Press, 2007)

Barclay, Barry, *Our Own Image* (Auckland: Longman Paul, 1990)

Belgrave, Michael, *Dancing with the King: The rise and fall of the King Country, 1864–1885* (Auckland: Auckland University Press, 2017)

Belgrave, Michael, *Historical Frictions: Maori claims and reinvented histories* (Auckland: Auckland University Press, 2005)

Belich, James, *I Shall Not Die: Titokowaru's War, New Zealand 1868–1869* (Wellington: Allen & Unwin/Port Nicholson Press, 1989)

———, *The New Zealand Wars and the Victorian Interpretation of Racial Conflict* (Auckland: Auckland University Press, 1986)

Bennett, James E. & Rebecca Beirne, *Making Film and Television Histories: Australia and New Zealand* (London: I.B. Tauris, 2012)

Binney, Judith, *Encircled Lands: Te Urewera, 1820–1921* (Wellington: Bridget Williams Books, 2009)

———, *Redemption Songs: A life of Te Kooti Arikirangi Te Turuki* (Auckland/Wellington: Auckland University Press/Bridget Williams Books, 1995)

Binney, Judith & Gillian Chaplin, *Ngā Mōrehu/The Survivors: The life histories of eight Māori women* (Auckland: Oxford University Press, 1986)

Binney, Judith, Gillian Chaplin & Craig Wallace, *Mihaia: The Prophet Rua Kenana and his community at Maungapohatu* (Auckland: Oxford University Press, 1979)

Blythe, Martin, *Naming the Other: Images of the Maori in New Zealand film and television* (Metuchen, NJ: Scarecrow Press, 1994)

Braithwaite, Errol, *The Evil Day* (London: Collins, 1967)

———, *The Flying Fish* (London: Collins, 1964)

———, *The Needle's Eye* (London: Collins, 1965)

Bruno, Frank, *Black Noon at Ngutu* (London: R. Hale, 1960)

Burgoyne, Robert, *Film Nation: Hollywood looks at U.S. History* (Minneapolis: University of Minnesota Press, 1997)

Byrnes, Giselle, *The Waitangi Tribunal and New Zealand History* (Auckland: Oxford University Press, 2004)

Campbell, Russell, *Observations: Studies in New Zealand documentary* (Wellington: Victoria University Press, 2011)

Conrich, Ian & Stuart Murray (eds), *New Zealand Film-makers* (Detroit: Wayne State University Press, 2007)

Dalton, B.J., *War and Politics in New Zealand 1855–1870* (Sydney: Sydney University Press, 1967)

Dawson, Graham, *Making Peace with the Past? Memory, trauma, and the Irish Troubles* (Manchester: Manchester University Press, 2007)

Dunleavy, Trisha, *Ourselves in Primetime: A history of New Zealand television drama* (Auckland: Auckland University Press, 2005)

Dunleavy, Trisha & Hester Joyce, *New Zealand Film and Television: Institution, industry and cultural change* (Bristol: Intellect Books, 2011)

Dyer, Richard, *White* (London: Routledge, 1997)

Evans, Brad & Aaron Glass (eds), *Return to the Land of the Headhunters: Edward S. Curtis, the Kwaka'wakw, and the making of modern cinema* (Seattle: University of Washington Press, 2014)

Fleming, Dan, *Making the Transformational Moment in Film: Unleashing the power of the image* (Los Angeles: Michael Wiese Productions, 2011)

Fox, Alistair, Barry Keith Grant & Hilary Radner (eds), *New Zealand Cinema: Interpreting the past* (Bristol: Intellect Books, 2011)

Gentry, Kynan, *History, Heritage and Colonialism: Historical consciousness, Britishness and cultural identity in New Zealand, 1870–1940* (Manchester: Manchester University Press, 2015)

Green, David, *Battlefields of the New Zealand Wars: A visitor's guide* (Auckland: Penguin, 2010)

Halbwachs, Maurice, *On Collective Memory*, trans. Lewis A. Coser (Chicago: University of Chicago, 1992)

Harris, Aroha, *Hikoi: Forty years of Maori protest* (Wellington: Huia, 2004)

Hjort, Mette & Duncan Petrie (eds), *The Cinema of Small Nations* (Edinburgh: Edinburgh University Press, 2007)

Hokowhitu, Brendan & Vijay Devadas (eds), *The Fourth Eye: Māori media in Aotearoa New Zealand* (Minneapolis: University of Minnesota Press, 2013)

Holman, Jeffrey Paparoa, *Best of Both Worlds: The story of Elsdon Best and Tutakangahau* (Auckland: Penguin, 2010)

Hooks, Bell, *Black Looks: Race and Representation* (Boston: South End Press, 1992)

Horrocks, Roger, *Re-inventing New Zealand: Essays on the arts and the media* (Pokeno: Atuanui Press, 2016)

Jaikumar, Priya, *Cinema at the End of Empire: A politics of transition in Britain and India* (Durham: Duke University Press, 2006)

Kawharu, Hugh, *Waitangi: Maori and Pakeha perspectives of the Treaty of Waitangi* (Auckland: Oxford University Press, 1989)

Keenan, Danny (ed.), *Terror in our Midst? Searching for terror in Aotearoa New Zealand* (Wellington: Huia, 2008)

Keenan, Danny, *Te Whiti o Rongomai and the Resistance of Parihaka* (Wellington: Huia Books, 2015)

———, *Wars Without End: The Land Wars in nineteenth-century New Zealand* (Auckland: Penguin, 2006)

Kilpatrick, Jacquelyn, *Celluloid Indians: Native Americans and film* (Lincoln: University of Nebraska Press, 1999)

King, Michael, *Te Puea: A biography* (Auckland: Hodder & Stoughton, 1977)

Limbrick, Peter, *Making Settler Cinemas: Film and colonial encounters in the United States, Australia, and New Zealand* (NY: Palgrave Macmillan, 2010)

Little, Paul, *Temuera Morrison: From haka to Hollywood* (Auckland: Penguin, 2009)

Marubbio, M. Elise, *Killing the Indian Maiden: Images of Native American women in film* (Lexington: University Press of Kentucky, 2006)

Miller, Harold, *Race Conflict in New Zealand* (Wellington: Blackwood & Janet Paul, 1966)

Mulgan, Alan, 'Cowan's history of the Maori Wars', in *Great Days in New Zealand Writing* (Wellington: A.H. & A.W. Reed, 1962)

Murphy, Geoff, *Geoff Murphy: A life on film* (Auckland: HarperCollins, 2015)

O'Malley, Vincent, *The Great War for New Zealand* (Wellington: Bridget Williams Books, 2016)

Orange, Claudia, *The Treaty of Waitangi* (Wellington: Allen & Unwin/Port Nicholson Press, 1987)

Petrie, Duncan, *Shot in New Zealand: The art and craft of the Kiwi cinematographer* (Auckland: Random House, 2007)

Pivac, Diane, with Frank Stark & Lawrence McDonald (eds), *New Zealand Film: An illustrated history* (Wellington: Te Papa Press, 2011)

Poata, Tama Te Kapua, *Poata – Seeing beyond the Horizon: A memoir* (Wellington: Steele Roberts, 2012)

Pope, Diana & Jeremy Pope, *Mobil South Island Travel Guide* (Auckland: Penguin, 1995)

——, *North Island: Penguin New Zealand travel guide* (Auckland: Penguin, 2009)

Prickett, Nigel, *Landscapes of Conflict: A field guide to the New Zealand Wars* (Auckland: Random House NZ, 2002)

Rosenstone, Robert A., *History on Film/Film on History* (Harlow: Pearson, 2006)

Ryan, Tim & Bill Parham, *The Colonial New Zealand Wars* (Wellington: Grantham House, 1986)

Said, Edward, *Culture and Imperialism* (NY: Knopf, 1993)

Salesa, Damon Ieremia, *Racial Crossings: Race, intermarriage, and the Victorian British Empire* (Oxford: Oxford University Press, 2011)

Scott, Dick, *Ask That Mountain: The story of Parihaka* (Auckland: Heinemann/Southern Cross, 1975)

——, *The Parihaka Story* (Auckland: Southern Cross Books, 1954)

Shadbolt, Maurice, *Monday's Warriors* (Auckland: Hodder & Stoughton, 1990)

——, *The House of Strife* (London/Auckland: Bloomsbury/Hodder & Stoughton, 1993)

——, *Season of the Jew* (London: Hodder & Stoughton, 1986)

Shepard, Deborah, *Reframing Women: A history of New Zealand film* (Auckland: Harper Collins, 2000)

Simpson, Tony, *Te Riri Pakeha: The white man's anger* (Martinborough: Alister Taylor, 1979)

Sinclair, Keith, *A Destiny Apart: New Zealand's search for national identity* (Wellington: Unwin Paperbacks/Port Nicholson Press, 1986)

——, *A History of New Zealand* (London: Oxford University Press, 1959)

——, *The Origins of the Maori Wars* (Wellington: New Zealand University Press, 1957; 2nd edn 1961)

Smith, Jo, *Māori Television: The first ten years* (Auckland: Auckland University Press, 2016)

Sole, Tony, *Ngāti Ruanui: A history* (Wellington: Huia, 2005)

Tapsell, Paul (ed.), *Ko Tawa: Maori treasures of New Zealand* (Auckland: David Bateman, 2006)

Vitali, Valentina & Paul Willemen (eds), *Theorising National Cinema* (London: British Film Institute, 2006)

Walker, Ranginui, *Ka Whawhai Tonu Mātou: Struggle Without End* (Auckland: Penguin, 1990)

Wanhalla, Angela, *Matters of the Heart: A history of interracial marriage in New Zealand* (Auckland: Auckland University Press, 2013)

Ward, Alan, *A Show of Justice: Racial 'amalgamation' in nineteenth century New Zealand* (Auckland: Auckland University Press, 1973)

Ward, Vincent with Alison Carter, Geoff Chapple & Louis Nowra, *The Edge of the Earth: Stories and images from the antipodes* (Auckland: Heinemann Reed, 1990)

Ward, Vincent with Lani-Rain Feltham & Louis Nowra, *The Past Awaits: People, images, film* (Nelson: Craig Potton, 2010)

Wards, Ian, *The Shadow of the Land: A study of British policy and racial conflict in New Zealand 1932–1852* (Wellington: Historical Branch, Internal Affairs, 1968)

Webster, Peter, *Rua and the Maori Millennium* (Wellington: Victoria University Press, 1979)

Wolfe, Patrick, *Settler Colonialism and the Transformation of Anthropology: The politics and poetics of an ethnographic event* (London: Cassell, 1999)

Wright, Matthew, *Two Peoples, One Land: The New Zealand Wars* (Auckland: Reed, 2006)

White, Hayden, *Tropics of Discourse: Essays in cultural criticism* (Baltimore: Johns Hopkins, 1978)

Young, Robert, *White Mythologies: Writing history and the West* (London: Routledge, 1990)

Dictionary of Biography and Encyclopedia

Belich, James, 'McDonnell, Thomas': www.teara.govt.nz/en/biographies/1m33/mcdonnell-thomas

Blainey, Ann & Mary Lazarus, 'Rusden, George William (1819–1903)' *Australian Dictionary of Biography*, vol. 6 (Melbourne: Melbourne University Press, 1976)

Gilling, Bryan D., 'George Hamilton-Browne': www.teara.govt.nz/en/biographies/2h10/hamilton-browne-george

Temara, Pou, 'Te Pairi Tuterangi': www.teara.govt.nz/en/biographies/3t16/te-pairi-tuterangi

ACKNOWLEDGEMENTS

This book has taken too long, of course, but it has been a great journey. On the way I interviewed, talked with, and consulted many talented and knowledgeable people. They generously shared their mātauranga and, in the process, gave me an education upon which this work rests. These people are included in the list of interviewees in the bibliography, so I will not name them separately now: they are the people who helped to make the films, and the people whose whanaunga were caught up in the past that the films are about. Through them I was taken into the world of filmmaking, into stories of the past and how colonial warfare still resonates today, and into rich accounts of the many ways that te ao pikitia and te ao Māori have encountered each other. He mihi nunui ki a koutou katoa. I have tried to ensure that your knowledge is reflected in this book, that your contributions are made apparent and your voices are heard often in its pages.

Several people have been touchstones and sounding boards throughout this long project. Catherine Fitzgerald provided advice and many useful pieces of information as well as her delicious food and a bed in Wellington. Diane Pivac smoothed my path in many ways and shared her great knowledge of Rudall Hayward with me. Helen and Alun Bollinger were a generous source of knowledge about the film world. Angela Wanhalla and Lachy Paterson have been ready sources of advice. Tom Roa gave his quiet, thoughtful comments. Paerau Warbrick was, as ever, an astonishing fund of information about the Bay of Plenty; Hilary Radner was similarly informative about the intricacies and the big picture of film. Helen and Alun Bollinger, Melissa Cross, Erik Olssen, Diane Pivac, Tom Roa, Mark Seymour and Paerau Warbrick all did me the favour of reading and commenting on different parts of the book. (Remaining faults are, of course, my own.)

My dear friends and writing compadres Barbara Brookes and Mark Seymour nursed my ego, banished my doubts, and made me stop for lunch – Mark often made it, which always improved the day. I count myself lucky to belong to a supportive department (my thanks go to Chris Brickell, Rebecca Stringer, Fairleigh Gilmour, Marcelle Dawson, Patrick Vakaoti and Hugh Campbell as well as all the rest), with wonderful support staff (Bronwyn Craig, Pam Jemmett and Helen O'Sullivan). The Centre for Research on Colonial Culture and my friends and colleagues there, Tony Ballantyne, Lachy Paterson and Angela Wanhalla, nurtured the project in many ways. Also at the University of Otago, Takashi

Shogimen, Paola Voci and Catherine Fowler; and further afield, Minette Hillyer, Lynn Jenner, Danny Keenan, Bronwyn Labrum, Charlotte McDonald, Jock Phillips and Bridget Williams – have all provided various kinds of encouragement, information and practical assistance.

I would also like to thank Ellen Pullar, a stellar research assistant; Catherine Smith, who undertook heroic bibliographic and proofreading labours; and Cam Olssen, who wheeled in cheerfully to do last-minute cross-checking.

This book could not have happened without the resources of Ngā Taonga Sound and Vision, and I am indebted in many ways to that institution's staff: as well as Diane Pivac, whom I have mentioned, Lawrence Wharerau and Honiana Love, especially but not only for helping me to find the right people to interview; Mish Muagututi`a, Steve Russell, Kiri Griffin, Owen Mann and Tania Loughlin for help with archives, and accessing images. Special thanks are due to Kurt Otzen for his superb work in creating the beautiful frame enlargements for the earlier chapters.

Kim Baker of NZ On Screen appeared like an angel just when I despaired of accessing many of the images, providing me with a long list of contacts and illuminating the complexities of copyright law. NZ On Screen was a miracle in its own right: over the course of the project several productions that had formerly been accessible only through a pre-arranged visit to Avalon in Lower Hutt appeared online, and so did NZ On Screen's excellent screentalk series, a great asset for researchers.

Lesley Mensah of TVNZ assisted with permissions to reproduce TVNZ material; Trisha Dunleavy's advice was also helpful in this regard. Staff of the Alexander Turnbull Library once again earned my gratitude, especially my friends Ariana Tikao and Paul Diamond. Thank you to Rohi Kaimārama, Tapara Reid-Hiakita and Hamish Petengell for their manaakitanga at Whakatāne Museum, and Kat Jehly and Stephanie Lambert at Te Awamutu Museum. The Auckland Institute and Museum assisted with images from their collection, and the Hocken Collection staff were, as always, invaluable in providing access to periodicals. I give warm thanks to Christy Paterson of the University of Otago Library, a deeply appreciated ally for many years. Lloyd Walker and his team at the Audio-Visual Unit, University of Otago, compensated for my technical naiveté as I created frame enlargements for the later chapters.

*

Many individuals, whānau and organisations granted me permission to reproduce their images, some of taonga and tīpuna: this book is as much a visual as a written story, and I could not have achieved this without the support of these kaitiaki. I acknowledge them formally in the image credits, but I thank them warmly here. Several people went out of their way to provide images directly or helped me with access, especially Helen Bollinger, Graeme Cowley, Stephen Ellis, Peter Janes, Colin McRae, John Milligan, Geoff Murphy, Gerd Pohlmann and Gaylene Preston. My thanks especially to Graeme Cowley and Park Road Post for the cover image. Other people introduced me to interviewees and contacts, gave advice on specific matters or helped with access to documents: my thanks go to Russell Campbell, Te Rau Oriwa Davis, Dean Parker, Gaylene Preston, Natalie Robertson, Pou Temara and Che Wilson, among others. Tēnā koutou katoa.

The project has benefitted enormously from ongoing and generous support from the University of Otago, through research grants from the Humanities and Otago research committees, a Prestigious Writing Grant that provided teaching relief for a semester, and two periods of research leave. A residency early in the project at the Stout Centre, Victoria University, gave me valuable time in Wellington, and the History Department at Waikato University hosted me for two months, allowing fieldwork in the central North Island.

Otago University Press sent the manuscript to three superb readers who all waived their anonymity – Michael Belgrave, Vincent O'Malley and Jo Smith. They wrote searching and insightful reports, and provoked the book into better shape. The press itself has once again been superb to work with, and in this case patient and tolerant as well as talented. I am grateful to Rachel Scott for her ongoing confidence. To Fiona Moffat, Gillian Tewsley, Imogen Coxhead and the rest of the team at Otago University Press: thank you for your fantastic work. It has been a privilege to be in your skilful hands.

Friends in other cities put me up and asked about my work: Cathy Lee and Richard Olssen, Karen Salmon and Paul Goulter, Susie Clark, and Maureen Molloy and Doug Sutton. My mother Joey Cooper and sisters Sandy and Mary Cooper and their families have been there for the long haul providing food, transport, love and fun, and keeping me well shod and clad. Thanks!

*

To those nearest, I owe the most. To Erik Olssen, thank you for warm love, excellent company, intellectual nourishment and challenge, and many domestic labours; but especially, for your faith in the work. To Cam Olssen and Susie Olssen: this project went on hold for a decade as you arrived and grew. There was never a more welcome delay. You are the best kids ever, and this book is for you and your dad.

Images

Almost all the images included here were created especially for this book. Wherever possible, I have sought to access images through the copyright holders. All the early productions were accessed through Ngā Taonga Sound and Vision, with permissions gained from kaitiaki where appropriate and images created at Ngā Taonga. For later productions, some images have been obtained through the purchase of licenses from the copyright holders, and for the rest I created frame enlargments under the copyright waiver. Except for professional actors, I contacted Māori subjects, or their descendants, for permission to reproduce images, and I thank them for their consent, which is acknowledged specifically in the credit lines. Where I have not gained consent I have not included images, with one exception: that of Napi Waaka in chapter 3. Reverend Waaka passed away before I could ask for his consent, but I was confident from the tone of my earlier interview with him, that he would have liked to be included in the book.

Acknowledgements

An earlier version of sections of chapter 5 has appeared in 'Televisual memory and the New Zealand Wars: Bicultural identities, masculinity and landscape', *European Journal of Cultural Studies*, 14 (2011), 446–65; and sections of chapters 3, 5 and 8 in 'Tracking Tītokowaru over text and screen: Pākehā narrate the warrior, 1906–2005', in A. Fox, B.K. Grant and H. Radner (eds), *New Zealand Cinema: Interpreting the past* (Bristol: Intellect Books, 2011), 135–52.

INDEX

Page numbers in **bold** refer to illustrations.

1846 War in Wellington app 267

Aberdein, Keith 94, 95, 106, 107–08, 110, 117, 118, 122, 126, 130, 132, 142, 143, 145, 154, 156
activism 95, 130–33, 134
actors 106, 109; professional actors 28, 80, 136, 212, 221, 235; *see also* casting; heroes and heroines; Māori actors; and names of individual actors
Albert, Gerrard 226, 228, 235, 245
Albert Park, Auckland 177
Alien Weaponry, *Raupatu* (song) 263, **264**, 265
Amohanga, R. 71
Anderson, Rovina Maniapoto 170
Anderson, Waimārama 34, 250, **261**
Animation Research 174, 175, 269, 270
Anzac Day 163, 250; RNZ coverage of New Zealand Wars, 2016 268
Aotearoa pā, Arohena 74
Arawa Contingent, Arawa Flying Column 12, 38–39, 52, 55, 56–57, 58, 59
Avalon studios, TV One 122
Awatere, Donna, *Maori Sovereignty* 95

Babington, Bruce 34, 35, 38, 58, 78, 236
Bailey, Chris 186, 188, 189
Barclay, Barry 92, 96, 124, 167, 201, 248
Barry, Alister 133
Bastion Point 95, 123, 124, 131, 133
Bastion Point – Day 507 **130**, 130–31

Battle of Gate Pā Told with Sand, The (sand-box projection) **258**, 258–59
Baxter, James K. 204, 206
Bay of Plenty 10, 12, 26, 54, 58, 67, 140
BBC 183, 184, 185–86, 188, 190
Belgrave, Michael 18
Belich, James 17, 18, 19, 22, 23, 74, 126, 159–60, 161, **168**, **173**, 192, 203–05, 232, 263, 274, 278; *I Shall Not Die: Titokowaru's War, New Zealand* 17, 159, 162–63, 231, 234, 235, 244, 276; *The New Zealand Wars* (book) 159, 162, 163–64, 167, 170, 179; *see also New Zealand Wars, The* (documentary series)
Bell, Leah 34, 250, **261**
Bennett, Cameron 269
Bennett, Michael 196, 254
Bennett, Simon 269
Bent, Kimble 15, 17, 99, 100, 101, 102, 163, 189, 231, 233, 234, 238, 278
Best, Elsdon 98, 203
Beyond International 183
Binney, Judith 17, 18, 61, 197, 198, 200, 203, 204, 207, 210, 217, **219**, 220–21, 224, 254; *Mihaia* 209, 210, **211**; *Ngā Mōrehu* 209, 232
Black, Awanuiārangi 257, 268
Black, Michael, *Pictures* 126–27
Black Robe (feature film) 236
Black, Sebastian **219**
Black, Taiarahia 222, 224
Black, Whirimako 176

Blakeney, Don 129
Blaxendale, Jack 72
Blythe, Martin 35, 78
Bodle, Frank 47
Boldrewood, Rolf 16
Bolger, Jim 261
Bollinger, Alun 202, 214, 226, 228, 229, 235, 236, 244
Booth, Captain 169
Boulcott's Farm, Battle of 173
Bourne, George 208, 217
Braithwaite, Errol 16, 97, 236
Bridge, The: A story of men in dispute (documentary) 131, **131**
Bristowe, Tania **20**, 140, **146**, 157
Broadcasting Commission of New Zealand (BCNZ) 32, 96, 160; *see also* New Zealand Broadcasting Corporation (NZBC); NZ On Air
Browne, Thomas Gore 74, 166
Brunning, Nancy 187
Bruno, Frank 16
Buck, Peter (Te Rangi Hīroa) 40
Buick, Lindsay 14
Buist, Alastair 98
Burke, Vincent 196
Burns, Ken, *The Civil War* 160, 161, 164, 168, 175, 191
Burton, Alfred 239; *Through the King Country with a Camera* 126–27
Burton, Walter 127, 239

Butcher, Margot 228–29
Byrnes, Giselle 18
Byrt, Anthony 224

Calder, Peter 244
Cameron, Duncan 10, 87, 117–18, **118**, 119–20, 121, 122, 167, 275
Campbell, Russell 124, 133
Campion, Richard 110, 123
Carr, Leo 98
Casselli, Nola 42
casting 8; and appeal to international markets 186–87; appropriateness of actors 28, 54, 55, 59–61, 69, 72, 73, 79, 80, 107; documentaries 28; fiction features 28; *The Governor* 28, 106, 107–08, 248; *Rewi's Last Stand* (with sound, 1940) 69, 70, 71, 72, 73, 79–81; *The Te Kooti Trail* 54–57, 59–61; *see also* actors; Māori actors
censorship 63, 64–65, 66
centennial of Treaty of Waitangi signing 68, 72
Chaplin, Gillian 17; *Mihaia* 209, 210; *Ngā Mōrehu* 209, 232
Chatham Islands (Wharekauri) 10, 12, 63, 254
children and youth 13, 28, 66, 70, 78, 82, 85, 87, 90, 98, 99, 103, 113, **120–21**, 124, 129, 149, 158, 178, 182, 194, 196, 203, 206–08, 210–12, 214, 217, 219, 22–22, 233, 235–36, **242**, 249, 252–53, 256, 260, 262, 272, 274, 278, 282, 298; images frontispiece, **120**, **121**, **139**, **147**, **207**, **213**, **215**, **237**, **242**, **243**, **252**, **255**, **261**, **266**, **271**; *see also Rain of the Children* and *Tātarakihi: The children of Parihaka*
Clayton, Hamish 17
Close to Home (television series) 105
collaboration in filmmaking 8, 25–27, 34, 38, 59, 93, 247, 248, 250, 273, 280; *The Governor* 106–09, 114, 116, 124, 126; *Greenstone* 185–86; *The Killing of Kane* 124, 126; *The New Zealand Wars* 164, 169–70, 176; *NZ Wars: Stories of Ruapekapeka* 269; *Rain of the Children* 218–21, **219**, 224; *Rewi's Last Stand* 68–70, 72, 73, 74, 86; *River Queen* 225–26, 228, 232, 241–42, 244–46; *Utu* 133–37; *Waka Huia* 257; *see also*

cultural and historical advisors; international funding, co-production and markets
colonial history: changing ideologies 22, 26, 117, 119, 129, 139, 273, 275–76; critique 29, 30, 123; divisions and injustices 8–9, 13, 16, 17, 18, 93, 95, 123, 162, 197, 200, 274–75, 280; George Grey 105–06, 275; 'good colonial and bad imperial' 275; *Greenstone* 184–85, 186, 188–90; Hayward's portrayal 47, 51, 54, 93, 128–29; *Heart of Darkness* (Conrad) 236; Māori perspectives 108, 117, 123, 124, 126, 200; narratives of colonial expansion 37, 38; *Pictures* 127, 239; *The Prophets* 254, 255; *River Queen* 232–33, 236, 238–39, 246; settler-colonial legacy 25, 40, 68, 273, 274–75; Te Awamutu Historical Society approaches 69–70; *Utu* 128–29, 144, 155–56; *Von Tempsky's Ghost* 192, 194; *see also* decolonisation; Māori-Pākehā relationships
Communicado 183
Coney, Sandra 127, 239
Conrad, Joseph, *Heart of Darkness* 236
Cooper, Whina 95
costume drama 183, 184–85, 188, 189
Coubray, Ted 37, 42, 61; *The Te Kooti Trail* **6**
Cowan, James 13–14, **15**, 18, 22, 64–65, 76, 98, 208; 'A Bush Court Martial' 140–45, 150, 151, 152; *The Adventures of Kimble Bent* 15, 36, 40, 98, 99, 100, 231, 233; historical advisor, and present influence on films 15, 38, 40, 42, 43–44; linking of defence of Ōrākau with Battle of Britain lead-up 91; *The New Zealand Wars* 14–15, 39, 46, 47, 48, 49, 54, 58, 63, 69, 74, 82, 84, 85, 105, 129, 144, 159, 235; *The Old Frontier* 76; *Rewi's Last Stand* 73; *Settlers and Pioneers* 68, 89; *Tales of the Maori Bush* 141
Cowley, Graeme 135, 157
creative control 24–27, 274–75; documentaries 9, 27, 130; international co-production 33, 184, 185–86, 188; Māori 9, 25, 27, 130, 154, 157, 217, 225–26, 247–63, 272, 275, 280–81; *see also* actors; directors; Māori actors
creative freedom 25
crew, Māori 26, 27, 134, 138–39, 247

Cross, Melissa 35, 84
cultural and historical advisors 8, 15, 25–26, 70, 126, 197, 225, 247, 280; *The Governor* 106–09, 114, 116, 124, 126; *Greenstone* 184, 186–87, 188, 189, 190; *The Killing of Kane* 102, 124, 126; *Rain of the Children* 205, 207, 210, 217; *Rewi's Last Stand* 40, 73, 74, 80–81; *River Queen* 225, 226, 228; *Utu* 134, 135, 136–37, 138, 139
Curtis, Cliff 228, 230, **237**, 243–44, 248, 274, 278

Davis, Te Rau Oriwa 102–03
Debrett, Mary 35, 161, 180
decolonisation 16–17, 22, 29, 94–95, 273; and political documentary 130–33
Deleau, Pierre-Henri 155
Dennis, Jonathan 35
Dennison, Julian 249
Department of Conservation 267
deregulation 29, 32, 160–61, 182, 183, 191, 200
Diamond, Paul 178
Dibble, Warren, *The Killing of Kane* 97–104, 235
digital histories 265, 267
digital media and technologies 27, 248, 251, 272, 281; *see also* online content and streaming
directors 25, 30; impact of New Zealand Wars films on 26, 34, 106, 274; international productions 32, 33, 184, 188; Māori 24, 26–27, 92, 104, 130, 133, 134–35, 138–39, 154, 155, 157, 160, 164, 196, 247, 248, 281; Pākehā men 24–26, 34, 136–37, 280; women 24, 27, 92, 133, 248, 281; *see also* names of individual directors
documentaries 19, 22, 96, 97, 275; connections between Māori performers and iwi speakers and their tīpuna 28; growing market 27, 248; historical documentary 33, 161, 180, 182–83, 272; industry deregulation impacts 160–61, 182, 191, 200; Māori creative control 9, 130, 247, 248, 249–50, 268, 275, 278, 279; online 9, 251, 268–72; 'our stories' 28, 29, 191, 194; political documentaries 130–32; market pressures 182; short life of on-demand access 24; TV One's *Documentary New Zealand* series 191; as a 'vehicle for the

delivery of cultural rights' 161; *see also* titles of individual documentaries
Domett, Alfred 119
Donaldson, Roger, *Sleeping Dogs* 123, 155
Douglas, Graeme 123
Douglas, Megan 254
drone cameras 251, 270
Dunleavy, Trisha 35, 96, 110, 160, 189–90

East Coast 10, 12, 41, 138, 140
East Coast Wars 55, 105, 167
Eisenstein, Sergei 18
Elizabeth II, Queen 263
Elliott, Peter 197
Ellis, Ngārino 256
Ellis, Stephen 164, 174, 175
Ellison, Rāniera 253
Emslie, Barry **119**
Endgame (United States) 229
Epitaph (television series) 191
Eripitana meeting house 256
Evans, Anne 231, 233, 236, 238, 240
Evans, Ripeka 154

Film Consortium (Britain) 229
Film Fund *see* New Zealand Film Production Fund
films: absence of Māori-led films on New Zealand Wars 248–49; afterlife 24; fiction features 20–21, 26, 28, 32–33, 34; influx of transnational films 29; instruments of cultural change 26; international funding and markets 32–33, 40, 45, 156, 158, 228, 229, 275; 'our stories' 28–30, 32, 33, 38–39, 218, 275; portrayals of Māori 23; potential for creating national origin stories 18–19, 24, 274, 275; relationship to histories and memory 18–24, 93, 246, 249–50, 273–74; state-supported films 30, 129; 'tax shelter years' 30, 32, 129–30, 157–58; *see also* documentaries; historical drama; screen industries; television; westerns; and titles of individual films
Finlayson, Chris 34
Finney, Edmund 42, **43**, **44**
Fitzgerald, Catherine 214
FitzGerald, James Edward 14, 45, 82

FitzRoy, Robert 111, 166
Fleming, Dan 241
Flight of Te Hookioi, The (documentary) 9, 26, 27, 251
Forbes, Mihingārangi 24, 25, 28, 249, 250, 268, **270**, 281; *NZ Wars: Stories of Ruapekapeka* 9, 24, 268–72, **270**, **271**
Ford, John, *The Searchers* 236–38
Forest Rangers 12, 38–39, 42–43, 77–78, 88, 191, 194
Fox, William 119
Fraser, Alistair **264**, 265
Fraser, Toa 225
Frontier Films 38, 69, 70
Frontier of Dreams (documentary series) 17, 182, 196–200, **197**, **198**, **199**, 254
Fry, Alexander 103–04
Fullers 37
funding and budgets: historical documentary 33, 161, 182–83, 272; historical drama 182, 183, 225, 228–29, 248, 251; NZ On Air 160–61, 182, 183, 191, 196, 205, 259, 268; in the 1980s 129–30; screen industries 8, 30, 32–33, 34, 35, 129–30, 182, 228–29; tax breaks for feature films 30, 32, 129–30, 157–58; *see also* deregulation, international funding, co-production and markets; and under titles of individual productions

Gardiner, Irene 192
Gardiner, Sir Wira 259
Gate Pā *see* Pukehinahina (Gate Pā)
Gifford, Gavin 70
Gittins, Paul 191
globalisation 29, 32
Gloyne, Paraone 257, 268
go-between figures, cultural 21, 22–23, 75, 143, 233, 234, 240, 243, 249, 275–76, 278, 281
Goodbye Pork Pie (Murphy) 27, 129, 134
Gorst, John 74, 75, 113, 251
Gosden, Bill 154
Governor, The (television series) 9, 22, 23, 105–25, 159, 161, 163, 165, 167, 182–83, 197, 248, 250, 262, 275, 276, 279; aftermath 94, 97, 122–24, 183; audience 112, 179; awards 122; budget 30, 94, 105, 122, 194; casting 26–27, 28, 106, 107–09, 248, 276; compared to *Greenstone* 188; episodes 110–22; involvement of Māori communities in production 25, 106–09, 114, 116, 124, 126; locations 107; images **11**, **27**, **110**, **111**, **113**, **114**, **115**, **116**, **119**, **120**, **121**; te reo Māori 34, 117, 123
Grace, David, *Rua Kēnana* (song) 263
Graham, Doug 178
Great South Road 10, 74, **173**, 267
Great Southern Television 268
Green, David, *Battlefields of the New Zealand Wars* 267
Greenstone (television series) 33, 182, 183–91, **185**, **187**, **190**, 197, 200, 236, 276, 278; co-production with BBC 183, 184, 185–86, 188, 190, 200; international funding and sales considerations 183, 184, 187, 188, 189–90, 200
Grey, Eliza 110, 112, 122–23
Grey, George 16, 52, 54, 74, 93, 105–06, 110, 166, 167, 258, 262, 275, 278; 'Good Governor Grey' 94, 105, 112; *see also Governor, The* (television series)
Grierson, John 72, 90
Griffith, D.W., *Birth of a Nation* 18, 39, 57–58
Guerrin, Erihapeti 46, 47, 48, 49, 50, 52, 56, 57, 58–59
Guerrin, Jean 46, 48–49, 52, 53, 54, 59, 93
guidebooks 267

Haami, Brad 66, 259, 263
Haddon, Oriwa 98, 100
Haddon, Tahupōtiki 98, 100–01
Hairini 74
Hakaraia, Jacob 170
Hakaraia, Libby: *Hautoa Ma!* 27, 248; *The Prophets* 254
Halbwachs, Maurice 23–24
Hall, Ria 25; *Rules of Engagement* music video 24, 265, **266**
Hamer, D.A. 122
Hamilton, Arapeta 269
Hamilton-Browne, George: *Camp Fire Yarns of the Lost Legion* 16; *With the Lost Legion in New Zealand* 16, 47, 51–52

Hanly, Gil 208
Hare, Turuhira Julie 219–20
Harris, George, *Von Tempsky* 104, **104**
Haumēne, Te Ua 10, 254
Hautoa Ma! The rise of Māori cinema (documentary) 27, 248
Hawea-Stephens, Wiha Te Raki 228
Hāwera 98, 100, 101, 102, **125**
Hawes, Peter 190
Hawke's Bay 137
Hayward, Henry 37, 40
Hayward, Hilda 42, 81; *The Te Kooti Trail* **6**, 9, 46, 56
Hayward, Ramai 66, 72, 81, 89, 91, 92, 93, 148, 199; *To Love a Maori* 92
Hayward, Rudall 19, 22, 26, 28, 36, 66, 92, 126, 129, 248, 279; accountability to film shareholders 30; treatment of ordinary soldiers 38–39, 42–43, 50, 51–52, 275; concern for nationhood 39, 47–48, 65, 76, 78, 90, 92, 149; Cowan as advisor and source of information 15, 38, 39, 40, 42, 43–44, 46, 47, 58, 63, 70, 74, 76, 82, 84, 85, 86, 89, 93; influence and legacy 93, 275; interracial relations 29, 39, 40, 43, 44, 47–48, 52, 54, 59, 65, 72, 87, 89, 90, 92, 128–29, 153
Hayward, Rudall: films: *The Bloke from Freeman's Bay* 36; *On the Friendly Road* 69, 80; *To Love a Maori* 92; *My Lady of the Cave* 38; *see also Last Stand, The* (1949); *Rewi's Last Stand* (silent film, 1925); *Rewi's Last Stand* (with sound, 1940); *Te Kooti Trail, The* (Hayward)
Hei Tiki (feature film) 26
Heke Pōkai, Hōne 9, 17, 103, 107, 108, 110–11, 112, 163, 164, 171, 181, 232, 271
Hēnare, George 26, 106, **110**, 126, **187**
Hēnare, Hirini 269
Hēnare, Sir James 176, 181
Hēnare, Peeni 268, 269, 271
Henty, G.A. 16
Hērangi, Te Puea 40, 41, 70, 74, 89
Heretaunga, Wī 141–42
Heritage New Zealand 267; Māori Heritage team 267

Heritage Taranaki 267
heroes and heroines 37, 39, 46, 48, 53, 54, 59, 75, 88, 143, 144, 146, 152, 255, 278; colonial 39, 46, 48, 50–52, 53, **54**, 58, 75–78, 143–44, 152, 276; Māori 43, 47, 49, 50, 52, **54**, **57**, 58–60, 75–79, 88, 129, 140, 143–44, 146, 152, 186, 188, 234, 255, 278
heroism 8, 37–41, 44–45, 48, 50, 52, 53, **54**, 165, 180, 195, 285, 287, 291; at Ōrākau 29, 39, 40, 41–42, 43–45, **44**, 69, 70, 71, 72–73, **73**, 78–79, 80, 82–87, 90–91, **199**, 274, 279, 285; *Rewi's Last Stand* (silent film, 1925) 76; *Rewi's Last Stand* (with sound, 1940) 75, 76; *The Te Kooti Trail* 76
Herrick, Linda 190
Hetaraka, Te Warahi 269, 272
Hika, Hongi 185, 187
Hill, Alfred 72, 84, 88, 91
Hill, Connie 138
Hilliard, Chris 89
Hillman, Marewa 221
Hirschfeld, Carol 268
historical drama 182–83, 272; costs and funding 182, 183, 225, 228–29, 248, 251; international co-production 32–33, 183, 184, 188–90, 228, 229, 275; *see also* costume drama; and names of individual drama productions
historiography: New Zealand film and television 35; New Zealand Wars 14–18, 97, 122, 162–63, 232, 265, 267, 271
History of Britain, The (television series) 196
Hobson, William 111, 114
Hohaia, Te Miringa 194, 195
Hohepa, Huru 252
Holman, Jeffrey Paparoa 203
Horo, Horomona 264, 265
Horrocks, Roger 35, 160
Horton, Mike 157
Hotene, Steve 56, **57**
Hunt for the Wilderpeople (feature film) 249
Hunt, Tina **6**, 41, 43, **44**, **49**, 49–50, **50**, 54–55, **57**, 65

Iharaira or Israelites, images of 208–09, 217
Ihimaera, Witi 17, 154–55
In Spring One Plants Alone (documentary) 26, 201–05, 207, 211, 212, 214, 218, 222, 233, 246, **277**
international funding, co-production and markets: casting factors 186–87; creative control 32, 33, 184, 185–86, 188; films 32–33, 40, 45, 156, 158, 228, 229, 275; historical drama 32–33, 183, 184, 188–90, 228, 229, 275; television 32, 33, 183, 184, 187, 188, 189–90, 200, 275
intermarriage *see* Māori–Pākehā relationships
inter-tribal conflict 10, 12, 140–41, 167
Invicta (Britain) 229
Irish characters and Irishness **51**, 51–53, **55**, **59**, 188–89, 203, 222, 225, 229–31, 238–89, **242**, 275
Isaac, Tony 94, 95, 96, 105, 106–07, 108, 117, 122
Iti, Tame 222

Jackson, Bob and June 102
Jerusalem, Whanganui River 204, 206
Jervis, Alan 100, **101**
Johnston, Kelly 139, **146**
Johnstone, Kirsten 265
Jones, Pei Te Hurinui 80
Joseph, Paora Te Oti Takarangi 25; *Tātarakihi: The children of Parihaka* 9, 27, 252–54, 279
Joyce, Hester 35, 110, 160

Kaa, Hirini 254, 255, 256–57
Kaa, Hone 132
Kaa, Keri 108–09, 116
Kaa, Sylvia 28, 137, 154
Kaa, Wī Kuki 106, 157; *The Governor* 26, 106, 108, 109, **115**, **121**; *River Queen* 229, 230, **231**, 241; *Utu* and *Utu: Redux* 28, 136–37, 139, **150**, **151**, 154, 155, 157, 243
Kael, Pauline 155–56
Kākahi, Tohu 13, 161, 253, 254, 255
Kahi, Tearepa 25; *The Flight of Te Hookioi* (documentary) 9, 26, 27, 251; *Mt Zion* 249; *Poi E!* 249
Kane, Charles 98, 99, 100, 101
Kāpiti Island 166

INDEX

Karaitiana, Wiremu (Billy Christian) 175
Karetu, Sam 201
Katipa, Heeni 259
kaumātua and kuia, kōrero in documentaries and films 8, 96, 214, 249, 255, 257, 259, 269, 280
Kawana, Nicola 194
Kawiti, Te Ruki 9, 17, 107, 112, 161, 163, 165, 171, 181, 269, 271, 281
Keenan, Danny 17, 18, 194, 195, 243, 265
Kelly, Hemi 17
Kēnana Hepetipa, Rua 13, 61, 164, 171, 201, 202, 203, 207, 210, 211, 212, 220, 256; photographs of 208–09, 216, **216**, 217
Kenny, Katie 253
Kessell, Simone **185**, 186–87
Kightley, Oscar 249
Kihikihi 40, 69, 74; *see also* Ōrākau, Battle of
Kiingitanga, The (documentary) 8, 23, 259–63, **260**, **261**, **262**, 278
Killing of Kane, The (television drama) 9, 23, 30, 97–104, 124, 126, 161, 194, 231, 233, 234, 235, 275, 276, 279; images **99**, **100**, **101**, **103**, **125**
Kilpatrick, Jacquelyn 37
King Country *see* Rohe Pōtae, Te
King, Michael 96, 124, 154, 167
King, Mike 28, **191**, 192, 194, 195, 196
Kingi, Merewakana **49**, **50**, 55, **56**, 66
Kīngi, Wiremu *see* Te Rangitāke, Wiremu Kīngi
Kīngitanga 10, 41, 74, 75, 82, 89, 96, 107, 113, 116, 123, 166, 167, 176, 197, 250, 258, 274
Knight, Stanley **77**, 80
Knowles, Marc 154
Kofoed, Rick 236
Koha (television programme) 27
Kōhanga Reo ('language nest') movement 162
Kohiti Kohiti **255**
Kora, Robin **187**, **193**, 194
Korokī, King 70, 89
Kororāreka 9, 16, 170, 251
Kotahitanga 114, 203
kūpapa (Crown-allied) Māori 12, 14, 50, 52–53, 59, 137, 141, 167, 226, 228, 230, 234, 243, 250, 256, 278, 279
Kurosawa, Akira 140, 155

Lacey, Cherie 35, 127
Lakshman, Brandon **243**
land, Māori 75, 78, 91, 92, 98, 103, 105, 123, 137, 138, 149, 166, 189, 197–98, 234, 271, 272, 280; film locations 25, 171–73, 280; individualisation of titles 13, 88, 198, 200; land rights 29, 95, 96, 113–14, 117, 119–20, 123, 124, 126, 130, 250, 260, 263; primary cause of conflicts 18, 89, 99, 100, 116, 171, 258, 261, 275, 279; purchases 10, 14, 74, 110, 113, 114, 117, 122, 123, 166, 260, 261; *see also* landscape, raupatu (land confiscations), whenua
'Land Wars,' use of term 18, 108
Landmarks (television series) 124
Landscape 137, 140, 164, 168, 171–78, 197, 201, 221, 224, 226, 236, 238, 245, 256, 265, 267, 269–70, 272, 280; *see also* locations, historical *and* whenua
Last Stand, The (feature film) 72, 82, 84, 85, 87, 88, 89, 91–92, 93, 105, 120; see also *Rewi's Last Stand*
Lattin, Mike 183, 187
Lawrence, Bruno 95, 104, **104**, 139, **150**, 154
Lawrence, David 154
Lee-Harris, Annabelle 269
Leeming, Cedric 102
Leonard, Carmen 269, 271
Leone, Sergio 140, 154
Lesser, Anton **21**, 230, 241
Lichtner, Giacomo 23
Limbrick, Peter 26, 29, 35
Little Big Man (feature film) 23
locations, historical 25–26, 34, 59, 61, 66, 72–74, 98, 102, 107, 137, 169, 171–73, 175, 228, 254, 256, 273, 280
Longford, Raymond 37, 42
Lord, Arthur 51
Lord, Robert, *Pictures* 126–27
Lowe, Stephen 184, 185–86, 188

Macassey, Olivia 238
Macbeth, references to in *Utu* 140, 144, 150, 152, 154
Mahana 157

Mahuta, Nanaia 259
Mahuta, Robert 261, 263
Mair, Gilbert 12, 39, 41, 46–47, 48, 49, 50, 52, 53, 54, 56, 59, 69, 75, 129, 141, 142–43, 275
Mair, William 12, 80, 85, 86, 87, 120, 121
Makarini, Peka 47, 48, 52, 53, 56, **57**, 57–59, 63, **64**
Making Utu (documentary) **27**, 129, 133, **134**, **135**, 137, 138, **139**, 153, **157**, 225
Malcolm, Joe 25, 134, 135, **135**, 136, 137, 138, 139, 153
mana whenua 7, 8, 25, 26, 34, 73, 75, 102, 103, 130, 164, 173, 201, 232, 247, 273, 274
Mandler, Peter 19
Mane-Wheoki, Jonathan 66
Mangatāwhiri Stream 10, 117, 262
Māngere Bridge strike 131, **131**
Maniapoto, Rewi 69, 74, 80, 232, 276; defence of Ōrākau 40, 70, 85, 86–87, 91, 92, 93, 120, 121; *The Governor* 108, 113, 114, 116–17, 120, 121, 126; *The Kiingitanga* 262; *The New Zealand Wars* 167, 181; *see also Rewi's Last Stand*
Manning, David 154
Manuera, Monika 34, 46–47, 49–50, 52–53, 55, 57–59, 61, 76, 145–46, 278, 288, 293–94; images **49**, **50**, **57**, **59**
Māori economic independence, pre-war period 75, 77, 197, 271
Māori actors 95–96, 106; agency of 38, 77; connections to characters 8, 28, 37–38, 54–57, 69, 70, 72, 73, 79, 80–81, 96, 107–08, 126, 137, 158, 212, 276, 278; cast from different iwi 28, 41, 221, 224, 244; performance and production roles 8, 26–27, 126, 157, 247, 248; *see also* casting; heroes and heroines; and names of individual actors; women
Māori Land Court 198, 200, 250
Māori renaissance 29
Māori Television 27, 33, 159, 248, 250, 251, 254, 256, 259, 263, 272
Maori Theatre Trust 106
Maori War Films Ltd 38, 40
'Māori Wars,' use of term 16, 18
Māoriland Film Festival 248
Māoriland Hub, Ōtaki 181

Māori–Pākehā relationships: challenges to national myths 16, 29, 94, 95, 132, 165–66; changing understandings 8, 26, 35, 94–95, 96, 97, 98–99, 129, 133, 139, 275–76; Cowan's idealisation 16, 149; economic and social disparities 13, 70, 73, 89, 200, 263, 272; alliances, 1970s, 80s and 90s 133, 162, 203, 204–05; European settlers' dependence on Māori agriculture and trade 75, 77, 197; go-between figures 21, 143, 233, 234, 240, 243, 249, 275–76, 278, 281; *The Governor* 94, 108, 124; Hayward's films 29, 39, 40, 43, 44, 47–48, 52, 54, 59, 65, 72, 87, 89, 90, 92, 128–29, 153; interracial marriage and people of mixed descent 57–58, 75, 76, 78, 79, 108, 186–87, 231, 233, 238, 276, 278–79; and nationhood 128–29, 149, 153; *The New Zealand Wars* 165–66, 169–70, 180; Pākehā assimilation into Māori world 101, 231, 233–34, 236, 238–40; *River Queen* 231, 233–34, 236, 238–40, 241–42, 246; *Utu* 7, 128–29, 133, 134, 136, 145, 146, 149–50, 152, 153, 154, 155; views of mid-twentieth-century white New Zealand 23, 29, 94, 98, 132, 165; Waipā district 75, 76, 77; *see also* collaboration in filmmaking

Mareikura, Charles 228
Markey, Alexander 37
Martin, Janine 253
masculinity *see* men and masculinity
Matahī 201, 203, 205, 209, 211, 222, 256
Matatahi, Huirama 262
Matawhero 255
Matetu, J. 70
Maungapōhatu 13, 61, 164, 167, 171, 176, 201, 207–13, **211–13**, 214, 217–18, 222, 224, 256, 279, 282, 297; histories 208; images of 208–09, 212, **216**, 217; *see also* Tūhoe
Mauri (feature film) 157
Maxwell, Te Kahautu 268
Maxwell, Warren 255
McCahon, Colin 224
McDermott, Tom **49, 53**
McDonald, James 216, 217
McDonnell, Thomas 21, 42–43, 75, 99, 100, 234
McGarvey, Te Uru 219–20, **219**
McGee, Greg 182, 184, 185, 186, 187

McGlashan, Don and the Muttonbirds 162
McLean, Donald 114, 1116
McLean, Edward Baker *see* Makarini, Peka
McNeilage, Dermot **104**
McRae, Colin 160, 161, 164, 170, 175, 179, 200, 269
Méliès, Gaston 37, 41
memory, forgetting, memorials and commemoration 9, 13–14, 16, 19, 23–24, 28, 30, 34, 39–40, 45–50, 52–55, 58–60, 63, 65, 66, 68, 82, 85, 90–91, 93, 94, 97, 110, 112, 119–20, 128, 137, 153, 157–58, 163, 168–69, 178, 179, **191**, 196, 201, 203–05, 207, 222, 224, 226, 246, 249, 250–55, 257–58, 261, 267–68, 272–74, 276, 281; *see also* New Zealand Wars, relationship between films, histories and memory
men and masculinity 75, 153, 160, 180, 232, 276; colonial 38–39, 42–43, 48, 51–54, 75, 143; Māori warriors and fighters 23, 163–64, 278; Native Americans 23; *see also* directors, New Zealand Wars troops, *and* heroes and heroines
Menehira, Makuini 114
Mikaere, Buddy **197**, 198
Milligan, John 182, 191–92, 194
Milroy, Wharehuia 207, 257
Ministry of Culture and Heritage 267
Mission, The (feature film) 236
missionaries 112
Mita, Merata 25, 92, 130, 131, 133, 134, **134**, 135, 136, 138, 139, 140, 153, 157, 222, 281; 'The Soul and the Image' 28, 247–48
Mōhaka 141–42
Monika, *see* Manuera, Monika
Morgan, John 74, 75, 76, 77, 78, 88, 93
Morgan, Tukoroirangi 259, 263
Morrison, Temuera 210, **211**, **213**, 221, 228, 229, 230, **234**, 235–36, 244
Morton, Samantha 229, 230, **237**, **239**, 239–42, **241**, 244
Moturoa Pā 12
Muldoon, Robert 94, 95, 105, 122, 123, 129
Murphy, Geoff 21, 29, 95, **125**, **135**, 281; *Goodbye Pork Pie* 27, 129, 134, 153; *Uenuku* 96, 137; *see also Utu* (Murphy)
music video 9, 24, 263–65
Musket Wars 185, 189

Napier–Taupō road 137
Narbey, Leon 130, 202, 217, 218, 219, 250, 256
narrators and other speakers 20, 131, 249, 250, 281; first Māori narrator of primetime programme 192; *Frontier of Dreams* 197; *The Governor* 22, 110; kaumātua and kuia 8, 96, 214, 249, 255, 257, 259, 269, 280; *The Kiingitanga* 259–60, 262, 263; *The Killing of Kane* 99–100; Māori women 278; *The New Zealand Wars* 22, 159, 168–70, 176–77, 268–69, 276, 278; *NZ Wars: Stories of Ruapekapeka* 268–69, 271–72; *The Prophets* 254, 256; *Rain of the Children* 22, 217–21; *Rewi's Last Stand* (with sound, 1940) 68, 78, 90; *River Queen* 244; *In Spring One Plants Alone* 214; *Tangata Whenua* 96; *Von Tempsky's Ghost* 192; *Waka Huia* 257
National Film Library 91
National Film Unit 30, 91; *One Hundred Crowded Years* 68, 197
national identity, New Zealand 19, 29, 30, 32, 275
nationhood 29–30, 278; Hayward's concern 39, 47–48, 65, 76, 78, 90, 92, 149; and Māori–Pākehā relationships 128–29, 149, 153; *Utu* (Murphy) 29, 128–29
Native Americans, portrayal in films 8, 23, 37, 92, 278
Neill, Sam 249
Nene, Tamati Waka 107, 114
Nevill, Hugh 122
New Zealand Broadcasting Corporation (NZBC) 32, 91, 95, 96, 97, 102; *see also* Broadcasting Commission of New Zealand (BCNZ); NZ On Air
New Zealand Company 166
New Zealand Cross 46
New Zealand Film Archive 66; *see also* Ngā Taonga Sound and Vision
New Zealand Film Commission 29–30, 32, 129, 205, 225, 229, 245
New Zealand Film Production Fund 32, 225, 228–29
New Zealand International Film Festival 222, 224, 248, 253
New Zealand Opera Company 106

New Zealand Wars: attraction to filmmakers 29; changing European perspectives 117, 119, 181, 204; commemorations 8, 9, 34, 250–51, 261, **261**, **268**, 268–69, 272, 281; coverage on Anzac Day, 2016 268; digital histories 265, 267; Grey's governorship 105–06; historical overview 9–13; interpreted through filter of World War One 14, 39, 53–54, 164, 274; legacies 8–9, 10, 13, 93; legally inflected approach to history 18; Māori unity 167; Māori perspectives, strategy and agency 17, 108, 117, 123, 124, 126, 163–68, 180, 181, 196, 205, 262, 263, 271, 276, 278, 281; memorials and historic sites 267; naming 18; neglected side of the 'national story' 16, 18–19, 24, 26, 34, 162–63; newspaper reports 14; official history 14–15; oral traditions, formal and informal 13–14, 15, 16, 17, 26, 273 (*see also* narrators and other speakers); as 'Pākehā Wars' 117, 123, 126; pivotal events in New Zealand's history 163; relationship between films, histories and memory 18–24, 93, 246, 249–50, 273; reshaping of stories over time 8, 13, 14, 15–16, 17, 35, 194–96, 273, 275–76; state-supported films 30–31; stories of women and others caught up in war and its aftermath 205, 209, 225, 231, 232–34, 235, 236, 238, 271–72, 278; te reo Māori in films and documentaries 33–34, 117, 170; 'the most resonant genre' in screen stories 34; written records and histories 13, 14–18, 97, 122, 159, 162–63, 164, 232, 273; *see also* East Coast Wars; Northern War; Taranaki Wars; Waikato War; Wellington War; and names of individual battles

New Zealand Wars, The (Cowan) 14–15, 39, 46, 47, 48, 49, 54, 58, 63, 69, 74, 82, 84, 85, 105, 129, 144, 159, 235

New Zealand Wars, The (documentary series) 9, 17, 22, 23, 27, 29, 30, **31**, 97, 159–60, 164–81, 247, 249, 253, 262, 268–69, 271, 275, 279; audiences 177–81, 263; Belich's persona as central component 168; episodes 164–65, 166–68; involvement of Māori communities 169–70, 176; Māori responses 176, 178, 181; narrators and other voices 168–70, 176–77, 268–69; Pākehā responses 178–79; images **165**, **168**, **169**, **170**, **171**, **172**, **173**, **174**, **177**; proposal and funding 161, 180; reconstituting Belich's book as a script 164–68; sites and landscapes 169, 171–75, 256, 280; soundscapes 175–77; te reo Māori 170

New Zealand Wars troops: British forces 9, 10, 12, 163–64, 165, 262, 275, 279; colonial troops 12, 38–39, 50, 51–52, 59, 173, 195, 230, 234, 275–76, 278, 279; Hayward's treatment of ordinary soldiers 38–39, 42–43, 50, 51–52, 275; kūpapa (Crown-allied) Māori 12, 14, 50, 52–53, 59, 137, 141, 167, 226, 228, 230, 234, 243, 250, 256, 278, 279

Newnham, Charles 37
Newton, John 204, 206
Ngā Aho Whakaari, *The Brown Book* 248
Ngā Ruahine 12, 101, 102, 232, 245
Ngā Tamatoa 95, 124
Ngā Taonga Sound and Vision 24, 34, 38; *see also* New Zealand Film Archive
Ngāi te Rangi **11**
Ngāi Tūhoe *see* Tūhoe
Ngāpuhi 75, 77, 107, 108, 170, 263, 269, 270, 271, 272
Ngāruahoe **177**
Ngāruawāhia 119
Ngata, Āpirana 63, 64
Ngata, Whai 160, 161, 170
Ngātai, Hori 169
Ngātai, Kihi 169
Ngātai, Tom 170, **171**, 181, 232
Ngāti (feature film) 157
Ngāti Apakura 257, 260
Ngāti Awa 6, 46, 55–57, 66, 140–41
Ngāti Hau 204, 206
Ngāti Hauā 28, 80, 107, 112, 178
Ngāti Hine 107, 268
Ngāti Kahungunu 12, 41, 141
Ngāti Kohera 41, 70
Ngāti Kuri 28, 107
Ngāti Maniapoto 13, 40, 41, 69, 70, 74, 76–77, 78, 80, 85, 86, 87, 108, 109, 257

Ngāti Porou 12, 30, 107, 108, 136, 137, 141, 167, 256
Ngāti Pūkeko 46, 52, 54, 55, 105
Ngāti Pūkenga 268
Ngāti Rangiwehiwehi 142
Ngāti Raukawa 41, 70, 80, 181, 268
Ngāti Ruanui 102
Ngāti Toa 9, 80, 107, 173
Ngāti Tūwharetoa 41, 80, 259–60
Ngāti Whare 255
Ngāti Whātua 95, 123, 130
ngeri 173, 176
Ngoungou, Queenie, *see* Perrett, Caroline
Nicols, Spenser Percival 169
Niki (son of Te Puhi Tatu), *see* Takao, Niki
Noonan, Michael 26, 94, 95, 96, 105, 106–07, 108, 109, 117
Northern War 9, 105, 110, 111, 165–66, 176, 181, 197, 250, 269, 271; long economic aftermath 272
NZ On Air 32, 33; editorial authority 161, 177; funding 160–61, 182, 183, 191, 196, 205, 259, 268; minimum Māori content requirement 161; programming of cultural significance 33, 160, 180; representation of Māori and Pacific Islanders 161; *see also* Broadcasting Commission of New Zealand (BCNZ)
NZ On Screen 24, 124, 210
NZ Wars: Stories of Ruapekapeka (online documentary) 9, 24, 268–72, **270**, 271

Ōhaeawai 9, 165, 170, 269
Ōhinemutu 47, 48
Ohlson, Jack **255**
Oliphant, James 69, 70–71, 73, 75, 86, 89
Oliver, Bill 18
O'Malley, Vincent 18, 74, 113, 250, 260, 261, 262, 263, 269, 271
Once Were Warriors (feature film) 157, 183, 247, 263
One Hundred Crowded Years (documentary) 68, 197
online content and streaming 9, 24, 251; *NZ Wars: Stories of Ruapekapeka* 9, 24, 268–72, **270**, **271**

Ōpōtiki 10, 55, 142
Ōrākau, Battle of 10, 14, 33, 119, 168, 198; and Māori heroism 39, 40, 41, 44, 45, 68, 80, 82, 84, 85, 87, 90, 91, 92; commemoration 94, 250–51, 257; Cowan's comparison of defence with Battle of Britain lead-up 91; *The Governor* 120–21, **121**, 126, **199**; mythologising as a site of 'interracial respect' 16, 29, 87, 90; see also *Rewi's Last Stand* (all versions)
Orange, Claudia 197; *The Treaty of Waitangi* 162
O'Regan, Stephen (Tipene) 155
O'Shea, John 30, 92, 126, 127
Owen, Rena 214, 221

Pacific Films 30
Paerata, Te Rongonui 70, 80, **81**
Pai Mārire movement 10, 12, 47, 137, 167, 226, 254
Paiaka, Raureti 69, 85, 86
Pākaitore/Moutoa Gardens 226
Pākehā: character of 22–23; more frequent use as a descriptor 162
'Pākehā Wars' 117, 123, 126
Paki, Korotangi 259
Paki, Ngāwai 259
Papa, Rāhui 259
Pāpāwai marae 203, 231, 240, **240**, 241
Parawera School 69
Paretekawa 80
Parham, Bill 17
Parihaka 13, 14, 16, 97, 98, 249, 250, 255, 256, 265, 279; *Tātarakihi: The children of Parihaka* (documentary) 9, 27, 252–54
Park Road Post 157
Parker, Cynthia Ann 236, 238
Parker, Dean 184, 185, 186, 187
Pātea Maori Club 102, 226; 'Poi E' 162, 249
Pāterangi 10
Patu! (documentary) 131–32, **132**, 133
Pene, Rāwiti 230, **237**, **242**
Perrett, Caroline ('Queenie') (later Queenie Ngoungou) 231, 232, 233–34, 235, 240, **240**, 241
Perrott, Lisa 35, 176, 178

Petrie, Duncan 29, 32
Phillips, Jock 196
phone apps 9, 251, 267
Piano, The (feature film) 228, 238
Pictures (feature film) 126–27, 239
Pihama, Leonie 245
Pihama, Mahanga 25, 26, 249, 259, 262, 263
Pilcher, Leo **76**, **77**, **79**, 80, 81, 86–87
Pipiriki 226
Pirongia 12
Pivac, Diane 35, 58
Poata, Tom (Tama) 95, 132, **132**, **134**, 140, 157, 247, 248
Pohlmann, Gerd 130, 131, 133
Pōmāre, Māui 40, 63, 64
Pope, Diana 267
Pope, Jeremy 267
Porgy and Bess (New Zealand Opera Company production) 106
Porourangi whare whakairo 30, **31**
Porter, Thomas William 14
poukai 263
Pounamu (television series) 161–62
Poverty Bay 12, 141
Preece, George 12, 41, 141, 143
Preston, Gaylene 157–58, 252; *Making Utu* 129, 133, **134**, **135**, 137, 138, **139**, 153, **157**, 225
Prickett, Nigel, *Landscapes of Conflict* 267
production companies 38, 182–83; Māori 248, 272; *see also* names of individual companies
Prophets, The (documentary series) 8, 250, 254–57, **255**, **256**, 278
Prosser, Rod 133
protest movements 95, 96, 130–33, 134; increasing authority of Māori 133
Puhi, *see* Tatu, Te Puhi
Puhirake, Rāwiri 121, 265
Pukehinahina (Gate Pā) 9, 10, **11**, 121–22, 126, 169, 265, **266**; *The Battle of Gate Pā Told with Sand* 258, 258–59; commemoration 257, 258
Pukemanu (television series) 95–96, 106
Puketakauere pā 166, 168
Puketutu 165
Pūniu River 10, 82, 170

Rain of the Children (documentary) 9, 17, 22, 26, 201, 204, 205–24, 232, 246, 247, 250, 276, 279; actors 28, 212, 214; Binney as historical advisor 210; composition 211–12, 214–15; dramatisations 219–20, 221–22; footage from *In Spring One Plants Alone* 214, 217; exploration of the past 206–11; funding 205; historical photographs 212, **216**, 217; inclusion of whānau 218–20, **219**; interviews 212, 214, 217–21, **219**, 256; iwi ownership 221, 222, 224; images **207**, **212**, **213**, **215**, **216**, **217**, **219**, **223**, **277**; reception 222, 224; and *River Queen* 205, 208
Rakena, Tamati 269
Rangiāowhia 10, 74, 82, 119, **120**, 126, 167, 196, 262, 279–80; commemoration 257
Rangihau, John 201, 202
Ranginui, Julie 226
Rangiriri 96, 119, 181, **197**, 198, **198**, 258, 267; commemoration 257
Rangitukia 137
Rastafarianism 138
Ratana Church 256
ratings performance 33, 112, 160, 161, 163, 179, 180, 200
raupatu (land confiscations) 13, 18, 90, 162, 198; Bay of Plenty 12, 55; Taranaki 10, 12; Waikato 10, 12, 68, 69, 70, 73, 88, 89, 90, 117, 119, 185, 198, **262**, 262, 263
Raupatu (music video) 263, **264**, 265
Rauporoa pā 46, 55
Raureti, Te Huia 69, 86
Rea, Iain, *Hundred Birds – Manu Rau* 194
Rea, Stephen 229, 230
Read, Lynette 35, 202
Redgrave, Corin 106, **113**
Redmond, H. **49**, 55
Reed, A.W. 71
Reeves, William Pember 14, 105
Reid, Nicholas 154
Reuben, Faenza 140
Rewi Maniapoto Memorial Committee 71
Rewi's Last Stand (Hayward and Reed, novelisation, 1939) 71, 72, 76, 85, 88, 89, 90

Rewi's Last Stand (silent film, 1925) 7, 9, 22, 38, 42–45, **43**, **44**, 69, 70, 82, 194, **195**, 275, 276; budget 40, 41, 42; historical value 18, 68, 274; international markets 40, 45; location 40–41; original title: 'The Victorious Defeat' 40; preparation and negotiations 40–42

Rewi's Last Stand (sound film, 1940) 9, 23, 26, 29, 34, 35, 38, 65, 68–93, 155, 275, 276, 278, 279; additional scenes 68, 69; budget 70, 71, 72; casting 69, 70, 71, 72, 73, 79–81; endings 88–90; historical settings and connections 72–79; *The Last Stand* (cut-down version, 1949) 72, 82, 84, 85, 87, 88, 89, 91–92, 93, 105, 120; loss of original film 72, 81; novelisation of plot 71, 72, 76; Ōrākau and the negotiation 82–87; images **73**, **76**, **77**, **79**, **81**, **82**, **83**, **84**, **86**, **89**; poster **199**; preparation and negotiations 68–71; reception and aftermath 90–92; romantic plot 75–79; shareholders 70, 73, 89; sound 72

Reynolds, Don 225–26

Ringatū faith 25, 46, 56, 58, 59, 60, 63–65, 96, 137–38, 209

River Queen (feature film) 9, 20–21, **21**, 26, 157, 201, 204, 205, 225–46, 247, 275, 276, 278, 280; background research 230–31; connections with history 232–36, 238–44; funding 225, 228–29; international co-production 33, 229; Irish stories and characters 225, 229–31, 238–39, **242**; Māori stories and characters 242–44, 245; images **21**, **227**, **228**, **231**, **234**, **237**, **239**, **241**, **243**; plot 230; production dilemmas 228–30, 241; Pākehā women characters and stories 230–34, 236–42; and *Rain of the Children* 205, 208; reception 244–46; reconfiguration of colonial conflict narrative 232, 233; Whanganui iwi 225, 226, 228, **228**, 230

RNZ (formerly Radio New Zealand) 251, 268; *Te Ahi Kaa* 254

Roa, Tom 92, **192**, 194, 195, 196, 257, 258, 259, 261, 262

Roberton, James 69, 70

Robinson, Sir Dove-Myer 123

Rochfort, John 126–27

Roger, Warwick 112

Rohe Pōtae, Te 126–27, 168, 263

Roia, Paoi 56–57

Rokoroko, Hōhepa 140

Rongowhakaata 12

Rosenstone, Robert 19

Rotorua: location of *Rewi's Last Stand* 40–41; filmmakers and 37, 41; Te Kooti campaign 47, 52, 54

Royal Visit of the Duke and Duchess of Cornwall to New Zealand, 1901, The 36–37

Rua, Toko 211

Rua, Whatu 210, 211

Rua Kēnana (song, David Grace) 263

Ruapekapeka pā 9, **111**, 111–12, 126, 159, 165, 166, **168**, 170, 177, 267, 274; *NZ Wars: Stories of Ruapekapeka* 9, 268–72, **270**, **271**

Ruapekapeka Trust 267, 269

Ruapekapeka website 9, 267

Ruatāhuna 13, 61, 209, 210

Ruka, Mark **21**

Rules of Engagement (Ria Hall) 24, 265, **266**

Rusden, George 14

Russell, Marcia 164

Russell, Thomas 185

Ryan, Tim 17, 194

Sanderson, Martyn 117, 119, **120**, 122, 132, **143**

Sandilands, Aline 154

Satchell, William 16, 75

Savage, Michael Joseph 72

Schama, Simon 196

Scholes, Robin 183–84, 186, 188, 190

Scott, Dick 16, 97, 163

Scott, Khai **190**

Scottie Productions 254

Scott-Smith, Michael 105

screen industries 29–34, 129–30; deregulation 32, 33, 160–61, 182, 183, 191, 200; funding 8, 30, 32–33, 34, 35, 129–30, 182, 228–29; historiography 35; independent industries 30, 129; rising presence and seniority of Māori 8, 27; *see also* films; television

screen technologies, impact of lower cost 27, 248, 251, 272

Seekers, The (feature film) 26

Selwyn, Don 25, 95, 96, 112, 281; *The Governor* 26–27, **27**, 28, 96, 106–09, 112, **113**, **116**, **120**, 126, 248, 276; *Greenstone* 184, 186–87, 188, 189, 190

Selwyn, George Augustus 110

Shadbolt, Maurice 17, 163, 231

Shaw, Barry 124

Shelton, Leo **125**

Shipwreck (television series) 191

Short, Chris 138

Short, Erica 154

Shortland, Waihoroi 109, 184, 186, 187, 188, 221, **223**

silent films, impact of talkies 65

Silver Scrolls Awards, Maioha Award 263, 265

Simpson, Tony 17

Sinclair, Keith 16, 98, 105, 114, 122, 123–24, 167, 232

Sklar, Robert 23, 92

Sleeping Dogs (feature film) 123, 155

smartphones 9, 251, 265, 267

Smith, Beaumont 37

Smith, Cheryl 244

Smith, Jo 35

Smith, Miriama 187

Smith, Philip 269

Snowden, Larry **190**

Soldiers *see* New Zealand Wars troops

South Africa, sporting contact 95, 130, 131–32

sovereignty 16, 18; Crown 68, 113; Māori 10, 68, 95, 111, 126, 271

Springbok tour, 1981 131–32, **132**, 133, 149, 152, 153

Stables, Kate 244

Stephens, Tainui 25, 191, 248, 281; *Hautoa Ma!* 27, 248; *The New Zealand Wars* 160, 164, 170, 172, 175, 176, 177, 178, 181, 226, 247, 249, 254, 256, 276, 278, 280, 281; *The Prophets* 254; *Rain of the Children* 205, 217, 222, 226, 247; *River Queen* 205, 225–26, 228, 230, 232, 241, 247

Stevanon, Adrian 269

Stevens, Geoff, *Te Matakite o Aotearoa: The Maori Land March* 96

Stewart, Albert Oliphant (Arapeta Tuati) **50**, 56

Stewart, Frank 42, 45
Stories of Ruapekapeka 9, 24, 268–72, **270**, **271**
Stowers, Richard 194
Strand Theatre, Auckland 45, 90
Sutherland, Kiefer 229, 230
Swarbrick, H.A. 69, 70, 71, 73, 75, 80, 86, **86**, 89, 91

Taane, Tiki 265
tablets 251, 265, 267
Tahuparae, Rangitihi (John) 226, 228, 230, 245
Tainui 10, 70, 73, 82, 88, 89, 92, 108, 116, 119, 196, 250, 251, 259–63; Waitangi Tribunal claim settlement 261, 263
Tainui Corporation 190
Tait, Kēro Nancy 217, 219, 221
Takao, Niki (son of Te Puhi Tatu) 202, 205, 206, 207, 209, 211, 214, 218, 221, 222
Takiora, Lucy 194, 195, 278
Tamahori, Lee 26, 27, **27**, 134–35, **135**, 136, 138, 157, 183, 247, 248–49
Tāmati, Kepa 42
Tāmihana, Wiremu 25, 28, 107–09, 112–13, 116–17, 119–20, 126, **165**, 166–67, 181, 198, 260, 261, 262, 276
Tāneatua 56, 274, 280
Tānenui-a-rangi meeting house 61
Tangata Whenua (television series) 96, 97, 124, 161, 167, 201
taonga pūoro 176, **264**
Taranaki iwi 72, 173, 231, 232, 235, 250, 256
Taranaki region 10, 166, 170, 233; Mt Taranaki **172**, 172–73, 175, 253, **256**
Taranaki Wars 9, 14, 17, 94, 97, 102, 103, 166–67, 201, 250, 275, 279; commemorations 250; First War (1860–63) 10, 16, 105, 116, 168, 172, 197, 267; Second War (1863–66) 10, 168
Taranaki Wars app 267
Taratoa, Hēnare 258, 265
Tarr, George 37
Tātarakihi: The children of Parihaka (documentary) 9, 27, 252–54, 279
'Tattooed Generals, The' (film script) 248
Tatu, Te Puhi 201–02, 203, 204, 205–06, **207**, 207–08, 209–11, 212, **213**, 214, **215**, 217, 218, 219, 221, 222, 224, 232, **277**, 278, 279

Tauranga Ika Pā 12, **174**, 235
Tauranga Moana 257, 265
Tauroa, Hiwi 153
Taurua, Kīngi 269
Tawhai, Bill 116
Tawhara, Mikaira **213**
Tāwhiao, King 12, 23, 74, 167, 181, 260, **260**, 261, 262, 263, 278
tax shelter 30, 32, 129–30, 157–58
Taylor, Ian 175, 269
Taylor, Robert **255**, 255–6
Te Ahi Kā Roa, Te Ahi Kātoro Taranaki War 1860-2010 exhibition 250
Te Ahuru, Kepa 141, 142, 143
Te Aitanga o Māhaki 255
Te Arawa 12, 38–39, 41, 46, 47, 48, 52, 53, 54, 55, 58, 59, 141, 143, 243, 244; *see also* Arawa Contingent and Arawa Flying Column
Te Atairangikaahu, Te Arikinui Dame 28, 107–08, 261
Te Auetū, Harata 258
Te Aupōuri 28, 107
Te Awamutu 74
Te Awamutu Historical Society 26, 68–69, 71, 73, 80
Te Hāroto 137–38
Te Heuheu Tukino III, Iwikau 259–60
Te Hokioi 251
Te Huia, Raureti 13, 25, 69, 70, 73, 80, 85, 86, **86**, 89
Kani, Turirangi 265
Te Karere (television programme) 250
Te Kiri Karamū, Hēni (Hēni Porei) 158, **158**, 169, **169**
Te Kohia 166
Te Kooti Arikirangi Te Turuki 12, 13, 15, 16, 17, 26, 38, 39, 46, 55–56, 58, 137, 161, 163, 181, 209, 232, 249; pardon 12, 58; *Pounamu* 161; *The Prophets* episode 254, 255–56; *Tangata Whenua* episode 96; *The Te Kooti Trail* as a memorial 58–61, 63–65, 276; *Utu* 9, 28, 137–38, 142, 143, 144, 276, 280
Te Kooti campaign ('Te Kooti's War') 18, 38–39, 41–42, 45–48, 143, 212, 232, 280; Cowan, 'A Bush Court Martial' 140–41

Te Kooti Trail, The (feature film) 9, 23, 25, 29, 34, 35, 38, 45–67, 91, 105, 128–29, 274, 276, 279, 280; authenticity and historical embeddedness 66–67; comparisons with *Utu* 143–44, 145–46, 149, 153; local pride 28, 65–66; Māori cast 54–57, 278; as memorial 48–54, 57–61, 63–65; images **6**, **49**, **50**, **51**, **53**, **54**, **55**, **57**, **59**, **60**, **62**, **64**; post production and editing 46; publicity **67**; reviews 65; serialised version of plot 47
Te Kura o Tamarongo 252
Te Māngai Pāho 33, 205
Te Matakite o Aotearoa: The Maori Land March (television documentary) 96
Te Miha, Ramai 25, 26, **79**, 81, 89, **89**, 90–91; *see also* Hayward, Ramai
Te Ngutu o te Manu 12, 98, 101, 187, 189, 191, **191**, 234, 235
Te Niho o Te Ātiawa marae 252
Te Oti Takarangi 254
Te Paerata 70
Te Paerata, Ahumai 70, 78, 85, 87, 120
Te Paerata, Hītiri 70, 80, 81
Te Paerata, Hone Teri 70
Te Pairi Tūterangi **6**, 25, 59–60, **60**, 61 **62**, 63, 65, 80, 281
Te Pihoihoi Mokemoke i Runanga i te Tuanui 74
Te Pōhue 137
Te Pōrere **177**
Te Poronu mill 39, 46, 48, 52, 54, 55, 56
Te Rā Maumahara National Day of Commemoration 34, 251, 265, 268, 272, 281
Te Ranga 257, 265
Te Rangihaeata 9, 166
Te Rangihīroa 46, 50, 56, 57
Te Rangihiwinui, Te Kēpa 12, 21
Te Rangitāke, Wiremu Kīngi 116, 166
Te Rārawa 176
Te Rau, Kereopa 55, 142
Te Rauparaha 9, 17, 107, 110, 112, 166, 173, 181
Te Rauparaha, Tamihana 260
te reo Māori 29, 33–34, 95, 102, 105, 117, 123, 136–37, 154, 162, 170, 187, 256, 257, 263, 269; official language of Aotearoa 162

Te Rerehau, Hemara 251
Te Tuhi, Nīkora 141
Te Urewera 10, 12, 13, 17, 41–42, 59, 140, 141, **148**, 164, 171, 201–03, 204, 208, 209, 211, 217, 231, 249, 256, 267, 279, 280; police 'terror raids,' 2007 222
Te Waharoa 112–13
Te Waharoa, Wiremu Tāmihana Tarapīpipi *see* Tāmihana, Wiremu
Te Whai a te Motu meeting house 13
Te Whāiti 255
Te Wherowhero, Pōtatau 74, 108–09, 114, 116, 166–67, 260–61
Te Whiti o Rongomai, Erueti 13, 17, 161, 253, 254, 255
Te Whiu 60
Te Whiwhi, Mātene 260
Te Wiata, Rima 249
Te Winika 70, 74, 91
television: community of viewers 96–97; cultural requirement 30, 96, 160, 180; drama 24, 30, 32, 95–96, 97, 160; dynamic between creators and programmers 182; international funding, co-production and markets 32, 33, 183, 184, 187, 188, 189–90, 200, 275; Māori programming 27; 'our stories' 29, 32, 33, 191, 194, 275; programming as product 182, 183; public service requirement 182; two-channel period 96–97; *see also* documentaries; films; screen industries; TV3; TV One; and titles of individual productions
Television New Zealand Act 2003 182
Television New Zealand (TVNZ) 160, 161, 177, 179, 183, 184, 197; Māori Programming Department 248; profit requirement 182
Temara, Pou 60, 63, 207, 218, 221, 222, 257
Tempsky, Gustavus von 21, 22, 28, 42, 43, 74, 98, 120, 234, 278; Māori commentators on 194; *Von Tempsky* (Harris, documentary) 104, **104**; *Von Tempsky's Ghost* (Milligan, documentary) 22, 182, **191**, 191–92, **192**, **193**, 194–96, **195**. 200
They Come Marching (music video) 265, 266
Thompson, Richard **195**

Thomson, Chris 102, **125**
Thomson, E. 70
tikanga Māori 25, 29, 95, 99, 102, 109, 136, 269
Tikao, Ariana **264**, 265
Tilly, Grant 110
Tinirau, Tamahina 107
Tioriori 119
tīpuna: associations in *Frontier of Dreams* 197; connections with Māori performers and iwi speakers 28, 81; films as permanent records of 28, 66; knowledge of descendants 25–26; representation of, and responsibility to 25, 108, 249, 276; Tūhoe 209
Tītokowaru, Riwha 12, 16, 17, 163, 187, 189, 248, 276, 279, 281; *The Killing of Kane* 97–98, 99–103; *The New Zealand Wars* 171, 172, **172**, 174, 181; *River Queen* 204, 230, 231, 232, 233, 234–36, 240, 244, 245, 276; *Von Tempsky's Ghost* 192
Tītokowaru's War 12, 18, 97–104, 167, 191, 226, 233, 246; *I Shall Not Die: Titokowaru's War, New Zealand* 17, 159, 162–63, 231, 234, 235, 244, 276
Toetoe, Wiremu 251
Toka, Hēnare 77, 81, **81**
Top Shelf Productions 196
Tracy, Mona 16
Treaty of Waitangi 13, 95, 108, 110–11, 114, 186, 269; centennial of signing 68, 72; recognition as nation's founding document 162; 'Treaty backlash' 162
Trinity Roots 255
troops *see* New Zealand Wars troops
Tuati, Arapeta *see* Stewart, Albert
Tuckett, Graeme 244
Tūheitea, King 23, 259, 260, 261
Tūhoe 6, 14, 41, 60, 63, 203, 204; government military invasion, 1860s and 70s 12, 211; Judith Binney's relationship and work with 17, 204, 207, 209, 210, 220–21; *The New Zealand Wars* 176; police invasion of 1916 13, 164, 167, 201, 209–13, **211-13**, 217, 222, 224, 282, 297; police raids of 2007 222; *The Prophets* 255, 256; protection of Te Kooti 12,

59–60, 141; *Rain of the Children* 206, 207, 208, 209–11, 212, 214, 217–20, 221–22, 224; *In Spring One Plants Alone* 201–02, 203, 204, 206; *Utu* 59, 141; *Waka Huia* 257
Tū-mātahi, Manahi 41–42
Tunui, Tom 56
Tupotahi, Winitana 85
Tūrangawaewae marae 40, 41, 70
Turuturumōkai 98, 100, 102, 189, 194
Tūtakangahau 203
Tūterangiwhiu 30, **31**
Tūwhakaruru, Wiremu Kātene 234–35, 236
Tūwhāngai, Hēnare 108, 109
TV3 161; *The Café* 265
TV One 94, 96, 97, 105, 112, 122, 124, 159, 179, 182, 263; *Documentary New Zealand* series 191

Uenuku (television drama) 96, 137
UK Film Council 229
Utu (feature film) 7, 9, 20, **20**, 21, 23, 26, 43, 128–58, 163, 201, 232, 247, 248, 274, 275, 276, 278, 279–80; adaptation of Cowan's story 'A Bush Court Martial' 140–45, 150, 151, 152; aftermath 156–58; beginning and end, historical and contemporary issues 144–46, 149–50, 152–53; budget 30, 129–30, 157–58; casting 28, 134, 138; references to *Macbeth* 140, 144, 150, 152, 154; filmmaking and funding in the 1980s 129–30; Gaylene Preston, *Making Utu* **27**, 129, 133, **134**, **135**, 137, 138, **139**, 153; location and local cultures 137–39; nationalism 29, 128–29; plot 139–40, 243; political documentary 130–37; reception 153–56; recut film for international release 156; te reo Māori 34, 136–37, 154; training ground for Māori filmmakers 27, 138
Utu: Redux (feature film) 28, 128, **134**, 142, **143**, **146**, **147**, **148**, **150**, **151**, **152**, 156–57, 158

Vanguard Films 133
Vanishing Race, The (feature film) 37
Vere Jones, Peter 95, 100, **101**, 102, 127

Vietnam War 95, 97, 130
violence in films 279–80
Völkner, Reverend Carl 10, 55, 142, 143
Von Tempsky (Harris, documentary) 104, **104**
Von Tempsky's Ghost (Milligan, documentary) 22, 182, **191**, 191–96, **192**, **193**, **195**, 200, 257

Waaka, Reverend Napi 25, **100**, 101–03, **103**, 107
Waerenga-a-hika 10, 12
Wahawaha, Rāpata 12, 30
Waikato (iwi) 14, 28, 41, 72, 89, 116, 166, 172
Waikato (region) 10, 73, 74, 75, 76, 77, 89, 96, 176
Waikato River 172
Waikato War 9, 10, 14–15, 16, 18, 41, 74, 89, 90, 97, 250, 275, 279; commemorations 94, 250, 257–58; *The Flight of Te Hookioi* 251; *Frontier of Dreams* 197; *The Governor* 105, 117–18, 119; *Greenstone* 185; *The Kiingitanga* 261, 262; *The New Zealand Wars* 167, 168, 169, 170, 172, 178, 181; *Von Tempsky's Ghost* 191; *Waka Huia* 257–58; *see also* individual battles
Waikato War Driving Tour app 267
Waikerepuru, Huirangi 254
Waimana 209, 212, 217, 218, 221, 224
Waipā district 73, 74, 75, 76, 82, 85, 88
Wairau Affray 9
Wairoa 141
Wairoa Māori Film Festival 248, 251
Waitangi Tribunal 13, 14, 18, 95, 162, 198, 204, 261, 263
Waitara land purchase 10, 14, 113, 166
Waititi, Mabel 181
Waititi, Taika 248; *Hunt for the Wilderpeople* 249
Waka Huia (television programme) 9, 27, 250, 257–58
Walker, Ranginui 17, 124
Wallace, Anzac (Zac) **130**, 131, **131**, 136, 137, 139, 144, 153, 154, 157, 158

Wallace, Craig 17, 208–09; *Mihaia* 209, 210, **211**
Warbrick, Paerau 59, 63
Warbrick, Pātiti **6**, **53**, 54, 55, 65
Ward, Alan 18
Ward, Ingrid 225, 230–31
Ward, Vincent 21, 26, 170, **202**, 203–04, 206, **215**, 279; *Breathe* (exhibition of paintings) 224; *Edge of the Earth* 209–10; *The Last Samurai* 204, 231; *Map of the Human Heart* 204; *The Navigator* 204, 208; *The Past Awaits* (book) 207, **207**, 217; *In Spring One Plants Alone* 26, 201–05, 207, 211, 212, 214, 218, 222, 233, 246, 276; *Vigil* 204, 208; *see also Rain of the Children* (Ward); *River Queen* (Ward)
Wards, Ian 16
Waru (feature film) 248
Waru, Ray 196
Wearing, Michael 184, 186
Webster, James 264, 265
Webster, Peter 204, 208, 209
Wellington War 9, 110, 112, 166, 173; 1846 War in Wellington app 267
westerns 8, 20, 21, 22, 23, 29, 36, 37, 38, 46, 57, 128, 130, 137, 140, 152, 153, 155, 276
Whakatāne 28, 46, 47, 55, 56, 60, 66, 233
Whakatane Films 38
Whakatāne River 46
Whakatōhea 268
Whanganui Awa Film Working Party 226, 245
Whanganui iwi 12, 141, 225, 226, 228, **228**, 230, 232, 243, 245–46
Whanganui River 201, 204, 225, **227**, 228, 229, 230, 232, 244
Whanganui River Trust Board 226
Wharehoka, Maata 252, 253, 254
Wharekauri (Chatham Islands) 10, 12, 63, 254
Whareongaonga 255, 256

whenua 8, 28, 96, 103, 118, 130, 170–73, **171**, 201, 256, 270, 273, 280; *see also* landscape *and* land, Māori
White, Hayden 19–20
White, Margo 179
White, Rob 154
Wichtel, Diana 180, 190–91
Wigby-Ngatai, Viv 259
Wild Horses 157
Willemen, Paul 29
Williams, Bob 154
Williams, Derek **125**
Williams, Haare 255
Williams, Henry 68, 110–11, 112
Williams, Joe 198, 200
Williams, Wayne **125**
Winitana, Chris 259–60
Winter, Marcus 258–59; *see also Battle of Gate Pā Told with Sand, The*
Wiremu, Bill 170, **171**
Wirepa, Ivan 208–09
women 13, 23, 24, 27, 50, 70, 95, 232, 279; colonial 230, 231, 238–40, 276; Māori 23, 39, 45, 46, 78, 82, 84–85, 87, 88, 90, 91, 95, 100, 114, 119, **120**, **121**, 120–21, 141, 145–46, 149, 196, 200, 201–02, 204, 209, 217, 220, 231, 235, 238–40, 244, 248, 253, 255, 272, 278, 282; *see also* directors *and* heroes and heroines
Wood, Gregory 35
World War One 23, 39, 53–54, 163, 164, 210, 250, 274; Māori participation 14, 39
World War Two 39, 71, 72, 91, 163

York, Nathan 190
Young Deer, James, *White Fawn's Devotion* 37
Young, Rose **192**, 194
YouTube 258, 263